ESSAYS IN COMPUTING SCIENCE

Prentice Hall International
Series in Computer Science

C.A.R. Hoare, Series Editor

WELSH, J., and ELDER, J., *Introduction to Pascal (Now in 3rd edn)*
BACKHOUSE, R. C., *Syntax of Programming Languages: Theory and practice*
DUNCAN, F., *Microprocessor Programming and Software Development*
JONES, C. B., *Software Development: A rigorous approach (OOP)*
WELSH, J., and MCKEAG, M., *Structured System Programming*
HENDERSON, P., *Functional Programming: Application and implementation*
DE BAKKER, J. W., *Mathematical Theory of Program Correctness*
TENNENT, R. D., *Principles of Programming Languages*
REYNOLDS, J. C., *The Craft of Programming*
BJÖRNER, D., and JONES, C. B., *Formal Specification and Software Development*
GOLDSCHLAGER, L., and LISTER, A., *Computer Science: A modern introduction (Now in 2nd edn)*
JACKSON, M. A., *System Development*
MACCALLUM, I., *Pascal for the Apple*
CLARK, K. L., and MCCABE, F. G., *micro-Prolog: Programming in logic*
INMOS LTD, *occam Programming Manual*
JOSEPH, M., PRASAD, V. R., and NATARAJAN, N., *A Multiprocessor Operating System*
WELSH, J., ELDER, J., and BUSTARD, D., *Sequential Program Structures*
ELDER, J., *Construction of Data Processing Software*
HEHNER, E. C. R., *The Logic of Programming*
DROMEY, R. G., *How to Solve it by Computer*
HOARE, C. A. R., and SHEPHERDSON, J. C. (eds), *Mathematical Logic and Programming Languages*
LEW, A., *Computer Science: A mathematical introduction*
JOHNSTON, H., *Learning to Program*
HOARE, C. A. R., *Communicating Sequential Processes*
MARTIN, J. J., *Data Types and Data Structures*
MACCALLUM, I., *UCSD Pascal for the IBM PC*
WELSH, J., and HAY, A., *A Model Implementation of Standard Pascal*
JONES, C. B., *Systematic Software Development using VDM*
BACKHOUSE, R. C., *Program Construction and Verification*
POMBERGER, G., *Software Engineering and Modula-2*
HAYES, I. (ed.), *Specification Case Studies*
BORNAT, R., *Programming from First Principles*
SLOMAN, M., and KRAMER, J., *Distributed Systems and Computer Networks*
JONES, G., *Programming in occam*
WATT, D. A., WICHMANN, B. A., and FINDLAY, W., *ADA: Language and methodology*
PEYTON JONES, S. L., *The Implementation of Functional Programming Languages*
WELSH, J., and ELDER, J., *Introduction to Modula-2*
WIKSTRÖM, Å., *Functional Programming using Standard ML*
INMOS LTD, *occam 2 Reference Manual*
BUSTARD, D., ELDER, J., and WELSH, J., *Concurrent Program Structures*
BIRD, R., and WADLER, P., *Introduction to Functional Programming*
MEYER, B., *Object-oriented Software Construction*
GORDON, M. J. C., *Programming Language Theory and its Implementation*
CROOKES, D., *Introduction to Programming in Prolog*
HUGHES, J. G., *Database Technology: A software engineering approach*
RYDEHEARD, D. E., and BURSTALL, R. M., *Computational Category Theory*
JONES, G., and GOLDSMITH, M., *Programming in occam 2*
SPIVEY, M., *The Z Notation: A reference manual*
ELLIOTT, SIR ROGER, and HOARE, C. A. R., *Scientific Applications of Multiprocessors*
HOARE, C. A. R., and JONES, C. B., *Essays in Computing Science*

ESSAYS IN COMPUTING SCIENCE

C. A. R. Hoare

Oxford University Computing Laboratory

C. B. Jones

(editor)

Department of Computer Science,
Manchester University

PRENTICE HALL

NEW YORK LONDON TORONTO SYDNEY TOKYO

First published 1989 by
Prentice Hall International (UK) Ltd,
66 Wood Lane End, Hemel Hempstead,
Hertfordshire, HP2 4RG
A Division of
Simon & Schuster International Group

Printed and bound in Great Britain at the
University Press, Cambridge.

Library of Congress Cataloging-in-Publication Data

Hoare, C. A. R. (Charles Antony Richard), 1934–
Essays in computing science / C. A. R. Hoare ;
C. B. Jones, editor.
p. cm. – (Prentice Hall international series in computer science)
'Bibliography of works by C. A. R. Hoare': p.
Includes index.
ISBN 0-13-284027-8 : $40.00
1. Electronic data processing. 2. Computers.
I. Jones, C. B. (Cliff B.), 1944– . II. Title. III. Series.
QA76.H56 1989
004–dc19 88-23169

British Library Cataloguing in Publication Data

Hoare, C. A. R. (Charles Anthony Richard), *1934–*
Essays in computing science. – (Prentice
Hall International series in computer science).
1. Computer systems
I. Title II. Jones, C. B., *1944–*
004

ISBN 0-13-284027-8

1 2 3 4 5 92 91 90 89 88

Contents

Foreword

Language – notation – shapes thought and mind. Our languages, and how they are defined, have a tremendous influence on what we can express and how simply. Often, a concept becomes clear only when a suitable notation for it has been defined and when rules for manipulating the notation have been developed: a concept and its expression are inextricably intertwined.

Notation has been particularly important in computer science. For forty years we have been searching for notations to express new algorithmic concepts, so that algorithms can be written clearly and with more assurance that they are correct. Complicating our search has been the need for efficient implementation. Indeed, this entirely new requirement of efficiency has too often overshadowed other important requirements, such as the ability to manipulate in order to analyse and prove results.

For twenty-five years, C. A. R. Hoare has been leading the way in our search for notations – elucidating the principles on which their design should (or should not) be based, warning us of pitfalls, pointing out the paths to take, and walking ahead for us to follow. Had we listened to him more, and had more of us listened, I venture to say that we would now be further along in our search than we are.

Why should we have been listening to Hoare? What makes him special? First, in the mid-1960s he was made acutely aware of the problems of software development by the absolute failure of a large software project he was managing: thirty man-years of effort were completely abandoned (see his Turing Award Lecture)! At the least, this failure gave him the right to expound on how software should *not* be done. Moreover, this failure induced him to search seriously for the principles of our field, and his amazing forward leaps in this ensuing search have established him as one of the pre-eminent scientists of the field. There are few whom I consider his equal.

In retrospect, this failure in the mid-1960s was probably the best thing that happened to the field of programming-language design.

Let me mention briefly some of his accomplishments. First, of course, was his brilliant sorting algorithm 'Quicksort', still of practical use after 27 years. In 1968–69, when the software world was admitting that it was in the throes of a crisis, he developed a good part of the scientific insight for its long-range solution: his axiomatic basis for computer programming provided, at last, the basic manipulative method for reasoning about programs. Throughout the 1970s, he continued to build on this framework, showing how to handle procedures, parameters, for-loops, and functions. His 1972 paper on proof of correctness of data representations is still the first paper to read on implementations of abstract data types. His axiomatic definition of Pascal in 1973 was the first such definition of a language.

Concurrency, once the purview of operating systems, became part of the field of programming-language design as a result of several of Hoare's early papers. He provided major notational tools for the two basic paradigms of concurrency: the Monitor for shared-memory models and CSP (communicating sequential processes) for message passing. And, although for some time CSP was a major example of the fact that our notational studies can have intellectual depth without an implementation, it was the major influence in the architectural design of the transputer.

Early in the game, Hoare recognized the need for various kinds of formal definitions. Besides his axiomatic basis for computer programming, he was involved in the first proof of consistency of an axiomatic language definition with an operational model, and he was responsible for several significant theories of semantics of programming languages. His theoretical work has been guided by his acute sense of the need to manipulate, reason about, and analyse programs.

Until now, the Prentice Hall International Series in Computer Science, edited by Hoare, consisted of forty-nine books. It is fitting that the fiftieth book be a treasure-house of works by Hoare himself. Read it for a sense of history. Read it for the facts – about Quicksort, proving programs correct, CSP, etc. Read it for its expositions of the principles of programming and programming language design and for its admonitions to stay on the right path in our search. And read it for the style: the clarity, taste, elegance, and precision that has become associated with Hoare.

David Gries
Cornell University

Editorial preface

Charles Antony Richard Hoare is one of the most productive and prolific computer scientists. This volume contains a selection of his published papers. There is a need, as in a Shakespearian Chorus, to offer some apology for what the book manifestly fails to achieve. It is not a complete 'collected works'. Selection between papers of this quality is not easy and, given the book's already considerable size, some difficult decisions as to what to omit have had to be made. Pity the editor weighing the choice between a seminal paper, perhaps widely republished, and a lesser known gem overtaken by subsequent developments. The only defence that can be offered is to reassure the reader that Tony Hoare was consulted.

The paper published as Chapter 1 is so placed because it provides biographical context. With this exception, the papers appear in chronological order of main publication.

Each paper is introduced by 'link material'. Here again, there is need (at least) for explanation: how can one embellish such papers? The idea behind the link material is to record things which could not have been written in the original paper. Sometimes, it is possible to explain better the context in which a paper was conceived; the subsequent development of the ideas introduced can only be written with hindsight. Apart from these inputs, the papers speak so well for themselves that it has been possible to keep the link material brief. Because the editor's text varies in length, the (abstract and) paper follow immediately rather than being laid out on separate pages. In order to avoid confusion, the link material is set in a smaller fount. Again to assuage the reader's doubts, Hoare does have the last word in the Postscript.

An attempt has been made to trace some of the key dates of drafts, submissions, etc. leading up to publication. For a scientist who points out that 'writing the paper is my method of research' this is both necessary and difficult. Some of Hoare's papers go through many drafts which are circulated to colleagues (sometimes changing title, sometimes using the same title on a complete rewrite.) A complete historiography has not been attempted. In particular, many of Hoare's papers have been reprinted (sometimes in several places): normally, only the first source is given.

With some caution, Hoare's work can be divided under a number of headings. These themes are not disjoint, the whole output comes from a single person. Hoare's work on language definition is seen in Chapters 3, 13, 14, 16 (and also, to a lesser extent, in Chapters 11, 12); his contribution to methods of reasoning about programs is covered in Chapters 4–6, 8, 9, 11, 12, 14, 15, 17, 19, 20; his seminal work on parallelism can be traced through Chapters 10, 12, 15–17. Amidst writing these, often difficult, papers Hoare has produced a number of articles aimed at a wider audience: here, Chapters 1, 2, 7, 18, 21, 22 represent this form of his writing.

The papers themselves have all been re-typeset and only minimal changes have been made. The form of references to other publications has been made uniform and all references have been collected at the end of this volume. In order to provide a useful snapshot, all papers by Hoare (even if there are co-authors) have been gathered into a separate list of references. (Except where they are referred to, Technical Reports etc. are not included: only true 'publications' are listed.) The form of reference to these is '[72]' or 'Hoare([72])', the list being ordered, and numbers accordingly assigned, on a chronological basis. (This results in the use of 'Hoare' as a key even where the article lists a co-author before Hoare. No disrespect to his erstwhile colleagues is intended.) The other list of references gives works to which Hoare has not contributed. It is listed alphabetically, and references take the form 'Dijksta (1976)', with a, b etc. to distinguish publications in the same year.

The editor and the publishers acknowledge, with thanks, permission to reprint the copyrighted articles in this book that have been published in various journals, proceedings, and books. Individual credits, with details of the sources of the papers, are given as a footnote to each chapter opening.

The task of editing these essays has been most rewarding. The fact that it did not become a burden is largely thanks to the support I have received. I should like to thank Julie Hibbs who has typed and controlled the evolving book; Alison McCauley undertook all of the bibliographic research with real enthusiasm. Thanks are also due to the staff at Prentice Hall International who provided enormous support and encouragement. I am also very grateful to those other computer scientists who have offered advice and/or references. In particular I should like to thank John Reynolds, Jim Horning, Bob Tennant, Brian Randell, David Gries, and Jim King. Finally, I should like to thank Tony Hoare, with whom co-operation is always so stimulating.

C. B. Jones

ONE

The Emperor's old clothes

The ACM Turing Award is the most prestigious given in Computer Science. Hoare received it in 1980. The citation includes:

> Professor Hoare was selected by the General Technical Achievement Award Committee for his fundamental contributions to the definition and design of programming languages. His work is characterized by an unusual combination of insight, originality, elegance, and impact. He is best known for his work on axiomatic definitions of programming languages through the use of techniques popularly referred to as axiomatic semantics. He developed ingenious algorithms such as Quicksort and was responsible for inventing and promulgating advanced data-structuring techniques in scientific programming languages. He has also made important contributions to operating systems through the study of monitors. His most recent work is on communicating sequential processes.
>
> Prior to his appointment to the University of Oxford in 1977, Professor Hoare was Professor of Computer Science at The Queen's University in Belfast, Ireland from 1968 to 1977 and was a Visiting Professor at Stanford University in 1973. From 1960 to 1968 he held a number of positions with Elliott Brothers, Ltd, England.
>
> Professor Hoare has published extensively and is on the editorial boards of a number of the world's foremost computer science journals. In 1973 he received the ACM Programming Systems and Languages Paper Award. Professor Hoare became a Distinguished Fellow of the British Computer Society in 1978 and was awarded the degree of Doctor of Science *Honoris Causa* by the University of Southern California in 1979.

This paper is placed first in the collection because of its autobiographical comments. Hoare was born in 1934 and studied at Oxford before doing National Service in the Royal Navy where he obtained an interpreter's qualification in Russian. (This explains his work on [1].) He joined Elliott Bros. in 1960. The 'Miss Pym' in this article is now Mrs Jill Hoare. Since 1977

C. A. R. Hoare, The Emperor's old clothes, *Comm. ACM* **24**(2), 75–83 (February 1981).

This paper was originally given as the ACM Turing Award Lecture in 1980, and appeared as [73].

he has been Professor of Computation at the University of Oxford. Further Honorary Doctorates have followed that from the University of Southern California. Hoare was also awarded the IEE Faraday medal in 1985.

Apart from its ability to set the context of the scientific material in subsequent chapters, this account provides an unusual opportunity to learn from mistakes as well as successes. Hoare's industrial career also shows the origin of the practical insight which guides so much of his theoretical work.

The text leads up to a very severe warning about the dangers inherent in using the Ada language for safety-critical systems. The stimulus for this was the claim that this language could be used as a basis for proven programs. Hoare spoke in disappointment rather than in rage and used a stern tone because the danger appeared imminent. In the event it took far longer to create implementations of Ada than had been expected and people's expectations of its security have moderated. This must in part be due to the impact of this article.

The Turing Award Lecture was delivered at the ACM '80 Conference in Nashville, Tennessee on 27 October 1980; the original publication is [73].

Abstract

The author recounts his experiences in the implementation, design, and standardization of computer programming languages, and issues a warning for the future.

My first and most pleasant duty in this lecture is to express my profound gratitude to the Association for Computing Machinery for the great honour which they have bestowed on me and for this opportunity to address you on a topic of my choice. What a difficult choice it is! My scientific achievements, so amply recognized by this award, have already been amply described in the scientific literature. Instead of repeating the abstruse technicalities of my trade, I would like to talk informally about myself, my personal experiences, my hopes and fears, my modest successes, and my rather less modest failures. I have learned more from my failures than can ever be revealed in the cold print of a scientific article and now I would like you to learn from them, too. Besides, failures are much more fun to hear about afterwards; they are not so funny at the time.

I start my story in August 1960, when I became a programmer with a small computer manufacturer, a division of Elliott Brothers (London) Ltd, where in the next eight years I was to receive my primary education in computer science. My first task was to implement for the new Elliott 803 computer, a library subroutine for a new fast method of internal sorting just invented by Shell. I greatly enjoyed the challenge of maximizing efficiency in the simple decimal-addressed machine code of those days. My boss and tutor, Pat Shackleton, was very pleased with my completed program. I then said timidly that I though I had invented a sorting method that would usually run faster than Shellsort, without taking much extra store. He bet me sixpence that I had not. Although my method was very difficult to explain, he finally agreed that I had won my bet.

I wrote several other tightly coded library subroutines but after six months I was given a much more important task—that of designing a new advanced high-level programming language for the company's next computer, the Elliott 503, which was to have the same instruction code as the existing 803 but run sixty times faster. In spite of my education in classical languages, this was a task for which I was even less qualified than those who undertake it today. By great good fortune there came into my hands a copy of the Report on the International Algorithmic Language ALGOL 60. Of course, this language was obviously too complicated for our customers. How could they ever understand all those **begins** and **ends** when even our salesmen couldn't?

Around Easter 1961, a course on ALGOL 60 was offered in Brighton, England, with Peter Naur, Edsger W. Dijkstra, and Peter Landin as tutors. I attended this course with my colleague in the language project, Jill Pym, our divisional Technical Manager, Roger Cook, and our Sales Manager, Paul King. It was there that I first learned about recursive procedures and saw how to program the sorting method which I had earlier found such difficulty in explaining. It was there that I wrote the procedure, immodestly named Quicksort, on which my career as a computer scientist is founded. Due credit must be paid to the genius of the designers of ALGOL 60 who included recursion in their language and enabled me to describe my invention so elegantly to the world. I have regarded it as the highest goal of programming language design to enable good ideas to be elegantly expressed.

After the ALGOL course in Brighton, Roger Cook was driving me and my colleagues back to London when he suddenly asked, 'Instead of designing a new language, why don't we just implement ALGOL 60?' We all instantly agreed – in retrospect, a very lucky decision for me. But we knew we did not have the skill or experience at that time to implement the whole language, so I was commissioned to design a modest subset. In that design I adopted certain basic principles which I believe to be as valid today as they were then.

(1) The first principle was *security*: The principle that every syntactically incorrect program should be rejected by the compiler and that every syntactically correct program should give a result or an error message that was predictable and comprehensible in terms of the source-language program itself. Thus no core dumps should ever be necessary. It was logically impossible for any source-language program to cause the computer to run wild, either at compile time or at run time. A consequence of this

principle is that every occurrence of every subscript of every subscripted variable was on every occasion checked at run time against both the upper and the lower declared bounds of the array. Many years later we asked our customers whether they wished us to provide an option to switch off these checks in the interests of efficiency on production runs. Unanimously, they urged us not to – they already knew how frequently subscript errors occur on production runs where failure to detect them could be disastrous. I note with fear and horror that even in 1980, language designers and users have not learned this lesson. In any respectable branch of engineering, failure to observe such elementary precautions would have long been against the law.

(2) The second principle in the design of the implementation was *brevity of the object code produced by the compiler and compactness of run time working data.* There was a clear reason for this: The size of main storage on any computer is limited and its extension involves delay and expense. A program exceeding the limit, even by one word, is impossible to run, especially since many of our customers did not intend to purchase backing stores.

This principle of compactness of object code is even more valid today, when processors are trivially cheap in comparison with the amounts of main store they can address, and backing stores are comparatively even more expensive and slower by many orders of magnitude. If as a result of care taken in implementation the available hardware remains more powerful than may seem necessary for a particular application, the applications programmer can nearly always take advantage of the extra capacity to increase the quality of his program, its simplicity, its ruggedness, and its reliability.

(3) The third principle of our design was that *the entry and exit conventions for procedures and functions should be as compact and efficient as for tightly coded machine-code subroutines.* I reasoned that procedures are one of the most powerful features of a high-level language, in that they both simplify the programming task and shorten the object code. Thus there must be no impediment to their frequent use.

(4) The fourth principle was that *the compiler should use only a single pass.* The compiler was structured as a collection of mutually recursive procedures, each capable of analysing and translating a major syntactic unit of the language – a statement, an expression, a declaration, and so on. It was designed and documented in ALGOL 60, and then coded into decimal machine code using an explicit stack for recursion. Without the ALGOL 60 concept of recursion, at that time highly controversial, we could not have written this compiler at all.

I can still recommend single-pass top-down recursive descent both as an implementation method and as a design principle for a programming language. First, we certainly want programs to be read by *people* and people prefer to read things once in a single pass. Second, for the user of a time-sharing or personal computer system, the interval between typing in a program (or amendment) and starting to run that program is wholly unproductive. It can be minimized by the high speed of a single-pass compiler. Finally, to structure a compiler according to the syntax of its input language makes a great contribution to ensuring its correctness. Unless we have absolute confidence in this, we can never have confidence in the results of any of our programs.

To observe these four principles, I selected a rather small subset of ALGOL 60. As the design and implementation progressed, I gradually discovered methods of relaxing the restrictions without compromising any of the principles. So in the end we were able to implement nearly the full power of the whole language, including even recursion, although several features were removed and others were restricted.

In the middle of 1963, primarily as a result of the work of Jill Pym and Jeff Hillmore, the first version of our compiler was delivered. After a few months we began to wonder whether anyone was using the language or taking any notice of our occasional re-issue, incorporating improved operating methods. Only when a customer had a complaint did he contact us and many of them had no complaints. Our customers have now moved on to more modern computers and more fashionable languages but many have told me of their fond memories of the Elliott ALGOL System, and the fondness is not due just to nostalgia, but to the efficiency, reliability, and convenience of that early simple ALGOL System.

As a result of this work on ALGOL, in August 1962 I was invited to serve on the new Working Group 2.1 of IFIP, charged with responsibility for maintenance and development of ALGOL. The group's first main task was to design a subset of the language which would remove some of its less successful features. Even in those days and even with such a simple language, we recognized that a subset could be an improvement on the original. I greatly welcomed the chance of meeting and hearing the wisdom of many of the original language designers. I was astonished and dismayed at the heat and even rancour of their discussions. Apparently the original design of ALGOL 60 had not proceeded in that spirit of dispassionate search for truth which the quality of the language had led me to suppose.

In order to provide relief from the tedious and argumentative task of designing a subset, the working group allocated one afternoon to discussing the features that should be incorporated in the next design of the language. Each member was invited to suggest the improvement he considered most important. On 11 October 1963, my suggestion was to pass on a request of our customers to relax the ALGOL 60 rule of compulsory declaration of variable names and adopt some reasonable default convention such as that of FORTRAN. I was astonished by the polite but firm rejection of this seemingly innocent suggestion: It was pointed out that the redundancy of ALGOL 60 was the best protection against programming and coding errors which could be extremely expensive to detect in a running program and even more expensive not to. The story of the Mariner space rocket to Venus, lost because of the lack of compulsory declarations in FORTRAN, was not to be published until later. I was eventually persuaded of the need to design programming notations so as to maximize the number of errors which cannot be made, or if made, can be reliably detected at compile time. Perhaps this would make the text of programs longer. Never mind! Wouldn't you be delighted if your Fairy Godmother offered to wave her wand over your program to remove all its errors and only made the condition that you should write out and key in your whole program three times! The way to shorten programs is to use procedures, not to omit vital declarative information.

Among the other proposals for the development of a new ALGOL was that the **switch** declaration of ALGOL 60 should be replaced by a more general feature, namely an array of label-valued variables, and that a program should be able to change the values of these variables by assignment. I was very much opposed to this idea, similar to the assigned **GOTO** of FORTRAN, because I had found a surprising number of tricky problems in the implementation of even the simple labels and switches of ALGOL 60. I could see even more problems in the new feature including that of jumping back into a block after it had been exited. I was also beginning to suspect that programs that used a lot of labels were more difficult to understand and get correct and that programs that assigned new values to label variables would be even more difficult still.

It occurred to me that the appropriate notation to replace the ALGOL 60 switch should be based on that of the conditional expression of ALGOL 60, which selects between two alternative actions according to the value of a Boolean expression. So I suggested the notation for a 'case expression' which selects between any number of alternatives according to the value of an integer expression. That was my second language-design proposal. I am still most proud of it, because it raises essentially no problems either for the implementor, the programmer, or the reader of a program. Now, after more than fifteen years, there is the prospect of international standardization of a language incorporating this notation – a remarkably *short* interval compared with other branches of engineering.

Back again to my work at Elliott's. After the unexpected success of our ALGOL Compiler, our thoughts turned to a more ambitious project: To provide a range of operating-system software for larger configurations of the 503 computer, with card readers, line printers, magnetic tapes, and even a core backing store which was twice as cheap and twice as large as main store, but fifteen times slower. This was to be known as the Elliott 503 Mark II software system.

It comprised:

(1) An assembler for a symbolic assembly language in which all the rest of the software was to be written.
(2) A scheme for automatic administration of code and data overlays, either from magnetic tape or from core backing store. This was to be used by the rest of the software.
(3) A scheme for automatic buffering of all input and output on any available peripheral device – again, to be used by all the other software.
(4) A filing system on magnetic tape with facilities for editing and job control.
(5) A completely new implementation of ALGOL 60, which removed all the nonstandard restrictions which we had imposed on our first implementation.
(6) A compiler for FORTRAN as it was then.

I wrote documents which described the relevant concepts and facilities and we sent them to existing and prospective customers. Work started with a team of fifteen programmers and the deadline for delivery was set some eighteen months ahead in March 1965. After initiating the design of the Mark II software, I was suddenly promoted to the dizzying rank of Assistant Chief Engineer, responsible for advanced development and design of the company's products, both hardware and software.

Although I was still managerially responsible for the 503 Mark II software, I gave it less attention than the company's new products and almost failed to notice when the deadline for its delivery passed without event. The programmers revised their implementation schedules and a new delivery date was set some three months ahead in June 1965. Needless to say, that day also passed without event. By this time, our customers were getting angry and my managers instructed me to take personal charge of the project. I asked the senior programmers once again to draw up revised schedules, which again showed that the software could be delivered within another three months. I desperately wanted to believe it but I just could not. I disregarded the schedules and began to dig more deeply into the project.

It turned out that we had failed to make any overall plans for the allocation of our most limited resource – main storage. Each programmer expected this to be done automatically, either by the symbolic assembler or by the automatic overlay scheme. Even worse, we had failed to simply count the space used by our own software which was already filling the main store of the computer, leaving no space for our customers to run *their* programs. Hardware address length limitations prohibited adding more main storage.

Clearly, the original specifications of the software could not be met and had to be drastically curtailed. Experienced programmers and even managers were called back from other projects. We decided to concentrate first on delivery of the new compiler for ALGOL 60, which careful calculation showed would take another four months. I impressed upon all the programmers involved that this was no longer just a prediction; it was a promise; if they found they were not meeting their promise, it was their personal responsibility to find ways and means of making good.

The programmers responded magnificently to the challenge. They worked nights and days to ensure completion of all those items of software which were needed by the ALGOL compiler. To our delight, they met the scheduled delivery date; it was the first major item of working software produced by the company over a period of two years.

Our delight was short-lived; the compiler could not be delivered. Its speed of compilation was only two characters per second which compared unfavourably with the existing version of the compiler operating at about a thousand characters per second. We soon identified the cause of the problem: It was thrashing between the main store and the extension core backing store which was fifteen times slower. It was easy to make some simple improvements, and within a week we had doubled the speed of compilation – to four characters per second. In the next two weeks of investigation and reprogramming, the speed was doubled again – to eight characters per second. We could see ways in which within a month this could be still further improved; but the amount of reprogramming required was increasing and its effectiveness was decreasing; there was an awful long way to go. The alternative of increasing the size of the main store so frequently adopted in later failures of this kind was prohibited by hardware addressing limitations.

There was no escape: The entire Elliott 503 Mark II software project had to be abandoned, and with it, over thirty man-years of programming effort, equivalent to nearly one man's working life, and I was responsible, both as designer and as manager, for wasting it.

A meeting of all our Elliott 503 customers was called and Roger Cook, who was then manager of the computing division, explained to them that not a single word of the long-promised software would ever be delivered to them. He adopted a very quiet tone of delivery, which ensured that none of the customers could interrupt, murmur in the background, or even shuffle in their seats. I admired but could not share his calm. Over lunch our customers were kind to try to comfort me. They had realized long ago that software to the original specification could never have been delivered, and even if it had been, they would not have known how to use its sophisticated features, and anyway many such large projects get cancelled before delivery. In retrospect, I believe our customers were fortunate that hardware limitations had protected them from the arbitrary excesses of our software designs. In the present day, users of microprocessors benefit from a similar protection – but not for much longer.

At that time I was reading the early documents describing the concepts and features of the newly announced OS 360, and of a new time-sharing project called Multics. These were far more comprehensive, elaborate, and sophisticated than anything I had imagined, even in the first version of the 503 Mark II software. Clearly IBM and MIT must be possessed of some secret of successful software design and implementation whose nature I could not even begin to guess at. It was only later that they realized they could not either.

So I still could not see how I had brought such a great misfortune upon my company. At the time I was convinced that my managers were planning to dismiss me. But no, they were intending a far more severe punishment. 'O.K. Tony,' they said. 'You got us into this mess and now you're going to get us out.' 'But I don't know how,' I protested, but their reply was simple. 'Well then, you'll have to find out.' They even expressed confidence that I could do so. I did not share their confidence. I was tempted to resign. It was the luckiest of all my lucky escapes that I did not.

Of course, the company did everything they could to help me They took away my responsibility for hardware design and reduced the size of my programming teams. Each of my managers explained carefully his own theory of what had gone wrong and all the theories were different. At last, there breezed into my office the most senior manager of all, a general manager of our parent company, Andrew St Johnston. I was surprised that he had even heard of me. 'You know what went wrong?' he shouted – he aways shouted – 'You let your programmers do things which you yourself do not understand.' I stared in astonishment. He was obviously out of touch with present-day realities. How could one person ever understand the whole of a modern software product like the Elliott 503 Mark II software system?

I realized later that he was absolutely right; he had diagnosed the true cause of the problem and he had planted the seed of its later solution.

I still had a team of some forty programmers and we needed to retain the goodwill of customers for our new machine and even regain the confidence of the customers for our old one. But what should we actually plan to do when we knew only one thing – that all our previous plans had failed? I therefore called an all-day meeting of our senior programmers on 22 October 1965, to thrash out the question between us. I still have the notes of that meeting. We first listed the recent major grievances of our customers: Cancellation of products, failure to meet deadlines, excessive size of software, '...not justified by the usefulness of the facilities provided,' excessively slow programs, failure to take account of customer feedback; 'Earlier attention paid to quite minor requests of our customers might have paid as great dividends of goodwill as the success of our most ambitious plans.'

We then listed our own grievances: Lack of machine time for program testing, unpredictability of machine time, lack of suitable peripheral equipment, unreliability of the hardware even when available, dispersion of programming staff, lack of equipment for keypunching of programs, lack of firm hardware delivery dates, lack of technical writing effort for documentation, lack of software knowledge outside of the programming group, interference from higher managers who imposed decisions, '... without a full realization of the more intricate implications of the matter,' and over-optimism in the face of pressure from customers and the Sales Department.

But we did not seek to excuse our failure by these grievances. For example, we admitted that it was the duty of programmers to educate their managers and other departments of the company by '... presenting the necessary information in a simple palatable form.' The hope '... that deficiencies in orginal program specifications could be made up by the skill of a technical writing department ... was misguided; the design of a program and the design of its specification must be undertaken in parallel by the same person, and they must interact with each other. A lack of clarity in specification is one of the surest signs of a deficiency in the program it describes, and the two faults must be removed simultaneously before the project is embarked upon.' I wish I had followed this advice in 1963; I wish we all would follow it today.

My notes of the proceedings of that day in October 1965 include a complete section devoted to failings within the software group; this section rivals the most abject self-abasement of a revisionist official in the Chinese cultural revolution. Our main failure was over-ambition. 'The goals which we have attempted have obviously proved to be far beyond our grasp.' There was also failure in prediction, in estimation of program size and speed, of effort required, in planning the co-ordination and interaction of programs, in providing an early warning that things were going wrong. There were faults in our control of program changes, documentation, liaison with other departments, with our management, and with our customers. We failed in giving clear and stable definitions of the responsibilities of individual porgrammers and project leaders – Oh, need I go on? What was amazing was that a large team of highly intelligent programmers could labour so hard and so long on such an unpromising project. You know, you shouldn't trust us intelligent programmers. We can think up such good arguments for convincing ourselves and each other of the utterly absurd. Especially don't believe us when we promise to repeat an earlier success, only bigger and better next time.

The last section of our inquiry into the failure dealt with the criteria of quality of software. 'In the recent struggle to deliver any software at all, the first casualty has been consideration of the quality of the software delivered. The quality of software is measured by a number of totally incompatible criteria, which must be carefully balanced in the design and implementation of every program.' We then made a list of no less than seventeen criteria which has been published in a guest editorial in Volume 2 of the journal, *Software Practice and Experience.*

How did we recover from the catastrophe? First, we classified our Elliott 503 customers into groups, according to the nature and size of the hardware configurations which they had bought – for example, those with magnetic tapes were all in one group. We assigned to each group of customers a small team of programmers and told the team leader to vist the customers to find out what they wanted; to select the easiest request to fulfil, and to make plans (but not promises) to implement it. In no case would we consider a request for a feature that would take more than three months to implement and deliver. The project leader would then have to convince *me* that the customers' request was reasonable, that the design of the new feature was appropriate, and that the plans and schedules for implementation were realistic. Above all, I did not allow anything to be done which I did not myself understand. It worked! The software requested began to be delivered on the promised dates. With an increase in our confidence and that of our customers, we were able to undertake fulfilling slightly more ambitious requests. Within a year we had recovered from the disaster. Within two years, we even had some moderately satisfied customers.

Thus we muddled through by common sense and compromise to something approaching success. But I was not satisfied. I did not see why the design and implementation of an operating system should be so much more difficult than that of a compiler. This is the reason why I have devoted my later research to problems of parallel programming and language constructs which would assist in clear structuring of operating systems – constructs such as monitors and communicating processes.

While I was working at Elliott's, I became very interested in techniques for formal definition of programming languages. At that time, Peter Landin and Christopher Strachey proposed to define a programming language in a simple functional notation that specified the effect of each command on a mathematically defined abstract machine. I was not happy with this proposal because I felt that such a definition must incorporate a number of fairly arbitrary representation decisions and would not be much simpler in principle than an implementation of the language for a real machine. As an alternative, I proposed that a programming language definition should be formalized as a set of axioms, describing the desired properties of programs written in the language. I felt that carefully formulated axioms would leave an implementation the necessary freedom to implement the language efficiently on different machines and enable the programmer to prove the correctness of his programs. But I did not see how to actually do it. I thought that it would need lengthy research to develop and apply the necessary techniques and that a university would be a better place to conduct such research than industry. So I applied for a chair in Computer Science at the Queen's University of Belfast where I was to spend nine happy and productive years. In October 1968, as I unpacked my papers in my new home in Belfast, I came across an obscure preprint of an article by Bob Floyd entitled, 'Assigning Meanings to Programs'. What a stroke of luck! At last I could see a way to achieve my hopes for my research. Thus I wrote my first paper on the axiomatic approach to computer programming, published in the *Communications of the ACM* in October 1969 (Chapter 4 of this book).

Just recently, I have discovered that an early advocate of the assertional method of program proving was none other than Alan Turing himself. On 24 June 1950 at a conference in Cambridge, he gave a short talk entitled, 'Checking a Large Routine' which explains the idea with great clarity. 'How can one check a large routine in the sense of making sure that it's right? In order that the man who checks may not have too difficult a task, the programmer should make a number of definite *assertions* which can be checked individually, and from which the correctness of the whole program easily follows.'

Consider the analogy of checking an addition. If the sum is given (just as a column of figures with the answer below) one must check the whole at one sitting. But if the totals for the various columns are given (with the carries added in separately), the checker's work is much easier, being split up into the checking of the various assertions (that each column is correctly added) and the small addition (of the carries to the total). This principle can be applied to the checking of a large routine but we will illustrate the method by means of a small routine viz. one to obtain *n* factorial without the use of a multiplier. Unfortunately there is no coding system sufficiently generally known to justify giving this routine in full, but a flow diagram will be sufficient for illustration. That brings me back to the main theme of my talk, the design of programming languages.

During the period, August 1962 to October 1966, I attended every meeting of the IFIP ALGOL working group. After completing our labours on the IFIP ALGOL subset, we started on the design of ALGOL X, the intended successor to ALGOL 60. More suggestions for new features were made and in May 1965, Niklaus Wirth was commissioned to collate them into a single language design. I was delighted by his draft design which avoided all the known defects of ALGOL 60 and included several new features, all of which could be simply and efficiently implemented, and safely and conveniently used.

The description of the language was not yet complete. I worked hard on making suggestions for its improvement and so did many other members of our group. By the time of the next meeting in St Pierre de Chartreuse, France in October 1965, we had a draft of an excellent and realistic language design which was published in June 1966 as 'A Contribution to the Development of ALGOL', in the *Communications of the ACM*. It was implemented on the IBM 360 and given the title ALGOL W by its many happy users. It was not only a worthy successor of ALGOL 60, it was even a worthy predecessor of Pascal.

At the same meeting, the ALGOL committee had placed before it, a short, incomplete and rather incomprehensible document, describing a different, more ambitious and, to me, a far less attractive language. I was astonished when the working group, consisting of all the best-known international experts of programming languages, resolved to lay aside the commissioned draft on which we had all been working and swallow a line with such an unattractive bait.

This happened just one week after our inquest on the 503 Mark II software project. I gave desperate warnings against the obscurity, the complexity, and over-ambition of the new design, but my warnings went unheeded. I conclude that there are two ways of constructing a software design: One way is to make it so simple that there are *obviously* no deficiencies and the other way is to make it so complicated that there are no *obvious* deficiencies.

The first method is far more difficult. It demands the same skill, devotion, insight, and even inspiration as the discovery of the simple physical laws which underlie the complex phenomena of nature. It also requires a willingness to accept objectives which are limited by physical, logical, and technological constraints, and to accept a compromise when conflicting objectives cannot be met. No committee will ever do this until it is too late.

So it was with the ALGOL committee. Clearly the draft which it preferred was not yet perfect. So a new and final draft of the new ALGOL language design was promised in three months' time; it was to be submitted to the scrutiny of a subgroup of four members including myself. Three months came and went, without a word of the new draft. After six months, the subgroup met in the Netherlands. We had before us a longer and thicker document, full of errors corrected at the last minute, describing yet another, but to me equally unattractive, language. Niklaus Wirth and I spent some time trying to get removed some of the deficiencies in the design and in the description, but in vain. The completed final draft of the language was promised for the next meeting of the full ALGOL committee in three months' time.

Three months came and went – not a word of the new draft appeared. After six months, in October 1966, the ALGOL working group met in Warsaw. It had before it an even longer and thicker document, full of errors corrected at the last minute, describing equally obscurely yet another different, and to me equally unattractive, language. The experts in the group could not see the defects of the design and they firmly resolved to adopt the draft, believing it would be completed in three months. In vain, I told them it would not. In vain, I urged them to remove some of the technical mistakes of the language, the predominance of references, the default type conversions. Far from wishing to simplify the language, the working group actually asked the authors to include even more complex features like overloading of operators and concurrency.

When any new language design project is nearing completion, there is always a mad rush to get new features added before standardization. The rush is mad indeed, because it leads into a trap from which there is no escape. A feature which is omitted can always be added later, when its design and its implications are well understood. A feature which is included before it is fully understood can never be removed later.

At last, in December 1968, in a mood of black depression, I attended the meeting in Munich at which our long-gestated monster was to come to birth and receive the name ALGOL 68. By this time, a number of other members of the group had become disillusioned, but too late: The committee was now packed with supporters of the language, which was sent up for promulgation by the higher committees of IFIP. The best we could do was to send with it a minority report, stating our considered view that, '... as a tool for the *reliable creation* of sophisticated programs, the language was a failure.' This report was later suppressed by IFIP, an act which reminds me of the lines of Hilaire Belloc,

> But scientists, who ought to know,
> Assure us that it must be so.
> Oh, let us never, never doubt
> What nobody is sure about.

I did not attend any further meetings of that working group. I am pleased to report that the group soon came to realize that there was something wrong with their language and with its description; they laboured hard for six more years to produce a revised description of the language. It is a great improvement but I'm afraid that, in my view, it does not remove the basic technical flaws in the design, nor does it begin to address the problem of its overwhelming complexity.

Programmers are always surrounded by complexity; we cannot avoid it. Our applications are complex because we are ambitious to use our computers in ever more sophisticated ways. Programming is complex because of the large number of conflicting objectives for each of our programming projects. If our basic tool, the language in which we design and code our programs, is also complicated, the language itself becomes part of the problem rather than part of its solution.

Now let me tell you about yet another over-ambitious language project. Between 1965 and 1970 I was a member and even chairman of the Technical Committee No. 10 of the European Computer Manufacturers Association. We were charged first with a watching brief and then with the standardization of a language to end all languages, designed to meet the needs of all computer applications, both commercial and scientific, by the greatest computer manufacturer of all time. I had studied with interest and amazement, even a touch of amusement, the four initial documents describing a language called NPL, which appeared between 1 March and 30 November 1964. Each was more ambitious and absurd than the last in its wishful speculations. Then the language began to be implemented and a new series of documents began to appear at six-monthly intervals, each describing the final frozen version of the language, under its final frozen name PL/I.

But to me, each revision of the document simply showed how far the initial *F*-level implementation had progressed. Those parts of the language that were not yet implemented were still described in free-flowing flowery prose giving promise of unalloyed delight. In the parts that *had* been implemented, the flowers had withered; they were choked by an undergrowth of explanatory footnotes, placing arbitrary and unpleasant restrictions on the use of each feature and loading upon a programmer the responsibility for controlling the complex and unexpected side-effects and interaction effects with all the other features of the language.

At last, 11 March 1968, the language description was nobly presented to the waiting world as a worthy candidate for standardization. But it was not. It had already undergone some 7000 corrections and modifications at the hand of its original designers. Another twelve editions were needed before it was finally published as a standard in 1976. I fear that this was not because everybody concerned was satisfied with its design, but because they were thoroughly bored and disillusioned.

For as long as I was involved in this project, I urged that the language be simplified, if necessary by subsetting, so that the professional programmer would be able to understand it and be able to take responsibility for the correctness and cost-effectiveness of his programs. I urged that the dangerous features such as defaults and ON- conditions be removed. I knew that it would be impossible to write a wholly reliable compiler for a language of this complexity and impossible to write a wholly reliable program when the correctness of each part of the program depends on checking that every other part of the program has avoided all the traps and pitfalls of the language.

At first I hoped that such a technically unsound project would collapse but I soon realized it was doomed to success. Almost anything in software can be implemented, sold, and even used given enough determination. There is nothing a mere scientist can say that will stand against the flood of a hundred million dollars. But there is one quality that cannot be purchased in this way – and that is reliability. The price of reliability is the pursuit of the utmost simplicity. It is a price which the very rich find most hard to pay.

All this happened a long time ago. Can it be regarded as relevant in a conference dedicated to a preview of the Computer Age that lies ahead? It is my gravest fear that it can. The mistakes which have been made in the last twenty years are being repeated today on an even grander scale. I refer to a language design project which has generated documents entitled *strawman*, *woodenman*, *tinman*, *ironman*, *steelman*, *green* and finally now Ada. This project has been initiated and sponsored by one of the world's most powerful organizations, the United States Department of Defense. Thus it is ensured of an influence and attention quite independent of its technical merits and its faults and deficiencies threaten us with far greater dangers. For none of the evidence we have so far can inspire confidence that this language has avoided any of the problems that have afflicted other complex language projects of the past.

I have been giving the best of my advice to this project since 1975. At first I was extremely hopeful. The original objectives of the language included reliability, readability of programs, formality of language definition, and even simplicity. Gradually these objectives have been sacrificed in favour of power, supposedly achieved by a plethora of features and notational conventions, many of them unnecessary and some of them, like exception handling, even dangerous. We relive the history of the design of the motor car. Gadgets and glitter prevail over fundamental concerns of safety and economy.

It is not too late! I believe that by careful pruning of the Ada language, it is still possible to select a very powerful subset that would be reliable and efficient in implementation and safe and economic in use. The sponsors of the language have declared unequivocally, however, that there shall be no subsets. This is the strangest paradox of the whole strange project. If you want a language with no subsets, you must make it *small.*

You include only those features which you know to be needed for *every* single application of the language and which you know to be appropriate for *every* single hardware configuration on which the language is implemented. Then extensions can be specially designed where necessary for particular hardware devices and for particular applications. That is the great strength of Pascal, that there are so few unnecessary features and almost no need for subsets. That is why the language is strong enough to support specialized extensions – Concurrent Pascal for real time work, Pascal Plus for discrete event simulation, UCSD Pascal for microprocessor work stations. If only we could learn the right lessons from the successes of the past, we would not need to learn from our failures.

And so, the best of my advice to the originators and designers of Ada has been ignored. In this last resort, I appeal to you, representatives of the programming profession in the United States, and citizens concerned with the welfare and safety of your own country and of mankind: Do not allow this language in its present state to be used in applications where reliability is critical, i.e., nuclear power stations, cruise missiles, early warning systems, anti-ballistic missile defence systems. The next rocket to go astray as a result of a programming language error may not be an exploratory space rocket on a harmless trip to Venus: It may be a nuclear warhead exploding over one of our own cities. An unreliable programming language generating unreliable programs constitutes a far greater risk to our environment and to our society than unsafe cars, toxic pesticides, or accidents at nuclear power stations. Be vigilant to reduce that risk, not to increase it.

Let me not end on this sombre note. To have our best advice ignored is the common fate of all who take on the role of consultant, ever since Cassandra pointed out the dangers of bringing a wooden horse within the walls of Troy. That reminds me of a story I used to hear in my childhood. As far as I recall, its title was:

The Emperor's old clothes

Many years ago, there was an Emperor who was so excessively fond of clothes that he spent all his money on dress. He did not trouble himself with soldiers, attend banquets, or give judgement in court. Of any other king or emperor one might say, 'He is sitting in council,' but it was always said of him, 'The emperor is sitting in his wardrobe.' And so he was. On one unfortunate occasion, he had been tricked into going forth naked to his chagrin and the glee of his subjects. He resolved never to leave his throne, and to avoid nakedness, he ordered that each of his many new suits of clothes should be simply draped on top of the old.

Time passed away merrily in the large town that was his capital. Ministers and courtiers, weavers and tailors, visitors and subjects, seamstresses and embroiderers went in and out of the throne room about their various tasks, and they all exclaimed, 'How magnificent is the attire of our Emperor.'

One day the Emperor's oldest and most faithful Minister heard tell of a most distinguished tailor who taught at an ancient institute of higher stitchcraft, and who had developed a new art of abstract embroidery using stitches so refined that no one could tell whether they were actually there at all. 'These must indeed be splendid stitches,' thought the minister. 'If we can but engage this tailor to advise us, we will bring the adornment of our Emperor to such heights of ostentation that all the world will acknowledge him as the greatest Emperor there has ever been.'

So the honest old Minister engaged the master tailor at vast expense. The tailor was brought to the throne room where he made obeisance to the heap of fine clothes which now completely covered the throne. All the courtiers waited eagerly for his advice. Imagine their astonishment when his advice was not to add sophistication and more intricate embroidery to that which already existed, but rather to remove layers of the finery, and strive for simplicity and elegance in place of extravagant elaboration. 'This tailor is not the expert that he claims', they muttered. 'His wits have been addled by long contemplation in his ivory tower and he no longer understands the sartorial needs of a modern Emperor.' The tailor argued loud and long for the good sense of his advice but could not make himself heard. Finally, he accepted his fee and returned to his ivory tower.

Never to this very day has the full truth of this story been told: That one fine morning, when the Emperor felt hot and bored, he extricated himself carefully from under his mountain of clothes and is now living happily as a swineherd in another story. The tailor is canonized as the patron saint of all consultants, because in spite of the enormous fees that he extracted, he was never able to convince his clients of his dawning realization that their clothes have no Emperor.

TWO

Quicksort

The background to the *Quicksort* algorithm is given in Hoare's Turing Lecture (cf. Chapter 1). The algorithm was discovered whilst Hoare was a British Council Exchange Student at Moscow State University. His original purpose was to study probability theory in Kolmogorov's department. While he was there, he received an offer of employment from the National Physical Laboratory (NPL) at Teddington to work on a new project for mechanical translation from Russian to English (cf. [2]). At that time, dictionaries were held on magnetic tape, so it was necessary to sort the words of a sentence into alphabetical order before they could be located. The first method that occurred to Hoare would have taken time proportional to the square of the length of the sentence. The second method was the algorithm '*Quicksort*'. The only language he knew was Mercury Autocode and his attempts to code it foundered after the first partition. (Hoare later decided that machine translation of natural languages was impractical, and declined the NPL offer of employment.)

The original difficulty in describing the algorithm and the part played by ALGOL 60 illustrate the rôle of programming languages in design. This paper, which was published as [4] in 1962, is included because of its clarity of description and discussion of performance; the algorithm itself is given in [3]. In fact, it was the discovery of the recurrence equation which predicts the speed of the algorithm that prompted Hoare to write the paper. A related algorithm is used as an example of formal program development in Chapter 5 and a proof of this algorithm is covered in [19].

Abstract

A description is given of a new method of sorting in the random-access store of a computer. The method compares very favourably with other known methods in speed, in economy of storage, and in ease of programming. Certain refinements of the method, which may be useful in the optimization of inner loops, are described in the second part of the paper.

C. A. R. Hoare, QUICKSORT, *BCS Computer Journal*, **5**(1), 10–15 (1962). This paper is republished by kind permission of the British Computer Society.

2.1 Theory

The sorting method described in this paper is based on the principle of resolving a problem into two simpler subproblems. Each of these subproblems may be resolved to produce yet simpler problems. The process is repeated until all the resulting problems are found to be trivial. These trivial problems may then be solved by known methods, thus obtaining a solution of the original more complex problem.

2.1.1 Partition

The problem of sorting a mass of items, occupying consecutive locations in the store of a computer, may be reduced to that of sorting two lesser segments of data, provided that it is known that the keys of each of the items held in locations lower than a certain dividing line are less than the keys of all the items held in locations above this dividing line. In this case the two segments may be sorted separately, and as a result the whole mass of data will be sorted.

In practice, the existence of such a dividing line will be rare, and even if it did exist its position would be unknown. It is, however, quite easy to rearrange the items in such a way that a dividing line is brought into existence, and its position is known. The method of doing this has been given the name *partition.* The description given below is adapted for a computer which has an *exchange* instruction; a method more suited for computers without such an instruction will be given in the second part of this paper.

The first step of the partition process is to choose a particular key value which is known to be within the range of the keys of the items in the segment which is to be sorted. A simple method of ensuring this is to choose the actual key value of one of the items in the segment. The chosen key value will be called the *bound.* The aim is now to produce a situation in which the keys of all items below a certain dividing line are equal to or less than the bound, while the keys of all items above the dividing line are equal to or greater than the bound. Fortunately, we do not need to know the position of the dividing line in advance; its position is determined only at the end of the partition process.

The items to be sorted are scanned by two pointers; one of them, the *lower pointer,* starts at the item with lowest address, and moves upward in the store, while the other, the *upper pointer*, starts at the item with the highest address and moves downward. The lower pointer starts first. If the item to which it refers has a key which is equal to or less than the bound, it moves up to point to the item in the next higher group of locations. It continues to move up until it finds an item with key value greater than the bound. In this case the lower pointer stops, and the upper pointer starts its scan. If the item to which it refers has a key which is equal to or greater than the bound, it moves down to point to the item in the next lower locations. It continues to move down until it finds an item with key value less than the bound. Now the two items to which the pointers refer are obviously in the wrong positions, and they must be exchanged. After the exchange, each pointer is stepped one item in its appropriate direction, and the lower pointer resumes its upward scan of the data. The process continues until the pointers cross each other, so that the lower pointer refers to an item in higher-addressed locations than the item referred to by the upper pointer. In this case the exchange of items is suppressed, the dividing line is drawn between the two pointers, and the partition process is at an end.

An awkward situation is liable to arise if the value of the bound is the greatest or the least of all the key values in the segment, or if all the key values are equal. The danger is that the dividing line, according to the rule given above, will have to be placed outside the segment which was supposed to be partitioned, and therefore the whole segment has to be partitioned again. An infinite cycle may result unless special measures are taken. This may be prevented by the use of a method which ensures that at least one item is placed in its correct position as a result of each application of the partitioning process. If the item from which the value of the bound has been taken turns out to be in the lower of the two resulting segments, it is known to have a key value which is equal to or greater than that of all the other items of this segment. It may therefore be exchanged with the item which occupies the highest-addressed locations in the segment, and the size of the lower resulting segment may be reduced by one. The same applies, *mutatis mutandis*, in the case where the item which gave the bound is in the upper segment. Thus the sum of the numbers of items in the two segments, resulting from the partitioning process, is always one less than the number of items in the original segment, so that it is certain that the stage will be reached, by repeated partitioning, when each segment will contain one or no items. At this stage the process will be terminated.

2.1.2 Quicksort

After each application of the partitioning process there remain two segments to be sorted. If either of these segments is empty or consists of a single item, then it may be ignored, and the process will be continued on the other segment only. Furthermore, if a segment consists of less than three or four items (depending on the characteristics of the computer), then it will be advantageous to sort it by the use of a program specially written for sorting a particular small number of items. Finally, if both segments are fairly large, it will be necessary to postpone the processing of one of them until the other has been fully sorted. Meanwhile, the addresses of the first and last items of the postponed segment must be stored. It is very important to economize on storage of the segment details, since the number of segments altogether is proportional to the number of items being sorted. Fortunately, it is not necessary to store the details of all segments simultaneously, since the details of segments which have already been fully sorted are no longer required.

The recommended method of storage makes use of a *nest,* i.e. a block of consecutive locations associated with a pointer. This pointer always refers to the lowest-addressed location of the block whose contents may be overwritten. Initially the pointer refers to the first location of the block. When information is to be stored in the nest, it is stored in the location referred to by the pointer, and the pointer is stepped on to refer to the next higher location. When information is taken from the nest, the pointer is stepped back, and the information will be found in the location referred to by the pointer. The important properties of a nest are that information is read out in the reverse order to that in which it is written, and that the reading of information automatically frees the locations in which is has been held, for the storage of further information.

When the processing of a segment has to be postponed, the necessary details are placed in the nest. When a segment is found to consist of one or no items, or when it has been sorted by some other method which is used on small segments, then it is possible to turn to the processing of one of the postponed segments; the segment chosen should always be the one most recently postponed, and its details may therefore be read from the nest. During the processing of this segment, it may be necessary to make further postponements, but now the segment details may overwrite the locations used during the processing of the previous segment. This is, in fact, achieved automatically by the use of a nest.

It is important to know in advance the maximum number of locations used by the nest; in order to ensure that the number of segments postponed at any one time never exceeds the logarithm (base 2) of the number of items to be sorted, it is sufficient to adopt the rule of always postponing the processing of the larger of the two segments.†

2.1.3 Estimate of time taken

The number of key comparisons necessary to partition a segment of N items will depend on the details of the method used to choose the bound, or to test

---

†A description of *Quicksort* in ALGOL [3] is rather deceptively simple, since the use of recursion means that the administration of the nest does not have to be explicitly described. The claim to a negative sorting time in the reference is, of course, due to a misprint.

for the completion of the partition process. In any case the number of comparisons is of the form $N+k$, where k may be -1, 0, 1, 2.

The number of exchanges will vary from occasion to occasion, and therefore only the expected number can be given. An assumption has to be made that the value of the bound is a random sample from the population of key values of the items in the segment. If this assumption is not justified by the nature of the data being sorted, it will be advisable to choose the item which yields the bound value *at random,* so that in any case the assumption of randomness will be valid.

In the calculations which follow, use is made of the principle of conditional expectation. We consider separately the case where the bound is the rth in order of magnitude of all the key values in the segment; the value of the conditional expectation of the quantity which interests us may now be expressed quite simply as a function of r. The rule of conditional expectation states that if each conditional expectation is multiplied by the probability of occurrence of the condition, and they are summed over the whole range of conditions, the result gives the unconditional or absolute expectation. According to the assumption of randomness, all the values of r between 1 and N inclusive are equally likely, so that they each have a probability of $1/N$. If, therefore, the expression which gives the conditional expectation on assumption of a given r is summed with respect to r and divided by N, we obtain the value of the absolute expectation of the quantity concerned.

Consider the situation at the end of the partition process, when the bound was the rth key value in order of magnitude. As a result of the final exchange, the item which yielded this key value will occupy the rth position of the segment, and the $r-1$ items with lesser key value will occupy the $r-1$ positions below it in the store. The number of exchanges made in the course of the partition process is equal to the number of items which originally occupied the $r-1$ positions of the lower resulting segment, but which were removed because they were found to have key values greater than the bound. The probability of any key value being greater than the bound is $(N-r-1)/N$, and therefore the expected number of such items among the $r-1$ items which originally occupied what was to be the lower resulting segment is:

$$\frac{(N-r-1)(r-1)}{N}$$

Summing with respect to r, dividing by N, and adding one for the final exchange of the item which yielded the bound, we get the absolute expectation of the number of exchanges:

$$\frac{N}{6}+\frac{5}{6N}$$

This figure may be reduced by $1/N$ if the final exchange is always omitted in the case when the item which provided the bound is already in its correct position. In general it will not be worthwhile to test for this case.

Given the expected theoretical number of comparisons and exchanges, it should be quite easy to calculate the expected time taken by a given program on a given computer. The formula for the time taken to partition a segment of N items will take the form

$$aN + b + \frac{c}{N},$$

where the coefficients a, b and c are determined by the loop times of the program. The expected time taken to sort N items will be denoted T_N. We shall suppose that a different method of sorting is used on segments of size less than M. The values of T_r for $r < M$ are taken as given. We shall find a recursive relationship to give the values of T_r for $r \geqslant M$.

Suppose that the value of the bound chosen for the first partition is the rth in order of magnitude. Then the time taken to sort the whole segment of N items is equal to the time taken to partition the N items, plus the time taken to sort the $r - 1$ items of the lower resulting segment, plus the time taken to sort the $N - r - 1$ items of the upper resulting segment. This assertion must also be true of the expected times

$$T_N = T_r + T_{N-r} + aN + b + \frac{c}{N},$$

on condition that the first bound was the rth. Summing with respect to r and dividing by N we get the unconditional expectation

$$T_N = \frac{2}{N} \sum_{1}^{N-1} T_r + aN + b + \frac{c}{N}, \qquad N \geqslant M.$$

The exact solution of this recurrence equation is†

$$\begin{aligned} T_N = {} & \frac{2(N+1)}{M(M+1)} \sum_{1}^{M-1} T_r + \frac{(N+1)c}{M(M+1)} \\ & + \left[\frac{2(N+1)}{M+1} - 1\right] b \\ & + \left[2(N+1) \sum_{M+1}^{N} \frac{1}{r} - \frac{4(N+1)}{M+1} + N + 4\right] a. \end{aligned}$$

The validity of the solution may be proved by substituting in the original equation, and showing that the result is an algebraic identity. For simplicity, the coefficients of $\sum_{1}^{M-1} T_r$, c, b, and a should be considered

†We adopt the convention that a sum is zero if its upper bound is less than its lower bound.

separately. The correctness of the first three coefficients is easily established. In verifying the coefficient of a, the following identities are used. Writing W_N for

$$\sum_{M+1}^{N} \frac{1}{r} + \frac{2}{N+1} - \frac{2}{M+1}$$

and V_N for the coefficient of a in T_N, we get

$$V_N = (N+1)(N+2)\,W_{N+1} - N(N+1)\,W_N \qquad (1)$$

$$= \frac{2}{N}\,N(N+1)\,W_N + N$$

$$= \frac{2}{N} \sum_{M}^{N-1} V_r + N. \qquad \text{from (1)}$$

It is interesting to compare the average number of comparisons required to sort N items, where N is very large, with the theoretical minimum number of comparisons. We consider the case $M = 2$, and find the expected number of comparisons by putting $a = 1$, $b = c = T_1 = 0$ in the formulae of the last paragraph. When N is very large, all terms except the largest may be ignored. The figure obtained for the expected number of comparisons is

$$2N \sum_{1}^{N} \frac{1}{r} \sim 2N \log_e N.$$

The theoretical minimum average number of comparisons required to sort N unequal randomly ordered items may be estimated on information-theoretic considerations. As a result of a single binary comparison, the maximum entropy which may be destroyed is $-\log 2$, while the original entropy of the randomly ordered data is $-\log N!$; the final entropy of the sorted data is zero. The minimum number of comparisons required to achieve this reduction in entropy is

$$\frac{-\log N!}{-\log 2} = \log_2 N! \sim N \log_2 N.$$

The average number of comparisons required by *Quicksort* is greater than the theoretical minimum by a factor of $2 \log_e 2 \sim 1.4$. This factor could be reduced by the expedient of choosing as the bound for each partition the median of a small random sample of the items in the segment. It is very difficult to estimate the saving which would be achieved by this, and it is possible that the extra complication of the program would not be justified. Probably more worthwhile is the attempt to reduce as far as possible the actual time taken by the innermost comparison cycle, and a number of simple programming devices to achieve this will be described in Part 2 of this paper.

2.1.4 A comparison of *Quicksort* with merge sorting

The National-Elliott 405 computer has a delay-line working store of 512 locations, and a magnetic-disk backing store of 16 384 words. The average access time for the working store is 0.8 ms and the average access time for a block of 64 words in the backing store is 32 ms. There are 19 words of immediate-access storage, which are used to contain instructions and working space of the inner loops; the time taken by such loops is about 0.15 ms per instruction.

Table 2.1 gives a comparison of times taken by *Quicksort* and a merge-sorting method, both programmed by Mr P. Shackleton for the 405. The times were measured automatically by the computer in tests on random data conducted by Mr D. J. Pentecost. The figures relate to six-word items with a single-word key.

Table 2.1

Number of items	*Merge sort*	*Quicksort*
500	2 min 8 s	1 min 21 s
1000	4 min 48 s	3 min 8 s
1500	8 min 15 s*	5 min 6 s
2000	11 min 0 s*	6 min 47 s

*These figures were computed by formula, since they cannot be achieved on the 405 owing to limited store size.

2.2 Implementation

In the implementation of a sorting method on a given computer, it is often possible to make adaptations which will ensure optimization of the innermost loops. *Quicksort* turns out to be exceptionally flexible; a number of possible variations are described below. The choice of which variation is adopted on any given computer will, of course, depend on the characteristics of the computer. In making the decision, the theoretical estimate of time taken for various values of a, b, c, and M should be used to determine the optimal method; it will not be necessary to write and test a large number of different programs.

2.2.1 Partition without exchange

On some computers the exchange operation would involve copying one of the items into workspace while the other item overwrites the locations which it occupied. On such a computer it would be advantageous to avoid exchanging altogether, and a method of achieving this is described below.

The item chosen to yield the bound should always be that which occupies the highest-addressed locations of the segment which is to be partitioned. If it is feared that this will have a harmfully nonrandom result, a randomly chosen item should be initially placed in the highest-addressed locations. The item which yielded the bound is copied into working space. Then the upper and lower pointers are set to their initial values, and the lower pointer starts its upward scan of the store. When it finds an item with key greater than the bound, this item is copied into the locations to which the upper pointer now refers. The upper pointer is stepped down, and proceeds on its downward scan of the data. When it finds an item with key lower than the bound, this item is copied into the locations referred to by the lower pointer. The lower pointer is then stepped up, and the process is repeated until both the pointers are referring to the same item. Then the item which has supplied the bound is copied from working space into the locations to which the pointers refer. Throughout the process, the stationary pointer refers to locations whose contents have been copied elsewhere, while the moving pointer searches for the item to be copied into these locations. The expected number of copying operations is obviously twice the corresponding figure for exchanges.

2.2.2 Cyclic exchange

On a machine with single-address instructions and the facility of exchanging the contents of accumulator and store, it is more economicalto perform long sequences of exchanges at one time. A single-exchange operation involves reading to the accumulator, exchanging with store, and writing to store, giving $3N$ instructions to perform N exchanges. If these exchanges are perfomed cyclically all at the same time, one exchange instruction can take the place of a read and a write instruction in all the exchanges except the first and the last. Thus only one read instruction, one write instruction, and $2N-1$ exchange instructions are required. Further economy is achieved in the case of multi-word items by the fact that the count of words exchanged need be tested only once for each N-fold exchange of each word of the item.

The method of *Quicksort* allows all exchanges to be saved up until the end of the partitioning process, when they may be executed together in a cyclic movement. In practice, the values of the pointers at the time when they come to a halt are stored in a list for later exchanging. The number of locations which can be spared to hold this list will be a limiting factor in the gain of efficiency.

2.2.3 Optimization of the key-comparison loop

Most sorting methods require that a test be made every time that a pointer is stepped, to see whether it has gone outside its possible range. *Quicksort* is one of the methods which can avoid this requirement by the use of sentinels. Before embarking on the sort, sentinels in the form of items with impossibly large and small key values are placed at each end of the data to be sorted. Now it is possible to remove the pointer test from the key comparison cycle; the test is made only when both pointers are stopped and an exchange is just about to be made. If, at this time, the pointers have not crossed, the exchange is made and the partition process is continued. If they have crossed over, the partition process is at an end.

If the value of the bound is the greatest or the least (or both) of the key values of items in the segment being partitioned, then one (or both) of the pointers will move outside the segment; but no harm can result, provided neither pointer moves outside the area in which the whole mass of data is stored. The upper sentinel, having a key value necessarily greater than that of the bound, will stop the lower pointer, while the lower sentinel will stop the upper pointer. The fact that two extra key comparisons are made on every application of the partition process will be more than compensated on fairly large segments by the omission of pointer comparison from the innermost loop.

2.2.4 Multiword keys

When the keys, with respect to which the sorting is performed, extend over more than one computer word, then a long time may be spent on comparing the second and subsequent words of the key. This is a serious problem, since it often happens that a large number of items share a very few values for the first words of their keys. The problem is aggravated when the items are nearly sorted, and it is necessary to make many comparisons between keys which are identical except in their last word. The method described below is due to Mr P. Shackleton.

The principle of the method is to compare only a single word of the keys on each application of the partitioning process. When it is known that a segment comprises all the items, and only those items, which have key values identical to a given value over their first n words, then, in partitioning this segment, comparison is made of the $(n + 1)$th word of the keys. A variation of the method of partitioning is adopted to ensure that all items with identical values of the key word currently being compared (and consequently identical over earlier words of their keys) are gathered together in one segment as quickly as possible.

The variation consists in altering the criteria which determine the stopping of the pointers. If we ensure that all items with key values equal to the bound are placed in the upper of the resulting segments, then we may associate with each segment its so-called *characteristic value,* which is the greatest value equal to or less than all the key values of the segment (using the expression *key value* to mean the value of the word of the key which will be compared when the segment is partitioned). Furthermore, each segment must contain all the items with key value equal to the characteristic value of the segment. This is easily achieved by making the lower pointer stop whenever it meets an item with key value equal to the bound, so that such an item will be transferred to the upper segment. The value of the bound may obviously be taken as the characteristic value of the upper resulting segment, while the characteristic value of the lower resulting segment is the same as that of the original segment which has just been partitioned. Where this rule does not determine the characteristic values (as in the case of the original mass of data), then no harm will be occasioned by choosing as characteristic value the lowest possible value of the key word.

Now whenever a segment is to be partitioned, the value chosen as the bound is compared with the characteristic value of the segment. If it is greater, partitioning is performed with the modification described in the last paragraph. If, however, they are equal, then it is the upper pointer which is made to stop on encountering an item with key value equal to the bound. Thus all items with key values equal to the characteristic value are collected together in the *lower* resulting segment, and when this segment comes to be partitioned, comparison may be made of the next word of the keys (if any).

The adoption of this refinement means that when the processing of a segment is postponed, the position of the key word which is next to be considered, and the characteristic value for the segment, must be stored together with the positions of the first and last items. On many machines, the extra book-keeping will be justified by the consequent optimization of the innermost comparison loop.

2.2.5 Multilevel storage

Quicksort is well suited to machines with more than one level of storage, for instance a fast-access working store on magnetic cores and a backing store on magnetic disks or drums. The data in the backing store are partitioned repeatedly until each resulting segment may be contained in the fast-access store, in which it may be sorted at high speed.

The partitioning process can be applied quite economically to data held on a magnetic drum or disk backing store. The reason for this is that the movement of the pointers allows serial transfer of information held adjacently in the backing store, and such transfers are usually faster than if more scattered random access were required. This is particularly true if information can only be transferred between the backing store and main store in large blocks. The time lost in searching for information on the backing store may be reduced to insignificant proportions, provided that it does not take an exceptionally long time to search for information at one end of the store immediately after transferring information at the other end. This condition is satisfied by many magnetic drums or disk stores; it is obviously not satisfied by a magnetic-tape store, on which the method of *Quicksort* cannot usefully be applied.

2.3 Conclusion

Quicksort is a sorting method ideally adapted for sorting in the random-access store of a computer. It is equally suited for data held in core storage and data held in high-volume magnetic drum or disk backing stores. The data are sorted *in situ*, and therefore the whole store may be filled with data to be sorted. There is no need to sort simultaneously with input or output. The number of cycles of the innermost comparison loop is close to the theoretical minimum, and the loop may be made very fast. The amount of data movement within the store is kept within very reasonable bounds. *Quicksort* is therefore likely to recommend itself as the standard sorting method on most computers with a large enough random-access store to make internal sorting worthwhile.

THREE

A contribution to the development of ALGOL

One of the themes of the work in this collection is the design of programming languages. The language described in this paper (co-authored with Niklaus Wirth) was implemented as ALGOL W and is referred to in Hoare's Turing Lecture as 'a worthy successor of ALGOL 60, ... a worthy predecessor of Pascal.' Interesting features include the **case** construct and result parameters. The most important contribution was undoubtedly the **record** construct. Hoare discussed this at greater length in a paper presented at the IFIP Working Conference on Symbol Manipulation Languages in Pisa, September 1966 (subsequently published as [11]). It is interesting to note that the idea of records is here linked to that of heap storage and even automatic garbage collection. The discussion of possible 'language extensions' is interesting, as is the allusion (in 1966) to the need for 'a conceptual framework for teaching, reasoning and research in both theoretical and practical aspects of the science of computation.'

This paper was submitted in January 1966, revised in February and published in June of the same year. Here, only Part I of the paper is reprinted; the subsequent parts contain a full description of the language in the style of the ALGOL report and can be found in the original publication ([9]). ALGOL W was implemented by Niklaus Wirth at Stanford and by Sue Graham and others for the then new IBM/360 architecture. Although now defunct, the language was used for teaching in several universities in Europe.

Abstract

A programming language similar in many respects to ALGOL 60, but incorporating a large number of improvements based on six years' experience with that language, is described in detail. The original paper consists of three Parts, of which only Part I is presented here. Part I consists of an introduction to the new language and a summary of the changes made to ALGOL 60, together with a discussion of the motives behind the

N. Wirth and C. A. R. Hoare, 'A contribution to the development of ALGOL', *Comm. ACM* **9**(6) 413–32 (June 1966).

revisions. Part II is a rigorous definition of the proposed language. Part III describes a set of proposed standard procedures to be used with the language, including facilities for input/output.

3.1 Historical background

A preliminary version of this report was originally drafted by the first author on an invitation made by IFIP Working Group 2.1 at its meeting in May 1965 at Princeton. It incorporated a number of opinions and suggestions made at that meeting and in its subcommittees, and it was distributed to members of the Working Group (Wirth 1965).

However, at the following meeting of the Group at Grenoble in October 1965, it was felt that the report did not represent a sufficient advance of ALGOL 60, either in its manner of language definition or in the content of the language itself. The draft therefore no longer had the status of an official Working Document of the Group and by kind permission of the Chairman it was released for wider publication.

At that time the authors agreed to collaborate on revising and supplementing the draft. The main changes were:

(1) Verbal improvements and clarifications, many of which were kindly suggested by recipients of the original draft.
(2) Additional or altered language features, in particular the replacement of tree structures by records as proposed by the second author.
(3) Changes which appeared desirable in the course of designing a simple and efficient implementation of the language.
(4) Addition of introductory and explanatory material, and further suggestions for standard procedures, in particular on input/output.
(5) Use of a convenient notational facility to abbreviate the description of syntax, as suggested by van Wijngaarden (1965).

The incorporation of the revisions is not intended to reinstate the report as a candidate for consideration as a successor to ALGOL 60. However, it is believed that its publication will serve three purposes:

(1) To present to a wider public a view of the general direction in which the development of ALGOL is proceeding.
(2) To provide an opportunity for experimental implementation and use of the language, which may be of value in future discussions of language development.
(3) To describe some of the problems encountered in the attempt to extend the language further.

3.2 Aims of the language

The design of the language is intended to reflect the outlook and intentions of IFIP Working Group 2.1, and in particular their belief in the value of a common programming language suitable for use by many people in many countries. It also recognizes that such a language should satisfy as far as possible the following criteria:

(1) The language must provide a suitable technique for the programming of digital computers. It must therefore be closely oriented toward the capabilities of these machines, and must take into account their inherent limitations. As a result it should be possible to construct a fast, well-structured and reliable translator, translating programs into machine code which makes economic use of the power and capacity of a computer. In addition, the design of the language should act as an encouragement to the programmer to conceive the solution of his problems in terms which will product effective programs on the computers he is likely to have at his disposal.

(2) The language must serve as a medium of communication between those engaged in problems capable of algorithmic solution. The notational structure of programs expressed in the language should correspond closely with the dynamic structure of the processes they describe. The programmer should be obliged to express himself explicitly clearly and fully, without confusing abbreviations or implicit presuppositions. The perspicuity of programs is believed to be a property of equal benefit to their readers and ultimately to their writers.

(3) The language must present a conceptual framework for teaching, reasoning and research in both theoretical and practical aspects of the science of computation. It must therefore be based on rigorous selection and abstraction of the most fundamental concepts of computational techniques. Its power and flexibility should derive from unifying simplicity, rather than from proliferation of poorly integrated features and facilities. As a consequence, for each purpose there will be exactly one obviously appropriate facility, so that there is minimal scope for erroneous choice and misapplication of facilities, whether due to misunderstanding, inadvertence or inexperience.

(4) The value of a language is increased in proportion to the range of applications in which it may effectively and conveniently be used. It is hoped that the language will find use throughout the field of algebraic and numeric applications, and that its use will begin to spread to non-numeric data processing in areas hitherto the preserve of special-purpose languages, for example, the fields of simulation studies, design automation, information retrieval, graph theory, symbol manipulation and linguistic research.

To meet any of these four requirements, it is necessary that the language itself be defined with utmost clarity and rigor. The Report on ALGOL 60 has set a high standard in this respect, and in style and notation its example has been gratefully followed.

3.3 Summary of new features

A large part of the language is, of course, taken directly from ALGOL 60. However, in some respects the language has been simplified, and in others extended. The following paragraphs summarize the major changes to ALGOL 60, and relate them to the declared aims of the language.

3.3.1 Data types

The range of primitive data types has been extended from three in ALGOL 60 to seven, or rather nine, if the long variants are included. In compensation, certain aspects of the concept of type have been simplified. In particular, the **own** concept has been abandoned as insufficiently useful to justify its position, and as leading to semantic ambiguities in many circumstances.

3.3.1.1 Numeric data types

The type **complex** has been introduced into the language to simplify the specification of algorithms involving complex numbers.

For the types **real** and **complex**, a long variant is provided to deal with calculations or sections of calculations in which the normal precision for floating-point number representation is not sufficient. It is expected that the significance of the representation will be approximately doubled.

No provision is made for specifying the exact required significance of floating-point representation in terms of the number of binary or decimal digits. It is considered most important that the value of primitive types should occupy a small integral number of computer words, so that their processing can be carried out with the maximum efficiency of the equipment available.

3.3.1.2 Sequences

The concept of a *sequence* occupies a position intermediate between that of an array and of other simple data types. Like single-dimensional arrays, they consist of ordered sequences of elements; however, unlike arrays, the most frequent operations performed on them are not the extraction or insertion of single elements, but rather the processing of whole sequences, or possibly subsequences of them.

Sequences are represented in the language by two new types, **bits** (sequence of binary digits), and **string** (sequence of characters). Operations defined for bit sequences include the logical operations $\neg$, $\wedge$ and $\vee$, and those of shifting left and right.

The most important feature of a bit sequence is that its elements are sufficiently small to occupy only a fraction of a 'computer word', i.e. a unit of information which is in some sense natural to the computer. This means that space can be saved by 'packing,' and efficiency can be gained by operating on such natural units of information. In order that use of such natural units can be made by an implementation, the maximum number of elements in a sequence must be specified, when a variable of that type is declared. Operations defined for string sequences include the catenation operator **cat**.

3.3.1.3 Type determination at compile time

The language has been designed in such a way that the type and length of the result of evaluating every expression and subexpression can be uniquely determined by a textual scan of the program, so that no type testing is required at run time, except possibly on procedure entry.

3.3.1.4 Type conversions

The increase in the number of data types has caused an even greater number of possibilities for type conversion; some of these are intended to be inserted automatically by the translator, and others have to be specified by the programmer by use of standard transfer functions provided for the purpose.

Automatic insertion of type conversion has been confined to cases where there could be no possible confusion about which conversion is intended: from **integer** to **real**, and **real** to **complex**, but not vice versa. Automatic conversions are also performed from shorter to longer variants of the data types; and in the case of numbers, from long to short as well.

For all other conversions explicit standard procedures must be used. This ensures that the complexity and possible inefficiency of the conversion process is not hidden from the programmer; furthermore, the existence of additional parameters of the procedure, or a choice of procedures, will draw his attention to the fact that there is more than one way of performing the conversion, and he is thereby encouraged to select the alternative which corresponds to his real requirements, rather than rely on a built-in 'default' conversion, about which he may have only vague or even mistaken ideas.

3.3.2 Control of sequencing

The only changes made to facilities associated with control of sequencing have been made in the direction of simplification and clarification, rather than extension.

3.3.2.1 Switches and the case construction

The switch declaration and the switch designator have been abolished. Their place has been taken by the **case** construction, applying to both expressions and statements. This construction permits the selection and execution (or evaluation) of one from a list of statements (or expressions); the selection is made in accordance with the value of an integer expression.

The **case** construction extends the facilities of the ALGOL conditional to circumstances where the choice is made from more than two alternatives. Like the conditional, it mirrors the dynamic structure of a program more clearly than **goto** statements and switches, and it eliminates the need for introducing a large number of labels in the program.

3.3.2.2 Labels

The concept of a label has been simplified so that it merely serves as a link between a **goto** statement and its destination; it has been stripped of all features suggesting that it is a manipulable object. In particular, designational expressions have been abolished, and labels can no longer be passed as parameters of procedures.

A further simplification is represented by the rule that a **goto** statement cannot lead from outside into a conditional statement or **case** statement, as well as iterative statement.

The ALGOL 60 integer labels have been eliminated.

3.3.2.3 Iterative statements

The purpose of iterative statements is to enable the programmer to specify iterations in a simple and perspicuous manner, and to protect himself from the unexpected effects of some subtle or careless error. They also signalize to the translator that this is a special case, susceptible of simple optimization.

It is notorious that the ALGOL 60 **for** statement fails to satisfy any of these requirements, and therefore a drastic simplification has been made. The use of iterative statements has been confined to the really simple and common cases, rather than extended to cover more complex requirements, which can be more flexibly and perspicuously dealt with by explicit program instructions using labels.

The most general and powerful iterative statement, capable of covering all requirements, is that which indicates that a statement is to be executed repeatedly while a given condition remains true. The only alternative type of iterative statement allows a formal counter to take successive values in a finite arithmetic progression on each execution of the statement. No explicit assignments can be made to this counter, which is implicitly declared as local to the iterative statement.

3.3.3 Procedures and parameters

A few minor changes have been made to the procedure concept of ALGOL 60, mainly in the interests of clarification and efficiency of implementation.

3.3.3.1 Value and result parameters

As in ALGOL 60, the meaning of parameters is explained in terms of the 'copy rule', which prescribes the literal replacement of the formal parameter by the actual parameter. As a counterpart to the 'value parameter', which is a convenient abbreviation for the frequent case where the formal parameter can be considered as a variable local to the procedure and initialized to the value of the actual parameter, a 'result parameter' has been introduced. Again, the formal parameter is considered as a local variable, whose value is assigned to the corresponding actual parameter (which therefore always must be a variable) upon termination of the procedure.

The facility of calling an array parameter by value has been removed. It contributes no additional power to the language, and it contravenes the general policy that operations on entire arrays should be specified by means of explicit iterations, rather than concealed by an implicit notation.

3.3.3.2 Statement parameters

A facility has been provided for writing a statement as an actual parameter corresponding to a formal specified as **procedure**. The statement can be considered as a proper procedure body without parameters. This represents a considerable notational convenience, since it enables the procedure to be specified actually in the place where it is to be used, rather than disjointly in the head of some embracing block.

The label parameter has been abolished; its function may be taken over by placing a **goto** statement in the corresponding actual parameter position.

3.3.3.3 Specifications

The specification of all formal parameters, and the correct matching of actuals to formals, has been made obligatory. The purpose of specifications is to inform the user of the procedure of the correct conditions of its use, and to ensure that the translator can check that these conditions have been met.

One of the most important facts about a procedure which operates on array parameters is the dimensionality of the arrays it will accept as actual parameters. A means has therefore been provided for indicating this in the specification of the parameter.

To compensate for the obligatory nature of specifications, their notation has been simplified by including them in the formal parameter list, rather than placing them in a separate specification part, as in ALGOL 60.

3.3.4 Data structures

The concept of an array has been taken from ALGOL 60 virtually unchanged, with the exception of a slight notational simplification.

To supplement the array concept, the language has been extended by the addition of a new type of structure (the **record**) consisting, like the array, of one or more elements (or *fields*). With each record there is associated a unique value of type **reference** which is said to refer to that record. This reference may be assigned as the value of a suitable field in another record, with which the given record has some meaningful relationship. In this way, groups of records may be linked in structural networks of any desired complexity.

The concept of records has been pioneered in the AED-I language by D. T. Ross.

3.3.4.1 Records and fields

Like the array, a record is intended to occupy a given fixed number of locations in the store of a computer. It differs from the array in that the types of the fields are not required to be identical, so that in general each field of a record may occupy a different amount of storage. This, of course, makes it unattractive to select an element from a record by means of a computed ordinal number, or index; instead, each field position is given a unique invented name (identifier), which is written in the program whenever that field is referred to.

A record may be used to represent inside the computer some discrete physical or conceptual object to be examined or manipulated by the program, for example, a person, a town, a geometric figure, a node of a graph, etc. The fields of the record then represent properties of that object, for example, the name of a person, the distance of a town from some starting point, the length of a line, the time of joining a queue, etc.

Normally, the name of the field suggests the property represented by that field.

In contrast to arrays, records are not created by declarations; rather, they are created dynamically by statements of the program. Thus their lifetimes do not have to be nested, and stack methods of storage control must be supplemented by more sophisticated techniques. It is intended that automatic 'garbage collection' will be applicable to records, so that records which have become inaccessible may be detected, and the space they occupy released for other purposes.

3.3.4.2 References

The normal data types (**string**, **real**, **integer**, etc.) are sufficient to represent the properties of the objects represented by records; but a new type of data is required to represent relationships holding between these objects. Provided that the relationship is a functional relationship (i.e. many–one or one–one), it can be represented by placing as a field of one record a reference to the other record to which it is related. For example, if a record which represents a person has a field named *father*, then this is likely to be used to contain a reference to the record which represents that person's father. A similar treatment is possible to deal with the relationship between a town and the next town visited on some journey, between a customer and the person following him in some queue, between a directed line and its starting point, etc.

References are also used to provide the means by which the program gains access to records; for this purpose, variables of type **reference** should be declared in the head of the block which uses them. Such variables will at any given time refer to some subset of the currently existing records. Fields of records can be referred to directly by associating the name of the field with the value of the variable holding a reference to the relevant record. If that record itself has fields containing references to yet further records outside the initial subset, then fields of these other records may be accessed indirectly by further associating their names with the construction which identified the reference to the relevant record. By assignment of references, records previously accessible only indirectly can be made directly accessible, and records previously directly accessible can lose this status, or even become totally inaccessible, in which case they are considered as deleted.

Thus, for example, if B is a variable of type **reference** declared in the head of some enclosing block, and if *age* and *father* are field identifiers, and if B contains a reference to a certain person, then

$$age(B)$$

(called a field designator) gives that person's age;

$$father(B)$$

is a reference to that person's father, and

$$age(father(B))$$

gives his father's age.

3.3.4.3 *Record classes*

Two records may be defined as similar if they have the same number of fields, and if corresponding fields in the two records have the same names and the same types. Similarity in this sense is an equivalence relation and may be used to split all records into mutually exclusive and exhaustive equivalence classes, called *record classes*. These classes tend to correspond to the natural classification of objects under some generic term, for example: *person*, *town* or *quadrilateral*. Each record class must be introduced in a program by means of a record class declaration, which associates a name with the class and specifies the names and types of the fields which characterize the members of the class.

One of the major pitfalls in the use of references is the mistaken assumption that the value of a reference variable, -field or -parameter refers to a record of some given class, whereas on execution of the program it turns out that the reference value is associated with some record of quite a different class. If the programmer attempts to access a field inappropriate to the actual class referred to, he will get a meaningless result; but if he attempts to make an assignment to such a field, the consequences could be disastrous to the whole scheme of storage control. To avoid this pitfall, it is specified that the programmer can associate with the definition of every reference variable, -field or -parameter the name of the record class to which any record referred to by it will belong. The *translator* is then able to verify that the mistake described can never occur.

3.3.4.4 *Efficiency of implementation*

Many applications for which record handling will be found useful are severely limited by the speed and capacity of the computers available. It has therefore been a major aim in the design of the record-handling facilities that in implementation the accessing of records and fields should be accomplished with the utmost efficiency, and that the layout of storage be subject only to a minimum administrative overhead.

3.4 Possibilities for language extension

In the design of the language a number of inviting possibilities for extensions were considered. In many cases the investigation of these extensions seemed to reveal inconsistencies, indecisions and difficulties which could not readily be solved. In other cases it seemed undesirable to make the extension into a standard feature of the language, in view of the extra complexity involved.

In this section, suggested extensions are outlined for the consideration of implementors, users and other language designers.

3.4.1 Further string operations

For some applications it seems desirable to provide facilities for referring to subsequences of bits and strings. The position of the subsequence could be indicated by a notation similar to subscript bounds, viz.

$S[i:j]$ the subsequence of S consisting of the ith to jth elements inclusive

This notation is more compact than the use of a standard procedure, and it represents the fact that extraction is more likely to be performed by an open subroutine than a closed one. However, the notational similarity suggests that the construction might also appear in the left part of an assignment, in which case it denotes insertion rather than extraction, i.e. assignment to a part of the quantity. Apart from the undesirability of the same contruction denoting two different operations, this would require that strings be classified as structured values along with arrays.

3.4.2 Further data types

Suggestions have been made for facilities to specify the precision of numbers in a more 'flexible' way, e.g. by indicating the number of required decimal places. This solution has been rejected because it ignores the fundamental distinction between the number itself and one of its possible denotations, and as a consequence is utterly inappropriate for calculators not using the decimal number representation. As an alternative, the notion of a precision hierarchy could be introduced by prefixing declarations with a sequence of symbols **long**, where the number of **long**s determines the precision class. For reasons of simplicity, and in order that an implementation may closely reflect the properties of a real machine (single vs. double precision real arithmetic), allowing for only one **long** was considered as appropriate. Whether an implementation actually distinguishes between **real** and **long real** can be determined by an environment enquiry.

3.4.3 Initial values and local constants

It is a minor notational convenience to be able to assign an initial value to a variable as part of the declaration which introduces that variable. A more important advantage is that the notation enables the programmer to express a very important feature of his calculations, namely, that this is a unique initial assignment made once only on the first entry to the block; furthermore it completely rules out the possibility of the elementary but all too common error of failing to make an assignment before the use of a variable.

However, such a facility rests on the notions of 'compile time' and 'run time' action, which, if at all, should be introduced at a conceptually much more fundamental level.

In some cases it is known that a variable only ever takes one value throughout its lifetime, and a means may be provided to make these cases notationally distinct from those of initial assignment. This means that the intention of the programmer can be made explicit for the benefit of the reader, and the translator is capable of checking that the assumption of constancy is in fact justified. Furthermore, the translator can sometimes take advantage of the declaration of constancy to optimize a program.

3.4.4 Array constructors

To provide the same technique for the initialization of arrays as for other variables, some method should be provided for enumerating the values of an array as a sequence of expressions. This would require the definition of a reference denotation for array values, which, if available, would consequently suggest the introduction of operations on values of type **array**. The reasons for not extending the language in this direction have already been explained.

3.4.5 Record class discrimination

In general, the rule that the values of a particular reference variable or field must be confined to a single record class will be found to present little hardship; however, there are circumstances in which it is useful to relax this rule, and to permit the value of a reference variable to range over more than one record class. A facility is then desirable to determine the record class to which a referred record actually belongs.

Two possibilities for record class discriminations are outlined as follows:

(1) A record union declaration is introduced with the form

union⟨record union identifier⟩ (⟨record class identifier list⟩)

The record class identifier accompanying a reference variable declaration could then be replaced by a record union identifier, indicating that the values of that reference variable may range over all record classes included in that union. An integer primary of the form

⟨record union identifier⟩ (⟨reference expression⟩)

would then yield the ordinal number of the record class in that union to which the record referred to by the reference expression belongs.

(2) Record class specifications in reference variable declarations are omitted, and a logical primary of the form

⟨reference primary⟩ **is** ⟨record class identifier⟩

could be introduced with the value **true** if and only if the reference primary refers to a record of the specified record class.

While the introduction of a new kind of declaration (1) may seem undesirable, solution (2) reintroduces the dangerous pitfalls described in Section 3.3.4.3.

3.4.6 Procedure parameters

It has been realized that in most implementations an actual parameter being an expression constitutes a function procedure declaration, and that one being a statement constitutes a proper procedure declaration. These quasi-procedure declarations, however, are confined to being parameterless. Samelson (1965) has suggested a notation for functionals which essentially does nothing more than remove this restriction: an actual parameter may include in its heading formal parameter specifications. In a paper by Wirth and Weber (1966), the notational distinction between procedure declarations and actual parameters has been entirely removed. This was done along with the introduction of a new kind of actual parameters similar in nature to the references introduced here in connection with records.

However, neither *ad hoc* solutions nor a radical change from the parameter mechanism and notation of ALGOL 60 seemed desirable.

FOUR

An axiomatic basis for computer programming

This paper can be taken as the first in Hoare's output on the formal verification of programs. It provided the most important single stimulus to the work on axiomatic semantics of programming languages. This is one of the most widely cited papers in computing science and it has been reprinted many times. It is worth considering the ideas current prior to its publication. Hoare cites the work of Floyd (discussed further below), Naur and van Wijngaarden. Naur (1966) is clearly less formal than the style chosen for the axiom system presented. An early piece of work which could have influenced his thinking, had Hoare been aware of it, was Turing (1949) – see Morris and Jones (1984). However, the prevalent view of language definition at that time was based on the operational semantics approach.

Hoare had attended the 1964 IFIP Working Conference on Formal Language Description Languages at Baden-bei-Wien in 1964 (the proceedings of which are published as Steel (1966). Although he did not give a talk, a comment was made (see pp. 142–3) on 'the need to leave languages undefined'. At the meeting of W.G. 2.1, which followed the Baden conference, Hoare discussed the definition of functions like **mod** via their properties (in this case, its result is non-negative and equal to either its argument or the negation thereof). In 1965, he attended, with other members of ECMA TC10, a course on the IBM Laboratory Vienna's work on operational semantics and he stayed at the Imperial Hotel on whose notepaper a first sketch of the axiomatic work was written. A two-part draft dated December 1967, one part of which axiomatized execution traces as a partial order on states, clearly states the goals of what was to become axiomatic semantics and discusses a wide range of language features. This draft was written during a brief period of employment at the National Computing Centre at Manchester.

Although the objectives are clear in the 1967 draft, there is no coherent notion of how to axiomatize programming language constructs. Among

C. A. R. Hoare, 'An axiomatic basis for computer programming', *Comm. ACM.* **12**(10), 576–80, 583 (October 1969).

others, Hoare sent these notes to Peter Lucas of the IBM Vienna group. On arrival in Belfast to take up his chair in October 1968, Hoare 'stumbled upon the mimeographed draft' (this was dated 20 May 1966) of what was to be published as Floyd (1967). This clearly had a major impact on the paper reproduced here. A further two-part draft dated December 1968 strongly resembles the final paper. The first part on data manipulation outlines the ideas at the beginning of this chapter, while the part on program execution uses the assertion form now known as Hoare triples (they are written here as $P\{S\}R$ but are now normally written as $\{P\}S\{R\}$ to emphasize the role of assertions as comments).

Floyd's paper uses a forward assignment rule which requires an existential quantifier; this was also used in Hoare's 1968 draft; the paper here uses a far more useful backwards rule which was first published in Jim King's thesis although he attributes it to Floyd; Hoare was made aware of this form by David Cooper who had been on sabbatical in Carnegie and had given a talk at Belfast University.

This paper, which has been reprinted many times, has had a major influence on formal methods of program development (extension of the method to cope with other language features is discussed in Chapters 6 and 11). The impact can be traced in Apt (1981) and in the enormous number of citations to the paper. Very few actual languages have been designed using this method. Euclid is perhaps the most notable attempt; Ada's objectives in this area were not met; the design of occam™ is discussed in Chapter 16.

The axiomatic system is presented as a way of proving the correctness of extant programs. Subsequent work (including Chapter 5) showed how the same system could be used in program design. The emphasis on control structures was also a limitation to the usefulness of the system presented; Hoare's approach to the problem of data abstraction is described in Chapter 8. The restriction to 'partial correctness' is explained in Section 5 of the paper. Another, more subtle, restriction is the assumption that post-conditions are predicates of the final state alone. Hoare adopted post-conditions which are predicates of initial and final states in his talks at the Newcastle seminar in 1982 (see also Chapter 20). This paper was published as [15] in October 1969.

Abstract

In this paper an attempt is made to explore the logical foundations of computer programming by use of techniques which were first applied in the study of geometry and have later been extended to other branches of mathematics. This involves the elucidation of sets of axioms and rules of inference which can be used in proofs of the properties of computer programs. Examples are given of such axioms and rules, and a formal proof of a simple theorem is displayed. Finally, it is argued that important advantages, both theoretical and practical, may follow from a pursuance of these topics.

4.1 Introduction

Computer programming is an exact science in that all the properties of a program and all the consequences of executing it in any given environment can, in principle, be found out from the text of the program itself by means of purely deductive reasoning. Deductive reasoning involves the application of valid rules of inference to sets of valid axioms. It is therefore desirable and interesting to elucidate the axioms and rules of inference which underlie our reasoning about computer programs. The exact choice of axioms will to some extent depend on the choice of programming language. For illustrative purposes, this paper is confined to a very simple language, which is effectively a subset of all current procedure-oriented languages.

4.2 Computer arithmetic

The first requirement in valid reasoning about a program is to know the properties of the elementary operations which it invokes, for example, addition and multiplication of integers. Unfortunately, in several respects computer arithmetic is not the same as the arithmetic familiar to mathematicians, and it is necessary to exercise some care in selecting an appropriate set of axioms. For example, the axioms displayed in Table 4.1 are rather a small selection of axioms relevant to integers. From this incomplete set of axioms it is possible to deduce such simple theorems as:

$$x = x + y \times 0$$

$$y \leqslant r \Rightarrow r + y \times q = (r - y) + y \times (1 + q)$$

The proof of the second of these is:

A5	$(r - y) + y \times (1 + q) = (r - y) + (y \times 1 + y \times q)$
A9	$= (r - y) + (y + y \times q)$
A3	$= ((r - y) + y) + y \times q$
A6	$= r + y \times q$ provided $y \leqslant r$

The axioms A1–A9 are, of course, true of the traditional infinite set of integers in mathematics. However, they are also true of the finite sets of 'integers' which are manipulated by computers provided that they are confined to *nonnegative* numbers. Their truth is independent of the size of the set; furthermore, it is largely independent of the choice of technique applied in the event of 'overflow'; for example:

(1) Strict interpretation: the result of an overflowing operation does not

Table 4.1

A1	$x + y = y + x$	addition is commutative
A2	$x \times y = y \times x$	multiplication is commutative
A3	$(x + y) + z = x + (y + z)$	addition is associative
A4	$(x \times y) \times z = x \times (y \times z)$	multiplication is associative
A5	$x \times (y + z) = x \times y + x \times z$	multiplication distributes through addition
A6	$y \leqslant x \Rightarrow (x - y) + y = x$	addition cancels subtraction
A7	$x + 0 = x$	
A8	$x \times 0 = 0$	
A9	$x \times 1 = x$	

exist; when overflow occurs, the offending program never completes its operation. Note that in this case, the equalities of A1 to A9 are strict, in the sense that both sides exist or fail to exist together.

(2) Firm boundary; the result of an overflowing operation is taken as the maximum value represented.

(3) Modulo arithmetic: the result of an overflowing operation is computed modulo the size of the set of integers represented.

These three techniques are illustrated in Table 4.2 by addition and multiplication tables for a trivially small model in which 0, 1, 2, and 3 are the only integers represented.

Table 4.2

1. Strict interpretation

+	0	1	2	3
0	0	1	2	3
1	1	2	3	*
2	2	3	*	*
3	3	*	*	*

×	0	1	2	3
0	0	0	0	0
1	0	1	2	3
2	0	2	*	*
3	0	3	*	*

* nonexistent

2. Firm boundary

+	0	1	2	3
0	0	1	2	3
1	1	2	3	3
2	2	3	3	3
3	3	3	3	3

×	0	1	2	3
0	0	0	0	0
1	0	1	2	3
2	0	2	3	3
3	0	3	3	3

3. Modulo arithmetic

+	0	1	2	3
0	0	1	2	3
1	1	2	3	0
2	2	3	0	1
3	3	0	1	2

×	0	1	2	3
0	0	0	0	0
1	0	1	2	3
2	0	2	0	2
3	0	3	2	1

It is interesting to note that the different systems satisfying axioms A1–A9 may be rigorously distinguished from each other by choosing a particular one of a set of mutually exclusive supplementary axioms. For example, infinite arithmetic satisfies the axiom:

A10_I $\qquad \neg\exists x \forall y (y \leqslant x)$,

whereas all finite arithmetics satisfy:

A10_F $\qquad \forall x (x \leqslant \max)$

where 'max' denotes the largest integer represented.

Similarly, the three treatments of overflow may be distinguished by a choice of one of the following axioms relating to the value of max + 1:

A11_S $\qquad \neg\exists x (x = \max + 1)$ $\qquad$ (strict interpretation)

A11_B $\qquad \max + 1 = \max$ $\qquad$ (firm boundary)

A11_M $\qquad \max + 1 = 0$ $\qquad$ (modulo arithmetic)

Having selected one of these axioms, it is possible to use it in deducing the properties of programs; however, these properties will not necessarily obtain, unless the program is executed on an implementation which satisfies the chosen axiom.

4.3 Program execution

As mentioned above, the purpose of this study is to provide a logical basis for proofs of the properties of a program. One of the most important properties of a program is whether or not it carries out its intended function. The intended function of a program, or part of a program, can be specified by making general assertions about the values which the relevant variables will take *after* execution of the program. These assertions will usually not ascribe particular values to each variable, but will rather specify certain general properties of the values and the relationships holding between them. We use the normal notations of mathematical logic to express these assertions, and the familiar rules of operator precedence have been used wherever possible to improve legibility.

In many cases, the validity of the results of a program (or part of a program) depend on the values taken by the variables before that program is initiated. These initial preconditions of successful use can be specified by the same type of general assertion as is used to describe the results obtained on termination. To state the required connection between a precondition (P), a program (Q) and a description of the result of its execution (R), we introduce a new notation:

$$P\{Q\}\ R.$$

This may be interpreted 'If the assertion P is true before initiation of a program Q, then the assertion R will be true on its completion.' If there are no preconditions imposed, we write **true** $\{Q\}\ R$.†

The treatment given below is essentially due to Floyd (1967) but is applied to texts rather than flowcharts.

4.3.1 Axiom of assignment

Assignment is undoubtedly the most characteristic feature of programming a digital computer, and one that most clearly distinguishes it from other branches of mathematics. It is surprising therefore that the axiom governing our reasoning about assignment is quite as simple as any to be found in elementary logic.

Consider the assignment statement:

$$x := f$$

where

x is an identifier for a simple variable;

f is an expression of a programming language without side effects, but possibly containing x.

Now any assertion $P(x)$ which is to be true of (the value of) x *after* the assignment is made must also have been true of (the value of) the expression f, taken *before* the assignment is made, i.e. with the old value of x. Thus if $P(x)$ is to be true after the assignment, then $P(f)$ must be true before the assignment. This fact may be expressed more formally:

D0 Axiom of assignment

$\vdash P_0\ \{x := f\}\ P$

where

x is a variable identifier;

f is an expression;

P_0 is obtained from P by substituting f for all occurrences of x.

It may be noticed that D0 is not really an axiom at all, but rather an axiom schema, describing an infinite set of axioms which share a common pattern. This pattern is described in purely syntactic terms, and it is easy to check whether any finite text conforms to the pattern, thereby qualifying as an axiom, which may validly appear in any line of a proof.

†If this can be proved in our formal system, we use the familiar logical symbol for theoremhood: $\vdash P\{Q\}\ R$

4.3.2 Rules of consequence

In addition to axioms, a deductive science requires at least one rule of inference, which permits the deduction of new theorems from one or more axioms or theorems already proved. A rule of inference takes the form 'If $\vdash X$ and $\vdash Y$ then $\vdash Z$', i.e. if assertions of the form X and Y have been proved as theorems, then Z also is thereby proved as a theorem. The simplest example of an inference rule states that if the execution of a program Q ensures the truth of the assertion R, then it also ensures the truth of every assertion logically implied by R. Also, if P is known to be a precondition for a program Q to produce result R, then so is any other assertion which logically implies P. These rules may be expressed more formally:

D1 Rules of consequence
If $\vdash P\{Q\}R$ and $\vdash R \Rightarrow S$ then $\vdash P\{Q\}S$
If $\vdash P\{Q\}R$ and $\vdash S \Rightarrow P$ then $\vdash S\{Q\}R$

4.3.3 Rule of composition

A program generally consists of a sequence of statements which are executed one after another. The statements may be separated by a semicolon or equivalent symbol denoting procedural composition: $(Q_1; Q_2; \ldots; Q_n)$. In order to avoid the awkwardness of dots, it is possible to deal initially with only two statements $(Q_1; Q_2)$, since longer sequences can be reconstructed by nesting, thus $(Q_1; (Q_2; (\cdots (Q_{n-1}; Q_n)\cdots)))$. The removal of the brackets of this nest may be regarded as convention based on the associativity of the ';-operator', in the same way as brackets are removed from an arithmetic expression $(t_1 + (t_2 + (\cdots (t_{n-1} + t_n)\cdots)))$.

The inference rule associated with composition states that if the proven result of the first part of a program is identical with the precondition under which the second part of the program produces its intended result, then the whole program will produce the intended result, provided that the precondition of the first part is satisfied.

In more formal terms:

D2 Rule of composition
If $\vdash P\{Q_1\}R_1$ and $\vdash R_1\{Q_2\}R$ then $\vdash P\{(Q_1; Q_2)\}R$

4.3.4 Rule of iteration

The essential feature of a stored program computer is the ability to execute some portion of program (S) repeatedly until a condition (B) goes false. A simple way of expressing such an iteration is to adapt the ALGOL 60 **while** notation:

$$\textbf{while } B \textbf{ do } S$$

In executing this statement, a computer first tests the condition B. If this is false, S is omitted, and execution of the loop is complete. Otherwise, S is executed and B is tested again. This action is repeated until B is found to be false. The reasoning which leads to a formulation of an inference rule for iteration is as follows. Suppose P to be an assertion which is always true on completion of S, provided that it is also true on initiation. Then obviously P will still be true after any number of iterations of the statement S (even no iterations). Furthermore, it is known that the controlling condition B is false when the iteration finally terminates. A slightly more powerful formulation is possible in light of the fact that B may be assumed to be true on initiation of S:

D3 Rule of iteration

$$\text{If } \vdash P \wedge B\,\{S\}\,P \quad \text{then} \quad \vdash P\,\{\textbf{while } B \textbf{ do } S\}\neg B \wedge P$$

4.3.5 Example

The axioms quoted above are sufficient to construct the proof of properties of simple programs, for example, a routine intended to find the quotient q and remainder r obtained on dividing x by y. All variables are assumed to range over a set of nonnegative integers conforming to the axioms listed in Table 4.1. For simplicity we use the trivial but inefficient method of successive subtraction. The proposed program is:

$$((r := x;\ q := 0);\ \textbf{while } y \leqslant r \textbf{ do } (r := r - y;\ q := 1 + q))$$

An important property of this program is that when it terminates, we can recover the numerator x by adding to the remainder r the product of the divisor y and the quotient q (i.e. $x = r + y \times q$). Furthermore, the remainder is less than the divisor. These properties may be expressed formally:

$$\textbf{true } \{Q\}\ \neg y \leqslant r \wedge x = r + y \times q$$

where Q stands for the program displayed above. This expresses a necessary (but not sufficient) condition for the 'correctness' of the program.

A formal proof of this theorem is given in Table 4.3. Like all formal proofs, it is excessively tedious, and it would be fairly easy to introduce notational conventions which would significantly shorten it. An even more powerful method of reducing the tedium of formal proofs is to derive general rules for proof construction out of the simple rules accepted as postulates. These general rules would be shown to be valid by demonstra-

Table 4.3

Line number	Formal proof	Justification
1	**true** $\Rightarrow x = x + y \times 0$	Lemma 1
2	$x = x + y \times 0 \{r := x\}\ x = r + y \times 0$	D0
3	$x = r + y \times 0 \{q := 0\}\ x = r + y \times q$	D0
4	**true** $\{r := x\}\ x = r + y \times 0$	D1 (1, 2)
5	**true** $\{r := x;\ q := 0\}\ x = r + y \times q$	D2 (4, 3)
6	$x = r + y \times q \wedge y \leqslant r \Rightarrow$ $x = (r - y) + y \times (1 + q)$	Lemma 2
7	$x = (r - y) + y \times (1 + q)\ \{r := r - y\}$ $x = r + y \times (1 + q)$	D0
8	$x = r + y \times (1 + q)\ \{q := 1 + q\}$ $x = r + y \times q$	D0
9	$x = (r - y) + y \times (1 + q)\{r := r - y;\ q := 1 + q$ $x = r + y \times q$	D2 (7, 8)
10	$x = r + y \times q \wedge y \leqslant r\ \{r := r - y;\ q := 1 + q\}$ $x = r + y \times q$	D1 (6, 9)
11	$x = r + y \times q$ **while** $y \leqslant r$ **do** $(r := r - y;\ q := 1 + q)\}$ $\neg y \leqslant r \wedge x = r + y \times q$	D3 (10)
12	**true** $\{((r := x;\ q := 0);$ **while** $y \leqslant r$ **do** $(r := r - y;\ q := 1 + q))\}$ $\neg y \leqslant r \wedge x = r + y \times q$	D2 (5, 11)

NOTES

(1) The left-hand column is used to number the lines, and the right-hand column to justify each line, by appealing to an axiom, a lemma or a rule of inference applied to one or two previous lines, indicated in brackets. Neither of these columns is part of the formal proof. For example, line 2 is an instance of the axiom of assignment (D0); line 12 is obtained from lines 5 and 11 by application of the rule of composition (D2).

(2) Lemma 1 may be proved from axioms A7 and A8.

(3) Lemma 2 follows directly from the theorem proved in Section 4.2.

ting how every theorem proved with their assistance could equally well (if more tediously) have been proved without. Once a powerful set of supplementary rules has been developed, a 'formal proof' reduces to little more than an informal indication of how a formal proof could be constructed.

4.4 General reservations

The axioms and rules of inference quoted in this paper have implicitly assumed the absence of side effects of the evaluation of expressions and conditions. In proving properties of programs expressed in a language permitting side effects, it would be necessary to prove their absence in each case before applying the appropriate proof technique. If the main purpose of a high-level programming language is to assist in the construction and verification of correct programs, it is doubtful whether the use of functional notation to call procedures with side effects is a genuine advantage.

Another deficiency in the axioms and rules quoted above is that they give no basis for a proof that a program successfully terminates. Failure to terminate may be due to an infinite loop; or it may be due to violation of an implementation-defined limit, for example, the range of numeric operands, the size of storage, or an operating system time unit. Thus the notation '$P\{Q\}\ R$' should be interpreted as 'provided that the program successfully terminates, the properties of its results are described by R.' It is fairly easy to adapt the axioms so that they cannot be used to predict the 'results' of nonterminating programs; but the actual use of the axioms would now depend on knowledge of many implementation-dependent features, for example, the size and speed of the computer, the range of numbers, and the choice of overflow technique. Apart from proofs of the avoidance of infinite loops, it is probably better to prove the 'conditional' correctness of a program and rely on an implementation to give a warning if it has had to abandon execution of the program as a result of violation of an implementation limit.

Finally it is necessary to list some of the areas which have not been covered: for example, real arithmetic, bit and character manipulation, complex arithmetic, fractional arithmetic, arrays, records, overlay definition, files, input/output, declarations, subroutines, parameters, recursion, and parallel execution. Even the characterization of integer arithmetic is far from complete. There does not appear to be any great difficulty in dealing with these points, provided that the programming language is kept simple. Areas which do present real difficulty are labels and jumps, pointers, and name parameters. Proofs of programs which made use of these features are likely to be elaborate, and it is not surprising that this should be reflected in the complexity of the underlying axioms.

4.5 Proofs of program correctness

The most important property of a program is whether it accomplishes the intentions of its user. If these intentions can be described rigorously by making assertions about the values of variables at the end (or at intermediate points) of the execution of the program, then the techniques described in this paper may be used to prove the correctness of the program, provided that the implementation of the programming language conforms to the axioms and rules which have been used in the proof. This fact itself might also be established by deductive reasoning, using an axiom set which describes the logical properties of the hardware circuits. When the correctness of a program, its compiler, and the hardware of the computer have all been established with mathematical certainty, it will be possible to place great reliance on the results of the program, and predict their properties with a confidence limited only by the reliability of the electronics.

The practice of supplying proofs for nontrivial programs will not become widespread until considerably more powerful proof techniques become available, and even then will not be easy. But the practical advantages of program proving will eventually outweigh the difficulties, in view of the increasing costs of programming error. At present, the method which a programmer uses to convince himself of the correctness of his program is to try it out in particular cases and to modify it if the results produced do not correspond to his intentions. After he has found a reasonably wide variety of example cases on which the program seems to work, he believes that it will always work. The time spent in this program testing is often more than half the time spent on the entire programming project; and with a realistic costing of machine time, two thirds (or more) of the cost of the project is involved in removing errors during this phase.

The cost of removing errors discovered after a program has gone into use is often greater, particularly in the case of items of computer manufacturers' software for which a large part of the expense is borne by the user. And finally, the cost of error in certain types of program may be almost incalculable – a lost spacecraft, a collapsed building, a crashed aeroplane, or a world war. Thus the practice of program proving is not only a theoretical pursuit, followed in the interests of academic respectability, but a serious recommendation for the reduction of the costs associated with programming error.

The practice of proving programs is likely to alleviate some of the other problems which afflict the computing world. For example, there is the problem of program documentation, which is essential, firstly, to inform a potential user of a subroutine how to use it and what it accomplishes, and secondly, to assist in further development when it becomes necessary to update a program to meet changing circumstances or to improve it in the light of increased knowledge. The most rigorous method of formulating the purpose of a subroutine, as well as the conditions of its proper use, is to make assertions about the values of variables before and after its execution. The proof of the correctness of these assertions can then be used as a lemma in the proof of any program which calls the subroutine. Thus, in a large program, the structure of the whole can be clearly mirrored in the structure of its proof. Furthermore, when it becomes necessary to modify a program, it will always be valid to replace any subroutine by another which satisfies the same criterion of correctness. Finally, when examining the detail of the algorithm, it seems probable that the proof will be helpful in explaining not only *what* is happening but *why*.

Another problem which can be solved, insofar as it is soluble, by the practice of program proofs is that of transferring programs from one design of computer to another. Even when written in a so-called machine-independent programming language, many large programs inadvertently take advantage of some machine-dependent property of a particular implementation, and unpleasant and expensive surprises can result when attempting to transfer it to another machine. However, presence of a machine-dependent feature will always be revealed in advance by the failure of an attempt to prove the program from machine-independent axioms. The programmer will then have the choice of formulating his algorithm in a machine-independent fashion, possibly with the help of environment enquiries; or if this involves too much effort or inefficiency, he can deliberately construct a machine-dependent program, and rely for his proof on some machine-dependent axiom, for example, one of the versions of A11 (Section 4.2). In the latter case, the axiom must be explicitly quoted as one of the preconditions of successful use of the program. The program can still, with complete confidence, be transferred to any other machine which happens to satisfy the same machine-dependent axiom; but if it becomes necessary to transfer it to an implementation which does not, then all the places where changes are required will be clearly annotated by the fact that the proof at that point appeals to the truth of the offending machine-dependent axiom.

Thus the practice of proving programs would seem to lead to solution of three of the most pressing problems in software and programming, namely, reliability, documentation, and compatibility. However, program proving, certainly at present, will be difficult even for programmers of high calibre; and may be applicable only to quite simple program designs. As in other areas, reliability can be purchased only at the price of simplicity.

4.6 Formal language definition

A high-level programming language, such as ALGOL, FORTRAN, or COBOL, is usually intended to be implemented on a variety of computers of differing size, configuration, and design. It has been found a serious problem to define these languages with sufficient rigour to ensure compatibility among all implementors. Since the purpose of compatibility is to facilitate interchange of programs expressed in the language, one way to achieve this would be to insist that all implementations of the language shall 'satisfy' the axioms and rules of inference which underlie proofs of the properties of programs expressed in the language, so that all predictions based on these proofs will be fulfilled, except in the event of hardware failure. In effect, this is equivalent to accepting the axioms and rules of inference as the ultimately definitive specification of the meaning of the language.

Apart from giving an immediate and possibly even provable criterion for the correctness of an implementation, the axiomatic technique for the definition of programming language semantics appears to be like the formal syntax of the ALGOL 60 report, in that it is sufficiently simple to be understood both by the implementor and by the reasonably sophisticated user of the language. It is only by bridging this widening communication gap in a single document (perhaps even provably consistent) that the maximum advantage can be obtained from a formal language definition.

Another of the great advantages of using an axiomatic approach is that axioms offer a simple and flexible technique for leaving certain aspects of a language *undefined*, for example, range of integers, accuracy of floating point, and choice of overflow technique. This is absolutely essential for standardization purposes, since otherwise the language will be impossible to implement efficiently on differing hardware designs. Thus a programming language standard should consist of a set of axioms of universal applicability, together with a choice from a set of supplementary axioms describing the range of choices facing an implementor. An example of the use of axioms for this purpose was given in Section 4.2.

Another of the objectives of formal language definition is to assist in the design of better programming languages. The regularity, clarity, and ease of implementation of the ALGOL 60 syntax may at least in part be due to the use of an elegant formal technique for its definition. The use of axioms may lead to similar advantages in the area of 'semantics', since it seems likely that a language which can be described by a few 'self-evident' axioms from which proofs will be relatively easy to construct will be preferable to a language with many obscure axioms which are difficult to apply in proofs. Furthermore, axioms enable the language designer to express his general *intentions* quite simply and directly, without the mass of detail which usually accompanies algorithmic descriptions. Finally, axioms can be formulated in a manner largely independent of each other, so that the designer can work freely on one axiom or group of axioms without fear of unexpected interaction effects with other parts of the language.

4.7 Acknowledgements

Many axiomatic treatments of computer programming (Yanov 1958; Igarishi 1968; de Bakker 1968) tackle the problem of proving the equivalence, rather than the correctness, of algorithms. Other approaches

(McCarthy 1963b; Burstall 1968) take recursive functions rather than programs as a starting point for the theory. The suggestion to use axioms for defining the primitive operations of a computer appears in van Wingaarden (1966); Laski (1968). The importance of program proofs is clearly emphasized in (Naur 1966), and an informal technique for providing them is described. The suggestion that the specification of proof techniques provides an adequate formal definition of a programming language first appears in Floyd (1967). The formal treatment of program execution presented in this paper is clearly derived from Floyd. The main contributions of the author appear to be: (1) a suggestion that axioms may provide a simple solution to the problem of leaving certain aspects of a language undefined; (2) a comprehensive evaluation of the possible benefits to be gained by adopting this approach both for program proving and for formal language definition.

However, the formal material presented here has only an expository status and represents only a minute proportion of what remains to be done. It is hoped that many of the fascinating problems involved will be taken up by others.

FIVE

Proof of a program: *Find*

This chapter develops the formal approach to program correctness proposed in Chapter 4. As the (retiring) *ACM* editor and some referees know to their cost, the original draft of this paper presented a *post facto* proof of the complete program. The change to using the axiomatic approach in the design process was Hoare's own decision and resulted in a far more readable account. The influence of Edsger Dijkstra's work is acknowledged. It is clear that this paper, in turn, affected Dijkstra (1976) and Wirth (1973). A draft of April 1969 covered Partition and *Find*; the September 1969 proof of Partition was extremely hard to understand and was submitted to *ACM*; this was revised in May 1970; and the final version published in January 1971 as [16].

The formality of the published proof uncovered subtle considerations like that mentioned in connection with Lemma 8 which was a potential error in the first program sketch. The use of an axiomatic system which covers only partial correctness again manifests itself by a – quite difficult – separate termination proof. The difficulty with the argument about the result being a permutation of the initial value is exacerbated by the use of post conditions which refer only to the final state.

Abstract

A proof is given of the correctness of the algorithm *Find*. First, an informal description is given of the purpose of the program and the method used. A systematic technique is described for constructing the program proof during the process of coding it, in such a way as to prevent the intrusion of logical errors. The proof of termination is treated as a separate exercise. Finally, some conclusions relating to general programming methodology are drawn.

C. A. R. Hoare, 'Proof of a Program: FIND', *Comm. ACM* **14**(1), 39–45 (January 1971).

5.1 Introduction

In a number of papers (Naur 1966; Dijkstra 1968a; Chapter 4 of this book) the desirability of proving the correctness of programs has been suggested and this has been illustrated by proofs of simple example programs. In this paper the construction of the proof of a useful, efficient, and nontrivial program, using a method based on invariants, is shown. It is suggested that if a proof is constructed as part of the coding process for an algorithm, it is hardly more laborious than the traditional practice of program testing.

5.2 The program *Find*

The purpose of the program *Find* [3] is to find that element of an array $A[1:N]$ whose value is fth in order of magnitude; and to rearrange the array in such a way that this element is placed in $A[f]$; and furthermore, all elements with subscripts lower than f have lesser values, and all elements with subscripts greater than f have greater values. Thus on completion of the program, the following relationship will hold:

$$A[1], A[2], \ldots, A[f-1] < A[f] \leqslant A[f+1], \ldots, A[N]$$

This relation is abbreviated as *Found.*

One method of achieving the desired effect would be to sort the whole array. If the array is small, this would be a good method; but if the array is large, the time taken to sort it will also be large. The *Find* program is designed to take advantage of the weaker requirements to save much of the time which would be involved in a full sort.

The usefulness of the *Find* program arises from its application to the problem of finding the median or other quantiles of a set of observations stored in a computer array. For example, if N is odd and f is set to $(N+1)/2$, the effect of the *Find* program will be to place an observation with value equal to the median in $A[f]$. Similarly the first quartile may be found by setting f to $(N+1)/4$, and so on.

The method used is based on the principle that the desired effect of *Find* is to move lower-valued elements of the array to one end – the 'left-hand' end – and higher-valued elements of the array to the other end – the 'right-hand' end. (See Table 5.1(a)). This suggests that the array be scanned, starting at the left-hand end and moving rightward. Any element encountered which is small will remain where it is, but any element which is large should be moved up to the right-hand end of the array, in exchange for a small one. In order to find such a small element, a separate scan is made, starting at the right-hand end and moving leftward. In this scan, any

Table 5.1

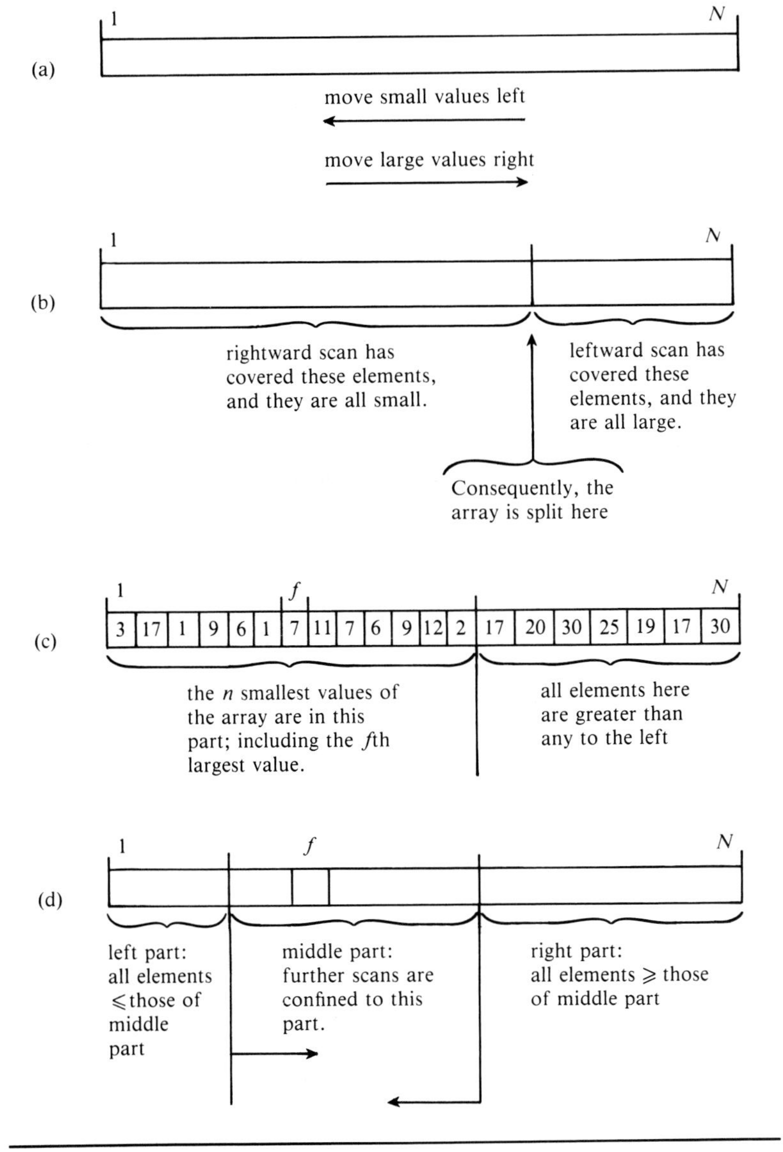

large element encountered remains where it is; the first small element encountered is moved down to the left-hand end in exchange for the large element already encountered in the rightward scan. Then both scans can be resumed until the next exchange is necessary. The process is repeated until the scans meet somewhere in the middle of the array. It is then known that all elements to the left of this meeting point will be small, and all elements to the right will be large. When this condition holds, we will say that the array is *split* at the given point into two parts (see Table 5.1(b)).

The reasoning of the previous paragraph assumes that there is some means of distinguishing small elements from large ones. Since we are interested only in their comparative values, it is sufficient to select the value of some arbitrary element before either of the scans starts; any element with lower value than the selected element is counted as small, and any element with higher value is counted as large. The fact that the discriminating value is arbitrary means that the place where the two scans will meet is also arbitrary; but it does not affect the fact that the array will be split at the meeting point, wherever that may be.

Now consider the question on which side of the split the *f*th element in order of value is to be found. If the split is to the right of $A[f]$, then the desired element must of necessity be to the left of the split, and all elements to the right of the split will be greater than it. In this case, all elements to the right of the split can be ignored in any future processing, since they are already in their proper place, namely to the right of $A[f]$ (see Table 5.1(c)). Similarly, if the split is to the left of $A[f]$, the element to be found must be to the right of the split, and all elements to the left of the split must be equal or less than it; furthermore, these elements can be ignored in future processing.

In either case, the program proceeds by repeating the rightward and leftward scans, but this time one of the scans will start at the split rather than at the beginning of the array. When the two scans meet again, it will be known that there is a second split in the array, this time perhaps on the other side of $A[f]$. Thus again, we may proceed with the rightward and leftward scans, but we start the rightward scan at the split on the left of $A[f]$ and the leftward scan at the split on the right, thus confining attention only to that part of the array that lies between the two splits; this will be known as the *middle part* of the array (see Table 5.1(d)).

When the third scan is complete, the middle part of the array will be split again into two parts. We take the new middle part as that part which contains $A[f]$ and repeat the double scan on this new middle part. The process is repeated until the middle part consists of only one element, namely $A[f]$. This element will now be equal to or greater than all elements to the left and equal to or less than all elements to the right; and thus the desired result of *Find* will be accomplished.

This has been an informal description of the method used by the program *Find*. Diagrams have been used to convey an understanding of how and why the method works, and they serve as an intuitive proof of its correctness. However, the method is described only in general terms, leaving many details undecided; and accordingly, the intuitive proof is far from watertight. In the next section, the details of the method will be filled in during the process of coding it in a formal programming language; and simultaneously, the details of the proof will be formalized in traditional logical notation. The end product of this activity will be a program suitable for computer execution, together with a proof of its correctness. The reader who checks the validity of the proof will thereby convince himself that the program requires no testing.

5.3 Coding and proof construction

The coding and proof construction may be split into several stages, each stage dealing with greater detail than the previous one. Furthermore, each stage may be systematically analyzed as a series of steps.

5.3.1 Stage 1: Problem definition

The first stage in coding and proof construction is to obtain a rigorous formulation of what is to be accomplished, and what may be assumed to begin with. In this case we may assume

(a) The subscript bounds of A are 1 and N.

(b) $1 \leqslant f \leqslant N$.

The required result is:

$$\forall\, p, q(1 \leqslant p \leqslant f \leqslant q \leqslant N \Rightarrow A[p] \leqslant A[f] \leqslant A[q]) \qquad [\mathit{Found}]$$

5.3.2 Stage 2: The general method

(1) The first step in each stage is to decide what variables will be required to hold intermediate results of the program. In the case of *Find*, it will be necessary to know at all times the extent of the middle part, which is currently being scanned. This indicates the introduction of variables m and n to point to the first element $A[m]$ and the last element $A[n]$ of the middle part.

(2) The second step is to attempt to describe more formally the purpose of each variable, which was informally described in the previous step. This purpose may be expressed as a formula of logic which is intended to remain true throughout the execution of the program, even when the value of the variable concerned is changed by assignment.† Such a formula is known as an *invariant*. As mentioned above, m is intended

†Except possibly in certain 'critical regions'.

to point to the leftmost element of the middle part of the array; and the middle part at all times contains $A[f]$; consequently m is never greater than f. Furthermore, there is always a split just to the left of the middle part, that is between $m-1$ and m. Thus the following formula should be true for m throughout execution of the program:

$$m \leqslant f \wedge \forall p, q(1 \leqslant p < m \leqslant q \leqslant N \Rightarrow A[p] \leqslant A[q]) \quad (m\text{-invariant})$$

Similarly, n is intended to point to the rightmost element of the middle part; it must never be less than f, and there will always be a split just to the right of it:

$$f \leqslant n \wedge \forall p, q(1 \leqslant p \leqslant n < q \leqslant N \Rightarrow A[p] \leqslant A[q]) \quad (n\text{-invariant})$$

(3) The next step is to determine the initial values for these variables. Since the middle part of the array is intended to be the part that still requires processing, and since to begin with the whole array requires processing, the obvious choice of initial values of m and n are 1 and N, respectively, indicating the first and last elements of the whole array. The code required is:

$$m := 1; \quad n := N$$

(4) It is necessary next to check that these values satisfy the relevant invariants. This may be done by substituting the initial value for the corresponding variable in each invariant, and ensuring that the result follows from facts already known:

$$1 \leqslant f \leqslant N \Rightarrow 1 \leqslant f \wedge \forall p, q(1 \leqslant p < 1 \leqslant q \leqslant N \Rightarrow A[p] \leqslant A[q]) \quad \text{(Lemma 1)}$$

$$1 \leqslant f \leqslant N \Rightarrow f \leqslant N \wedge \forall p, q(1 \leqslant p \leqslant N < q \leqslant N \Rightarrow A[p] \leqslant A[q]) \quad \text{(Lemma 2)}$$

The quantified clause of each lemma is trivially true since the antecedents of the implications are always false.

(5) After setting the initial values, the method of the program is repeatedly to reduce the size of the middle part, until it contains only one element. This may be accomplished by an iteration of the form:

while $m < n$ **do** *'reduce middle part'*

(6) It remains to prove that this loop accomplishes the objectives of the program as a whole. If we write the body of the iteration properly (i.e. in such a way as to preserve the truth of all invariants) then all invariants will still be true on termination. Furthermore, termination will occur only when $m < n$ goes false. Thus it is necessary only to show that the combination of the truth of the invariants and the falsity of the **while** clause expression $m < n$ implies the truth of *Found*.

$$m \leqslant f \wedge \forall p, q(1 \leqslant p < m \leqslant q \leqslant N \Rightarrow A[p] \leqslant A[q])$$
$$\wedge f \leqslant n \wedge \forall p, q(1 \leqslant p \leqslant n < q \leqslant N \Rightarrow A[p] \leqslant A[q]) \wedge \neg m < n$$
$$\Rightarrow \forall p, q(1 \leqslant p \leqslant f \leqslant q \leqslant N \Rightarrow A[p] \leqslant A[f] \leqslant A[q])$$
(Lemma 3)

The antecedents imply that $m = n = f$. If $1 \leqslant p \leqslant f \leqslant q \leqslant N$, then either $p = f$, in which case $A[p] \leqslant A[f]$ is obvious, or $p < f$, in which case substituting f for both m and q in the first quantified antecedent gives $A[p] \leqslant A[f]$. A similar argument shows that $A[f] \leqslant A[q]$.

At this point, the general structure of the program is as follows:

$m := 1$; $n := N$;
while $m < n$ **do** *'reduce middle part'*

Furthermore, this code has been proved to be correct, provided that the body of the contained iteration is correct.

5.3.3 Stage 3: Reduce the middle part

(1) The process for reducing the middle part involves a scan from the left and from the right. This requires two pointers, i and j, pointing to elements $A[i]$ and $A[j]$ respectively. In addition, a variable r is required to hold the arbitrary value which has been selected to act as a discriminator between 'small' and 'large' values.

(2) The i pointer is intended to pass over only those array elements with values smaller than r. Thus all array elements strictly to the left of the currently scanned element $A[i]$ will be known always to be equal to or less than r:

$$m \leqslant i \wedge \forall p(1 \leqslant p < i \Rightarrow A[p] \leqslant r) \qquad (i\text{-invariant})$$

Similarly the j pointer passes over only large values, and all elements strictly to the right of the currently scanned element $A[j]$ are known always to be equal to or greater than r:

$$j \leqslant n \wedge \forall q(j < q \leqslant N \Rightarrow r \leqslant A[q]) \qquad (j\text{-invariant})$$

Since the value of r does not change, there is no need for an r-invariant.

(3) The i pointer starts at the left of the middle part, i.e. at m; and the j pointer starts at the right of the middle part, i.e. at n. The initial value of r is taken from an arbitrary element of the middle part of the array. Since $A[f]$ is always in the middle part, its value is as good as any.

(4) The fact that the initial values satisfy the i- and j-invariants follows directly from the truth of the corresponding m- and n-invariants; this

is stated formally in the following lemmas:

$$f \leqslant N \wedge m \leqslant f \wedge \forall p, q(1 \leqslant p < m \leqslant q \leqslant N \Rightarrow A[p] \leqslant A[q])$$
$$\Rightarrow m \leqslant m \wedge \forall p(1 \leqslant p < m \Rightarrow A[p] \leqslant A[f])$$

(Lemma 4)

$$1 \leqslant f \wedge f \leqslant n \wedge \forall p, q(1 \leqslant p \leqslant n < q \leqslant N \Rightarrow A[p] \leqslant A[q])$$
$$\Rightarrow n \leqslant n \wedge \forall q(n < q \leqslant N \Rightarrow A[f] \leqslant A[q])$$

(Lemma 5)

The first of these is proved by setting q to f and the second by setting p to f.

(5) After setting the initial values, the method is to repeatedly add one to i and subtract one from j, until they cross over. This may be achieved by an iteration of the form:

while $i \leqslant j$ **do** *'increase i and decrease j'*

On exit from this loop, $j < i$ and all invariants are intended to be preserved.

If j and i cross over above f, the proposed method assigns j as the new value of n; if they cross over below f, i is assigned as the new value of m.

if $f \leqslant j$ **then** $n := j$
else if $i \leqslant f$ **then** $m := i$
else goto L

The destination of the jump will be determined later.

(6) The validity of these assignments is proved by showing that the new value of n or m satisfies the corresponding invariant whenever the assignment takes place. In these proofs it can be assumed that the i- and j-invariants hold; and furthermore, since the assignment immediately follows the iteration of (5), it is known that $j < i$. Thus the appropriate lemma is:

$$j < i \wedge \forall p(1 \leqslant p < i \Rightarrow A[p] \leqslant r) \wedge \forall q(j < q \leqslant N \Rightarrow r \leqslant A[q])$$
$$\Rightarrow \textbf{if } f \leqslant j \textbf{ then } f \leqslant j \wedge \forall p, q(1 \leqslant p \leqslant j < q \leqslant N) \Rightarrow A[p] \leqslant A[q])$$
$$\textbf{else if } i \leqslant f \textbf{ then } i \leqslant f \wedge \forall p, q(1 \leqslant p < i \leqslant q \leqslant N \Rightarrow A[p] \leqslant A[q])$$

(Lemma 6)

The proof of this is based on the fact that if $1 \leqslant p \leqslant j < q \leqslant N$, then $p < i$ (since $j < i$), and both $A[p] \leqslant r$ and $r \leqslant A[q]$. Hence $A[p] \leqslant A[q]$. Similarly, if $1 \leqslant p < i \leqslant q \leqslant N$, then $j < q$, and the same result follows.

It remains to determine the destination of the jump **goto** L. This jump is obeyed only if $j < f < i$, and it happens that in this case it can be proved that the condition *Found* has already been achieved. It is therefore legitimate to jump straight to the end of the program. The lemma which justifies this is:

$$1 \leqslant f \leqslant N \wedge j < f < i \wedge \forall p(1 \leqslant p < i \Rightarrow A[p] \leqslant r)$$
$$\wedge \forall q(j < q \leqslant N \Rightarrow r \leqslant A[q])$$
$$\Rightarrow \forall p, q(1 \leqslant p \leqslant f \leqslant q \leqslant N \Rightarrow A[p] \leqslant A[f] \leqslant A[q]) \qquad \text{(Lemma 7)}$$

This may be readily proved: if f is put for q in the antecedent, we obtain $r \leqslant A[f]$. Similarly, putting f or p in the antecedent we obtain $A[f] \leqslant r$. Hence $A[f] = r$. If $1 \leqslant p \leqslant f \leqslant q \leqslant N$, then $1 \leqslant p < i$ (since $f < i$) and $j < q \leqslant N$ (since $j < f$) and hence the i-invariant states that $A[p] \leqslant r$ and the j-invariant states that $r \leqslant A[q]$. But r has already been proved equal to $A[f]$.

This concludes the outline of the program required to reduce the middle part:

$r := A[f]$; $i := m$; $j := n$;
while $i \leqslant j$ **do** *'increase i and decrease j'*;
if $f \leqslant j$ **then** $n := j$
else if $i \leqslant f$ **then** $m := i$
else goto L

This program has been proved to be correct, in that it preserves the truth of the m- and n-invariants, provided that the body of the contained loop preserves these invariants as well as the i- and j-invariants.

5.3.4 Stage 4: Increase *i* and decrease *j*

At this stage there is no need to introduce further variables and no further invariants are required. The construction of the code is not therefore split into the steps as before.

The first action of this part of the program is to use the i-point to scan rightward, passing over all elements with value less than r. This is accomplished by the loop†

while $A[i] < r$ **do** $i := i + 1$

The fact that this loop preserves the truth of the invariant is expressed in the

†The reason for the strict inequality is connected with termination. See Section 5.4.

obvious lemma:

$$A[i] \leqslant r \wedge m \leqslant i \wedge \forall p(1 \leqslant p < i \Rightarrow A[p] \leqslant r)$$
$$\Rightarrow m \leqslant i+1 \wedge \forall p(1 \leqslant p < i+1 \Rightarrow A[p] \leqslant r) \qquad \text{(Lemma 8)†}$$

The next action is to use the j-pointer to scan leftward, passing over all elements greater than r. This is accomplished by the loop:

while $r < A[j]$ **do** $j := j - 1$

which is validated by the truth of:

$$r \leqslant A[j] \wedge j \leqslant n \wedge \forall q(j < q \leqslant N \Rightarrow r \leqslant A[q])$$
$$\Rightarrow j-1 \leqslant n \wedge \forall q(j-1 < q \leqslant N \Rightarrow r \leqslant A[q]) \qquad \text{(Lemma 9)}$$

On termination of the first loop, it is known that $r \leqslant A[i]$, and on termination of the second loop $A[j] \leqslant r$. If i and j have not crossed over, an exchange of the elements they point to takes place. After the exchange, it is obvious that

$$A[i] \leqslant r \leqslant A[j],$$

and hence Lemmas 8 and 9 justify a further increase in i and decrease in j:

if $i \leqslant j$ **then**
begin *'exchange* $A[i]$ *and* $A[j]$*'*;
 $i := i + 1$; $j := j - 1$
end

Thus the process of increasing i and decreasing j preserves the truth of all the invariants, provided that the exchange of $A[i]$ and $A[j]$ does so, and the program takes the form:

while $A[i] < r$ **do** $i := i + 1$;
while $r < A[j]$ **do** $j := j - 1$;
if $i \leqslant j$ **then**
begin *'exchange* $A[i]$ *and* $A[j]$*'*;
 $i := i + 1$; $j := j - 1$
end

5.3.5 Stage 5: Exchange $A[i]$ and $A[j]$

The code for performing the exchange is:

$$w := A[i];\ A[i] := A[j];\ A[j] := w$$

†This lemma is not strictly true for some implementations of computer arithmetic. Suppose that N is the largest number representable in the integer range, that $m = i = N$, and that modulo arithmetic is used. Then $i + 1$ will be the smallest number representable, and will certainly be less than m. The easiest way to evade this problem is to impose on the user of the algorithm the insignificant restriction that $N < maxint$, where *maxint* is the largest representable integer.

Although this code uses a new variable w, there is no need to establish an invariant for it, since its value plays a purely temporary role.

The proof that the exchange preserves the invariants is not trivial, and depends critically on the fact that $i \leqslant j$. Let A' stand for the value of the array as a whole after the exchange has taken place. Then obviously:

$$A'[i] = A[j] \tag{1}$$

$$A'[j] = A[i] \tag{2}$$

$$\forall s(s \neq i \wedge s \neq j \Rightarrow A'[s] = A[s]) \tag{3}$$

The preservation of the i-invariant is stated in the lemma:

$$m \leqslant i \leqslant j \wedge \forall p(1 \leqslant p < i \Rightarrow A[p] \leqslant r) \Rightarrow m \leqslant i \wedge \forall p(1 \leqslant p < i \Rightarrow A'[p] \leqslant r) \qquad \text{(Lemma 10)}$$

This is proved by observing that if $p < i \leqslant j$ then $p \neq i$ and $p \neq j$ and by (3), $A'[p] = A[p]$.

Similarly the preservation of the j-invariant is guaranteed by the lemma:

$$i \leqslant j \leqslant n \wedge \forall q(j < q \leqslant N \Rightarrow r \leqslant A[q]) \Rightarrow j \leqslant n \wedge \forall q(j \leqslant q \leqslant N \Rightarrow r \leqslant A'[q]) \qquad \text{(Lemma 11)}$$

The proof likewise proceeds by observing that $i \leqslant j < q$ implies that $q \neq i$ and $q \neq j$, and therefore by (3), $A'[q] = A[q]$.

The preservation of the m-invariant is guaranteed by the truth of the following lemma:

$$m \leqslant i \leqslant j \wedge \forall p, q(1 \leqslant p < m \leqslant q \leqslant N \Rightarrow A[p] \leqslant A[q]) \Rightarrow \forall p, q(1 \leqslant p < m \leqslant q \leqslant N \Rightarrow A'[p] \leqslant A'[q]) \qquad \text{(Lemma 12)}$$

Outline proof Assume $1 \leqslant p < m \leqslant q \leqslant N$; hence $p \neq i$ and $p \neq j$ (since $p < m \leqslant i \leqslant j$). Therefore by (3),

$$A'[p] = A[p]. \tag{4}$$

Substituting i and then j for q in the antecedent, we obtain $A[p] \leqslant A[i]$ and $A[p] \leqslant A[j]$. Consequently $A'[p] \leqslant A'[j]$ and $A'[p] \leqslant A'[i]$ (from (4), (1), and (2)). Furthermore, for all $q \neq i$ and $q \neq j$, $A'[p] = A[p] \leqslant A[q] = A'[q]$ (by (4) and (3)). Hence $A'[p] \leqslant A'[q]$ for all $q(m \leqslant q \leqslant N)$.

The preservation of the n-invariant is guaranteed by a similar lemma:

$$i \leqslant j \leqslant n \wedge \forall p, q(1 \leqslant p \leqslant n < q \leqslant N \Rightarrow A[p] \leqslant A[q]) \Rightarrow \forall p, q(1 \leqslant p \leqslant n < q \leqslant N \Rightarrow A'[p] \leqslant A'[q]) \qquad \text{(Lemma 13)}$$

The proof is very similar to that of Lemma 12, and is left as an exercise.

5.3.6 The whole program

The gradual evolution of the program code and proof through several stages has been carried out in the previous sections. In presenting the code of the program as a whole, the essential invariants and other assertions have been preserved as comments. Thus a well-annotated version of the program appears in Table 5.2.

Table 5.2

```
begin
  comment This program operates on an array A[1:N], and a value of
  f(1 ≤ f ≤ N). Its effect is to rearrange the elements of A in such a way that:

  ∀p, q(1 ≤ p ≤ f ≤ q ≤ N ⇒ A[p] ≤ A[f] ≤ A[q]);
  integer m, n;  comment
  m ≤ f ∧ ∀ p, q(1 ≤ p < m ≤ q ≤ N ⇒ A[p] ≤ A[q]),
  f ≤ n ∧ ∀ p, q(1 ≤ p ≤ n < q ≤ N ⇒ A[p] ≤ A[q]);
  m := 1;  n := N;
  while m < n do
  begin integer r, i, j, w;
    comment
    m ≤ i ∧ ∀ p(1 ≤ p < i ⇒ A[p] ≤ r),
    j ≤ n ∧ ∀ q(j < q ≤ N ⇒ r ≤ A[q]);
    r := A[f];  i := m;  j := n;
    while i ≤ j do
    begin while A[i] < r do i := i + 1;
      while r < A[j] do j := j − 1;
      comment  A[j] ≤ r ≤ A[i];
      if i ≤ j then
      begin w := A[i];  A[i] := A[j];  A[j] := w;
        comment  A[i] ≤ r ≤ A[j];
        i := i + 1;  j := j − 1;
      end
    end 'increase i and decrease j';
    if f ≤ j then n := j
    else if i ≤ f then m := i
    else goto L
  end 'reduce middle part';
L:
end Find
```

5.4 Termination

The proof given so far has concentrated on proving the correctness of the program supposing that it terminates; and no attention has been given to the problem of proving termination. It is easier in this case to prove termination of the inner loops first.

The proof of the termination of:

while $A[i] < r$ **do** $i := i + 1$

depends on the recognition that at all times there will be an element in the middle part to the right of $A[i]$ whose value is equal to or greater than r. This element will act as a 'stopper' to prevent the value of i from increasing beyond the value n. More formally, it is necessary to establish an additional invariant for i, which is true before and during the loop; i.e. throughout execution of '*reduce middle part*'. This invariant is:

$$\exists\, p(i \leqslant p \leqslant n \wedge r \leqslant A[p]) \tag{5}$$

Obviously if this is true, the value of i is necessarily bounded by n; it cannot increase indefinitely, and the loop must therefore terminate.

The fact that (5) is an invariant for the duration of the particular loop is established by the following lemmas:

$$m \leqslant f \leqslant n \Rightarrow \exists\, p(m \leqslant p \leqslant n \wedge A[f] \leqslant A[p]) \qquad \text{(Lemma 14)}$$

Proof Take f for p.

$$A[i] < r \wedge \exists\, p(i \leqslant p \leqslant n \wedge r \leqslant A[p]) \Rightarrow \exists\, p(i + 1 \leqslant p \leqslant n \wedge r \leqslant A[p]) \qquad \text{(Lemma 15)}$$

Proof Consider the p whose existence is asserted by the antecedent. Since $r \leqslant A[p] \wedge A[i] < r$, $p \neq i$. Hence $i + 1 \leqslant p$.

$$r \leqslant A[i] \wedge i + 1 \leqslant j - 1 \wedge j \leqslant n \Rightarrow \exists\, p(i + 1 \leqslant p \leqslant n \wedge r \leqslant A'[p]) \qquad \text{(Lemma 16)}$$

Proof Take j for p. Then $A'[p] = A'[j] = A[i] \geqslant r$.

Lemma 14 shows that the invariant is true after the initialization of '*reduce middle part*'. Lemma 15 shows that the invariant is preserved by **while** $A[i] < r$ **do** $i := i + 1$, and Lemma 16 shows that the invariant is preserved by the final compound statement of '*reduce middle part*', providing that $i \leqslant j$ after the execution of this statement. Since the body of the loop is not re-entered unless this condition is satisfied, the invariant is unconditionally true at the beginning of the second and subsequent repetitions of '*reduce middle part.*'

The termination of the loop

while $r < A[j]$ **do** $j := j - 1$

is established in a very similar manner. The additional invariant is

$$\exists\, q(m \leqslant q \leqslant j \wedge A[q] \leqslant r) \tag{6}$$

and the lemmas required are Lemma 14 and

$$r < A[j] \wedge \exists\, q(m \leqslant q \leqslant j \wedge A[q] \leqslant r)$$
$$\Rightarrow \exists\, q(m \leqslant q \leqslant j - 1 \wedge A[q] \leqslant r) \quad \text{(Lemma 17)}$$

$$A[j] \leqslant r \wedge i + 1 \leqslant j - 1 \wedge m \leqslant i$$
$$\Rightarrow \exists\, q(m \leqslant q \leqslant j - 1 \wedge A'[q] \leqslant r) \quad \text{(Lemma 18)}$$

The proofs of these lemmas are very similar to those for Lemmas 15 and 16.

This proof of termination is more than usually complex; if the program were rewritten to include an extra test ($i \leqslant n$ or $m \leqslant j$) in each loop, termination would have been obvious. However, the innermost loops would have been rather less efficient.

The proof of termination of the middle loop is rather simpler. The loop for increasing i and decreasing j must terminate; since if the conditional statement it contains is not obeyed then j is already less than i, and termination is immediate; whereas if $j \geqslant i$, then i is necessarily incremented and j decremented, and they must cross over after a finite number of such operations.

Proof of the termination of the outermost loop depends on the fact that on termination of the middle loop both $m < i$ and $j < n$. Therefore whichever one of the assignments $m := i$ or $n := j$ is executed, the distance between n and m is strictly decreased. If neither assignment is made, **goto** L is executed, and terminates the loop immediately.

The proof that at the end of the middle loop both $m < i$ and $j < n$ depends on the fact that on the first execution of the loop body the conditional **if** $i \leqslant j$ **then** ... is actually executed. This is because at this stage $A[f]$ is still equal to r, and therefore the rightward scan of i cannot pass over $A[f]$. Similarly the leftward scan of j cannot pass over $A[f]$. Thus on termination of both innermost loops $i \leqslant f \leqslant j$. Thus the condition $i \leqslant j$ is satisfied, and i is necessarily incremented, and j is necessarily decremented. Recall that this reasoning applies only to the first time round this loop – but once is enough to ensure $m < i$ and $j < n$, since i is a nondecreasing quantity and j is a nonincreasing quantity.

5.5 Reservation

In the proof of *Find*, one very important aspect of correctness has not been treated, namely that the program merely rearranges the elements of the array A, without changing any of their values. If this requirement were not stated, there would be no reason why the program *Find* should not be written trivially:

```
for i := 1 step 1 until N do
  A[i] := i
```

since this fully satisfies all the other criteria for correctness.

The easiest way of stating this additional requirement is to forbid the programmer to change the array A in any other way than by exchanging two of its elements. This requirement is clearly met by the *Find* program and not by its trivial alternative.

If it is desired to formulate the requirement in terms of conditions and invariants, it is necessary to introduce the concept of a permutation; and to prove that for arbitrary A_0,

$$A \text{ is a permutation of } A_0 \qquad (Perm)$$

is an invariant of the program. Informally this may be proved in three steps:

(a) '*exchange* $A[i]$ *and* $A[j]$' is the only part of the program which changes A,
(b) exchanging is a permutation,
(c) the composition of two permutations is also a permutation.

The main disadvantages of the formal approach are illustrated by this example. It is far from obvious that the invariance of *Perm* expresses exactly what we want to prove about the program; when the definition of *Perm* is fully and formally expressed, this is even less obvious; and finally, if the proof is formulated in the manner of the proofs of the other lemmas of this paper, it is very tedious.

Another problem which remains untreated is that of proving that all subscripts of A are within the bounds 1 to N.

5.6 Conclusion

This paper has illustrated a methodology for systematic construction of program proofs together with the programs they prove. It uses a 'top-down' method of analysis to split the process into a number of stages, each stage embodying more detail than the previous one; the proof of the correctness of the program at each stage leads to and depends upon an accurate formulation of the characteristics of the program to be developed at the next stage.

Within each stage, there are a number of steps: the decision on the nature of the data required; the formulation of the invariants for the data; the construction of the code; the formulation and proof of the lemmas. In this paper, the stages and steps have been shown as a continuous progress, and it has not been necessary to go back and change decisions made earlier. In practice, reconsideration of earlier decisions is frequently necessary, and this imposes on the programmer the need to re-establish the consistency of invariants, program, lemmas, and proofs. The motivation for taking this extra trouble during the design and coding of a program is that it is hoped to reduce or eliminate trouble at phases which traditionally come later – program testing, documentation, and maintenance.

Similar systematic methods of program construction are described in Naur (1969) and Dijkstra (1972c); this present paper, however, places greater emphasis on the formalization of the characteristics of the program as an aid to the avoidance of logical and coding errors. In future, it may be possible to enlist the aid of a computer in formulating the lemmas, and perhaps even in checking the proofs (Floyd 1967; King 1969).

5.7 Acknowledgements

The author is grateful to the referee and to the retiring editor for his meticulous comments and general encouragement in the preparation of this paper.

SIX

Procedures and parameters: an axiomatic approach

This paper applies the axiomatic approach of Chapter 4 to further features of programming languages. Much of this work had been sketched in the 1968 drafts of the axiomatic basis paper but did not appear in the published version. The problems of providing axiomatic definitions of procedures and parameter passing are intricate and interested readers should consult Apt (1981) for a full discussion. The problems of providing axiomatic definitions of procedures were the motivation for the wish to forbid 'aliasing' of parameters in Euclid and later in Ada. The formulation of a set of rules which were easy to check statistically but did not preclude certain efficient coding techniques proved difficult. Further progress has been made by Reynolds (1981).

This paper was published in 1971 as [17].

Procedures provide an elegant way of governing the control flow of programs. It comes as a surprise to find that jumps can also be handled by the familiar logical technique of subsidiary deductions from hypotheses. (This technique is possible only for partial correctness because, in a theory of total correctness, $\{P\}$**goto**$\{$**false**$\}$ is a contradiction.) A formal treatment of jumps is given in [26]. An inconsistency in this paper was discovered by Ed Ashcroft while lecturing on the article and led to [59]. The topic of jumps had been touched on in the 1968 draft of the axiomatic basis paper. There, after some discussion, the section concludes with '... If there is more than one label, yet further complexities arise. The unravelling of them is left to a reader with a sufficient enthusiasm for jumping.' In [26], the general aversion to jumps is tempered by an analysis of cases where they can actually improve program structure. (An interesting additional reference on this topic would be Knuth, 1974. It is amusing to note that, in 1987, the debate about goto statements is still occupying space in the *Communications of the ACM.*) Although one of the identified uses of jumps is for abnormal exits, Hoare expresses in the

C. A. R. Hoare, Procedures and parameters: an axiomatic approach. In E. Engeler (ed.), *Symposium on Semantics of Algorithmic Languages,* Lecture Notes in Mathematics Vol. 188, pp. 102–16 (1971). This paper is republished by kind permission of Springer-Verlag Berlin Heidelberg.

conclusion a dislike of PL/I's ON-conditions; this dislike he subsequently transferred to Ada's exception handling.

6.1 Introduction

It has been suggested (Chapter 4) that an axiomatic approach to formal language definition might simultaneously contribute to the clarity and reliability of programs expressed in the language, and to the efficiency of their translation and execution on an electronic digital computer. This paper gives an example of the application of the axiomatic method to the definition of procedure- and parameter-passing features of a high-level programming language. It reveals that ease of demonstrating program correctness and high efficiency of implementation may be achieved simultaneously, provided that the programmer is willing to observe a certain familiar and natural discipline in his use of parameters.

6.2 Concepts and notations

The notations used in this paper are mainly those of symbolic logic and particularly natural deduction. They are supplemented by conventions introduced in Chapter 4. The more important of them are summarized below.

(1) $P\{Q\}R$ – where P and R are propositional formulae of logic and Q is a part of a program. *Explanation: If P is true of the program variables* before executing the first statement of the program Q, and if the program Q terminates, then R will be true of the program variables after execution of Q is complete.

(2) S_e^x – where S is an expression or formula, x is a variable, and e is an expression. *Explanation:* The result of replacing all free occurrences of x in S by e. If e is not free for x in S, a preliminary systematic change of bound variables of S is assumed to be made.

(3) $\dfrac{A, B}{C}$ – where A, B, and C are propositional formulae. *Explanation:* A rule of inference which states that if A and B have been proved, then C may be deduced.

(4) $\dfrac{A, B \vdash C}{D}$ – where A, B, C, and D are propositional formulae. *Explanation:* A rule of inference which permits deduction of D if A and C are proved; however, it also permits B to be assumed as a hypothesis in the proof C. The deduction of C from B is known as a subsidiary deduction.

It is assumed that, with the exception of program material (usually enclosed in braces), all letters stand for formulae of some suitably chosen logical system. The formulae of this system are presumed to include:

(a) all expressions of the programming language;
(b) the familiar notations of predicate calculus (truth functions, quantifiers, etc.).

The properties of the basic operands, operators and built-in functions of the language are assumed to be specified by some suitably chosen axiom set; and the proof procedures are assumed to be those of the first-order predicate calculus.

As a simple example of the use of these notations, let Q stand for the single assignment statement $k := (m+n)/2$. We wish to prove that after execution of this statement, k will take a value between m and n, whenever $m \leqslant n$; or more formally that the desired result R of execution of Q is $m \leqslant k \leqslant n$. In Chapter 4 there was introduced the axiom schema

$$R_e^x \; \{x := e\} \; R \qquad \text{(Axiom of Assignment)}$$

This indicates that for an assignment $x := e$, if R is the desired result of the assignment, a sufficient precondition for this result to obtain is that R_e^x is true before execution. R_e^x is derived by replacing all occurrences of the target variable x in R by the assigned expression e. In the present case, the target variable is k, and the assigned expression is $(m+n)/2$. Thus we obtain, as an instance of the axiom schema,

$$m \leqslant (m+n)/2 \leqslant n \; \{k := (m+n)/2\} \; m \leqslant k \leqslant n$$

It is an obvious theorem of mathematics that $m \leqslant (m+n)/2 \leqslant n$ can be inferred from the truth of $m \leqslant n$. This may be written using the notation explained above:

$$m \leqslant n \vdash m \leqslant (m+n)/2 \leqslant n$$

Another obvious rule mentioned in Chapter 4 states that if $S \{Q\} R$ has been proved, and also that the truth of S may be inferred from the truth of P, then $P \{Q\} R$ is a valid inference, or more formally

$$\frac{S \{Q\} R, \; P \vdash S}{P \{Q\} R} \qquad \text{(Rule of Consequence)}$$

In applying this rule to our example, we take $m \leqslant n$ for P and $m \leqslant (m+n)/2 \leqslant n$ for S, and obtain

$$m \leqslant n \; \{k := (m+n)/2\} \; m \leqslant k \leqslant n$$

which is what was required to be proved.

A full list of rules of inference, together with associated conventions, is given in the Appendix. They are not supposed to give a 'complete' proof procedure for correctness of programs, but they will probably be found adequate for the proof of most practical algorithms.

6.3 Procedures

Before embarking on a treatment of parameters, it is convenient first to consider the simple case of a procedure without parameters. Suppose p has been declared as a parameterless procedure, with body Q. We introduce the notation

$$p \textbf{ proc } Q$$

to represent this declaration. A call of this procedure will take the form

$$\textbf{call } p$$

It is generally accepted that the effect of each call of a procedure is to execute the body Q of the procedure in the place of the call. Thus if we wish to prove that a certain consequence R will follow from a call of p (under some precondition P), all we have to do is to prove that this consequence will result from execution of Q (under the same precondition). This reasoning leads to an inference rule of the form

$$\frac{p \textbf{ proc } Q,\ P\,\{Q\}\,R}{P\,\{\textbf{call } p\}\,R} \qquad \text{(Rule of Invocation)}$$

6.4 Parameters

In dealing with parameterization, we shall treat in detail the case where all variables of the procedure body Q (other than locally declared variables) are formal parameters of the procedure. Furthermore, we shall make a clear notational distinction between those formal parameters which are subject to assignment in the body Q, and those which do not appear to the left of an assignment in Q nor in any procedure called by it.

These decisions merely simplify the discussion; they do not involve any loss of generality, since any program can fairly readily be transformed to one which observes the conventions.

Let $\mathbf{x}$ be a list of all non-local variables of Q which are subject to change by Q. Let $\mathbf{v}$ be a list of all other non-local variables of Q. We extend the notation for procedure declarations, thus

$$p(\mathbf{x}):(\mathbf{v}) \textbf{ proc } Q$$

This asserts that p is the name of a procedure with body Q and with formal parameters $\mathbf{x}, \mathbf{v}$.

The notation for a procedure call is similarly extended:

$$\textbf{call } p(\mathbf{a}):(\mathbf{e})$$

This is a call of procedure p with actual parameters $\mathbf{a}, \mathbf{e}$ corresponding to the formals $\mathbf{x}, \mathbf{v}$, where $\mathbf{a}$ is a list of variable names, and $\mathbf{e}$ is a list of expressions; and $\mathbf{a}$ is the same length as $\mathbf{x}$, and $\mathbf{e}$ is the same length as $\mathbf{v}$.

As before, we assume that $P\{Q\}R$ has been proved of the body Q. Consider the call

$$\textbf{call } p(\mathbf{x}):(\mathbf{v})$$

in which the names of the formal parameters have been 'fed back' as actual parameters, thus effectively turning the procedure back into a parameterless one. It is fairly obvious that this call has the same effect as the execution of the procedure body itself; thus we obtain the rule

$$\frac{p(\mathbf{x}):(\mathbf{v})\ \textbf{proc}\ Q,\ P\{Q\}R}{P\{\textbf{call } p(\mathbf{x}):(\mathbf{v})\}R} \qquad \text{(Rule of Invocation)}$$

Of course, this particular choice of actual parameters is most unlikely to occur in practice; nevertheless, it will appear later that the rule of invocation is a useful basis for further advance.

Consider next the more general call

$$\textbf{call } p(\mathbf{a}):(\mathbf{e})$$

This call is intended to perform upon the actual parameters $\mathbf{a}$ and $\mathbf{e}$ exactly the same operations as the body Q would perform upon the formal parameters $\mathbf{x}$ and $\mathbf{v}$. Thus it would be expected that $R^{\mathbf{x},\mathbf{v}}_{\mathbf{a},\mathbf{e}}$ would be true after execution of the call, provided that the corresponding precondition $P^{\mathbf{x},\mathbf{v}}_{\mathbf{a},\mathbf{e}}$ is true before the call. This reasoning leads to the rule

$$\frac{P\{\textbf{call } p(\mathbf{x}):(\mathbf{v})\}R}{P^{\mathbf{x},\mathbf{v}}_{\mathbf{a},\mathbf{e}}\{\textbf{call } p(\mathbf{a}):(\mathbf{e})\}R^{\mathbf{x},\mathbf{v}}_{\mathbf{a},\mathbf{e}}} \qquad \text{(Proposed Rule of Substitution)}$$

Unfortunately, this rule is not universally valid. If the actual parameter list $\mathbf{a}, \mathbf{e}$ contains the same variable more than once, the proof of the body of the subroutine is no longer valid as a proof of the correctness of the call. This may be shown by a trivial counterexample, contained in Table 6.1. In order to prevent such contradictions, it is necessary to formulate the conditions that all variables in $\mathbf{a}$ are distinct, and none of them is contained in $\mathbf{e}$. We shall henceforth insist that every procedure call satisfy these readily tested conditions, and thus re-establish the validity of the rule of substitution. We shall see later that, in a programming language standard, there are other reasons for leaving undefined the effect of a procedure call which fails to satisfy the conditions.

As an example of the successful use of the rule of substitution, assume that a declaration has been made,

$$random(k):(m, n)\ \textbf{proc}\ Q$$

Table 6.1 Counterexample

Assume:	$p(x):(v)$ **proc** $x:= v+1$		(1)
	$v+1=v+1\ \{x:= v+1\}\ x=v+1$	(Assignment)	(2)
	$true \vdash v+1=v+1$	(Logical theorem)	(3)
From 2, 3:	**true** $\{x:= v+1\}\ x=v+1$	(Consequence)	(4)
From 1, 4:	**true** $\{$**call** $p(x):(v)\}\ x=v+1$	(Invocation)	(5)
From 5:	**true** $\{$**call** $p(a):(a)\}\ a=a+1$	(Substitution)	(6)

Since the conclusion is an obvious contradiction, we must prohibit calls of the form **call** $p(a):(a)$.

where Q is a procedure body of which it has been proved that

$$m \leqslant n\ \{Q\}\ m \leqslant k \leqslant n.$$

The rule of invocation permits deduction of

$$m \leqslant n\ \{\textbf{call}\ random(k):(m, n)\}\ m \leqslant k \leqslant n$$

and applying the rule of substitution to a particular call, it is possible to obtain

$$1 \leqslant q+1\ \{\textbf{call}\ random(r):(1, q+1)\}\ 1 \leqslant r \leqslant q+1$$

In some cases it is necessary to use a slightly more powerful rule of substitution. Suppose P and/or R contain some variables $\mathbf{k}$ which do not occur in $\mathbf{x}$ or $\mathbf{v}$, but which happen to occur in $\mathbf{a}$ or $\mathbf{e}$. In such a case it is necessary first to substitute some entirely fresh variables, $\mathbf{k}'$ for $\mathbf{k}$ in P and R, before applying the rule given above. This is justified by a more powerful version of the rule

$$\frac{P\{\textbf{call}\ p(\mathbf{x}):(\mathbf{v})\}R}{P^{\mathbf{k},\,\mathbf{x},\,\mathbf{v}}_{\mathbf{k}',\,\mathbf{a},\,\mathbf{e}}\ \{\textbf{call}\ p(\mathbf{a}):(\mathbf{e})\}\ R^{\mathbf{k},\,\mathbf{x},\,\mathbf{v}}_{\mathbf{k}',\,\mathbf{a},\,\mathbf{e}}} \qquad \text{(Rule of Substitution)}$$

6.5 Declaration

In most procedures it is highly desirable to declare that certain of the variables are *local* to the procedure, or to some part of it, and that they are to be regarded as distinct from any other variables of the same name which may exist in the program. Since local variables do not have to be included in parameter lists, a considerable simplification in the structure of the program and its proof may be achieved. We will introduce the notation for declarations,

begin new x; Q **end**

where x stands for the declared variable identifier, and Q is the program statement (scope) within which the variable x is used; or, in ALGOL terms, the block to which it is local.

The effect of a declaration is merely to introduce a new working variable, and its introduction is not intended to have any effect on any of the other variables of the program; it cannot therefore affect the truth of any provable assertion about these variables.

Thus in order to prove

$$P\,\{\mathbf{begin\ new}\ x;\ Q\ \mathbf{end}\}\,R$$

all that is in principle necessary is to prove the same property of the body of the block, namely,

$$P\,\{Q\}\,R$$

However, this rule is not strictly valid if the variable x happens to occur in either of the assertions P or R. In this case, the validity of the rule can be re-established by first replacing every occurrence of x in Q by some entirely fresh variable y, which occurs neither in P, Q, nor R. It is a general property of declarations that such a systematic substitution can have no effect on the meaning of the program. Thus the rule of declaration takes the form

$$\frac{P\,\{Q_y^x\}\,R}{P\,\{\mathbf{new}\ x;\ Q\}\,R} \qquad \text{(Rule of Declaration)}$$

where y is not free in P or R, nor does it occur in Q (unless y is the same variable as x).

In practice it is convenient to declare more than one variable at a time, so that the rule of declaration needs to be strengthened to apply to lists $\mathbf{x}$ and $\mathbf{y}$ rather than single variables.

6.6 Recursion

The rules of inference given above are not sufficient for the proof of the properties of recursive procedures. The reason is that the body Q of a recursive procedure contains a call of itself, and there is no way of establishing what are the properties of this recursive call. Consequently, it is impossible to prove any properties of the body Q. This means that it is impossible to use even the simple rule of invocation,

$$\frac{p\ \mathbf{proc}\ Q,\ P\,\{Q\}\,R}{P\,\{\mathbf{call}\ p\}\,R}$$

since the proof of the second premise $P\,\{Q\}\,R$ remains forever beyond our grasp.

The solution to the infinite regress is simple and dramatic: to permit the use of the desired conclusion as a hypothesis in the proof of the body itself. Thus we are permitted to prove that the procedure body possesses a property, on the assumption that every recursive call possesses that property, and then to assert categorically that every call, recursive or otherwise, has that property. This assumption of what we want to prove before embarking on the proof explains well the aura of magic which attends a programmer's first introduction to recursive programming.

In formal terms, the rule of invocation for a recursive procedure is

$$\frac{p(\mathbf{x}):(\mathbf{v})\ \mathbf{proc}\ Q,\ P\,\{\mathbf{call}\ p(\mathbf{x}):(\mathbf{v})\}\,R \vdash P\,\{Q\}\,R}{P\,\{\mathbf{call}\ p(\mathbf{x}):(\mathbf{v})\}\,R}$$

(Rule of Recursive Invocation)

Unfortunately, this relatively simple rule is not adequate for the proof of the properties of recursive procedures. The reason is that it gives no grounds for supposing that the local variables of the procedure (other than those occurring in the left-hand parameter list) will remain unchanged during a recursive call. What is required is a rather more powerful rule which permits the assumed properties of a recursive call to be *adapted* to the particular circumstances of that call. The formulation of a rule of adaptation is designed in such a way as to permit a mechanically derived answer to the question, 'If S is the desired result of executing a procedure call, **call** $p(\mathbf{a}):(\mathbf{e})$, and $P\,\{\mathbf{call}\ p(\mathbf{a}):(\mathbf{e})\}\,R$ is already given, what is the weakest precondition W such that $W\,\{\mathbf{call}\ p(\mathbf{a}):(\mathbf{e})\}\,S$ is universally valid?'

It turns out that this precondition is

$$\exists\mathbf{k}(P \wedge \forall a(R \Rightarrow S)),$$

where $\mathbf{k}$ is a list of all variables free in P, R but not in $\mathbf{a}, \mathbf{e}$, or S. This fact may be formalized

$$\frac{P\,\{\mathbf{call}\ p(\mathbf{a}):(\mathbf{e})\}\,R}{\exists\mathbf{k}(P \wedge \forall a(R \Rightarrow S))\,\{\mathbf{call}\ p(\mathbf{a}):(\mathbf{e})\}\,S}$$

(Rule of Adaptation)

In the case where $\mathbf{k}$ is empty, it is understood that the $\exists$ will be omitted.

The rule of adaptation is also extremely valuable when applied to nonrecursive procedures, since it permits a single proof of the properties of the body of a procedure to be used again and again for every call of the procedure. In the absence of recursion, the rule of adaptation may be justified as a *derived* inference rule, since it can be shown that every theorem proved with its aid could also have been proved without it. However, successful use of the rule of adaptation to simplify proofs still depends on observance of the conditions of the disjointness of actual parameters.

Example

As an example of the application of the rules given above, we will take the trivial, but familiar, problem of the computation of the factorial r of a non-negative integer a. The procedure is declared:

```
fact(r):(a) proc
  if a = 0 then r:= 1
    else begin new w;
      call fact(w):(a − 1);
      r:= a×w
    end.
```

It is required to prove that

$$a \geqslant 0\ \{\mathbf{call}\ fact(r):(a)\}\ r = a! \qquad \text{(I)}$$

This is achieved by proving

$$a \geqslant 0\ \{Q\}\ r = a!$$

where Q stands for the body of the procedure, on the hypothesis that (I) already holds for the internal recursive call. The proof is given in Table 6.2; it contains a number of lemmas which can be readily proved as theorems in the arithmetic of integers. A list of inference rules used is contained in the Appendix.

Table 6.2 Proof of factorial program

Line number	*Formal proof*	*Justification*
1	$a\times w = a!\ \{r := a\times w\}\ r = a!$	D0
2	$a-1 \geqslant 0 \wedge \forall w(w = (a-1)! \Rightarrow a\times w = a!)\ \{\mathbf{call}\ fact(w):(a-1)\}\ axw = a!$	D6, D7, Hypothesis
3	$a > 0 \vdash a-1 \geqslant 0 \wedge \forall w(w = (a-1)! \Rightarrow a\times w = a!)$	Lemma 1
4	$a > 0\ \{\mathbf{begin\ new\ w;\ call}\ fact\ (w):(a-1);\ r := a\times w\ \mathbf{end}\}\ r = a!$	D1, D2, D8 (1, 2, 3)
5	$1 = a!\ \{r := 1\}\ r = a!$	D0
6	$\mathbf{if}\ a = 0\ \mathbf{then}\ 1 = a!\ \mathbf{else}\ a > 0\ \{Q\}\ r = a!$	D4(5, 4)
7	$a \geqslant 0 \vdash \mathbf{if}\ \mathrm{a} = 0\ \mathbf{then}\ 1 = a!\ \mathbf{else}\ a > 0$	Lemma 2
8	$a \geqslant 0\ \{Q\}\ r = a!$	D1(7, 6)
9	$a \geqslant 0\ \{\mathbf{call}\ fact\ (r):(a)\}\ r = a!$	D5 (8)

6.7 Implementation

It has been suggested by Floyd (1967) that a specification of proof techniques for a language might serve well as a formal definition of the semantics of that language, for it lays down, as an essential condition on any computer implementation, that every provable property of any program expressed in the language shall, in practice, obtain when the program is executed by the implementation. It is, therefore, interesting to inquire what implementation methods for parameter passing will be valid in a language whose definition includes the inference rules described in the previous sections. It appears that there is a wide choice of valid implementation methods, covering all the standard methods which have been used in implementations of widely familiar languages.

This means that each implementor of the language defined by these rules can make his selection of method in order to maximize the efficiency of his implementation, taking into account not only the characteristics of his particular machine, but also varying his choice in accordance with the properties of each particular procedure and each particular type of parameter; and he is free to choose the degree of automatic optimization which he will bring to bear, without introducing any risk that an optimized program will have different properties from an unoptimized one.

The remainder of this section surveys the various familiar parameter mechanisms, and assesses the circumstances under which each of them gives the highest efficiency. The reader may verify that they all satisfy the requirements imposed by the proof rules stated above, bearing in mind that every procedure call,

$$\textbf{call } p(\mathbf{a}):(\mathbf{e})$$

conforms to the condition that all the parameters **a** are distinct from each other, and none of them appears in any of the expressions **e**. The observance of this restriction is the necessary condition of the validity of most of the commonly used parameter-passing methods.

6.7.1 Compile-time macro-substitution

Macro-substitution is an operation which replaces all calls of a procedure by a copy of the body of the procedure, after this copy has itself been modified by replacing each occurrence of a formal parameter within it by a copy of the corresponding actual parameter. The normal process of translation to machine code takes place only after these replacements are complete. This technique has been commonly used for assembly languages and for business-oriented languages.

Macro-substitution will be found to be a satisfactory technique in any of the following circumstances:

(1) The procedure body is so short that the code resulting from macro-substitution is not appreciably longer than the parameter planting and calling sequence would have been.

(2) The procedure is called only once from within the program which incorporates it.
(3) The procedure is called several times, but on each occasion some or all of the parameters are identical. Substitution can be applied only to those parameters which are identical, leaving the remaining parameters to be treated by some run-time mechanism.
(4) In a highly optimizing compiler, macro-substitution will ensure not only that no time is wasted on parameter passing, but also that each call can be fully optimized in the knowledge of the identity and properties of its actual parameters.

The technique is not applicable to recursive procedures.

6.7.2 Run-time code construction

An alternative to substitution in the source code at compile time is the execution of a logically identical operation on the object code at run time. This involves planting the addresses of the actual parameters within the machine code of the procedure body on each occasion that the procedure is called. The technique may be favoured whenever all the following conditions are satisfied:

(1) The computer has an instruction format capable of direct addressing of the whole store.
(2) The actual parameter is an array (or other large structure) which would be expensive to copy.
(3) The called procedure is not recursive.
(4) The called procedure contains at least one iteration.

This technique was used in FORTRAN implementations on the IBM 704/709 series of computers.

6.7.3 Indirect addressing

Before jumping to the procedure body, the calling program places the addresses of the actual parameters in machine registers or in the local workspace of the called procedure. Whenever the procedure refers to one of its parameters, it uses the corresponding address as an indirect pointer (modifier).

This technique is suitable in the following circumstances:

(1) The computer has an instruction format with good address-modification facilities.
(2) The actual parameter is an array (or other large structure) which would be expensive to copy.

If a single parameter mechanism is to be used in all circumstances, this is undoubtedly the correct one. However, on fast computers with slave stores, operand pre-fetch queues, or paging methods of storage control, it could cause some unexpected inefficiencies.

This technique is used in PL/I and in many implementations of FORTRAN on the IBM 360 series of computers.

6.7.4 Value and result

Before jumping to the subroutine, the calling program copies the current values of the actual parameters into machine registers or local workspace of the called subroutine. After exist from the subroutine, the calling program copies back all values that might have been changed (i.e., those to the left of the colon in the actual-parameter list).

This technique is to be preferred when either of the following conditions hold:

(1) The size of the parameter is sufficiently small that copying is cheap, accomplished in one or two instructions.
(2) The actual parameter is 'packed' in such a way that it cannot readily be accessed by indirect addressing.

This technique is available in ALGOL W, and is used in several current implementations of FORTRAN.

6.7.5 Call by name (as in ALGOL 60)

The calling program passes to the procedure the addresses of portions of code corresponding to each parameter. When the procedure wishes to access or change the value of a parameter, it jumps to the corresponding portion of code.

Since the restrictions on the actual parameters prohibit the use of Jensen's device, there is no reason why this technique should ever be used. It is difficult to envisage circumstances in which it could be more efficient than the other techniques listed.

6.8 Conclusion

It has been shown that it is possible by axiomatic methods to define an important programming language feature in such a way as to facilitate the demonstration of the correctness of programs and at the same time to permit flexibility and high efficiency of implementation. The combination of these two advantages can be achieved only if the programmer is willing to observe certain disciplines in his use of the feature, namely that all actual parameters which may be changed by a procedure must be distinct from each other, and must not be contained in any of the other parameters. It is believed that this discipline will not be felt onerous by programmers who are interested in the efficient and reliable solution of practical problems in a machine-independent fashion.

It is interesting to note that the discipline imposed is a combination of the disciplines required by the ISO standard FORTRAN and by the IFIP recommended subset of ALGOL 60. The former insists on the distinctness of all parameters changed by a procedure, and the latter insists that each of them be an unsubscripted identifier.

6.9 Acknowledgement

The basic approach adopted in this paper was stimulated by an investigation reported in Foley (1969).

6.10 Appendix

P, P_1, P_2, R, S stand for propositional formulae.
Q, Q_1, Q_2 stand for program statements.
x, y stand for variable names (y not free in P or R).
e stands for an expression.
B stands for a Boolean expression.
p stands for a procedure name.
$\mathbf{x}$ stands for a list of nonlocal variables of Q which are subject to change in Q.
$\mathbf{v}$ stands for a list of other nonlocal variables of Q.
$\mathbf{a}$ stands for a list of distinct variables.
$\mathbf{e}$ stands for a list of expressions, not containing any of the variables in $\mathbf{a}$.
$\mathbf{k}$ stands for a list of variables not free in $\mathbf{x}, \mathbf{v}$.
$\mathbf{k}'$ stands for a list of variables not free in $\mathbf{a}, \mathbf{e}, S$.

D0 $$R_e^x \{x := e\}\ R$$ (Assignment)

D1 $$\frac{P\{Q\}\ S,\ S \vdash R}{P\{Q\}\ R} \quad \frac{P \vdash S,\ S\{Q\}\ R}{P\{Q\}\ R}$$ (Consequence)

D2 $$\frac{P\,\{Q_1\}\,S,\ S\,\{Q_2\}\,R}{P\,\{Q_1;\,Q_2\}\,R}$$ (Composition)

D3 $$\frac{P\,\{Q\}\,S,\ S \vdash \textbf{if } B \textbf{ then } P \textbf{ else } R}{P\,\{\textbf{while } B \textbf{ do } Q\}\,R}$$ (Iteration)

D4 $$\frac{P_1\,\{Q_1\}\,R,\ P_2\{Q_2\}\,R}{\textbf{if } B \textbf{ then } P_1 \textbf{ else } P_2\,\{\textbf{if } B \textbf{ then } Q_1 \textbf{ else } Q_2\}\,R}$$ (Alternation)

D5 $$\frac{p(\mathbf{x}):(\mathbf{v})\ \textbf{proc}\ Q,\ P\,\{\textbf{call}\ p(\mathbf{x}):(\mathbf{v})\}\,R \vdash P\,\{Q\}\,R}{P\,\{\textbf{call}\ p(\mathbf{x}):(\mathbf{v})\}\,R}$$ (Recursion)

D6 $$\frac{P\,\{\textbf{call}\ p(\mathbf{x}):(\mathbf{v})\}\,R}{P^{\mathbf{k},\,\mathbf{x},\,\mathbf{v}}_{\mathbf{k}',\,\mathbf{a},\,\mathbf{e}}\,\{\textbf{call}\ p(\mathbf{a}):(\mathbf{e})\}\,R^{\mathbf{k},\,\mathbf{x},\,\mathbf{v}}_{\mathbf{k}',\,\mathbf{a},\,\mathbf{e}}}$$ (Substitution)

D7 $$\frac{P\,\{\textbf{call}\ p(\mathbf{a}):(\mathbf{e})\}\,R}{\exists k'\,(P \wedge \forall \mathbf{a}(R \Rightarrow S))\,\{\textbf{call}\ p(\mathbf{a}):(\mathbf{e})\}\,S}$$ (Adaptation)

D8 $$\frac{P\,\{Q^x_y\}\,R}{P\,\{\textbf{new x};\,Q\}\,R}$$ (where y is not in Q unless y and x are the same)
(Declaration)

SEVEN

Computer science

This is the text of Hoare's inaugural lecture at The Queen's University of Belfast. It explains the challenge of computer science by describing, to a lay audience, the task of designing an algorithm. The chosen task is the partition problem used as an example for proof in Chapter 5. The example used was enacted with a carefully prearranged pack of playing cards.

The talk (published as [18]) was given on 10 February 1971. The content of the talk defined the objectives and structure of a modular degree course (joint with mathematics) which was developed and introduced over the subsequent years.

In University circles it is a pleasant and informative custom when introducing members of staff to mention the academic department to which they belong. The same custom is extended to our wives, who, like the wives of peers, assume their husbands' titles. But one drawback in this mode of introduction is that it frequently leads to further conversation on academic topics. In my case, this is often introduced by an open admission that my new acquaintance has never been able to understand computers. I wonder whether others have found an acceptable response to this conversational gambit. There is the temptation to joke:

'And I don't suppose computers could ever understand you', which is very feeble and quite rude. How about:

'Never mind, I expect there are things that you understand and I don't'? But this is excruciatingly condescending.

A more comforting remark would be:

'Well, there is no reason why you *should* understand computers'. But this is not quite honest. Certainly, a lot of the details of how to use computers can safely be left to the experts. But I believe it also to be most important that there should be a general understanding among the educated public of

C. A. R. Hoare, *Computer Science*, New Lecture Series No. 62 (1971). An Inaugural Lecture delivered at The Queen's University of Belfast on 10 February. This paper is republished by kind permission of The Queen's University Belfast.

the potentialities and limitations of computers; of their benefits and also of their dangers.

So the only remaining possibility is perhaps to give way to temptation, and attempt a short description of what computers are, and what they can and cannot do. Sometimes, I must confess, I step beyond any reasonable limit for talking shop at a social gathering. But what better gathering could present itself than the audience at this public lecture? That is why I have chosen to speak not on some fascinating side-line of my subject, but on the central core of the subject itself. I will address myself to the fundamental questions:

'What is computer science?'

'Is it even a science?'

and 'Why should it be taught in a university?'

In answering these questions, it is helpful to relate the subject to other, perhaps more familiar, academic disciplines with which it overlaps. The first such discipline is electrical (or more precisely electronic) engineering, which studies the physical properties of the electronic circuits from which all modern computers are constructed. Computer science is concerned not with the physical but rather with the logical properties of the circuits, and with effective methods of connecting them together into large networks which provide the logical and arithmetic functions required in a computer. The study of logic design and computer architecture could be important to an electronic engineer who wishes to design and develop circuits that will be useful in a modern computer; it is also important to a computer scientist who wishes to understand the engineering foundation on which his subject rests, and who wishes to influence the future design of computers to make them more suitable for their purposes.

Since their earliest days, computers have been most heavily used in the study of applied mathematics and theoretical physics, and have found numerical solutions to many problems which have hitherto been considered insoluble – for example, the multi-body problem of classical mechanics. A study of the effective methods of solving mathematical problems on a computer is known as numerical analysis. Some familiarity with this subject is indispensable to theoretical physicists and other scientists engaging in heavy use of the computer; it is also part of the province of a computer scientist who wishes to practise his art in this field.

The majority of computers in operation to-day are not used by scientists but by industrialists, administrators and accountants; they carry out the clerical routine required for the running of a business, a bank, or a government department. Any student of modern business methods must know something of the application of computers in this area of data processing; but the task of introducing a computer in a data-processing environment often forms the major part of the professional activities of a computer scientist.

Turning now to the theoretical aspects of the subject, we find similar connections between the theory of computation and other traditional academic disciplines – pure mathematics, linguistic studies, and logic. There are already a number of branches in the theory of computation – finite automata, Turing machines, Markov algorithms, recursive functions, formal grammars, formal language definition, and the proof of programs. Many of these topics could be studied by a pure mathematician, a theoretical linguist, or by a logician; they also form the conceptual foundation of the study of computer science, and can give a valuable practical insight into the solution of certain classes of problem on a computer.

Thus we see that computer science has strong links with many familiar disciplines, ranging from pure mathematics to electronic engineering, from linguistics to business studies, from logic to theoretical physics. This illustrates the fascinating range of the subject, from the most abstract of theoretical studies, to the most practical aspects of the construction and use of computers. It is a great challenge in education to convey an understanding of the closeness of the theory to its practice; for this is one of the fortunate academic subjects for which, in the span of an undergraduate curriculum, it is possible to convey something of an understanding of the underlying mathematical and logical principles, as well as an adequate knowledge of the engineering aspects of its practice.

Having surveyed the relationships of computer science with other disciplines, it remains to answer the basic questions: What is the central core of the subject? What is it that distinguishes it from the separate subjects with which it is related? What is the linking thread which gathers these disparate branches into a single discipline? My answer to these questions is simple – it is the art of programming a computer. It is the art of designing efficient and elegant methods of getting a computer to solve problems, theoretical or practical, small or large, simple or complex. It is the art of translating this design into an effective and accurate computer program. This is the art that must be mastered by a practising computer scientist; the skill that is sought by numerous advertisements in the general and technical press; the ability that must be fostered and developed by computer science courses in universities.

So in order to explain my understanding of computer science, it is essential to describe the nature of the activity of computer programming. To do this I have chosen an example of one of the first programs which I designed and wrote some ten years ago for the solution of a simple but nontrivial practical problem. It is a problem that can arise in the collection and tabulation of statistics, for example, the discovery of the median and other quantiles of a set of statistical observations. Suppose we have a large number of observations, say a hundred thousand – perhaps the heights of school entrants, or the distances of stars, or marks in some examination. It is required to single out those 20 thousand observations with smallest value;

perhaps the 20 thousand nearest stars, or the 20 thousand shortest schoolchildren, or the 20 thousand students with lowest marks.

The first guide in discovery of a method for computer solution of a problem is to see how the problem could be solved by hand by a human being. In order not to be overwhelmed by the sheer numbers involved, we will scale down the problem to only one hundred observations, of which the twenty with lowest values are to be selected. Imagine for convenience that the values of the observations are recorded on a hundred cards; these cards must be separated into two heaps, the left hand heap containing the twenty lowest cards, and the right hand heap containing the rest. We can now regard the problem as one of designing, as it were, the rules for a game of patience, whose outcome is the one we desire, and which has the delightful property that it always comes out.

Perhaps the first idea which occurs to us is to sort the cards into ascending order; for then the selection of the required twenty cards is trivial. All that is needed is to deal the first twenty cards off the top of the pack. So all we have to do is to find some efficient method of sorting the pack. But further consideration shows that it would be a waste of time to sort the *whole* pack, when all we require is to single out twenty of them, the twenty cards with smallest value. So we turn attention again to this problem.

Our second proposed method is to look through the whole pack for the smallest card, and remove it; then look for the smallest again in the reduced pack; and to repeat the process until twenty cards have been singled out. Before accepting this solution, we ask ourselves how efficient the method is. In order to find the lowest card in a pack it is in principle necessary to look at every card in the pack, i.e., a hundred cards; to find the second lowest card requires ninety-nine inspections, and so on. Thus assuming optimistically that each inspection takes a second, the total time taken will be about half an hour – a rather daunting prospect. Going back to the original computer problem of 100 thousand observations, and assuming that our computer can examine about a hundred thousand observations in one second, it would take about five hours to select the least 20 000 observations. So it is worth while to seek an alternative more efficient solution.

As our third idea, it may occur to us that if we happened to know the value of the observation which was the twenty-first smallest one, we could use this as a sort of *borderline* value in the process of splitting the pack into two heaps. For example, supposing we think that 376 is the twentieth smallest value. All we need to do is to go through the pack, putting all cards lower than the borderline value on a left-hand heap, and all cards higher than it on a right hand heap, and so on. At the end, we expect that the left-hand heap will contain exactly the required twenty values. This process requires only one scan of the entire pack, and will take just over one and a half minutes in our small manual example. Returning to the computer problem, it could carry out the whole process on a hundred thousand observations in one second – very much better than the five hours required if the previous method had been used. But it seems that this gain in speed can be achieved only if we have prior knowledge of the correct borderline value, and this knowledge we do not have.

But now suppose we make a *guess* of the correct borderline value, and carry out the partitioning process as before. I suggest that we choose the borderline as the value of an actual card in the pack, since this will ensure that we never choose a ridiculously high or low value. Now if our guess, say 376, was too high, the left-hand heap ends up too large, containing more than twenty cards; and the right-hand heap is too small, containing less than eighty cards. Similarly, if our guess was too low, the left-hand heap is too small and the right-hand heap too large. Thus we always know afterwards whether the first guess was too high or too low, and perhaps we can use this knowledge to make a better guess next time.

As before, it is a good idea to select as next guess an actual card of the pack, which is known to be better than the previously guessed wrong borderline. This can be done very easily by selecting a card from the appropriate heap, for example, the left-hand heap if the original guess was too high; for it is known that all cards in this heap are smaller than the previous (too high) borderline. So we can repeat the process with the new borderline.

But now consider the right-hand heap which was too small. This heap contains only cards which *should* be there, in the sense that they are already in the same heap as they will be in when the correct borderline is found. There is no point in scanning the cards of this heap again. This suggests that in any subsequent scan we can put these cards aside, say at the top of the card table. The importance of this suggestion arises from the fact that subsequent scans will be shorter than earlier ones, so eventually we will get down to a single card, which must then be the right borderline.

So having put to the top the right-hand heap which was too small, we move the other heap to the middle, select a new borderline, say 196, and proceed with the split. At the end of the second split, we will have a borderline value and three heaps:

(1) A top right heap, with cards higher than the first borderline 367.
(2) A bottom right heap, with cards lying between the two borderlines 196 and 367.
(3) A bottom left heap, with cards lower than the second smaller borderline 196.

It may happen now that it is the left of the two bottom heaps which is too small; it will therefore contain only cards which properly belong to the left heap; and as before, we can put it to the top of the card table, and omit it from future examination. Then we place the borderline value on that heap. Next we move the remaining bottom heap up to the middle and repeat the

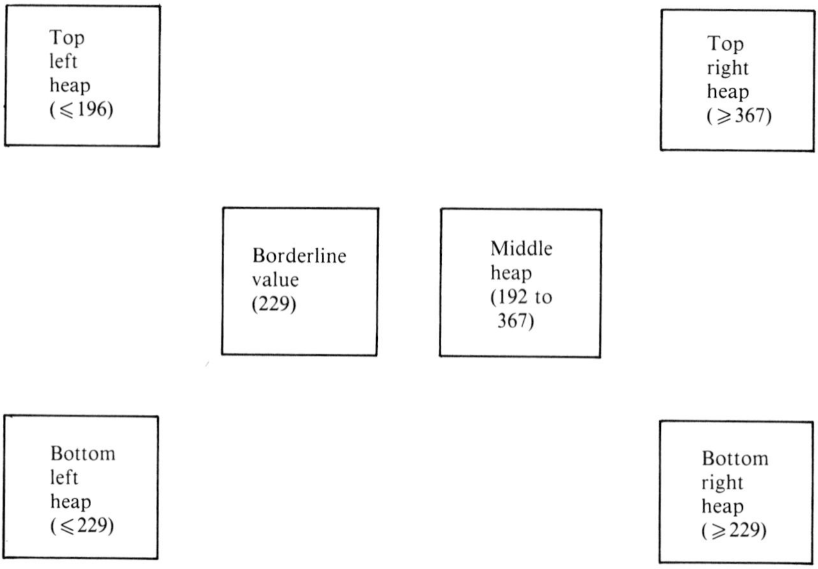

Figure 7.1 Layout of the game

process, selecting again an arbitrary trial borderline (say 229), and splitting the middle heap into a bottom left heap and a bottom right heap. Then we have a picture as shown in Fig. 7.1.

Obviously we don't want to continue to proliferate more and more heaps, and we must seek every opportunity to amalgamate them, for example by putting the bottom right heap on top of the top right heap. This operation is permissible whenever the resulting combined heap is not too large. Similarly the left-hand heaps can be amalgamated if this would not make the top left heap too large. It is evident that one at least of these amalgamations is always possible; and if they are both possible, the whole problem is solved. But if one of them cannot be amalgamated, we must continue the process of splitting on this remaining heap, and so continue until the problem is solved.

It seems now that we have a grasp of a solution to our original problem; and to verify this, it is worthwhile to write out the rules of the game rather more precisely, as is done in Fig. 7.2.

Notice how we have dealt with the borderline card. This is the most troublesome card of all. We must make sure that this borderline card is *always* put on to one of the two top heaps, because this is the only way we can guarantee that the middle heap will always be reduced in size; for if it is not reduced, there is a danger that our game of patience will not come out at all – and what is worse, it will go on forever. Consider, for example, the case when there is only one card left on the middle heap. This is necessarily

(1) Put all 100 cards on the middle heap.
(2) Repeat the following until the middle heap is empty:
  (2.1) Take a card from the middle heap as borderline.
  (2.2) Repeat the following until the middle heap is empty:
    If the top card of the middle heap is less than the borderline, put it on the bottom left heap; otherwise on the bottom right heap.
  (2.3) If the combined size of top left and bottom left heaps is less than 21, amalgamate them; and if it is still less than 20 put the borderline card on as well.
  (2.4) If the combined size of top right and bottom right heaps is less than 81, amalgamate them; and if it is still less than 80, put the borderline card on as well.
  (2.5) Move the remaining bottom heap (if any) to the middle heap.
(3) The required 20 observations will now be found on the top left heap.

Figure 7.2 Rules of the game

selected as the borderline value. After the split, both bottom heaps will, of course, be empty. Thus the borderline card must now be added directly to that top pile which needs it. On a careful interpretation of steps 2.3 and 2.4 it is possible to see that an amalgamation of an *empty* bottom heap with a top heap will still leave that heap too small, and thereby justify the addition of the borderline card. This is the kind of subtle reasoning that is often required to ensure the correct working of a computer program.

Let us see whether this approach is in fact faster than the previous one. Let us use the letter N to stand for the number of observations, a hundred in the manual case, a hundred thousand in the computer example. Consider first a so-called 'worst-case' analysis, which will give an upper bound for the time taken. The worst thing that can happen in each scan of the middle heap is for the value chosen as borderline to be the largest or smallest of the values in the middle heap. In this case, all the remaining cards will go into only one of the bottom heaps, the other bottom heap remaining empty. Then the borderline will be moved to a top heap, and the new middle heap will contain only one less card than before. Thus N operations will be required on the first scan, $N-1$ on the second, $N-2$ on the third, and so on; until the last scan involves only one observation. This adds up to about $\frac{1}{2}N^2$ operations in all; which take about an hour and a half on our manual example, and about fourteen hours for the computer. This is far worse than our previous approach, and suggests that we should take steps to minimize the chances that our borderline card will be the lowest or highest card in the middle heap.

At the other extreme, the best possible case is when the first selection of borderline happens to be the right one; for in this case the task is completed by a single scan of N operations, taking about a minute and a half by hand, or one second in the computer. Obviously, the average time taken will lie between these two extremes, and we hope very much closer to the best case than the worst.

So let us consider what we may call a 'typical' case, in which the value selected as borderline is roughly the middle value of the middle heap. In this case, the bottom left and bottom right heaps will each contain about half the cards. One of these will be moved to the top, and the other will form the new middle heap. Thus on each scan the size of the middle heap will be roughly halved. The first scan involves all N cards and so the second scan will take $\frac{1}{2}N$, the next one $\frac{1}{4}N$, and so on, until the size of the middle heap is reduced to one. The resulting sum is approximately equal to $2N$, which takes about three minutes on our manual example, and about two seconds on the computer. This seems fully satisfactory, and I doubt whether it is worthwhile to search for a basically more efficient approach, though there are one or two special techniques that can be used to speed up the suggested approach even further.

We have now worked out quite an efficient way of accomplishing our original objective. All that remains is to tell the computer by means of a program how to carry out the process. But now it is necessary to take into account the actual characteristics of computing machines. For example, computers are not capable physically of picking up and dealing sets of cards; they use quite different methods of manipulating numbers. Imagine, therefore, a long array of pigeonholes, numbered from one to a hundred thousand, each containing a single card with a single value written upon it (Fig. 7.3). We will call this array A, and the individual pigeonholes will be denoted by using square brackets: $A[i]$ stands for the ith pigeonhole of the internal store of a computer. Assume also that the operation which the computer can perform most efficiently on this array is to *exchange* the contents of two of the pigeonholes, say the ith pigeonhole and the jth. The process which we have discovered to be efficient for heaps of cards must now be adapted to work efficiently in this new environment.

Obviously, all five of our previous heaps are going to have to be accommodated somehow within this single long array of pigeonholes. So let

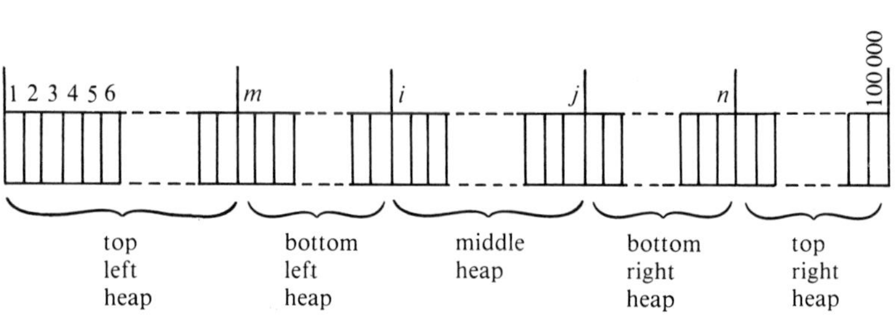

Figure 7.3 The computer's store

us use the left-hand end to hold the left heaps, and the right-hand end to hold the right heaps. More precisely, the top left-hand heap will be the contents of the pigeonholes numbered 1, 2, to $m - 1$:

$$A[1], A[2], \ldots, A[m-1];$$

and the top right-hand heap will be the contents of pigeonholes numbered $n+1$, $n+2$, to 100000, that is:

$$A[n+1], A[n+2], \ldots, A[100\,000],$$

where m and n are numbers marking the limits of these heaps. The middle heap will, of course, consist of the remaining pigeonholes:

$$A[m], A[m+1], \ldots, A[n].$$

If $m = 1$, this signifies that the left heap is empty.

If $n = 100\,000$, this signifies that the right heap is empty.

If n is less than m, this means that the middle heap is empty, and that our task is complete.

During the process of splitting the middle heap, two further heaps are required, the bottom left heap and the bottom right heap. As before, we introduce letters i and j, and decree that the bottom left heap shall comprise the contents of:

$$A[m], A[m+1], \ldots, A[i-1],$$

and the bottom right heap will be:

$$A[j+1], A[j+2], \ldots, A[n].$$

If $i = m$ this means that the bottom left heap is empty; and if $j = n$, this means the bottom right heap is empty. Since at the beginning of each scan of the middle heap both bottom heaps are empty, the value of i must initially be set to m and the value of j must be the same as n (see Fig. 7.3).

Next, the borderline value must be selected from the middle heap. Instead of removing the card from its pigeonhole, which is not allowed, we make a copy of the number on it. Then we look at one of the cards of the middle heap, say $A[i]$. If this is less than the borderline value we must put it in the bottom left heap. This can be done simply by adding one to the previous value of i, which is the value that marked the top of the bottom left heap. This will automatically achieve the desired effect of increasing the size of the heap by one and simultaneously including $A[i]$ in the bottom left heap.

Now what happens if the contents of $A[i]$ is larger than the borderline value, and needs to go into the bottom right heap? To do this it must obviously be moved to the top of the bottom right heap, namely to $A[j]$. This must be accomplished by an *exchange*, which puts the original content of $A[j]$ into $A[i]$. Then the size of the right-hand heap must be enlarged to contain its new card, by subtracting one from the previous value of j.

So we see that we can always move the contents of the pigeonhole $A[i]$, to the appropriate one of the two bottom heaps. All that now needs to be done is to repeat the process until the size of the middle heap has been reduced to nothing, that is, until j is less than i.

At this stage we must join one or both of the bottom heaps to the corresponding top heap. This may be done by a trick similar to that which we have used in adding single cards to the bottom heaps. In fact, to join the bottom left heap to the top left heap, all that is necessary is to change the value of m (marking the limit of the top left heap) so that it is equal to the current value of i (marking the limit of the bottom left heap); and similarly, to add the bottom right heap to the top right heap, we set the value of n (marking the limit of the top right heap) so that it is equal to the current value of j. But of course, before performing either of these two operations, it is necessary to check that the result of the operation would not make the top heap too large.

Thus we have worked towards the program shown in Fig. 7.4. In fact this program contains some of the special techniques to secure the highest degree of efficiency; and these are based on some rather subtle reasoning, which need not concern us here. Furthermore, this program is expressed in something close to ordinary English, and not in the kind of mathematical notation (programming language) which a computer can understand and interpret. But it is sufficient to illustrate the most important aspects of the art of programming, which is the keystone of the discipline of computer science. So allow me to conclude with a summary of the nature of the

(1) Set m to 1 and n to 100 000.
(2) Repeat the following until $n \leqslant m$:
  (2.1) If $A[m] > A[n]$ exchange them.
  (2.2) If $A[m] > A[m+1]$ exchange them, otherwise if $A[m+1] > A[n]$ exchange them instead.
  (2.3) Set i to $m+2$ and j to $n-1$ and b to $A[m+1]$.
  (2.4) Repeat the following until $j < i$:
    (2.4.1) Add one to i repeatedly until $A[i] \geqslant b$.
    (2.4.2) Subtract one from j repeatedly until $b \geqslant A[j]$.
    (2.4.3) If $i \leqslant j$ then exchange $A[i]$ and $A[j]$ and add one to i and subtract one from j.
  (2.5) Exchange $A[m+1]$ and $A[j]$ and subtract one from j.
  (2.6) If $j \leqslant 20\,000$ set m to i.
  (2.7). If $80\,000 \leqslant i$ then set n to j.
(3) The required observations will be found in

$$A[1], A[2], \ldots, A[20\,000].$$

Figure 7.4 The computer program

reasoning involved, and of some of the qualities that must be possessed by successful programmers.

The first requirement for the successful construction of programs is a rather careful analysis of the problem itself. Most problems in real life are poorly understood, in that the real problem is often something different from what it is orginally thought to be. Even in our relatively simple example, the original problem was formulated rather vaguely, and needed to be interpreted carefully to ensure that it was solvable at all. For example, suppose there is no twentieth value, but rather five values which are equal seventeenth. Do we know what we want in this case? Will our program even work at all? A good computer programmer must be able to recognize, pose, and answer questions far more subtle and difficult than these.

The second requirement is a thorough search for a suitable efficient (and preferably simple and elegant) technique for solving the problem. It is at this stage that imagination must be given the fullest rein; here is the scope for profound insight or spectacular invention. But the imagination must always be disciplined by a sound judgement of the value of each approach. This judgement must be exercised rapidly on incomplete evidence to reject unprofitable lines of inquiry even before their detailed implications have been worked out.

The next requirement is for careful elaboration of the chosen approach. At this stage, many further decisions about the details of the solution must be taken; and each of them must be taken in a manner that contributes to the overall quality of the end product. Large programs require many hundreds or even thousands of such decisions; and although inevitably some of them will be taken wrongly, the effect of making even slightly inappropriate choices on a large number of occasions will be cumulatively disastrous.

The programmer next needs the patience and understanding to go back and reconsider the entire approach to the problem in the light of the deeper understanding that has been gained in the design process. This is particularly important when the elaboration of detail has shown that the chosen approach does not have the properties of elegance and efficiency which were expected of it.

A further requirement is for meticulous accuracy in avoiding or detecting the numerous small oversights and errors which afflict all computer programs. This involves frequent exercise of the kind of subtle reasoning which was needed to find an appropriate treatment of the borderline value in our example problem.

An obvious further requirement is a clear understanding of the structure and capabilities of a digital computer; the sizes, speeds, access characteristics, and costs of the various forms of storage and other devices, and the range of known techniques for using them efficiently. For many important and interesting problems, it is a major challenge to find effective methods for solving them, when even the largest and fastest modern computers would seem initially to be too small and slow for the purpose.

Another important requirement, which is all too often forgotten by practising programmers, is to describe to others the working of his program, and to explain and justify the decisions which he has made. It is not enough in the present world for a programmer to act as a solitary genius, who produces the goods but can never explain how. Modern large programs are written by teams of people, and each decision taken by a programmer potentially impinges on the work of the whole team. Even after the program is launched into practical use there will be frequent requirements to alter it, either as a result of subsequently discovered improvements, or as a result of a change in the circumstances in which the program is used. Unless the entire program is fully and comprehensibly explained in writing, it will be literally impossible to make any change in any part of it. The inflexibility which frequently results from this is one of the most serious drawbacks involved in the introduction of computers, and apart from programming error, could lead to the most dangerous social or commercial consequences.

To add to this long list of desirable attributes, we must also require from the computer programmer a high degree of professional integrity, and a recognition of his responsibility to society for the purposes to which computers are put. I do not wish to exaggerate the social dangers of potential misuse of computers; but at the present time when there is little general understanding of the potentialities and limitations of computers, and even less of the arcane jargon of computer men, the programmer has especial responsibility for complete frankness and honesty in the pursuit of his profession.

The final requirement is of course that the computer scientist should enjoy the practice of his art. This attitude was well expressed by an old friend and colleague, Mr Cedric Dennis, who declared: computer programming is like doing crossword puzzles, and being paid for it.

This concludes my brief investigation into the nature of computer science. I have shown that it has strong links with other branches of learning – electronic engineering, numerical analysis, business studies, pure mathematics, formal linguistics and logic. But the essential core of the subject is computer programming, the design and implementation of efficient and effective programs for the solution of problems on a digital computer.

I have also implicitly given the answer to the question why computer science is a worthy subject to take its place in the curriculum of a university. Its study involves development of the ability to abstract the essential features of a problem and its solution, to reason effectively in the abstract plane, without confusion by a mass of highly relevant detail. The abstraction must then be related to the detailed characteristics of computers as the design of the solution progresses; and it must culminate in a program in which all the detail has been made explicit; and at this stage, the utmost care must be exercised to ensure a very high degree of accuracy. At all stages the programmer must be articulate about his activity. The need for abstract thought together with meticulous accuracy, the need for imaginative speculation in the search for a solution, together with a sound knowledge of the practical limitations of the tools available for its implementation, the combination of formal rigour with a clear style for its explanation to others – these are the combinations of attributes which should be inculcated and developed in a student by any university academic discipline; and which must be developed in high degree in students of computer science. I should like to conclude with a quotation from one of the earliest and most distinguished computer scientists, Edsger Dijkstra:

> Computers are extremely flexible and powerful tools, and many feel that their application is changing the face of the earth. I would venture the opinion that as long as we regard them primarily as tools, we might grossly underestimate their significance. Their influence as tools might turn out to be but a ripple on the surface of our culture, whereas I expect them to have a much more profound influence in their capacity of intellectual challenge.

It is this intellectual challenge that we have set out to meet in introducing computer science as a subject of university education.

EIGHT

Proof of correctness of data representations

This paper makes a key point about the formal development of programs. Data abstraction is essential for succinct specifications; the development of representations becomes a necessary design tool. (A beautiful example of this method is given in Chapter 9.) It is an accident of history that the work on operation decomposition preceded that on data representation. How unfortunate that this history has influenced so many subsequent authors to focus on operation decomposition even to the exclusion of the area of which Hoare still says 'data abstraction makes practical the use of proof during design.'

The style of presenting the data abstraction is via a model. Again, Hoare expresses 'amazement at the attention (the property-oriented approach) is still receiving.' He had, of course, used the axiomatic (or property-oriented) method for his 'axiomatic basis' work; whilst acknowledging its utility for basic data types he comments that 'the complexities of application seem to require the model-based approach, which takes for granted the basic properties of data and structures.'

The idea for this style of development came when Hoare was working on [31]. Unusually, there was only one draft and this document – dated 11 December 1971 – is very close to the published form of the paper which was submitted on 16 February 1972. The debt, among others, to Milner's work is acknowleged but the paper here presents the proof method much more in the spirit of program proofs than Milner's more algebraic view.

An important step in proving the correctness of representations with respect to given abstractions is to record a function from the representation to the abstraction: the direction is dictated by the fact that there can be many representations for any particular element of the abstract space. This realization came to Hoare when working on [36]. Although the choice of the function letter ($\mathscr{A}$) suggests a name like 'abstraction function', it is actually called a 'representation function' in the text.

This paper, which is published as [32], was widely influential and roughly this form of proof about data representation stood as a standard until

C. A. R. Hoare, Proof of correctness of data representations, *Acta Informatica,* **1**(4), 271–81 (1972). This paper is republished by kind permission of Springer-Verlag GmbH.

recently. A broadly equivalent rule is used in VDM (a recent reference to which is Jones 1986). But the rule is incomplete! A more complete rule has been discovered, two forms of which can be found in [97] and Nipkow (1986).

Abstract

A powerful method of simplifying the proofs of program correctness is suggested; and some new light is shed on the problem of functions with side-effects.

8.1 Introduction

In the development of programs by stepwise refinement (Wirth 1971b; Dijkstra 1972c; Dahl 1972; Hoare [30]), the programmer is encouraged to postpone the decision on the representation of his data until after he has designed his algorithm, and has expressed it as an 'abstract' program operating on 'abstract' data. He then chooses for the abstract data some convenient and efficient concrete representation in the store of a computer; and finally programs the primitive operations required by his abstract program in terms of this concrete representation. This paper suggests an automatic method of accomplishing the transition between an abstract and a concrete program, and also a method of proving its correctness; that is, of proving that the concrete representation exhibits all the properties expected of it by the 'abstract' program. A similar suggestion was made more formally in algebraic terms in Milner (1971) which gives a general definition of simulation. However, a more restricted definition may prove to be more useful in practical program proofs.

If the data representation is proved correct, the correctness of the final concrete program depends only on the correctness of the original abstract program. Since abstract programs are usually very much shorter and easier to prove correct, the total task of proof has been considerably lightened by factorizing it in this way. Furthermore, the two parts of the proof correspond to the successive stages in program development, thereby contributing to a constructive approach to the correctness of programs (Dijkstra, 1968a). Finally, it must be recalled that in the case of larger and more complex programs the description given above in terms of two stages readily generalizes to multiple stages.

8.2 Concepts and notations

Suppose in an abstract program there is some abstract variable t which is regarded as being of type T (say a small set of integers). A concrete representation of t usually consists of several variables $c_1, c_2, \ldots, c_n$ whose types are directly (or more directly) represented in the computer store. The primitive operations on the variable t are represented by procedures $p_1, p_2, \ldots, p_m$, whose bodies carry out on the variables $c_1, c_2, \ldots, c_n$ a series of operations directly (or more directly) performed by computer hardware, and which correspond to meaningful operations on the abstract variable t. The entire concrete representation of the type T can be expressed by declarations of these variables and procedures. For this we adopt the notation of the Simula 67 (Dahl *et al.* 1970) class declaration, which specifies the association between an abstract type T and its concrete representation:

class T;
  begin ... *declarations of* $c_1, c_2, \ldots, c_n$ ...;
    procedure p_1⟨*formal parameter part*⟩; Q_1;
    procedure p_2⟨*formal parameter part*⟩; Q_2;
      ... (8.1)
    procedure p_m⟨*formal parameter part*⟩; Q_m;
    Q
  end;

where Q is a piece of program which assigns initial values (if desired) to the variables $c_1, c_2, \ldots, c_n$. As in ALGOL 60, any of the ps may be functions; this is signified by preceding the procedure declaration by the type of the procedure.

Having declared a representation for a type T, it will be required to use this in the abstract program to declare all variables which are to be represented in that way. For this purpose we use the notation:

var$(T)t$;

or for multiple declarations:

var$(T)t_1, t_2, \ldots$;

The same notation may be used for specifying the types of arrays, functions, and parameters. Within the block in which these declarations are made, it will be required to operate upon the variables $t, t_1, \ldots,$ in the manner defined by the bodies of the procedures $p_1, p_2, \ldots, p_m$. This is accomplished by introducing a compound notation for a procedure call:

$t_i \cdot p_j$⟨*actual parameter part*⟩;

where t_i names the variable to be operated upon and p_j names the operation to be performed.

If p_j is a function, the notation displayed above is a function designator; otherwise it is a procedure statement. The form $t_i \cdot p_j$ is known as a *compound identifier*.

These concepts and notations have been closely modelled on those of Simula 67. The only difference is the use of **var**(T) instead of **ref**(T). This reflects the fact that in the current treatment, objects of declared classes are not expected to be addressed by reference; usually they will occupy storage space contiguously in the local workspace of the block in which they are declared, and will be addressed by offset in the same way as normal integer and real variables of the block.

8.3 Example

As an example of the use of these concepts, consider an abstract program which operates on several small sets of integers. It is known that none of these sets ever has more than a hundred members. Furthermore, the only operations actually used in the abstract program are the initial clearing of the set, and the insertion and removal of individual members of the set. These are denoted by procedure statements

$$s \cdot insert(i)$$

and

$$s \cdot remove(i).$$

There is also a function $s \cdot has(i)$, which tests whether i is a member of s.

It is decided to represent each set as an array A of 100 integer elements, together with pointer m to the last member of the set; m is zero when the set is empty. This representation can be declared:

```
class smallintset;
  begin integer m; integer array A[1 : 100];
  procedure insert(i); integer i;
    begin integer j;
      for j:= 1 step 1 until m do
        if A[j] = i then goto end insert;
        m:= m + 1;
        A[m]:= i;

  end insert: end insert;

  procedure remove(i); integer i;
    begin integer j, k;
      for j:= 1 step 1 until m do
        if A[j] = i then
          begin for k:= j + 1 step 1 until m do A[k − 1]:= A[k];
            comment close the gap over the removed member;
            m:= m − 1;
            goto end remove
          end;

    end remove: end remove;
```

```
Boolean procedure has(i); integer i;
  begin integer j;
    has:= false;
    for j:= 1 step 1 until m do
      if A[j] = i then
        begin
          has:= true
          goto end has
    end has: end has;
          end;
  m:= 0; comment intialize set to empty;
end smallintset;
```

Note: As in Simula 67, simple variable parameters are presumed to be called by value.

8.4 Semantics and implementation

The meaning of class declarations and calls on their constituent procedures may be readily explained by textual substitution; this also gives a useful clue to a practical and efficient method of implementation. A declaration:

var$(T)t$;

is regarded as equivalent to the unbracketed body of the class declaration with **begin** ... **end** brackets removed, after every occurrence of an identifier c_i or p_i declared in it has been prefixed by $t\cdot$. If there are any initializing statements in the class declaration these are removed and inserted just in front of the compound tail of the block in which the declaration is made. Thus if T has the form displayed in (1), **var**$(T)t$ is equivalent to:

```
... declarations for t · c1, t · c2, ..., t · cn ... ;
procedure t · p1(...); Q1';
procedure t · p2(...); Q2';
...
procedure t · pm(...); Qm';
```

where $Q_1', Q_2', \ldots, Q_m', Q'$ are obtained from $Q_1, Q_2, \ldots, Q_m, Q$ by prefixing every occurrence of $c_1, c_2, \ldots, c_n, p_1, p_2, \ldots, p_m$ by $t\cdot$. Furthermore, the initializing statement Q' will have been inserted just ahead of the statements of the block body.

If there are several variables of class T declared in the same block, the method described above can be applied to each of them. But in a practical implementation, only one copy of the procedure bodies will be translated.

This would contain as an extra parameter an address to the block of $c_1, c_2, \ldots, c_n$ on which a particular call is to operate.

8.5 Criterion of correctness

In an abstract program, an operation of the form

$$t_i \cdot p_j(a_1, a_2, \ldots, a_{n_j}) \tag{8.2}$$

will be expected to carry out some transformation on the variable t_i, in such a way that its resulting value is $f_j(t_i, a_1, a_2, \ldots, a_{nj})$, where f_j is some primitive operation required by the abstract program. In other words the procedure statement is expected to be equivalent to the assignment

$$t_i := f_j(t_i, a_1, a_2, \ldots, a_{n_j});$$

When this equivalence holds, we say that p_j *models* f_j. A similar concept of modelling applies to functions. It is desired that the proof of the abstract program may be based on the equivalence, using the rule of assignment (Hoare, [15]), so that for any propositional formula S, the abstract programmer may assume:

$$S^{t_i}_{f_j}(t_i, a_1, a_2, \ldots, a_{n_j})\{t_i \cdot p_j(a_1, a_2, \ldots, a_{n_j})\}S.\dagger$$

In addition, the abstract programmer will wish to assume that all declared variables are initialized to some designated value d_0 of the abstract space.

The criterion of correctness of a data representation is that every p_j models the intended f_j and that the initialization statement 'models' the desired inital value; and consequently, a program operating on abstract variables may validly be replaced by one carrying out equivalent operations on the concrete representation.

Thus in the case of *smallintset*, we require to prove that:

$$\begin{aligned}
&\mathbf{var}(i)t \text{ initializes } t \text{ to } \{\,\} \text{(the empty set)}\\
&t \cdot insert(i) \equiv t := t \cup \{i\}\\
&t \cdot remove(i) \equiv t := t \cap \neg\{i\}\\
&t \cdot has(i) \equiv i \in t.
\end{aligned} \tag{8.3}$$

8.6 Proof method

The first requirement for the proof is to define the relationship between the abstract space in which the abstract program is written, and the space of the

$\dagger S^x_y$ stands for the result of replacing all free occurrences of x in S by y: if any free variables of y would become bound in S by this substitution, this is avoided by preliminary systematic alteration of bound variables in S.

concrete representation. This can be accomplished by giving a function $\mathscr{A}(c_1, c_2, \ldots, c_n)$ which maps the concrete variables into the abstract object which they represent. For example, in the case of *smallintset*, the representation function can be defined as

$$\mathscr{A}(m, A) = \{i: integer \mid \exists k(1 \leqslant k \leqslant m \wedge A[k] = i)\} \qquad (8.4)$$

or in words, '(m, A) represents the set of values of the first m elements of A.' Note that in this and in many other cases $\mathscr{A}$ will be a many–one function. Thus there is no unique concrete value representing any abstract one.

Let t stand for the value of $\mathscr{A}(c_1, c_2, \ldots, c_m)$ before execution of the body Q_j of procedure p_j. Then what we must prove is that after execution of Q_j the following relation holds:

$$\mathscr{A}(c_1, c_2, \ldots, c_n) = f_j(t, v_1, v_2, \ldots, v_{n_j})$$

where $v_1, v_2, \ldots, v_{n_j}$ are the formal parameters of p_j.

Using the notations of [15], the requirement for proof may be expressed:

$$t = \mathscr{A}(c_1, c_2, \ldots, c_n)\ \{Q_j\}\ \mathscr{A}(c_1, c_2, \ldots, c_n) = f_j(t, v_1, v_2, \ldots, v_{n_j})$$

where t is a variable which does not occur in Q_j. On the basis of this we may say: $t \cdot p_j(a_1, a_2, \ldots, a_n) \equiv t := f_j(t, a_1, a_2, \ldots, a_n)$ with respect to $\mathscr{A}$. This deduction depends on the fact that no Q_j alters or accesses any variables other than $c_1, c_2, \ldots, c_n$; we shall in future assume that this constraint has been observed.

In fact for practical proofs we need a slightly stronger rule, which enables the programmer to give an invariant condition $I(c_1, c_2, \ldots, c_n)$, defining some relationship between the constituent concrete variables, and thus placing a constraint on the possible combinations of values which they may take. Each operation (except initialization) may assume that I is true when it is first entered; and each operation must in return ensure that it is true on completion.

In the case of *smallintset*, the correctness of all operations depends on the fact that m remains within the bounds of A, and the correctness of the remove operation is dependent on the fact that the values of $A[1], A[2], \ldots, A[m]$ are all different; a simple expression of this invariant is:

$$size(\mathscr{A}(m, A)) = m \leqslant 100. \qquad (I)$$

One additional complexity will often be required; in general, a procedure body is not prepared to accept arbitrary combinations of values for its parameters, and its correctness therefore depends on satisfaction of some precondition $P(t, a_1, a_2, \ldots, a_n)$ before the procedure is entered. For example, the correctness of the inset procedure depends on the fact that the size of the resulting set is not greater than 100, that is

$$size(t \cup \{i\}) \leqslant 100$$

This precondition (with t replaced by $\mathscr{A}$) may be assumed in the proof of the body of the procedure; but it must accordingly be proved to hold before every call of the procedure.

It is interesting to note that any of the ps that are functions may be permitted to change the values of the cs, on condition that it preserves the truth of the invariant, and also that it preserves unchanged the value of the abstract object $\mathscr{A}$. For example, the function *has* could re-order the elements of A; this might be an advantage if it is expected that membership of some of the members of the set will be tested much more frequently than others. The existence of such a concrete side-effect is wholly invisible to the abstract program. This seems to be a convincing explanation of the phenomenon of 'benevolent side-effects', whose existence I was not prepared to admit in [15].

8.7 Proof of *smallintset*

The proof may be split into four parts, corresponding to the four parts of the class declaration:

8.7.1 Initialization

What we must prove is that after initialization the abstract set is empty and that the invariant I is true:

$$\textbf{true}\ \{m := 0\}$$
$$\{i \mid \exists k(1 \leqslant k \leqslant m \wedge A[k] = i)\} = \{\} \wedge size(\mathscr{A}(m, a)) = m \leqslant 100$$

Using the rule of assignment, this depends on the obvious truth of the lemma

$$\{i \mid \exists k(1 \leqslant k \leqslant 0 \wedge A[k] = i\} = \{\} \wedge size(\{\}) = 0 \leqslant 100$$

8.7.2 *Has*

What we must prove is

$$\mathscr{A}(m, A) = k \wedge I\ \{Q_{has}\}\ \mathscr{A}(m, A) = k \wedge I \wedge has = i \in \mathscr{A}(m, A)$$

where Q_{has} is the body of *has*. Since Q_{has} does not change the value of m or A, the truth of the first two assertions on the right-hand side follows directly from their truth beforehand. The invariant of the loop inside Q_{has} is:

$$j \leqslant m \wedge has = i \in \mathscr{A}(j, A)$$

as may be verified by a proof of the lemma:

$$\begin{aligned} &j < m \wedge j \leqslant m \wedge has = i \in \mathscr{A}(j, A) \\ &\Rightarrow \textbf{if } A[j+1] = i \textbf{ then } (\textbf{true} = i \in \mathscr{A}(m, A)) \\ &\qquad\qquad\qquad \textbf{else } has = i \in \mathscr{A}(j+1, A). \end{aligned}$$

Since the final value of j is m, the truth of the desired result follows directly from the invariant; and since the 'initial' value of j is zero, we only need the obvious lemma

$$\textbf{false} = i \in \mathscr{A}(0, A)$$

8.7.3 *Insert*

What we must prove is:

$$P \wedge \mathscr{A}(m, A) = k \wedge I \,\{Q_{insert}\}\, \mathscr{A}(m, A) = (k \cup \{i\}) \wedge I,$$

where $P =_{\text{df}} size(\mathscr{A}(m, A) \cup \{i\}) \leqslant 100$.

The invariant of the loop is:

$$P \wedge \mathscr{A}(m, A) = k \wedge I \wedge i \notin \mathscr{A}(j, A) \wedge 0 \leqslant j \leqslant m$$

as may be verified by the proof of the lemma

$$\begin{aligned} &\mathscr{A}(m, A) = k \wedge i \notin \mathscr{A}(j, A) \wedge 0 \leqslant j \leqslant m \wedge j < m \\ &\qquad \Rightarrow \textbf{if } A[j+1] = i \textbf{ then } \mathscr{A}(m, A) = (k \cup \{i\}) \\ &\qquad\qquad\qquad \textbf{else } 0 \leqslant j+1 \leqslant m \wedge i \notin \mathscr{A}(j+1, A) \end{aligned}$$

(The invariance of $P \wedge \mathscr{A}(m, A) = k \wedge I$ follows from the fact that the loop does not change the values of m or A). That (8.6) is true before the loop follows from $i \notin \mathscr{A}(0, A)$.

We must now prove that the truth of (8.6), together with $j = m$ at the end of the loop, is adequate to ensure the required final condition. This depends on proof of the lemma

$$\begin{aligned} j = m \wedge (8.6) \cup \mathscr{A}(m+1, A') = (k \cup \{i\}) \wedge size(\mathscr{A}(m+1, A')) \\ = m + 1 \leqslant 100 \end{aligned}$$

where $A' = (A, m+1 : i)$ is the new value of A after assignment of i to $A[m+1]$.

8.7.4 *Remove*

What we must prove is

$$\mathscr{A}(m, A) = k \wedge I \,\{Q_{remove}\}\, \mathscr{A}(m, A) = (k \cap \neg \{i\}) \wedge I.$$

The details of the proof are complex. Since they add nothing more to the purpose of this paper, they will be omitted.

8.8 Formalities

Let T be a class declared as shown in Section 8.2, and let $\mathscr{A}, I, P_j, f_j$ be formulae as explained in Section 8.6 (free variable lists are omitted where convenient). Suppose also that the following $m+1$ theorems have been proved:

$$\textbf{true}\ \{Q\}\ I \wedge \mathscr{A} = d_0 \tag{8.7}$$

$$\mathscr{A} = t \wedge I \wedge P_j(t)\ \{Q_j\}\ I \wedge \mathscr{A} = f_j(t) \text{ for procedure bodies } Q_j \tag{8.8}$$

$$\mathscr{A} = t \wedge I \wedge P_j(t)\ \{Q_j\}\ I \wedge \mathscr{A} = t \wedge p_j = f_j(t) \text{ for function bodies } Q_j. \tag{8.9}$$

In this section we show that the proof of these theorems is a sufficient condition for the correctness of the data representation, in the sense explained in Section 8.5.

Let X be a program beginning with a declaration of a variable t of an abstract type, and initializing it to d_0. The subsequent operations on this variable are of the form

(1) $t := f_j\ t, a_1, a_2, \ldots, a_{n_j})$ if Q_j is a procedure
(2) $f_j(t, a_1, a_2, \ldots, a_{n_j})$ if Q_j is a function.

Suppose also that $P_j(t, a_1, a_2, \ldots, a_{n_j})$ has been proved true before each such operation.

Let X' be a program formed from X by replacements described in Section 8.4, as well as the following (see Section 8.5):

(1) initialization $t := d_0$ replaced by Q'
(2) $t := f_j(t, a_1, a_2, \ldots, a_{n_j})$ replaced by $t \cdot p_j(a_1, a_2, \ldots, a_{n_j})$
(4) $f_j(t, a_1, a_2, \ldots, a_{n_j})$ by $t \cdot p_j(a_1, a_2, \ldots, a_{n_j})$.

Theorem
Under conditions described above, if X and X' both terminate, the value of t on termination of X will be $\mathscr{A}(c_1, c_2, \ldots, c_n)$, where $c_1, c_2, \ldots, c_n$ are the values of these variables on termination of X'.

Corollary
If $R(t)$ has been proved true on termination of X, $R(\mathscr{A})$ will be true on termination of X'.

Proof Consider the sequence S of operations on t executed during the computation of X, and let S' be the sequence of subcomputations of X' arising from execution of the procedure calls which have replaced the corresponding operations on t in X. We will prove that there is a close elementwise correspondence between the two sequences, and that

(a) Each item of S' is the very procedure statement which replaced the corresponding operation in S.
(b) The values of all variables (and hence also the actual parameters) which are common to both 'programs' are the same after each operation.
(c) The invariant I is true between successive items of S'.
(d) If the operations are function calls, their results in both sequences are the same.
(e) And if they are procedure calls (or the initialization) the value of t immediately after the operation in S is given by $\mathscr{A}$, as applied to the values of $c_1, c_2, \ldots, c_n$ after the corresponding operation in S'.

It is this last fact, applied to the last item of the two sequences, that establishes the truth of the theorem.

The proof is by induction on the position of an item in S.

(1) *Basis.* Consider its first item of S, $t := d_0$. Since X and X' are identical up to this point, the first item of S' must be the subcomputation of the procedure Q which replaced it, proving (a). By (8.7), I is true after Q in S', and also $\mathscr{A} = d_0$, proving (c) and (e). (d) is not relevant. Q is not allowed to change any nonlocal variable, proving (b).

(2) *Induction step.* We may assume that conditions (a)–(e) hold immediately after the $(n-1)$th item of S and S', and we establish that they are true after the nth. Since the values of all other variables (and the result, if a function) were the same after the previous operation in both sequences, the subsequent course of the computation must also be the same until the very next point at which X' differs from X. This establishes (a) and (b). Since the only permitted changes to the values of $t \cdot c_1, t \cdot c_2, \ldots, t \cdot c_n$ occur in the subcomputations of S', and I contains no other variables, the truth of I after the previous subcomputation proves that it is true before the next. Since S contains *all* operations on t, the value of t is the same before the nth as it was after the $(n-1)$th operation, and it is still equal to $\mathscr{A}$. It is given as proved that the appropriate $P_j(t)$ is true before each call of f_j in S. Thus we have established that $\mathscr{A} = t \wedge I \wedge P_j(t)$ is true before the operation in S'. From (8.8) or (8.9) the truth of (c), (d), (e) follows immediately. (b) follows from the fact that the assignment in S changes the values of no other variable besides t; and similarly, Q_j is not permitted to change the value of any variable other than $t \cdot c_1, t \cdot c_2, \ldots, t \cdot c_n$.

This proof has been an informal demonstration of a fairly obvious theorem. Its main interest has been to show the necessity for certain restrictive conditions placed on class declarations. Fortunately these restrictions are formulated as scope rules, which can be rigorously checked at compile time.

8.9 Extensions

The exposition of the previous sections deals only with the simplest cases of the Simula 67 class concept; nevertheless, it would seem adequate to cover a wide range of practical data representations. In this section we consider the possibility of further extensions, roughly in order of sophistication.

8.9.1 Class parameters

It is often useful to permit a class to have formal parameters which can be replaced by different actual parameters whenever the class is used in a declaration. These parameters may influence the method of representation, or the identity of the initial value, or both. In the case of *smallintset*, the usefulness of the definition can be enhanced if the maximum size of the set is a parameter, rather than being fixed at 100.

8.9.2 Dynamic object generation

In Simula 67, the value of a variable c of class C may be reinitialized by an assignment:

$$c := new\ C\ \langle \text{actual parameter part} \rangle;$$

This presents no extra difficulty for proofs.

8.9.3 Remote identification

In many cases, a local concrete variable of a class has a meaningful interpretation in the abstract space. For example, the variable m of *smallintset* always stands for the size of the set. If the main program needs to test the size of the set, it would be possible to make this accessible by writing a function

integer procedure *size; size* := m;

But it would be simpler and more convenient to make the variable more directly accessible by a compound identifier, perhaps by declaring it

public integer m;

The proof technique would specify that

$$m = size(\mathscr{A}(m, A))$$

is part of the invariant of the class.

8.9.4 Class concatenation

The basic mechanism for representing sets by arrays can be applied to sets with members of type or class other than just integers. It would therefore be useful to have a method of defining a class *smallset*, which can then be used to construct other classes such as *smallrealset* or *smallcarset*, where *car* is another class. In Simula 67, this effect can be achieved by the class/subclass and virtual mechanisms.

8.9.5 Recursive class declaration

In Simula 67, the parameters of a class, or of a local procedure of the class, and even the local variables of a class, may be declared as belonging to that very same class. This permits the construction of lists and trees, and their processing by recursive procedure activation. In proving the correctness of such a class, it will be necessary to assume the correctness of all 'recursive' operations in the proofs of the bodies of the procedures. In the implementation of recursive classes, it will be necessary to represent variables by a null pointer (**none**) or by the *address* of their value, rather than by direct inclusion of space for their values in block workspace of the block to which they are local. The reason for this is that the amount of space occupied by a value of recursively defined type cannot be determined at compile time.

It is worthy of note that the proof technique recommended above is valid only if the data structure is 'well grounded' in the sense that it is a pure tree, without cycles and without convergence of branches. The restrictions suggested in this paper make it impossible for local variables of a class to be updated except by the body of a procedure local to that very same activation of the class; and I believe that this will effectively prevent the construction of structures which are not well grounded, provided that assignment is implemented by copying the complete value, not just the address.

8.10 Acknowledgements

I am deeply indebted to Doug Ross and to all authors of referenced works. Indeed, the material of this paper represents little more than my belated understanding and formalization of their original work.

NINE

Proof of a structured program: The Sieve of Eratosthenes

This paper provides a beautiful example of the development of a computer program from a version which works on abstract data types. Not only is there the obvious task of representing sets but also two different representations of integers are considered in order to develop an efficient program.

It is sometimes argued that such developments are published only for algorithms which are already known. An adequate rebuttal of this claim comes in Misra and Gries (1978), which was extended to an algorithm requiring sub-linear time in Pritchard (1981), both of which were stimulated by this paper. A survey of these algorithms is contained in Pritchard (1987).

This paper was submitted in March 1972 and published as [34]. Anyone who equates the term 'structured programming' with a narrow set of rules concerning the choice of control constructs might be surprised by the Appendix to this paper.

Abstract

This paper illustrates a method of constructing a program together with its proof. By structuring the program at two levels of abstraction, the proof of the more abstract algorithm may be completely separated from the proof of the concrete representation. In this way, the overall complexity of the proof is kept within more reasonable bounds.

9.1 Introduction

In a previous paper (Hoare, [16]) it was shown how a fairly rigorous proof technique could be applied to the development of a simple

C. A. R. Hoare, Proof of a structured program: The Sieve of Eratosthenes, *BCS Computer Journal* **15**(4), 321–5 (November 1972). This paper is republished by kind permission of the British Computer Society.

program, in order to inhibit the intrusion of programming and coding errors. The method involved making a careful formulation of what each part of the program is intended to do, and the invariants which it has got to preserve, before the program is coded. In general, it will then be intuitively obvious that the code is being written to meet its specification; but if confirmation is required, it is possible to extract formally (even mechanically, see Foley and Hoare [19]) the lemmas on which the correctness of the program depends, and give them a rigorous proof. Very often, these lemmas and proofs are both trivial and tedious, and it is to be hoped that the computer may in future be programmed to help in their extraction and verification (King 1969). But even in the absence of such aid, the most important lesson of this method of program construction is the clear statement of the purpose of each part of the program, and the assumptions which it needs to make in order to achieve this purpose. The formal derivation and proof of lemmas can be omitted if we have sufficient trust in our intuition.

The problem now arises, how can these techniques be applied to large programs, where they are so much more necessary? Their application even to small programs is already quite laborious, so their direct application to large programs is out of the question. The solution to this problem lies in the recognition (Dijkstra 1972c; Dahl 1972; Wirth 1971b) that a large program can and should be expressed as a small program written in a more powerful, higher-level programming language. This short program can then be constructed correctly using the same techniques as described in Hoare [16].

However, there remains the problem of 'implementing' the higher-level language in terms which the machine can understand, and of simultaneously proving that this implementation is correct. The programmer must select some efficient method of representation of the data used by the abstract program, and should formulate the function which maps the representation onto the abstract data which it represents. Then the various primitive operations on the abstract data must be implemented by procedures coded in a language closer to one that is comprehensible to the computer. Finally, it must be proved that each procedure operating on the representation has its intended effect on the abstract data which it represents.

The proof methods used in this paper are similar to those described and formalized in Milner (1971) and Hoare [32]. However, they are explained and justified rather informally, relying on intuition to verify that the lemmas quoted are indeed the ones that need to be proved in order to establish the correctness of the programs.

9.2 The abstract algorithm

The Sieve of Eratosthenes is an efficient method of finding all primes equal or less than a given integer N. The 'sieve' contains initially 2 and all odd numbers up to N; but numbers which are multiples of other numbers are gradually 'sifted out', until all numbers remaining in the sieve are prime.

The desired result of the algorithm is

$$sieve = primes(N)$$

where *sieve* is a set of integers and $primes(k)$ is the set of all primes up to and possibly including k.

Some important properties of the algorithm are that it never removes a prime from the sieve, and that it never adds to the sieve a number outside the range 2 to N. These properties may be formally defined by stating invariants of the algorithm – that is, facts which are true of the variables of the program thoughout its execution, except possibly in certain critical regions, or action clusters (Naur 1969), in which the individual variables of a structure are updated piecemeal. These invariants are:

$$primes(N) \subseteq sieve \subseteq range(N) \qquad (I)$$

where $range(k)$ is the set of numbers between 2 and k inclusive.

The sieve is said to be 'sifted' with respect to a number q if all multiples of q have been removed from it:

$$sifted(q) =_{\text{df}} \forall\, n \in sieve(q \text{ divides } n \Rightarrow q = n)$$

The sieve is said to be 'sifted up to p' if all multiples of any prime less than p have been removed from it:

$$sifted\ up\ to(p) =_{\text{df}} \forall\, q \in primes(p-1)(sifted(q))$$

We now prove the elementary lemmas on which the algorithm is based.

Lemma 1
$sieve = \{2\} \cup \{n \in range(N) \mid n \text{ is odd}\} \Rightarrow sifted\ up\ to\ (3)$

Proof No odd number is divisible by 2, so the only number in the sieve divisible by 2 is 2 itself. Therefore *sifted* (2), which implies the conclusion.

Lemma 2
$p^2 > N \wedge sifted\ up\ to\ (p) \wedge primes(N) \subseteq sieve \subseteq range(N) \Rightarrow sieve = primes(N)$

Proof Let $s \in sieve - primes(N)$ and let q be its smallest prime factor.
$\therefore$ $q^2 \leqslant s \leqslant N < p^2$ since s is a non-prime in $range(N)$
$\therefore$ $q \leqslant p - 1$
$\therefore$ $sifted(q)$ since $sifted\ up\ to(p) \wedge q$ is prime
$\therefore$ $s \notin sieve$ since q divides s (by hypothesis) and $q \neq s$

This contradiction shows that $sieve - primes(N)$ is empty. The conclusion follows from $primes(N) \subseteq sieve$.

The algorithm can be based on these two theorems:

begin p: *integer*;
  $sieve := \{2\} \cup \{n \in range(N) \mid n\ is\ odd\}$;
  $p := 3$;
  while $p^2 \leqslant N$ **do**
    begin $sift(p)$;
      $p :=$ *next prime after* (p)
    end
end

where $sift(p)$ is assumed to have the result

$$sifted(p)$$

and to preserve the invariance of

$$I \wedge sifted\ up\ to(p).$$

The correctness of the loop in preserving the invariance of *sifted up to*(p) now depends on the lemma.

Lemma 3
$p^2 \leqslant N \wedge sifted\ up\ to(p) \wedge sifted(p) \Rightarrow sifted\ up\ to(next\ prime\ after(p))$

Proof Let

$$q \in primes\ (next\ prime\ after(p) - 1)$$

(1) if $q \leqslant p - 1$, $sifted(q)$ follows from *sifted up to*(p)
(2) if $q = p$, $sifted(q)$ follows from $sifted(p)$
(3) since q is prime it is impossible that

$$p < q \leqslant next\ prime\ after(p) - 1,$$

$sifted(q)$ follows in both possible cases, and consequently *sifted up to* (*next prime after*(p)).

Of course, this algorithm would be rather pointless unless there were some especially fast way of computing the next prime after p in the context in which it is required. Summarizing all facts known at this stage we get:

$$I \wedge p^2 \leqslant N \wedge sifted\ up\ to\ (next\ prime\ after(p)) \qquad (P)$$

Now we can rely on the theorem

Lemma 4
$P \Rightarrow$ *next prime after*$(p) =$ *next after* $(p, sieve)$
where *next after* (n, s) is the smallest element of s which is greater than n.

Proof Let

$$p' = next\ after\ (p, sieve)$$

Since

$$primes(N) \subseteq sieve, \text{ and } p' \in sieve$$

it follows that

$$p < p' \leqslant next\ prime\ after(p)$$

To establish equality, it is sufficient to prove that p' is prime. Let r be the smallest prime factor of p', so $r \leqslant p'$.
Assume $r < p'$
then *sifted*(r) follows from $r < p' \leqslant$ *next prime after*(p)
and *sifted up to* (*next prime after* (p)).
$\therefore\ r = p'$ since $p' \in sieve \wedge r$ *divides* p'
Therefore p' is equal to its smallest prime factor.

It remains to prove that *next after* $(p, sieve)$ actually exists; this follows from $p^2 \leqslant N$ and the fact that there is always a prime between p and p^2. This is a deep result in number theory, and will not be proved here.

A second obvious improvement in efficiency is to replace the test

$$p^2 \leqslant N$$

by

$$p \leqslant rootN$$

where *rootN* has been precomputed as the highest integer not greater than *sqrt*(N).

9.3 Sifting

It remains to program the procedure *sift*(p). This procedure may assume the precondition that $p > 2$ is odd, and must produce the result that *sifted*(p). It must also preserve the invariants:

$$primes(N) \subseteq sieve$$
$$sieve \subseteq range(N)$$
$$sifted\ up\ to(p)$$

The only change made to global variables by the operation of sifting is the repeated removal of an integer s from the sieve:

$$sieve := sieve - \{s\};$$

where s is not prime. Removal of non-prime elements from the sieve can never alter any of these invariants from true to false, as may be verified by the trivial lemmas:

Lemma 5
$s \notin primes(N) \wedge primes(N) \subseteq sieve \Rightarrow primes(N) \subseteq sieve - \{s\}$

Lemma 6
$sieve \subseteq range(N) \Rightarrow sieve - \{s\} \subseteq range(N)$

Lemma 7
$$\forall q \in primes(p-1)\ \forall n \in sieve(q \text{ divides } n \Rightarrow q = n)$$
$$\Rightarrow \forall q \in primes(p-1)\ \forall n \in (sieve - \{s\})(q \text{ divides } n \Rightarrow q = n)$$

Proof After replacing $n \in (sieve - \{s\})$ by an equivalent form $n \in sieve \wedge n \notin \{s\}$, this is a tautology.

Now all that is necessary is to generate a sequence of multiples of p, and remove them from the sieve. However, it is known that $p > 2$, so that *sifted up to* (p) implies that *sifted*(2). Consequently, it is not necessary to remove *even* multiples of p, since they are already gone. Also all nonprimes less than p^2 will be gone as a result of *sifted up to* (p). We design the sifting process to preserve the invariance of

$$sifted\ up\ to(p) \wedge s \textbf{ mod } 2p = p \wedge s \geqslant 2 \wedge p \text{ is odd} \wedge p > 2 \wedge$$
$$\forall s' \in sieve \cap range(s-1)(p \text{ divides } s' \Rightarrow p = s')$$

Note that $s \textbf{ mod } 2p = p$ implies that s is non-prime, which we required to justify removal of s from sieve.

The program is:

```
sift: begin s, step: integer;
         step := p + p;
         s := p × p;
         while s ⩽ N do
            begin sieve := sieve − {s};
               s := s + step
            end
      end sift.
```

The correctness of the program depends on the following lemmas:

Lemma 8

p is odd $\Rightarrow (p \times p)$ **mod** $2p = p$

Lemma 9

$\mathit{sifted\ up\ to}\ (p) \wedge p > 2 \Rightarrow \ \forall s' \in \mathit{sieve} \cap \mathit{range}(p \times p - 1)$
$(p\ \mathit{divides}\ s' \Rightarrow p = s')$

Proof Let $s' \in \mathit{sieve} \cap \mathit{range}(p^2 - 1)$ and assume $p\ \mathit{divides}\ s'$. We shall prove that s' is prime, for then it follows immediately from $p\ \mathit{divides}\ s'$ that $s' = p$.

Let r be the smallest prime factor of s'.
There are two cases:

(1) if $r = s'$ then s' is prime anyway
(2) if $r^2 \leqslant s'$ then

$r^2 \leqslant s' < p^2$	since $s' \in \mathit{range}(p^2 - 1)$
$r \leqslant p - 1$	
$\mathit{sifted}(r)$	since $\mathit{sifted\ up\ to}(p)$
$\therefore\ r = s'$	since $r\ \mathit{divides}\ s' \in \mathit{sieve}$

hence s' is prime.

Lemma 10

s **mod** $2p = p \Rightarrow (s + 2p)$ **mod** $2p = p$

Lemma 11

$s \geqslant 2 \wedge p > 2 \Rightarrow s + 2p \geqslant 2$

Lemma 12

$\mathit{sifted}(2) \wedge s$ **mod** $2p = p \wedge s \geqslant 2 \wedge$
$\quad \forall s' \in \mathit{sieve} \cap \mathit{range}(s - 1)(p\ \mathit{divides}\ s' \Rightarrow p = s')$
$\quad \Rightarrow \ \forall s' \in (\mathit{sieve} - \{s\}) \cap \mathit{range}(s + 2p - 1)(p\ \mathit{divides}\ s' \Rightarrow p = s')$

Proof Consider s' satisfying the conditions
$s' \in (\mathit{sieve} - \{s\}) \wedge s' \leqslant s + 2p - 1 \wedge p\ \mathit{divides}\ s'$
There are three cases:

(1) if $s' < s$, then $p = s'$ follows from the antecedent
(2) $s' = s$ is impossible, since $s' \in \mathit{sieve} - \{s\}$
(3) if $s' > s$ then $s' = s + p$ since $s' \leqslant s + 2p - 1$ and p divides both s and s'

$\therefore\ s'$ **mod** $2p = 0$	since s **mod** $2p = p$
$\therefore\ 2\ \mathit{divides}\ s'$	
$\therefore\ s' = 2$	follows from $\mathit{sifted}(2)$

but this contradicts $s' > s \geqslant 2$. Thus case (3) is also impossible.

Lemma 13
$s > N \wedge sieve \subseteq range(N) \wedge$
$\forall s' \in sieve \cap range(s-1)(p \text{ divides } s' \Rightarrow p = s') \Rightarrow sifted(p)$

Proof $sieve \subseteq range(N) \subseteq range(s-1)$
$\therefore \quad sieve \cap range(s-1) = sieve.$

9.4 Concrete representation

The program developed and proved in the previous section is abstract, in the sense that it assumes the possibility of operating on integers and sets of integers of arbitrary size (up to N). Now, if N is smaller than $2\uparrow wordlength - 1$ (where *wordlength* is the number of bits in the word of the computer), the possibility of operating on integers of this size will have been provided by the hardware of the computer. Furthermore, if $N \leqslant 2 \times wordlength$, the sieve itself may be represented as a single word of the computer store which has the nth bit set to one if $(2n + 1)$ is in the sieve. The operations on the set are probably built into the instruction code of the computer in the form of logical and shifting instructions.

However, the case which interests us is when N is rather large compared with the computer wordlength, but still rather smaller than the total number of bits in the main store of the computer. A figure of the order of 10 000 may be typical. It is, therefore, necessary to represent the sieve by means of an array of words, and it is now the responsibility of the programmer to find an efficient way of implementing the required set operations on this array. A word may be regarded as representing a subset of the positive integers less than the wordlength.

Unfortunately, the access and manipulation of an arbitrary bit held in an array of words is rather an inefficient operation, involving a division to find the right wordnumber, with the remainder indicating the bitnumber within the word. On machines with wordlength equal to a power of two this will be less inefficient than on other machines. But the solution which we adopt here is to represent the integers p, s, and *step* as *mixed radix* numbers. Each of them contains two components, a wordnumber and a bitnumber within the word. Furthermore, only *odd* numbers need be represented in the case of p and s, whereas only *even* numbers need be represented for the step.

Since we have to test p and s against N and *rootN*, it is as well to represent these in the same way as odd numbers. If they are even, this means subtracting one from them. The validity of this is due to the fact that

$$a \text{ is odd} \wedge b \text{ is even} \Rightarrow (a \leqslant b \equiv a \leqslant b - 1).$$

We therefore need to implement the arithmetic operations required on this curious representation of odd integers, as well as the required set operations on the sieve; and for this purpose we will use the concepts and notations described in Chapter 8, and declare the representations as Simula classes. A class is a declaration of a data structure (its local variables), together with declarations of all the procedures which operate on data of that structure. The body of each procedure is a critical region inside which invariants may be temporarily falsified. We can outline the requirements by showing the class declarations, but replacing all the procedure bodies by a comment stating what they are intended to do:

```
class eveninteger(a: oddinteger);
  begin wd, bit;
    initialize: comment initialize to 2 × a;
  end;
class oddinteger(n: integer);
  begin wd, bit: integer;
    procedure add(b: eveninteger);
    comment ': + b';
    boolean procedure eqless(c: oddinteger);
    comment ' ⩽ c';
    procedure nextafter(sve: sieveclass);
    comment ': = nextafter(itself, sve)';
    procedure square(c: oddinteger);
    comment ': = c × c';
    comment initialize to ((n − 1) ÷ 2) × 2 + 1;
  end oddinteger;
class sieveclass(N: integer);
  begin constant W = (N ÷ 2) ÷ wordlength
    bitmap: array 0 .. W of word;
    procedure remove(s: oddinteger);
    comment ': − {s}';
    comment initialize to {2}∪{n: 3 .. N | n is odd};
  end sieveclass.
```

In these declarations the type (or class) of a variable or a formal parameter is written after the declaratory occurrence of its name, and separated from it by a colon.

We can now recode the algorithm using class on these procedures instead of the statements which they are intended to simulate.

```
sieve : sieveclass(N);
begin constant rootN : oddinteger(sqrt(N));
  comment rootN := (sqrt(N) − 1) ÷ 2 × 2 + 1;
  constant oddN : oddinteger(N);
  comment oddN := (N − 1) ÷ 2 × 2 + 1;
  p : oddinteger(3); s : oddinteger(3);
  comment p := s := 3;
  while p . eqless(rootN) do
    comment p ⩽ rootN;
    begin step : eveninteger(p);
      comment step := 2 × p;
      s . square(p);
      comment s := p × p;
    while s . eqless(oddN) do
      comment s ⩽ oddN;
      begin sieve . remove(s);
        comment sieve := sieve − {s};
        s . add(step)
        comment s := s + step;
      end sloop;
    p . next after (sieve)
    comment p := nextafter(p, sieve);
    end ploop
end sieve;
```

The variable changed by each procedure call is written to the left of it, separated by a dot. The comment gives the intended effect.

First it is necessary to define the abstract objects in terms of their concrete representations. We introduce abbreviations:

$$number(w, b) =_{\mathrm{df}} 2 \times w \times wordlength + 2 \times b + 1$$
$$w(n) =_{\mathrm{df}} ((n-1) \div 2) \div wordlength$$
$$b(n) =_{\mathrm{df}} ((n-1) \div 2) \ \mathbf{mod}\ wordlength$$

We now have

$$w(number(w, b)) = w \qquad \text{provided } 0 \leqslant b < wordlength$$
$$b(number(w, b)) = b \qquad \text{provided } 0 \leqslant b < wordlength$$
$$number(w(n), b(n)) = ((n-1) \div 2) \times 2 + 1$$
$$= \begin{cases} n & \text{if } n \text{ is odd} \\ n-1 & \text{if } n \text{ is even} \end{cases}$$

Now we can define the abstract objects implemented by each class, in terms of the local variable of that class.

$$oddinteger = number\ (wd, bit)$$

$$eveninteger = number\ (wd, bit) + 1$$

$$sieveclass = \{2\} \cup \{n \in range(N) \mid n \text{ is odd} \wedge b(n) \in bitmap[w(n)]\}.$$

We also need the following invariant for both the *oddinteger* and the *eveninteger* classes.

$$0 \leqslant bit < wordlength \qquad (bitrange)$$

We now proceed to code the bodies of the procedures, and formulate the lemmas on which their correctness depends. The proofs (like the procedure bodies) are rather trivial, though also tedious. They do not depend on any results of number theory, and they are of a sort that might in the future be readily checked by a computer. They will therefore be omitted in the remainder of the paper. The important point to note is that all the proofs are independent of each other.

As a preliminary we code an operation to perform any necessary carry between the bit and the wordnumber:

```
carry: if bit ≥ wordlength then
  begin bit := bit − wordlength;
        wd := wd + 1
  end
```

The label indicates that this piece of code is known as *carry*. We prove that *carry* leaves unchanged the value of *number*(*wd*, *bit*).

This depends on the truth of

Lemma 1A

$$number(wd, bit) = 2 \times (\textbf{if } bit \geqslant wordlength \textbf{ then } wd + 1 \textbf{ else } wd) \times wordlength + 2 \times (\textbf{if } bit \geqslant wordlength \textbf{ then } bit - wordlength \textbf{ else } bit) + 1$$

Next we prove $0 \leqslant bit < 2 \times wordlength\ \{carry\}\ 0 \leqslant bit < wordlength$, that is, if the assertion before the left brace is true before performing *carry*, the assertion after the right brace is true afterwards.

This depends on the truth of

Lemma 1B

$$0 \leqslant bit < 2 \times wordlength \Rightarrow 0 \leqslant (\textbf{if } bit \geqslant wordlength \textbf{ then } bit - wordlength \textbf{ else } bit) < wordlength$$

This means that we can ensure the truth of *bitrange* by invoking *carry* after each change to the value of *bit*, provided this change does not take the *bit* outside the range

$$0 \leqslant bit < 2 \times wordlength.$$

(1) initialize *eveninteger* (*a*: *oddinteger*):

```
begin wd := a.wd + a.wd;
   bit := a.bit + a.bit;
   carry
end
```

Lemma 2

$0 \leqslant a.bit < wordlength \Rightarrow 0 \leqslant a.bit + a.bit < 2 \times wordlength$

Lemma 3

$number(a.wd + a.wd,\ a.bit + a.bit) + 1 = 2 \times number(a.wd,\ a.bit)$

(2) initialize *oddinteger*(*n*: *integer*):

```
begin wd := ((n - 1) ÷ 2) ÷ wordlength;
   bit := ((n - 1) ÷ 2) mod wordlength
end
```

Lemma 4

$0 \leqslant ((n-1) \div 2) \textbf{ mod } wordlength < wordlength$

Lemma 5

$number(w(n), b(n)) = ((n-1) \div 2) \times 2 + 1$

(3) **procedure** *add*(*b*: *eveninteger*);

```
   begin wd : = wd + b.wd;
      bit := bit + b.bit + 1;
      carry
   end
```

Lemma 6

$0 \leqslant bit,\ b.bit < wordlength$
$\quad \Rightarrow 0 \leqslant bit + b.bit + 1 < 2 \times wordlength$

Lemma 7

$number(wd + b.wd,\ bit + b.bit + 1)$
$\quad = number(wd, bit) + (number(b.wd,\ b.bit) + 1)$

Note: The proof method reminds us to add one to *bit* here.

(4) **Boolean procedure** *eqless*(*c*: *oddinteger*);

```
   eqless := if wd = c.wd then (bit ≤ c.bit)
                else (wd < c.wd).
```

Lemma 8

$0 \leqslant bit,\ c.bit \leqslant wordlength$
$\Rightarrow$ (**if** $wd = c.wd$ **then** $(bit \leqslant c.bit)$ **else** $(wd < c.wd)$
$\equiv number(wd, bit) \leqslant number(c.wd,\ c.\mathrm{bit}))$

(5) **procedure** *remove*(*s*: *oddinteger*);

$bitmap[s.wd] := bitmap[s.wd] - \{s.bit\}$

Let *bitmap'* be the result of executing this statement; i.e.

$bitmap' = \lambda w : 0\,..\,W(\textbf{if } w = s.wd \textbf{ then } bitmap[w] - \{s.bit\} \textbf{ else } bitmap[w])$

Lemma 9

$0 \leqslant s.bit < wordlength$
$\Rightarrow \{2\} \cup \{n \in range(N) \mid b(n) \in bitmap'[w(n)]\}$
$= \{2\} \cup (\{n \in range(N) \mid b(n) \in bitmap[w(n)]\}$
$- \{number(s.wd, s.bit)\})$

(6) **procedure** *square*(*c*: *oddinteger*);

```
begin t: integer;
   t := 2 × c.bit × (c.bit + 1);
   bit := t mod wordlength;
   wd := 2 × c.wd × (c.wd × wordlength
      + 2 × c.bit + 1)
      + t ÷ wordlength
end
```

Lemma 10

$number(c.wd, c.bit)^2$
$= number(2 \times c.wd \times (c.wd \times wordlength + 2 \times c.bit + 1) + t \div wordlength,\ t \textbf{ mod } wordlength)$

where

$$t = 2 \times c.bit \times (c.bit + 1)$$

Lemma 11

$0 \leqslant t \textbf{ mod } wordlength < wordlength$

Note: Here we need all the confidence that we can get in the correctness of the algebra.

(7) initialize *sieveclass*:

for $w : 0\,..\,W$ **do** $bitmap[w] := \{n \mid 0 \leqslant n < wordlength\}$

(i.e. for all *w* in the range 0 to *W* **do** ...).

The result of this **for** statement is to set *bitmap* to the constant function (each word of it is 'all ones'):

$$bitmap_0 = \lambda w : 0\,..\,W(\{n \mid 0 \leqslant n < wordlength\})$$

Lemma 12
$\{2\} \cup \{n : 3 .. N \mid n \text{ is odd}\} =$
$\{2\} \cup \{n : 3 .. N \mid n \text{ is odd} \wedge b(n) \in \mathit{bitmap}_0[w(n)]\}$

(8) **procedure** *next after* (*sve*: *sieveclass*);
    with *sve* **do**
      begin *this*: *word*;
        this := *bitmap*[*wd*] ∩ {*n* | *bit* < *n* < *wordlength*};
        while *this* = *empty* **do**
          begin *wd* := *wd* + 1;
            this := *bitmap*[*wd*]
          end;
        bit := *min*(*this*); **comment** *smallest member of this*;
      end

The criterion of correctness is

$$(\mathit{number}(\mathit{wd}, \mathit{bit}) = n)\{\mathit{next\ after}\}R$$

where $R =_{\text{df}} n < \mathit{number}(\mathit{wd}, \mathit{bit}) \in \mathit{sieve}$
$$\wedge\ \forall s(n < s < \mathit{number}(\mathit{wd}, \mathit{bit}) \Rightarrow s \notin \mathit{sieve})$$

The proof of this is left to the reader.

9.5 Conclusion

The concrete representation has now been proved to be a valid implementation of the operations required by the abstract program. The final concrete program may be obtained from the text of the program given in Sections 9.2 and 9.3, together with the text of the class declarations, using the simple substitution method implemented in Simula 67 and described in Dahl (1972) and Chapter 8.

In presenting the lemmas on which the correctness of each procedure is based, we have relied on intuition to relate the procedures to the lemmas. In fact, it is possible to formalize the relationship between program and lemma in such a way that the required lemma could be mechanically generated from the definitions of the invariants of the class, the definition of the representation function, and the definition of the operation which each procedure is intended to carry out.

It is interesting to compare the structured program developed here with the corresponding unstructured program displayed in the Appendix. It can be readily seen that a direct proof of the correctness of the unstructured version would be much more laborious.

The structuring of programs is of great assistance, not only in their proof, but also in their design, coding and documentation. I would expect that programming languages of the future may be designed to encourage and assist the structuring of programs, and perhaps even to enforce the observance of those disciplines necessary to avoid breakdown of structure.

For another example of stepwise development and proof of a program, see Jones (1971).

9.6 Appendix: The unstructured program

```
bitmap: array 0 .. W .. of word;

for w:0 .. W do bitmap[w] := {n | 0 ≤ n < wordlength};
begin rootNwd, rootNbit, Nwd, Nbit, t, pwd, pbit: integer;
  t := (sqrt(N) − 1) ÷ 2;
  rootNwd := t ÷ wordlength;
  rootNbit := t mod wordlength;
  t := (N − 1) ÷ 2;
  Nwd := t ÷ wordlength;
  Nbit := t mod wordlength;
  pwd := 1 ÷ wordlength;
  pbit := 1 mod wordlength;
  while if pwd = rootNwd then pbit ≤ rootNbit
    else pwd < rootNwd do
    begin stepwd, stepbit, swd, sbit: integer;
      stepwd := pwd + pwd;
      stepbit := pbit + pbit;
      if stepbit ≥ wordlength then
        begin stepbit := stepbit − wordlength;
              stepwd := stepwd + 1
        end;
    t := 2 × pbit × (pbit + 1);
    sbit := t mod wordlength;
    swd := 2 × pwd × (pwd × wordlength + 2 × pbit + 1)
                                          + t ÷ wordlength;
    while if swd = Nwd then sbit ≤ Nbit
      else swd < Nwd do
      begin bitmap[swd] = bitmap[swd] − {sbit};
        swd := swd + stepwd;
        sbit := sbit + stepbit;
        if sbit ≥ wordlength then
          begin sbit := sbit − wordlength;
                swd := swd + 1
          end;
```

```
      end sloop;
      begin this: word;
         this := bitmap[pwd] ∩ {n | pbit < n < wordlength};
         while this = { } do
            begin pwd := pwd + 1
               this := bitmap[pwd]
            end;
         pbit := min(this)
      end nextafter
   end ploop
end sieve
```

TEN

A structured paging system

This paper contains a beautiful exposition of the design of a significant component of the design of an operating system. Hoare's work on such problems, which dated from his employment in the Elliott company, provided him with a fund of material against which he could evaluate and develop ideas for specifying and designing parallel algorithms.

The necessary mutual exclusion is achieved here by a version of 'monitors'. A fuller discussion of the place these have in the development of Hoare's ideas on parallelism is given in the link material to Chapter 12. The paper here was submitted in October 1972 and published as [36] in 1973. Hoare adds 'This paper went through six or seven completely rewritten versions, some of which were actually worse than their predecessors. The penultimate one was fortunately rejected outright by the referees.'

Abstract

The principles and practices of structured programming have been expounded and illustrated by relatively small examples (Dahl 1972; Dijkstra 1972c; Chapter 8 of this book). Systematic methods for the construction of parallel algorithms have also been suggested (Dijkstra 1968a, b). This paper attempts to extend structured programming methods to a program intended to operate in a parallel environment, namely a paging system for the implementation of virtual store. The design decisions are motivated by considerations of cost and effectiveness.

The purpose of a paging system is taken to be the sharing of main and backing store of a computer among a number of users making unpredictable demands upon them; and doing so in such a way that each user will not be concerned whether his information is stored at any given time on main or backing store. For the sake of definiteness, the backing store is taken here to be a sectored drum; but the system could readily be adapted for other devices. Our design does not rely on any particular paging hardware, and it should be implementable in any reasonable combination of hardware and software. Furthermore, it does not presuppose any particular structure of virtual store (linear, two-dimensional, 'cactus', etc.) provided to the user program.

C. A. R. Hoare, A structured paging system, *BCS Computer Journal* **16**(3), 209–15 (August 1973). This paper is republished by kind permission of the British Computer Society.

10.1 Introduction

The notations used in the paper are based on those of Pascal (Wirth 1971c) and Simula 67 (Dahl 1972). However, the reader is warned not to expect that any automatic compiler will be written to translate these notations into machine code – that must almost certainly be done by hand.

10.2 The hardware

A paging system is essentially concerned with the physical storage devices of a particular computer installation, and if it is to be designed for many installations, some degree of abstraction must be used in referring to the hardware. For example, symbolic constants must be used to refer to installation parameters such as

M the number of pages that will fit in main store
D the number of pages that will fit on the drum
L the number of words on a page.

We can now define certain ranges for variables, using the Pascal range definitions, for example:

type *mainpageframe* $= 0..M-1;$
type *drumpageframe* $= 0..D-1;$
type *line* $= 0..L-1;$

A page may now be regarded as an array of words, where a word has to be defined in a machine-dependent fashion;

type *word* =
type *page* = **array** *line* **of** *word;*

Furthermore, the physical main and backing store may be regarded abstractly as arrays of pages:

mainstore: **array** *mainpageframe* **of** *page*;
drumstore: **array** *drumpageframe* **of** *page*;

Individual pages of these stores will be denoted by single subscript:

$$mainstore[m], drumstore[d]$$

and individual words of *mainstore* by double subscript

$$mainstore[m, i].$$

Of course, the individual word *drumstore*[*d*, *i*] can never actually be referred to in our program, since a drum provides access only to complete pages.

10.3 Dynamic storage allocation

It is evident that a paging system is concerned with the dynamic allocation and deallocation of page frames to processes. We shall therefore require a dynamic storage allocation system for page frames. In this section we describe an allocator for main page frames; an allocator for drum page frames is sufficiently similar that it need not be separately described. The most important data item in any resource allocator is the pool of currently free items of resource. This can be declared:

pool: **powerset** *mainpageframe;*

In a sequential program we then use operations

$$m := \textit{anyone of}\ (\textit{pool});\ \textit{pool} := \textit{pool} - [m];$$

to acquire a free page frame m; and an operation:

$$\textit{pool} := \textit{pool} \cup \{m\};$$

to return m to the free pool.

However, in a parallel programming environment there are two additional problems, namely exclusion and synchronization.

10.3.1 Mutual exclusion

Suppose that one program calls the function *anyone of* (*pool*) just after another one has completed the same function. It will then obtain the same value. This will frustrate the whole purpose of the allocator, which is to prevent duplicate use of the same pageframe by two different user programs. A group of operations which must not be executed re-entrantly by several programs is known as a critical region.

The solution we adopt is to introduce a program structure known as a *monitor*. A monitor consists of one or more items of data, together with one or more procedures operating on that data. Thus a monitor is like an object in Simula 67 (Dahl 1972), with the additional understanding that the bodies of the procedures local to the object will not be executed in parallel or interleaved with each other.

In implementation, the necessary exclusion can be assured by associating a Boolean mutual exclusion semaphore (Dijkstra 1968b) with each monitor and by surrounding each call on a procedure of the monitor by a P and V on this semaphore. Alternatively, in suitable cases, the required effect can be achieved by inhibiting interrupts during execution of the procedure bodies. Since details of implementation are hardware-dependent, we shall introduce a high-level notation for declaration of monitors:

monitor *mfree*;
  begin *pool*: **powerset** *mainpageframe*;
  function *acquire*: *mainpageframe*;
    begin.. *body of acquire*.. **end**;
  procedure *release*(*m* : *mainpageframe*);
    begin.. *body of release*.. **end**;
    pool:= *all mainpageframes*;
  end *mfree*;

Calls on the two procedures will be written using the Pascal and Simula 67 notation for components of a structure:

m:= *mfree.acquire*;
mfree.release(*m*).

The monitor concept described here corresponds to the secretary mentioned at the end of (Dijkstra 1973).

10.3.2 Synchronization

Any resource allocator has to face the problem of exhaustion of its resource. In a single-programming environment, any further request for that resource will be refused, and often lead to immediate termination of the program; but if there are many processes, it is more reasonable merely to postpone the request until some other process kindly releases an item of the resource. Of course, if this never happens, we have deadlock; but this will be averted by a pre-emptive technique to be described later. What is required is some method whereby one process, on detecting that it cannot proceed, can wait until some other process brings about the condition that will enable it to proceed.

Methods of obtaining such synchronization are rather machine-dependent, so again we shall introduce a high-level notation which can probably be implemented on many machines with reasonable efficiency. For each condition on which a program may have to wait, we introduce a variable of type *condition*, for example:

nonempty: *condition*.

There are only two operations defined on a condition variable, namely waiting and signalling. When a process needs to wait until some condition becomes true, it 'waits on' the corresponding condition variable, for example:

nonempty.wait.

When some other process has made the condition true, it should issue a signal instruction on that variable:

nonempty.signal.

If there are no processes waiting on the condition, the instruction has no effect; otherwise it terminates the wait of the longest waiting process, and *only* that process. The convention that at most one process shall proceed after a signal differs from the familiar 'event' type signalling (Brinch Hansen 1972b); but it appears, at least in the cases considered here, to be both more convenient and more efficient.

It is important to clarify the relationship between synchronization and mutual exclusion. When a wait instruction is given from within a monitor, the mutual exclusion for that monitor is assumed to be released, since otherwise it would be impossible for any other process to enter a procedure of that monitor to make the condition true. Furthermore, when a wait ends as a result of a signal, the waiting program resumes *immediately* in place of the signalling program, and the signalling program resumes only when the previously waiting program releases exclusion again. Thus exclusion is *not* released between the signal and the resumption of the waiting process; since if it were there would be a risk that some other process might enter the monitor during the interval and make the condition false again.

Using the monitor concept for mutual exclusion and the condition variable for synchronization, the programming of a simple allocator for main page frames can be given:

```
monitor mfree;
  begin pool: powerset mainpageframe;
  nonempty: condition;
  function acquire: mainpageframe;
    begin m: mainpageframe;
      if pool = empty then nonempty.wait;
      m:= anyone of (pool);
      pool:= pool − [m];
      acquire:= m
    end acquire;
  procedure release (m: mainpageframe);
    begin pool:= pool ∪ {m};
      nonempty.signal
    end;
  pool:= all mainpageframes; note initial value of pool;
end mfree.
```

10.4 Drum transfers

It is evident that a paging system will also be concerned with input and output of pages between main and backing store. This will usually be effected by special hardware (a channel) which operates in parallel with all user programs, except possibly for the one which is waiting for completion of transfer. We shall therefore require a scheduler to prevent interference between transfer instructions given by separate programs, and to secure the necessary synchronization between the programs and the asynchronous channel. As before we shall use monitors and conditions; and to begin with we shall assume that the drum is capable of only one transfer per revolution.

The monitor for drum transfers will obviously have to store details of an outstanding transfer command; that is, its direction, and the relevant main and drum page frames. If there is no outstanding command, we use the convention that the direction is 'null':

direction : (*in, out, null*);
m : *mainpageframe*;
d : *drumpageframe*.

The operations provided by the monitor to the user are

input(*dest* : *mainpageframe*; *source* : *drumpageframe*);

and

output(*source* : *mainpageframe*; *dest* : *drumpageframe*).

These operations merely record the outstanding command; its execution is accomplished by an operation

execute,

which will be written here as part of the monitor, but will in practice be implemented by the hardware of the drum channel, and perhaps by its intimate interrupt routines.

There are two possible reasons for waiting by a user program; firstly, when there is already an outstanding command and therefore a new one cannot be recorded, and secondly when its command has been recorded but has not yet been finished. Thus we introduce two condition variables

free, finished : *condition*

The drum itself never waits; if there is nothing for it to do, it idles for one revolution.

The programming of the monitor is now simple.

```
monitor drummer;
  begin direction: (in, out, null);
    m: mainpageframe;
    d: drumpageframe;
    free, finished: condition;
  procedure input(dest: mainpageframe;
                    source: drumpageframe);
    begin if direction ≠ null then free.wait;
      direction:= in;
      m:= dest;
      d:= source;
      finished.wait; free.signal
    end input;
  procedure output ... very similar ...;
  procedure execute;
    begin
    case direction of
      in: mainstore[m]:= drumstore[d],
      out: drumstore[d]:= mainstore[m],
      null: do nothing for one revolution;
      direction:= null; finished.signal
    end execute;
    direction:= null
  end drummer.
```

The activity of the hardware of the drum channel may be described as a process:

```
  process drum hardware;
    while true do drummer.execute;
```

Suppose now that several drums are available, and capable of simultaneous transfers. It is important to have a separate monitor for each drum channel, so that simultaneity of transfers is not inhibited by the exclusion of the monitor. Since the monitors are identical it would be unfortunate to have to write out the whole text several times; instead we borrow the idea of a Simula 67 **class** (Dahl 1972) and declare each separate monitor as a different object of the class, each with its own workspace

```
  class drummer;
    monitor begin ... as before ...
           end;
```

We then declare several 'instances' of this class:

drum1, drum2 : drummer.

Operations on these drums are written

drum1.input(m, d); drum2.output(m, d), etc.

Thus a class declaration is very similar to a Pascal record type declaration with the addition of procedures as well as data components.

On most modern drums the number S of pages (sectors) that can in principle be transferred in a single revolution is considerably greater than one. Dijkstra has pointed out that such a sectored drum may be treated in the same way as S separate drums, each capable of one transfer per revolution. We therefore introduce a whole array of monitors, one for each sector:

sector drum: **array** $0..S-1$ **of** *drummer.*

The action of the drum channel hardware may be described as an autonomous process:

process *sector drum hardware*;
  while *true* **do**
    for $s = 0$ **to** $S-1$ **do** *sectordrum*[*s*]*.execute.*

Let *sectorof* be a function giving the sector of a drum page frame. Since the user is not interested in the sector structure of the drum, we provide the simple procedures:

procedure *input*(*dest* : *mainpageframe*; *source* : *drumpageframe*);
  sectordrum[*sectorof*(*source*)]*.input*(*dest, source*);
procedure *output ... very similar ...*

For convenience, we use the same identifiers *input* and *output* for procedures local to the monitors, and for global procedures, which are not inside a monitor, and which can therefore be shared in re-entrant fashion by all user programs.

Using these procedures, the programmer may maintain the illusion that all drum transfer instructions relating to different page frames are carried out in parallel with each other, since any necessary exclusion and synchronization is carried out behind the scenes. Successive instructions relating to the same drumpageframe are carried out in the right sequence.

10.5 Virtual store

A virtual store, like the actual stores, can be regarded as an array which maps virtual page frames onto virtual pages.

virtualstore : **array** *virtualpageframe* **of** *virtual page*;

where *virtual page* is a class to be defined in the next section. The concept of virtual page frame may be simply defined as a range

type *virtualpageframe* = 0 . . *V* − 1;

where *V* is a constant several times larger than *D*. This will give a single-dimensional structure of virtual store. In some operating systems, a two-dimensional structure is preferred, in which case the virtual page frame can be described as a record:

type *virtualpageframe* = *record s* : *segmento*; *p* : *pageno* **end**.

In this case the virtual store array may well be implemented as a tree structure, so that no space is wasted on storing unused pages at the end of segments. But the paging system designed in this paper will be equally valid for both these cases, and perhaps many others.

As far as the user program is concerned, the most important operations are:

(1) A function *fetch*(*i* : *virtual address*): *word,* which delivers the content of the *i*th 'location' of virtual store.
(2) A procedure *assign* (*i*: *virtual address*; *w*: *word*) which stores the value *w* in the *i*th 'location' of virtual store.

A virtual address is defined as a pair:

```
type virtual address = record p : virtualpageframe;
                              l : line
                       end.
```

These two procedures can be implemented using the same structure as input and output on a sectored drum, by calling on procedures of the same name local to the relevant virtual page.

```
function fetch (i: virtual address): word;
  fetch:= virtualstore[i.p].fetch(i.l);
procedure assign(i : virtual address; w : word);
  virtualstore[i.p].assign(i.l, w).
```

Note that these procedures are *not* protected by mutual exclusion, so that when one program is held up waiting for a page transfer, the other programs can continue to operate on other pages.

10.6 Virtual pages

In this section we implement the *virtual page* class which was introduced in the previous section. This class must obviously provide the user program with the procedures *fetch* and *assign*; in addition it contains:

(1) **procedure** *bring in*;

This has no effect on the apparent content of the page, but merely ensures that it is located in main store, where its individual words can be accessed.

(2) **procedure** *throw out*;

This also has no effect on the apparent content of the page; but it ensures that the page no longer occupies a main page frame.

The data local to each virtual page must include an indication of whether the content of the page is currently held in main or drum store; and we also admit a third possibility, that the content of the page is equal to an 'all clear' value, in which case no actual storage is allocated to it. This is the value to which each page is initialized. The required indication is given in a variable local to each virtual page:

where: (*in, out, clear*).

The physical location of the content of each page will be recorded in one of the two local variables:

$$m : mainpageframe;$$
$$d : drumpageframe;$$

In programming a paging system, it is essential to ensure that no two virtual pages ever point to the same actual page frame, and in particular, that they never point to a free page frame; in other words, every operation of the virtual page must preserve the truth of:

(1) $where = in \Rightarrow m \notin mfree.pool$
(2) $where = out \Rightarrow d \notin dfree.pool,$

and further, the only operations on m and d are acquiring and releasing them to their respective pools. We may also define the content of the virtual page by the formula

$$\begin{aligned} content = \textbf{case}\ &\text{where}\ \textbf{of} \\ &in : mainstore[m], \\ &out : drumstore[d], \\ &clear : all\ clear. \end{aligned}$$

The implementation of a simple virtual page is shown below.

```
class virtual page;
  monitor begin where: (in, out, clear);
    m : mainpageframe;
    d : drumpageframe;
    note content = case where of in : mainstore[m],
                                 out : drumstore[d],
                                 clear : allclear;
    note where = in ⇒ m ∉ mfree.pool ∧
         where = out ⇒ d ∉ dfree.pool;
    procedure bring in; note ensures where = in;
      if where ≠ in then
        begin m:= mfree.acquire;
          if where = clear then mainstore[m] := allclear
            else {input(m, d); dfree.release(d)};
          where:= in;
        end;
    procedure throwout; note ensures where ≠ in;
      if where = in then
        begin d:= dfree.acquire;
          output(m, d);
          mfree.release(m);
          where:= out
        end throwout;
    function fetch(l : line): word; note = content[l];
      begin bring in;
        fetch:= mainstore[m, l]
      end;
    procedure assign (l : line; w : word); note content[l] := w;
      begin bring in;
        mainstore[m, l] := w
      end;
    where:= clear; note initial value of each virtual page is allclear;
  end virtual page.
```

10.7 Automatic discard

The most characteristic feature of a paging system is that pages can throw themselves out automatically to drum, and release the main page frame they occupy, independently of the programs which may or may not be using them. Of course the rate at which pages throw themselves out must be regulated in such a way that the output and subsequent input do not overload the drum channel. Since the rate of input cannot persistently exceed the rate of output, it is sufficient to control the latter. To ensure that the average output rate does not exceed one page per drum revolution, it is sufficient to ensure that each page remains in main store for an average of M drum revolutions after it has been input, where M is the number of pages in main store.

Since each page is capable of independent activity, it is necessary to associate a process with each page, which is responsible for throwing the page out after it has been in store for long enough. This process will be called

process *automatic discard*;

It is invoked when the page is first brought into main store, and is then supposed to proceed 'in parallel' with the user program. However, the first thing the process does is to wait for M drum revolutions; and it is assumed that exclusion is released during this wait, so that other user programs may invoke the other operations on the page during the interval. Of course, at the end of the wait, the exclusion is seized again while the page is actually being thrown out.

The process is easily coded:

```
process automatic discard;
  begin wait about M drum revolutions;
    throwout
  end
```

It remains to design an efficient implementation of the wait; and we should try to ensure that it is impossible for pages to get into synchronization, and attempt to throw themselves out simultaneously. Our solution assumes the existence of a mechanism which will wait about one drum revolution.

With each main page frame we associate a condition on which the automatic discarder waits whenever it needs to delay for M revolutions:

delay: **array** *mainpageframe* **of** *condition*.

We also introduce a process known as the cyclic discarder which is responsible for signalling each condition at an interval of approximately M drum revolutions. This can be accomplished by a simple loop:

```
process cyclic discarder;
  while true do
    for m = 0 . to M − 1 do
      begin delay[m] . signal;
        wait one drum revolution
      end;
```

An important point to note is that the cyclic discarder has been carefully designed so that it is never held up. If, for example, it attempted to make a direct entry to *throw out,* it might be held up by normal exclusion during a *bring in* operation on the same page. If that *bring in* were itself held up waiting for a free main page frame, a deadly embrace would result.

10.8 Load control

The major defect of the system described above is that it reacts badly to an overload of the main store, which occurs when the rate at which programs wish to acquire page frames is consistently greater than the rate at which they are being released. In these circumstances, some or all of the programs running may spend nearly all their time waiting to acquire a main page frame; and by the time they get it, they may well find that one of their own pages has been automatically discarded, and a new main page frame must be acquired again immediately.

The only effective solution in these circumstances is to reduce the requirement for free page frames or to increase the supply. Both may be accomplished by suspending one of the programs currently under execution, since this program will no longer be able to acquire pages, and the pages which it currently possesses will be thrown out in due course by the automatic discarder. If there is only one program under execution, and it is spending most of its time waiting for main page frames, it too should be discontinued, since here the only solution is to redesign the program or to buy more main store.

After a program has been suspended, it would obviously be foolish to suspend another program until all its pages have been discarded. This suggests that the suspension should be carried out (when necessary) at the end of each scan of the store by the cyclic discarder. We will assume that the choice of a program to be suspended is not the responsibility of the paging system.

However, to ensure that no single program is subject to undue delay, we will at regular intervals resume the longest suspended program. If this causes overload again, some other program should be suspended. By controlling the rate of program resumption at once per twenty cycles of the cyclic discarder, we can control the frequency of suspension to an acceptable level, since suspension cannot in the long run occur more frequently than resumption.

The cyclic discarder takes the form:

```
process cyclic discarder;
  while true do
  begin for i = 0 to 19 do
    begin for m = 0 to M - 1 do
      begin delay[m].signal;
        wait one drum revolution
      end;
      if size (mfree) < 3 then suspend a program
    end;
    resume longest suspended program
  end cyclic discarder.
```

An alternative to load shedding is to allow the rate of automatic discard to increase when there are no free main page frames. This unfortunately leads to a phenomenon known as thrashing, in which pages are discarded as fast as the programs using them can bring them back. This all too common elementary mistake in control engineering is avoided by ensuring that the maximum rate of discard remains less than the minimum rate of recall.

10.9 Refinements

This section discusses a number of detailed refinements, which either improve efficiency or adapt the algorithm for more direct implementation on hardware.

10.9.1 Clearing

On some occasions, the programmer is no longer interested in the current content of a page, for example if it contains an array local to a block which he is about to exit. In this case it is possible immediately to release both the main and drum page frames, and return the apparent content of the page to its initial clear state. This is accomplished by a call on a procedure local to each virtual page:

```
procedure clear; note content:= all clear;
  begin case where of
    in : begin delay[m]:= null; mfree.release(m) end,
    out : dfree.release(d),
    clear : do nothing;
    where:= clear
  end.
```

Note that the instruction $delay[m] := null$ is intended to cancel the wait of the automatic discarder.

10.9.2 Unchanged

When a page is used to store code, it is likely that the content of the page remains unchanged for long periods. The same will be true of certain data pages as well. This means that when the time comes to throw out the page, the copy which already exists on the drum is still valid, and the output instruction can be avoided, provided that the relevant drumpageframe has not been released.

We therefore introduce for each virtual page a variable

$$unchanged : Boolean$$

which is set true after input of each page and set false by the first assignment to that page. Each operation of the paging system must preserve the truth of

$$where = in \wedge unchanged \Rightarrow mainstore[m] = drumstore[d] \wedge d \notin dfree$$

10.9.3 Locking

When a page is engaged in an autonomous peripheral transfer it is usually necessary to ensure that the page is not thrown out until the transfer is complete. Similarly, considerations of efficiency sometimes dictate that a copy of the absolute main store address be made, for example in an associative slave store; and the page must not be thrown out while this address is in use. We therefore provide a function

function *lock*(*v* : *virtualpageframe*) : *mainpageframe*;

which 'locks' the virtual page into main store, and delivers its address as result. The effect may be reversed by calling

procedure *unlock*(*v* : *virtualpageframe*).

If a virtual page is being shared among several programs, and more than one of them lock it, it is essential that the page remains locked until they have all unlocked it. It is therefore necessary to introduce for each main page frame a count of the number of times it has been locked:

lockcount : **array** *mainpageframe* **of** *integer*;

which is incremented by locking and decremented by unlocking.

10.9.4 Usebit

When a page automatically discards itself, it will frequently happen that this page will be accessed again almost immediately; and in this case an unnecessary delay of up to two revolutions has been inflicted upon at least one user program. An obvious symptom that a page is going to be used again in the near future is that is has been used in the recent past. We therefore associate with each virtual page a

$$usebit: Boolean$$

which is set to true by *bringin* in every *fetch* or *assign* instruction, and is set false by the automatic discard process at regular intervals. Thus the page will be thrown out only if it remains unaccessed throughout the interval.

```
process automatic discard;
  begin delay[m].wait;
    while usebit ∨ lockcount[m] > 0 do
    begin usebit:= false;
      delay[m].wait
    end;
    throw out.
  end;
```

Since at least two delays are involved before a page automatically discards itself, the rate at which the cyclic discarder scans the store should be increased by a factor of two.

10.9.5 Explicit discard

On occasions a programmer knows that he will not require to access a page again for a long period. For example it could be a completed page of an input or output file, or a piece of program that has been finished with. In this case it is kind to inform the paging system of this fact, so that the page may be sooner thrown out. This may be done by calling:

procedure *discardnow.*

But if there is any risk at all that the page is being shared by some other program, or that it may after all be required back in main store sooner than expected, it would be better to use a milder suggestion:

procedure *discardsoon.*

The implementation of these is trivial:

```
discardnow:
  begin usebit:= false;
    if where = in then
    delay[m].signal
  end;
discardsoon:
  if where = in then usebit:= false.
```

The explicit discard can also be used by the loadshedding mechanism, and before each interaction of a multiple access program, provided that the pages in private use by each program are known.

10.10 The complete program

This section describes the complete paging system, with all its refinements. The reader may study it to check compatibility of the refinements, or to confirm his understanding. Alternatively, he may consult it for reference or even omit it altogether.

```
class virtual page;
  monitor begin where: (in, out, clear);
    m: mainpageframe;
    d: drumpageframe;
    unchanged, usebit: Boolean;
  note where = in ⇒ m ∉ mfree ∧ content = mainstore[m],
       where = out ∨ where = in ∧ unchanged ⇒ d ∉ dfree ∧
         content = drumstore[d],
       otherwise content = all clear;

  procedure bringin; note ensures where = in, content unchanged;
  begin usebit:= true;
    if where ≠ in then
    begin m:= mfree.acquire;
      if where = clear
        then begin mainstore[m]:= all clear;
                unchanged:= false
              end
        else begin input(m, d);
                unchanged:= true
             end;
      where:= in;
      automatic discard
    end
  end bringin;
```

```
procedure throwout;
  note ensures where ≠ in, content unchanged;
  if where = in then
    begin if ¬ unchanged then begin d:= dfree.acquire; output(m, d)
                                   end;
      mfree.release(m);
      where:= out
    end throwout;

process automatic discard; note no change;
  begin delay[m].wait;
    while usebit ∨ lockcount[m] > 0 do
    begin usebit:= false;
      delay[m].wait
    end;
    throwout
  end automatic discard;

procedure clear; note content:= all clear;
  begin case where of
    in: begin delay[m]:= null;
          if unchanged then dfree.release(d);
          mfree.release(m)
        end;
    out: dfree.release(d);
    where:= clear
  end clear;

function fetch (l: line): word; note = content[l];
  begin bringin; fetch:= mainstore[m, l] end;

procedure assign(l: line; w: word); note content[l]:= w;
  begin bringin; mainstore[m, l]:= w;
    if unchanged then begin dfree.release(d);
                            unchanged:= false
                      end
  end;

function lock: mainpageframe;
  begin bringin; lockcount[m]:= lockcount[m] + 1;
                                lock:= m end;

procedure unlock;
  lockcount[m]:= lockcount[m] − 1;

procedure discard now;
  if where = in then
  begin usebit:= false;
    delay[m].signal
  end;
```

procedure *discard soon*; *usebit*:= *false*;
where:= *clear*
end *virtual page*;

10.11 Conclusion

If the reasoning of this paper is correct, there is nothing seriously wrong with the algorithm described; it is reasonably independent of machine characteristics and work load; and although it will not generally make the best decisions in individual cases, it will not persistently make disastrous ones. Having established the adequacy of the overall algorithm, the next step is to decide suitable representations of the data, including page size, and code the basic operations required compactly and efficiently in a suitable mixture of hardware and software.

The quality of the final product will depend critically on the skill and ingenuity of the implementors. For example, an entry in the virtual store table should occupy only a single word; and access to a page in main store must be highly optimized, even if this means extra book-keeping in the other case. The page size should be large enough to make demand paging an acceptable method of loading and reloading a program; and the implementors of commonly used programming languages must inhibit vagrancy of object code. Writers of large programs should also be willing to co-operate in this.

I hope that this structured paging system has been designed and described in such a way as to encourage future implementors to take it as a model; so that the validity of the reasoning and the quality of the documentation may be put to the test.

Since nothing is new about this algorithm (except possibly its structure), acknowledgement is due to M. Melliar Smith for the elegance of the cyclic discarder and loadshed mechanism; to E. W. Dijkstra for central concepts of structure, exclusion, and synchronization; and to these, together with R. M. McKeag, J. Bézivin, and P. Brinch Hansen, for ideas, discussion, inspiration, and criticism on points too numerous to recall.

ELEVEN

An axiomatic definition of the programming language Pascal

Hoare started writing this paper on a short family holiday in County Kerry Eire, just at the major peak of violence in Northern Ireland. The news on television was so bad that he could not concentrate on the business of enjoying himself and had to take to the comfort of scribbling formulae. The published version ([37]) was jointly authored with Niklaus Wirth and was submitted on 11 December 1972. (It had gone through a number of drafts, one of which appeared as an ETH Zurich report in November 1972; a version presented in August 1972 at a Symposium on Theoretical Programming in Novosibirsk appears in the proceedings only in 1974.) Here, the 'syntax diagrams' have been omitted – they can be found in [37].

This definition represents the culmination of the effort to tackle various features of imperative programming languages by the axiomatic approach (as well as those in preceding chapters, see [26, 33]). Although it by no means provides a proof system for the whole of Pascal as known today, it is an extremely interesting undertaking. The task of writing *post hoc* definitions of programming languages is both difficult and unrewarding. By now it is clear that the desire for a language about which formal proofs can be constructed must influence the choice and design of its features. Even a language such as Euclid, which was designed with proofs in mind, was by no means easy to axiomatize.

For a brief period, it appeared that this work might have an influence on the design of the language which has been christened 'Ada'. The so-called Ironman requirements did state that a formal definition should be provided in either the VDL style or in the axiomatic style of this paper. In the event, the formal definition of the 'Green' language was tackled by Bjørner and Oest (1980a,b); both papers were broadly denotational. There is now – after the fact – a relatively complete description of Ada created by CRAI and the DDC

C. A. R. Hoare and N. Wirth, An axiomatic definition of the programming language Pascal, *Acta Informatica,* **2**(4), 335–55 (1973). This paper is republished by kind permission of Springer-Verlag GmbH.

for the EEC, but this is a huge document which again shows the folly of designing languages without using formal models.

Abstract

The axiomatic definition method proposed in Chapter 4 is extended and applied to define the meaning of the programming language Pascal (Wirth 1971c). The whole language is covered with the exception of real arithmetic and goto statements.

11.1 Introduction

The programming language Pascal was designed as a general-purpose language efficiently implementable on many computers and sufficiently flexible to be able to serve in many areas of application. Its defining report (Wirth 1971c) was given in the style of the Algol 60 report (Naur 1963). A formalism was used to define the syntax of the language rigorously. But the meaning of programs was verbally described in terms of the meaning of individual syntactic constructs. This approach has the advantage that the report is easily comprehensible, since the formalism is restricted to syntactic matters and is basically straightforward. Its disadvantage is that many semantic aspects of the language remain sufficiently imprecisely defined to given rise to misunderstanding. In particular, the following motivations must be cited for issuing a more complete and rigorous definition of the language:

(1) Pascal is being implemented at various places on different computers (Wirth 1971a; Welsh and Quinn 1972). Since one of the principal aims in designing Pascal was to construct a basis for truly portable software, it is mandatory to ensure full compatibility among implementations. To this end, implementors must be able to rely on a rigorous definition of the language. The definition must clearly state the rules that are considered as binding, and on the other hand give the implementor enough freedom, to achieve efficiency by leaving certain less important aspects undefined.
(2) Pascal is being used by many programmers to formulate algorithms as programs. In order to be safe from possible misunderstandings and misconceptions they need a comprehensive reference manual acting as an ultimate arbiter among possible interpretations of certain language features.
(3) In order to prove properties of programs written in a language, the programmer must be able to rely on an appropriate logical foundation provided by the definition of that language.

(4) The attempt to construct a set of abstract rules rigorously defining the meaning of a language may reveal irregularities of structure or machine-dependent features. Thus the development of a formal definition may assist in better language design.

Among the available methods of language definition the axiomatic approach proposed and elaborated by Hoare (Chapters 4 and 11, [30] and [33]) seems to be best suited to satisfy the different aims mentioned. It is based on the specification of certain axioms and rules of inference. The use of notations and concepts from conventional mathematics and logic should help in making this definition more easily accessible and comprehensible. The authors therefore hope that the axiomatic definition may simultaneously serve as

(1) a 'contract' between the language designer and implementors (including hardware designers),
(2) a reference manual for programmers,
(3) an axiomatic basis for formal proofs of properties of programs, and
(4) an incentive for systematic and machine-independent language design and use.

This axiomatic definition covers exclusively the semantic aspects of the language, and it assumes that the reader is familiar with the syntactic structure of Pascal as defined in Wirth (1971c). We also consider such topics as rules about the scope of validity of names and priorities of operators as belonging to the realm of syntax.

The axiomatic method in language definition as introduced in Chapter 4 operates on four levels of discourse:

(1) *Pascal statements,* usually denoted by S.
(2) *Logical formulae* describing properties of data, usually denoted by P, Q, R
(3) *Assertions,* usually denoted by H, of which there are two kinds:
(a) Assertions obtained by quantifying on the free variables in a logical formula. They are used to axiomatize the mathematical structures which correspond to the various data types.
(b) Assertions of the form $P \{S\} Q$ which express that, if P is true before the execution of S, then Q is true after the execution of S. This kind of assertion is used to define the meaning of assignment and procedure statements. It is vacuously true if the execution of S does not terminate.
(4) *Rules of inference* of the form

$$\frac{H_1, \ldots, H_n}{H}$$

which state that whenever $H_1, \ldots, H_n$ are true assertions, then H is also a true assertion, or of the form

$$\frac{H_1, \ldots, H_n \vdash H_{n+1}}{H}$$

which states that if H_{n+1} can be proved from $H_1, \ldots, H_n$, then H is a true assertion. Such rules of inference are used to axiomatize the meaning of declarations and of structured statements, where $H_1, \ldots, H_n$ are assertions about the components of the structured statements.

In addition, the notation

$$P_y^x$$

is used for the formula which is obtained by systematically substituting y for all free occurrences of x in P. If this introduces conflict between free variables of y and bound variables of P, the conflict is resolved by systematic change of the latter variables.

$$P_{y_1 \ldots y_n}^{x_1 \ldots x_n}$$

denotes simultaneous substitution for all occurrences of any x_i by the corresponding y_i. Thus occurrences of x_i within any y_i are *not* replaced. The variables $x_1 \ldots x_n$ must be distinct; otherwise the simultaneous substitution is not defined.

In proofs of Pascal programs, it will be necessary to make use of the following two inference rules:

$$\frac{P\,\{S\}\,Q,\ Q \Rightarrow R}{P\,\{S\}\,R}$$

$$\frac{P \Rightarrow Q,\ Q\,\{S\}\,R}{P\,\{S\}\,R}$$

The axioms and rules of inference given in this article explicitly forbid the presence of certain 'side-effects' in the evaluation of functions and execution of statements. Thus programs which invoke such side-effects are, from a formal point of view, undefined. The absence of such side-effects can in principle be checked by a textual (compile-time) scan of the program. However, it is not obligatory for a Pascal implementation to make such checks.

The whole language Pascal is treated in this article with the exception of real arithmetic and **goto** statements (jumps). Also the type *alfa* is not treated. It may be defined as

type *alfa* = **array** [1 .. *w*] **of** *char*

where w is an implementation-defined integer.

The task of rigorously defining the language in terms of machine-independent axioms, as well as experience gained in use and implementation of Pascal have suggested a number of changes with respect to the original description. These changes are informally described in the subsequent section of this article, and must be taken into account whenever referring to Wirth (1971c). For easy reference, the revised syntax is summarized in the form of diagrams. (These appeared in the original paper [37], but are omitted here.)

Many of the axioms have been explained in previous papers, e.g. Chapters 4 and 11, [30] and [33]. However, the axioms for procedures are novel; an informal explanation and example are given in Appendix 2.

The authors are not wholly satisfied with the axioms presented for classes, and for procedures and functions, particularly with those referring to global variables. This may be due either to inadequacy of the axiomatization or to genuine logical complexity of these features of the language. The paper is offered as a first attempt at an almost complete axiomatization of a realistic programming language, rather than as a definitive specification of a language especially constructed to demonstrate the definition method.

11.2 Changes and extensions of Pascal

The changes which were made to the language Pascal since it was defined in 1969 and implemented and reported in 1970 can be divided into semantic and syntactic amendments. To the first group belong the changes which affect the meaning of certain language constructs and can thus be considered as essential changes. The second group was primarily motivated by the desire to simplify syntactic analysis or to coordinate notational conventions which thereby become easier to learn and apply.

11.2.1 File types

The notion of the *mode* of a file is eliminated. The applicability of the procedures *put* and *get* is instead reformulated by antecedent conditions in the respective rules of inference. The procedure *reset* repositions a file to its beginning for the purpose of reading only. A new standard procedure *rewrite* is introduced to effectively discard the current value of a file variable and to allow the subsequent generation of a new file.

11.2.2 Parameters of procedures

Constant parameters are replaced by so-called *value parameters* in the sense of ALGOL 60. A formal value parameter represents a variable local to the procedure to which the value of the corresponding actual parameter is initially assigned upon activation of the procedure. Assignments to value parameters from within the procedure are permitted, but do not affect the corresponding actual parameter. The symbol **const** will not be used in a formal parameter list.

11.2.3 Class and pointer types

The class is eliminated as a data structure, and pointer types are bound to a data type instead of a class variable. For example, the type definition and variable declaration

type $P = \uparrow c$;
var c: **class** n **of** T

are replaced and expressed more concisely by the single pointer-type definition

type $P = \uparrow T$.

This change allows the allocation of all dynamically generated variables in a single pool.

11.2.4 The for statement

In the original report, the meaning of the **for** statement is defined in terms of an equivalent conditional and repetitive statement. It is felt that this algorithmic definition resulted in some undesirable overspecification which unnecessarily constrains the implementor. In contrast, the axiomatic definition presented in this paper leaves the value of the control variable undefined after termination of the **for** statement. It also involves the restriction that the repeated statement must not change the initial value (Hoare [33]).

11.2.5 Changes of a syntactic nature

Commas are used instead of colons to separate (multiple) labels in **case** statements and variant record definitions.

Semicolons are used instead of commas to separate constant definitions.

The symbol **powerset** is replaced by the symbols **set of,** and the scale symbol $_{10}$ is replaced by the capital letter E.

The standard procedure *alloc* is renamed *new*, and the standard function *int* is renamed *ord.*

Declarations of labels are compulsory.

11.3 Data types

The axioms presented in this and the following sections display the relationship between a type declaration and the axioms which specify the properties of values of the type and operations defined over them. The treatment is not wholly formal, and the reader must be aware that:

(1) Free variables in axioms are assumed to be universally quantified.
(2) The expression of the 'induction' axiom is always left informal.
(3) The types of variables used have to be deduced either from the chapter heading or from the more immediate context.
(4) The name of a type is used as a transfer function constructing a value of the type. Such a use of the type identifier is not available in Pascal.
(5) Axioms for a defined type must be modelled after the definition and be applied only in the scope (block) to which the definition is local.
(6) A type name (other than that of a pointer type) may not be used directly or indirectly within its own definition.

11.3.1 Scalar types

1.1 $c_1, c_2, \ldots, c_n$ are distinct elements of T.
1.2 These are the only elements of T.
1.3 $c_{i+1} = succ(c_i) \quad$ for $i = 1, \ldots, n-1$
1.4 $c_i = pred\,(c_{i+1}) \quad$ for $i = 1, \ldots, n-1$
1.5 $\neg(x < x)$
1.6 $(x < y) \wedge (y < z) \Rightarrow (x < z)$
1.7 $(x \neq c_n) \Rightarrow (x < succ(x))$
1.8 $x > y \equiv y < x$
1.9 $x \leqslant y \equiv \neg(x > y)$
1.10 $x \geqslant y \equiv \neg(x < y)$
1.11 $x \neq y \equiv \neg(x = y)$

We define $\min_T = c_1$ and $\max_T = c_n$ (not available to the Pascal programmer).

The standard scalar type *Boolean* is defined as

$$\textbf{type } Boolean = (false, true).$$

The standard type *integer* stands for a finite, coherent set of the whole numbers. The logical operators $\vee$, $\wedge$, $\neg$, and the arithmetic operators $+$, $-$, $*$, and **div**, are those of the conventional logical calculus and of whole-number arithmetic. The modulus operator **mod** is defined by the equation

$$m \textbf{ mod } n = m - (m \textbf{ div } n) * n$$

whereas **div** denotes division with truncated fraction.

Implementations are permitted to refuse the execution of programs which refer to integers outside the range specified by their definition of the type *integer*.

11.3.2 The type *char*

2.1 The elements of the type *char* are the 26 (capital) letters, the 10 (decimal) digits, and possibly other characters defined by particular implementations. In programs, a constant of type **char** is denoted by enclosing the character in quote marks.

2.2
$$
\begin{array}{ll}
'A' < 'B' & '1' = succ('0') \\
'B' < 'C' & '2' = succ('1') \\
\vdots & \vdots \\
'Y' < 'Z' & '9' = succ('8').
\end{array}
$$

The sets of letters and digits are ordered, and the digits are coherent.

Axioms 1.5–1.11 apply to the *char* type. The functions *ord* and *chr* are defined by the following additional axioms:

2.3 if u is an element of *char*, then $ord(u)$ is a non-negative integer (called the *ordinal number of* u), and

$$chr(ord(u)) = u$$

2.4
$$u < v \equiv ord(u) < ord(v).$$

These axioms have been designed to make possible an interchange of programs between implementations using different character sets. It should be noted that the function *ord* does not necessarily map the characters onto consecutive integers.

11.3.3 Subrange types

$$\textbf{type } T = m..n$$

Let a, m, n be elements of T_0 such that

$$m \leqslant a \leqslant n$$

and let x, y be elements of T. Then we define

$$\min_T = m \qquad \text{and} \qquad \max_T = n.$$

3.1 $T(a)$ is an element of T.
3.2 These are the only elements of T.
3.3 $T^{-1}(T(a)) = a$.
3.4 If $\ominus$ is a monadic operator defined on T_0, then

$$\ominus x \text{ means } \odot T^{-1}(x).$$

3.5 If $\odot$ is a dyadic operator defined on $T_0 \times T_0$, then

$$x \odot y \text{ means } T^{-1}(x) \odot T^{-1}(y)$$
$$x \odot a \text{ means } T^{-1}(x) \odot a$$
$$a \odot x \text{ means } a \odot T^{-1}(x).$$

11.3.4 Array types

type $T =$ **array** $[I]$ **of** T_0

Let $m = \min_I$ and $n = \max_I$.

4.1 If x_i is an element of T_0 for all i such that $m \leqslant i \leqslant n$, then $T(x_m, \ldots, x_n)$ is an element of T.

4.2 These are the only elements of T.

4.3 $m \leqslant i \leqslant n \Rightarrow T(x_m, \ldots, x_n)[i] = x_i$.

4.4 **array** $[I_1, I_2, \ldots, I_k]$ **of** T_0 means **array** $[I_1]$ **of array** $[I_2, \ldots, I_k]$ **of** T_0.

4.5 $x[i_1, i_2, \ldots, i_k]$ means $x[i_1][i_2, \ldots, i_k]$.

We introduce the following abbreviation for later use (see rule 11.1): $(x, i: y)$ stands for $T(x[m], \ldots, x[pred(i)], y, x[succ(i)], \ldots, x[n])$.

11.3.5 Record types

type $T =$ **record** $s_1 : T_1; \ldots; s_m : T_m$ **end**

Let x_i be an element of T_i for $i = 1, \ldots, m$.

5.1 $T(x_1, x_2, \ldots, x_m)$ is an element of T.

5.2 These are the only elements of T.

5.3 $T(x_1, \ldots, x_m) . s_i = x_i$ for $i = 1, \ldots, m$.

11.3.6 Variant records

type $T =$ **record** $s_1 : T_1; \ldots; s_{m-1}: T_{m-1}$;
 case $s_m : T_m$ **of**
  $k_1 : (s'_1 : T'_1)$;
  $k_2 : (s'_2 : T'_2)$;
  ⋮
  $k_n : (s'_n : T'_n)$
 end

Let k_j be an element of T_m and let x'_j be an element of T'_j for $j = 1, \ldots, n$. Then axiom 5.1 is rewritten as

5.1(a) $T(x_1, \ldots, x_{m-1}, k_j, x'_j)$ is an element of T.

Axioms 5.2 and 5.3 apply to this record type unchanged, and in addition the following axiom is given:

5.4 $T(x_1, \ldots, x_{m-1}, k_j, x_j').s_j' = x_j'$ for $j = 1, \ldots, n$.

We introduce the following abbreviation for later use (see rule 11.1):

$(x, s_i : y)$ stands for $T(x.s_1, \ldots, x.s_{i-1}, y, x.s_{i+1}, \ldots, x.s_m)$

and

$(x, s_j' : y)$ stands for $T(x.s_1, \ldots, x.s_m, y)$

The case with a field list containing several fields

$$k_j : (s_{j1} : T_{j1} : \ldots s_{jh} : T_{jh})$$

is to be interpreted as

$$k_j' : (s_j : T_j')$$

where s_j' is a fresh identifier, and T_j' is a type defined as

type T_j' = **record** $s_{j1} : T_{j1}; \ldots; s_{jh} : T_{jh}$ **end**

In this case $x.s_{jt}$ is interpreted as $x.s_j'.s_{jt}$.

11.3.7 Set types

type T = **set of** T_0

Let x_0, y_0 be elements of T_0.

6.1 [ ] is an element of T.

6.2 If x is an element of T, then $x \vee [x_0]$ is a T.

6.3 These are the only elements of T.

6.4 $[x_1, x_2, \ldots, x_n]$ means $((([\ ] \vee [x_1]) \vee [x_2]) \vee \cdots \vee [x_n]$.

[ ] denotes the empty set, and $[x_0]$ denotes the singleton set containing x_0. The operators $\vee$, $\wedge$, and $-$, applied to elements of set type, denote the conventional operations of set union, intersection, and difference.

Note that Pascal allows implementations to restrict set types to be built only on base types T_0 with a specified maximum number of elements.

11.3.8 File types

type T = **file of** T_0

Let x_0 be an element of T_0.

7.1 $\langle\rangle$ is an element T.

7.2 If x is an element of T, then $x \wedge \langle x_0 \rangle$ is an element of T.
7.3 These are the only elements of T.
7.4 $(x \wedge y) \wedge z = x \wedge (y \wedge z)$.
7.5 $x \wedge \langle x_0 \rangle \neq \langle \rangle$.

$\langle \rangle$ denotes the empty file (sequence), and $\langle x_0 \rangle$ the singleton sequence containing x_0. The operator $\wedge$ denotes concatenation such that $x \wedge y = \langle x_1, \ldots, x_m, y_1, \ldots, y_n \rangle$, if $x = \langle x_1, \ldots, x_m \rangle$ and $y = \langle y_1, \ldots, y_n \rangle$. Neither the explicit denotation of sequences nor the concatenation operator are available in Pascal.

7.6 $\mathit{first}(\langle x_0 \rangle \wedge x) = x_0$, $\mathit{rest}(\langle x_0 \rangle \wedge x) = x$.

The functions *first* and *rest* are not explicitly available in Pascal. They will later be used to define the effect of file-handling procedures.

11.3.9 Pointer types

$$\textbf{type } T = \uparrow T_0$$

A pointer type consists of an arbitrary, unbounded set of values

$$\textbf{nil}, \varphi_1, \varphi_2, \varphi_3, \ldots$$

over which no operation except test of equality is defined. Associated with a pointer type T are a variable ξ of type *integer* (and initial value 0) and a variable τ with components τ_{φ_1}, $\tau_{\varphi_2}, \ldots$ which are all of type T_0. These components are the variables to which elements of T (other than **nil**) are 'pointing'. ξ is used in connection with the 'generation' of new elements of T (see rule 11.7). ξ and τ are not available to the Pascal programmer.

8.1 $x \neq \textbf{nil} \Rightarrow x\uparrow = \tau_x$.

11.4 Declarations

The purpose of a declaration is to introduce a named object (constant, type, variable, function, or procedure) and to prescribe its properties. These properties may then be assumed in any proof relating to the scope of the declaration.

11.4.1 Constant-, type-, and variable declarations

If D is a sequence of declarations and S is a compound statement, then

$$D; S$$

is called a *block,* and the following is its rule of inference (expressed in the usual notation for subsidiary deductions):

9.1
$$\frac{H \vdash P\,\{S\}\,Q}{P\,\{D;\, S\}\,Q}$$

H is the set of assertions describing the properties established by the declarations in D. The assertions P and Q may not contain any identifiers declared in D; if they do, the rule can be applied only after a systematic substitution of fresh identifiers local to the block. In the case of constant declarations the assertions in H are nothing but the list of equations themselves. In the case of type definitions they are the axioms derived from the declaration in the manner described above. In the case of a variable declaration $x: T$ it is the fact that x is an element of T.

11.4.2 File variable declarations

The declaration

var $x: T$

where

type $T =$ **file of** T_0,

introduces the *two* variables x of type T and $x\uparrow$ of type T_0. The variable $x\uparrow$ is called the *buffer variable* of x and is used implicitly by the standard file procedures. A so-called *file position* is associated with x; it splits x into a left part x_L and a right part x_R such that

9.2 x_L and x_R are of type T, and $x \equiv x_L \wedge x_R$.

x_L and x_R are not explicitly available to the programmer. Assignments to the buffer variable $x\uparrow$ are permitted only if $x_R = \langle\rangle$. This condition is denoted in Pascal by the Boolean function *eof* (end of file):

9.3 $eof(x) =_{df} x_R = \langle\rangle$.

In addition, the following axiom holds:

9.4 $x_R \neq \langle\rangle \Rightarrow x \Rightarrow x\uparrow = first(x_R)$.

9.5 The standard type *text*, and the standard variables *input* and *output* are defined as follows:

type *text* = **file of** *char*
var *input, output*: *text*.

11.4.3 Function and procedure declarations

function $f(L): T; S$

Let **x** be the list of parameters declared in L, and let **y** be the set of global variables occurring within S (implicit parameters). Given the assertion $P\ \{S\}\ Q$, where f does not occur free in P, and none of the variables of **x** occurs free in Q, we may deduce the following implication:

10.1 $P \Rightarrow Q^{f}_{f(\mathbf{x},\mathbf{y})}$ for all values of the variables involved in this assertion.

Note that the explicit parameter list **x** has been extended by the implicit parameters **y**, that **x** may not contain any variable parameters (specified by **var**), and that no assignments to nonlocal variables may occur within S. It is this property (10.1) that may be assumed in proving assertions about expressions containing calls of the function f, including those occurring within S itself and in other declarations in the same block. In addition, assertions generated by the parameter specifications in L may be used in proving assertions about S.

procedure $p(L): S$.

Let **x** be the list of explicit parameters declared in L; let **y** be the set of global variables occurring in S (implicit parameters), let $x_1, \ldots, x_m$ be the parameters declared in L as variable parameters, and let $y_1, \ldots y_n$ be those global variables which are changed within S. Given the assertion $P\ \{S\}\ Q$ where none of the value parameters of **x** occurs free in Q, we may deduce the existence of functions f_i and g_j satisfying the following implication:

10.2 $P \Rightarrow Q^{x_1, \ldots x_m, \quad y_1, \quad \ldots, y_n}_{f_1(\mathbf{x},\mathbf{y}), \ldots f_m(\mathbf{x},\mathbf{y}), g_1(\mathbf{x},\mathbf{y}), \ldots, g_n(\mathbf{x},\mathbf{y})}$

for all values of the variables involved in this assertion.

It is this property that may be assumed in proving assertions about calls of this procedure, including those occurring within S itself and in other declarations in the same block.

The functions f_i and g_j may be regarded as those which map the initial values of **x** and **y** on entry to the procedure onto the final values of $x_1, \ldots, x_m$ and $y_1, \ldots, y_n$ on completion of the execution of S.

11.5 Statements

Statements are classified into simple statements and structured statements. The meaning of simple statements is defined by axioms, and the meaning of structured statements is defined in terms of rules of inference permitting deduction of the properties of the structured statement from properties of its constituents. However, the rules of inference are formulated in such a way that the reverse process of deriving necessary properties of the constituents from postulated properties of the composite statement is facilitated. The reason for this orientation is that in deducing proofs of properties of programs it is most convenient to proceed in a 'top-down' direction.

11.5.1 Simple statements

Assignment statements

11.1 $P_y^x \{x := y\} P.$

We introduce the following conventions:

(1) If the type T of x is a subrange of the type of y,

$$P_y^x \text{ means } P_{T(y)}^x.$$

(2) If the type T of y is a subrange of the type of x,

$$P_y^x \text{ means } P_{T^{-1}(y)}^x.$$

(3) If x is an indexed variable

$$P_y^{a[i]} \text{ means } P_{(a,i:y)}^a.$$

(4) If x is a field designator

$$P_y^{r,s} \text{ means } P_{(r,s:y)}^r.$$

Procedure statements

11.2 $P_{f_1(\mathbf{x},\mathbf{y}) \ldots, f_m(\mathbf{x},\mathbf{y}), g_1(\mathbf{x},\mathbf{y}), \ldots, g_n(\mathbf{x},\mathbf{y})}^{x_1 \ldots, x_m, y_1, \ldots, y_n} \{p(\mathbf{x})\} P.$

$\mathbf{x}$ is the list of actual parameters; $x_1, \ldots, x_m$ are those elements of $\mathbf{x}$ which correspond to formal parameters specified as variable parameters, $\mathbf{y}$ is the set of all variables accessed nonlocally by the procedure p, and $y_1, \ldots, y_n$ are those elements of $\mathbf{y}$ which are subject to assignments by the procedure.

$f_1, \ldots, f_m$ and $g_1, \ldots, g_n$ are the functions introduced and explained in implication 10.2. Note that $x_1, \ldots, x_m, y_1, \ldots, y_n$ must be all distinct (in the sense that none can contain or be a variable which is contained in another); otherwise the effect of the procedure statement is undefined. Rule 11.2 states that the procedure statement $p(\mathbf{x})$ is equivalent with the sequence of assignments (executed 'simultaneously')

$$x_1 := f_1(\mathbf{x}, \mathbf{y}); \ldots x_m := f_m(\mathbf{x}, \mathbf{y});$$
$$y_1 := g_1(\mathbf{x}, \mathbf{y}); \ldots y_n := g_n(\mathbf{x}, \mathbf{y}).$$

11.5.2 Standard procedures

The following inference rules specify the properties of the standard procedures *put, get, reset*, and *rewrite*. The assertion P in rules 11.3–11.6 must not contain $x, x_L, x_R, x\uparrow$, except in those cases where they occur explicitly in the list of substituends.

11.3 $eof(x) \wedge P^{x_L}_{x_L \wedge \langle x\uparrow \rangle} \{put(x)\}\ P\ eof(x).$

This axiom specifies that the procedure $put(x)$ is applicable only if $eof(x)$ is true i.e. $x_R = \langle\rangle$. It thus leaves $eof(x)$ and $x_L = x$ invariant, makes $x\uparrow$ undefined, and corresponds to the assignment

$$x := x \wedge \langle x\uparrow \rangle.$$

11.4 $\neg\, eof(x) \wedge P^{x_L,\ \ x\uparrow,\ \ x_R}_{x_L \wedge \langle first(x_R)\rangle,\ first(rest(x_R)),\ rest(x_R)} \{get(x)\}\ P$

The operation $get(x)$ is applicable only if $\neg eof(x)$, i.e. $x_R \neq \langle\rangle$ and then corresponds to the three simultaneous assignments

$$x_L := x_L \wedge \langle first(x_R)\rangle; \qquad x\uparrow := first(rest(x_R)); \qquad x_R := rest(x_R).$$

11.5 $P^{x_L,\ x\uparrow,\ x_R}_{\langle\rangle,\ first(x),\ x} \{reset(x)\}\ P.$

The operation $reset(x)$ corresponds to the three assignments

$$x_L := \langle\rangle; \qquad x\uparrow := first(x); \qquad x_R := x.$$

11.6 $P^{x}_{\langle\rangle}\{rewrite(x)\}P.$

The procedure statement $rewrite(x)$ corresponds to the assignment

$$x := \langle\rangle.$$

The following rule specifies the effect of the standard procedure *new*.

11.7 If t is a pointer variable of type T, then

$$new(t) \quad \text{means} \quad \xi := succ(\xi); \quad t := \varphi_\xi$$

where ξ is the hidden variable associated with the pointer type T.

11.5.3 Structured statements

Compound statements

12.1 $$\frac{P_{i-1}\ \{S_i\}\ P_i \text{ for } i = 1, \ldots, n}{P_0\ \{\mathbf{begin}\ S_1; S_2; \ldots; S_n\ \mathbf{end}\}\ P_n}$$

If statements

12.2 $$\frac{P \wedge B\ \{S_1\}\ Q,\ P \wedge \neg B\ \{S_2\}\ Q}{P\ \{\textbf{if}\ B\ \textbf{then}\ S_1\ \textbf{else}\ S_2\}\ Q}$$

12.3 $$\frac{P \wedge B\ \{S\}\ Q,\ P \wedge \neg B \Rightarrow Q}{P\ \{\textbf{if}\ B\ \textbf{then},\ S\}\ Q}$$

Case statements

12.4 $$\frac{P \wedge (x = k_i)\ \{S_i\}\ Q \qquad \text{for } i = 1, \ldots, n}{(x \in [k_1, \ldots, k_n]) \wedge P\ \{\textbf{case}\ x\ \textbf{of}\ k_1 : S_1; \ldots; k_n : S_n\ \textbf{end}\}\ Q}$$

Note: $k_a, k_b, \ldots, k_m : S$ stands for $k_a : S; k_b : S; \ldots; k_m : S$.

While statements

12.5 $$\frac{P \wedge B\ \{S\}\ P}{P\ \{\textbf{while}\ B\ \textbf{do}\ S\}\ P \wedge \neg B}$$

Repeat statements

12.6 $$\frac{P\ \{S\}\ Q,\ Q \wedge \neg B \Rightarrow P}{P\ \{\textbf{repeat}\ S\ \textbf{until}\ B\}\ Q \wedge B}$$

For statements

12.7 $$\frac{(a \leqslant x \leqslant b) \wedge P([a\,..\,x))\ \{S\}\ P([a\,..\,x])}{P([\ ])\ \{\textbf{for}\ x := a\ \textbf{to}\ b\ \textbf{do}\ S\}\ P([a\,..\,b])}$$

$[u\,..\,v]$ denotes the closed interval $u \ldots v$, i.e. the set $\{i \mid u \leqslant i \leqslant v\}$ and $[u\,..\,v)$ denotes the half-open interval $u \ldots v$, i.e. the set $\{i \mid u \leqslant i < v\}$. Similarly, $(u\,..\,v]$ denotes the set $\{i \mid u < i \leqslant v\}$. Note that $[u\,..\,u) = (u\,..\,u]$ is the empty set.

$$\frac{(a \leqslant x \leqslant b) \wedge P((x\,..\,b])\ \{S\}\ P([x\,..\,b])}{P([\ ])\ \{\textbf{for}\ x := b\ \textbf{downto}\ a\ \textbf{do}\ S\}\ P([a\,..\,b])}$$

Note that S must not change x, a, or b.

With statements

12.9 $$\frac{P^{r\,.\,s_1, \ldots, r\,.\,s_m}_{s_1, \ldots, s_m}\ \{S\}\ Q^{r\,.\,s_1, \ldots, r\,.\,s_m}_{s_1, \ldots, s_m}}{P\ \{\textbf{with}\ r\ \textbf{do}\ S\}\ Q}$$

$s_1, \ldots, s_m$ are the field identifiers of the record variable r. Note that r must not contain any variables subject to change by S, and that

with $r_1, \ldots, r_n$ **do** S

stands for

with r_1 **do** ... **with** r_n **do** S.

11.6 Appendix: Procedures

Consider the trivial procedure, with only one variable parameter, one value parameter, and no nonlocal references.

procedure p(**var** a : *integer*; b : integer);
  begin $b := 2 * b$; **if** $a > b$ **then** $a := b$ **end**.

Letting S stand for the body of this procedure, it is easy to prove that

$$(b = b_0) \wedge (b > 0) \{S\}\ a \leqslant 2 * b_0.$$

The invocation of this procedure will (in general) change the value of a in some manner dependent on the initial values of a and b (and initial values of nonlocal variables, if referenced from within S). Let us introduce a new function symbol f to denote this dependency, so that the final value of a can be denoted as

$$f(a, b).$$

Now the effect of any call of $P(x, y)$ is (by definition of f) equivalent to the simple assignment

$$x := f(x, y),$$

and using the axiom of assignment 11.1, we may validly conclude for any R that

$$R^x_{f(x,y)}\{p(x, y)\}R.$$

But by itself, application of this rule would be useless, since f has been introduced as an arbitrary function symbol. We need therefore to know at least something of the properties of f, and these can only be derived from the properties of the body of the procedure p. Suppose that we have proved

$$P \{S\}\ Q.$$

Occurrences of a in Q refer to the value of a *after* the execution of S, namely $f(a, b)$. Suppose that Q does not refer to any other program variable (in particular, does not refer to b). Then the values of all free variables of $Q^a_{f(a,b)}$ will be the same as they were in P, since the (a, b) in $f(a, b)$ also refer to the initial values of the parameters. Thus we may validly form the implication

$$P \Rightarrow Q^a_{f(a,b)},$$

and this implication will be true for all values of the variables involved in it. Thus, in the case shown above, we have

$$\forall a, b, b_0((b = b_0) \wedge (b > 0) \Rightarrow f(a, b) \leqslant 2 * b_0)$$

or more simply

$$\forall a, b(b > 0 \Rightarrow f(a, b) \leqslant 2 * b).$$

TWELVE

Monitors: an operating system structuring concept

There is considerable evidence that designing languages whose programs can be safely reasoned about involves looking for increasingly structured expressions. The story of the **goto** statement, and the evolution of structured coding, is well known. Pascal shows the advantages of a strict type structure and further constraints are considered in Chapter 14.

The need for structured expressions is perhaps strongest in the area of parallelism. This chapter discusses the 'monitor' concept, which is also exhibited in Chapter 10. Dijkstra's p and v operators had provided a primitive tool for programming mutual exclusion: used with care and taste, programs could be made believable; used in an unstructured way, texts of programs become incomprehensible. Hoare had proposed 'conditional critical sections' in [22]. These were somewhat higher-level constructs, which 'attempted to incorporate structure', but they could be spread throughout the program text. Monitors provided the next step (but not the final one – see Chapter 16). Simula was a key influence in the way monitors were described. (The original intention of producing [29] was to publish Dijkstra (1972c). During this exercise, Hoare had become involved in the rewriting of a paper by Ole-Johan Dahl: this finally appeared as [31].) Like the classes of Simula, monitors collected all of the operations together with the data they manipulate.

The paper includes proposed implementations for monitors as well as many examples which have become standard challenges for parallel languages and proof methods. The fact that Hoare felt the need to show – in the first example – that monitors were as expressive as p and v provides an interesting reminder of the date of this work. He also showed that monitors could be implemented in terms of p and v.

The first draft of this paper was distributed to the participants of the 1971 Belfast symposium reported in [20]. Significant contributions were made by Per Brinch Hansen, who implemented his language Concurrent Pascal. Monitors were later implemented in Pascal-Plus (see Welsh and McKeag 1980). It was also taken as the basis of the redesign of the concurrency

C. A. R. Hoare, Monitors: an operating system structuring concept, *Comm. ACM* **17**(10), 549–57 (October 1974).

features of Mesa. But the implementation with the aid of pre-existing synchronization and scheduling facilities resulted in unacceptable inefficiency and many programmers developed their skill at bypassing the monitor discipline; this left them struggling with more complex multithreading techniques. The paper was first submitted in February 1973; the material was presented at an IRIA conference in France on 11 May 1973. The paper was revised in April 1974 and published ([42]) in October 1974.

Monitors were undoubtedly a move towards more tractable expression of parallelism and this paper, together with Chapter 10, helped their adoption in languages like Pascal Plus and Simone [55]. Even within the paper, reservations on monitors are expressed. The difficulty of constructing appropriate proof methods was to lead to further developments.

Abstract

This paper develops Brinch Hansen's concept of a monitor as a method of structuring an operating system. It introduces a form of synchronization, describes a possible method of implementation in terms of semaphores and gives a suitable proof rule. Illustrative examples include a single resource scheduler, a bounded buffer, an alarm clock, a buffer pool, a disk head optimizer, and a version of the problem of readers and writers.

12.1 Introduction

A primary aim of an operating system is to share a computer installation among many programs making unpredictable demands upon its resources. A primary task of its designer is therefore to construct resource allocation (or scheduling) algorithms for resources of various kinds (main store, drum store, magnetic tape handlers, consoles, etc.). In order to simplify his task, he should try to construct separate schedulers for each class of resource. Each scheduler will consist of a certain amount of local administrative data, together with some procedures and functions which are called by programs wishing to acquire and release resources. Such a collection of associated data and procedures is known as a *monitor*; and a suitable notation can be based on the *class* notation of Simula 67 (Dahl 1972).

monitorname: **monitor**
  begin...*declarations of data local to the monitor*;
    procedure *procname* (...*formal parameters*...);
    begin...*procedure body*...**end**;
    ...*declarations of other procedures local to the monitor*;
    ...*initialization of local data of the monitor*...
  end;

Note that the procedure bodies may have local data in the normal way.

In order to call a procedure of a monitor, it is necessary to give the name of the monitor as well as the name of the desired procedure, separating them by a dot:

monitorname.procname(...actual parameters...);

In an operating system it is sometimes desirable to declare several monitors with identical structure and behaviour, for example to schedule two similar resources. In such cases, the declaration shown above will be preceded by the word **class**, and the separate monitors will be declared to belong to this class:

monitor 1, *monitor* 2: *classname*;

Thus the structure of a class of monitors is identical to that described for a data representation in Chapter 8, except for addition of the basic word *monitor*. Brinch Hansen (1973) used the word *shared* for the same purpose.

The procedures of a monitor are common to all running programs, in the sense that any program may at any time attempt to call such a procedure. However, it is essential that only one program at a time actually succeed in entering a monitor procedure, and any subsequent call must be held up until the previous call has been completed. Otherwise, if two procedure bodies were in simultaneous execution, the effects on the local variables of the monitor could be chaotic. The procedures local to a monitor should not access any nonlocal variables other than those local to the same monitor, and these variables of the monitor should be inaccessible from outside the monitor. If these restrictions are imposed, it is possible to guarantee against certain of the more obscure forms of time-dependent coding error; and this guarantee could be underwritten by a visual scan of the text of the program, which could readily be automated in a compiler.

Any dynamic resource allocator will sometimes need to delay a program wishing to acquire a resource which is not currently available, and to resume that program after some other program has released the resource required. We therefore need: a 'wait' operation, issued from inside a procedure of the monitor, which causes the calling program to be delayed; and a 'signal' operation, also issued from inside a procedure of the same monitor, which causes exactly one of the waiting programs to be resumed immediately. If there are no waiting programs, the signal has no effect. In order to enable other programs to release resources during a wait, a wait operation must relinquish the exclusion which would otherwise prevent entry to the releasing procedure. However, we decree that a signal operation be followed immediately by resumption of a waiting program, without possibility of an intervening procedure call from yet a third program. It is only in this way that a waiting program has an absolute guarantee that it can acquire the resource just released by the signalling program without any danger that a third program will interpose a monitor entry and seize the resource instead.

In many cases, there may be more than one reason for waiting, and these need to be distinguished by both the waiting and the signalling operation. We therefore introduce a new type of 'variable' known as a *condition*; and the writer of a monitor should declare a variable of type *condition* for each reason why a program might have to wait. Then the wait and signal operations should be preceded by the name of the relevant condition variable, separated from it by a dot:

condvariable. wait;
condvariable. signal;

Note that a condition 'variable' is neither true nor false; indeed, it does not have any stored value accessible to the program. In practice, a condition variable will be represented by an (initially empty) queue of processes which are currently waiting on the condition; but this queue is invisible both to waiters and signallers. This design of the condition variable has been deliberately kept as primitive and rudimentary as possible, so that it may be implemented efficiently and used flexibly to achieve a wide variety of effects. There is a great temptation to introduce a more complex synchronization primitive, which may be easier to use for many purposes. We shall resist this temptation for a while.

As the simplest example of a monitor, we will design a scheduling algorithm for a single resource, which is dynamically acquired and released by an unknown number of customer processes by calls on procedures:

procedure *acquire*;
procedure *release*;

A variable†

busy : *Boolean*

determines whether or not the resource is in use. If an attempt is made to acquire the resource when it is busy, the attempting program must be delayed by waiting on a variable,

nonbusy : *condition*

which is signalled by the next subsequent release. The initial value of *busy* is *false*. These design decisions lead to the following code for the monitor:

single resource : **monitor**
begin *busy* : *Boolean*;
  nonbusy : *condition*;
  procedure *acquire*;
    begin if *busy* **then** *nonbusy . wait*;
      busy := *true*
    end;

†As in Pascal (1971c), a variable declaration is of the form: ⟨*variable identifier*⟩ : ⟨*type*⟩;

```
    procedure release;
      begin busy := false;
        nonbusy . signal
      end;
    busy := false; comment initial value;
end single resource
```

NOTES

(1) In designing a monitor, it seems natural to design the procedure headings, the data, the conditions, and the procedure bodies, in that order. All subsequent examples will be designed in this way.

(2) The *acquire* procedure does not have to retest that *busy* has gone *false* when it resumes after its wait, since the *release* procedure has guaranteed that this is so; and as mentioned before, no other program can intervene between the signal and the continuation of exactly one waiting program.

(3) If more than one program is waiting on a condition, we postulate that the signal operation will reactivate the longest waiting program. This gives a simple neutral queuing discipline which ensures that every waiting program will eventually get its turn.

(4) The single resource monitor simulates a Boolean semaphore (Dijkstra 1968b) with *acquire* and *release* used for *P* and *V* respectively. This is a simple proof that the monitor/condition concepts are not in principle less powerful than semaphores, and that they can be used for all the same purposes.

12.2 Interpretation

Having proved that semaphores can be implemented by a monitor, the next task is to prove that monitors can be implemented by semaphores.

Obviously, we shall require for each monitor a Boolean semaphore *mutex* to ensure that the bodies of the local procedures exclude each other. The semaphore is initialized to 1; a *P*(*mutex*) must be executed on entry to each local procedure, and a *V*(*mutex*) must usually be executed on exit from it.

When a process signals a condition on which another process is waiting, the signalling process must wait until the resumed process permits it to proceed. We therefore introduce for each monitor a second semaphore *urgent* (initialized to 0), on which signalling processes suspend themselves by the operation *P*(*urgent*). Before releasing exclusion, each process must test whether any other process is waiting on *urgent*, and if so, must release it instead by a *V*(*urgent*) instruction. We therefore need to count the number of processes waiting on *urgent*, in an integer *urgentcount* (initially zero). Thus each exit from a procedure of a monitor should be coded:

if *urgentcount* > 0 **then** *V*(*urgent*) **else** *V*(*mutex*)

Finally, for each condition local to the monitor, we introduce a semaphore *condsem* (initialized to 0), on which a process desiring to wait suspends itself by a *P*(*condsem*) operation. Since a process signalling this condition needs to know whether anybody is waiting, we also need a count of the number of waiting processes held in an integer variable *condcount* (initially 0). The operation *cond. wait* may now be implemented as follows (recall that a waiting program must release exclusion before suspending itself):

condcount := *condcount* + 1;
if *urgentcount* > 0 **then** *V*(*urgent*) **else** *V*(*mutex*);
P(*condsem*);
comment *This will always wait*;
condcount := *condcount* − 1

The signal operation may be coded:

urgentcount := *urgentcount* + 1;
if *condcount* > 0 **then** {*V*(*condsem*); *P*(*urgent*)};
urgentcount := *urgentcount* − 1

In this implementation, possession of the monitor is regarded as a privilege which is explicitly passed from one process to another. Only when no one further wants the privilege is *mutex* finally released.

This solution is not intended to correspond to recommended 'style' in the use of semaphores. The concept of a condition variable is intended as a substitute for semaphores, and has its own style of usage, in the same way that **while** loops or coroutines are intended as a substitute for jumps.

In many cases, the generality of this solution is unnecessary, and a significant improvement in efficiency is possible.

(1) When a procedure body in a monitor contains no wait or signal, exit from the body can be coded by a simple *V*(*mutex*), since *urgentcount* cannot have changed during the execution of the body.
(2) If a *cond.signal* is the last operation of a procedure body, it can be combined with monitor exit as follows:

    if *condcount* > 0 **then** *V*(*condsem*)
    else if *urgentcount* > 0 **then** *V*(*urgent*)
    else *V*(*mutex*)

(3) If there is no other wait or signal in the procedure body, the second line shown above can also be omitted.
(4) If *every* signal occurs as the last operation of its procedure body, the variables *urgentcount* and *urgent* can be omitted, together with all operations upon them. This is such a simplification that O-J. Dahl suggests that signals should always be the last operation of a monitor procedure; in fact, this restriction is a very natural one, which has been unwittingly observed in all examples of this paper.

Significant improvements in efficiency may also be obtained by avoiding the use of semaphores, and by implementing conditions directly in hardware, or at the lowest and most uninterruptible level of software (e.g. supervisor mode). In this case, the following optimizations are possible.

(1) *urgentcount* and *condcount* can be abolished, since the fact that someone is waiting can be established by examining the representation of the semaphore, which cannot change surreptitiously within non-interruptible mode.
(2) Many monitors are very short and contain no calls to other monitors. Such monitors can be executed wholly in non-interruptible mode, using, as it were, the common exclusion mechanism provided by hardware. This will often involve *less* time in non-interruptible mode than the establishment of separate exclusion for each monitor.

I am grateful to J. Bezivin, J. Horning, and R. M. McKeag for assisting in the discovery of this algorithm.

12.3 Proof rules

The analogy between a monitor and a data representation has been noted in the introduction. The mutual exclusion on the code of a monitor ensures that procedure calls follow each other in time, just as they do in sequential programming; and the same restrictions are placed on access to nonlocal data. These are the reasons why the same proof rules can be applied to monitors as to data representations.

As with a data representation, the programmer may associate an invariant $\mathcal{I}$ with the local data of a monitor, to describe some condition which will be true of this data before and after every procedure call. $\mathcal{I}$ must also be made true after initialization of the data, and before *every* wait instruction; otherwise the next following procedure call will not find the local data in a state which it expects.

With each condition variable b the programmer may associate an assertion B which describes the condition under which a program waiting on b wishes to be resumed. Since other programs may invoke a monitor procedure during a wait, a waiting program must ensure that the invariant $\mathcal{I}$ for the monitor is true beforehand. This gives the proof rule for waits:

$$\mathcal{I}\ \{b\,.\ wait\}\ \mathcal{I} \wedge B$$

Since a signal can cause immediate resumption of a waiting program, the conditions $\mathcal{I} \wedge B$ which are expected by that program must be made true before the signal; and since B may be made false again by the resumed program, only $\mathcal{I}$ may be assumed true afterwards. Thus the proof rule for a signal is:

$$\mathscr{I} \wedge B \{b.signal\} \mathscr{I}$$

This exhibits a pleasing symmetry with the rule for waiting.

The introduction of condition variables makes it possible to write monitors subject to the risk of deadly embrace (Dijkstra 1968b). It is the responsibility of the programmer to avoid this risk, together with other scheduling disasters (thrashing, indefinitely repeated overtaking, etc. (Dijkstra 1972a). Assertion-oriented proof methods cannot prove absence of such risk; perhaps it is better to use less formal methods for such proofs.

Finally, in many cases an operating system monitor constructs some 'virtual' resource which is used in place of actual resources by its 'customer' programs. This virtual resource is an abstraction from the set of local variables of the monitor. The program prover should therefore define this abstraction in terms of its concrete representation, and then express the intended effect of each of the procedure bodies in terms of the abstraction. This proof method is described in detail in Chapter 8.

12.4 Example: bounded buffer

A bounded buffer is a concrete representation of the abstract idea of a sequence of portions. The sequence is accessible to two programs running in parallel: the first of these (the producer) updates the sequence by appending a new portion x at the end; and the second (the consumer) updates it by removing the first portion. The initial value of the sequence is empty. We thus require two operations:

(1) *append*(x: *portion*);

which should be equivalent to the abstract operation

$$sequence := sequence \cap \langle x \rangle;$$

where $\langle x \rangle$ is the sequence whose only item is x and $\cap$ denotes concatenation of two sequences.

(2) *remove*(**result** x: *portion*);

which should be equivalent to the abstract operations

$$x := first(sequence);\ sequence := rest(sequence);$$

where *first* selects the first item of a sequence and *rest* denotes the sequence with its first item removed. Obviously, if the sequence is empty, *first* is undefined; and in this case we want to ensure that the consumer waits until the producer has made the sequence non-empty.

We shall assume that the amount of time taken to produce a portion or consume it is large in comparison with the time taken to append or remove it from the sequence. We may therefore be justified in making a design in which producer and consumer can both update the sequence, but not simultaneously.

The sequence is represented by an array:

$$buffer: \textbf{array } 0\,..\,N-1 \textbf{ of } portion;$$

and two variables:

(1) $lastpointer: 0\,..\,N-1;$

which points to the buffer position into which the next append operation will put a new item, and

(2) $count: 0\,..\,N;$

which always holds the length of the sequence (initially 0).

We define the function

$$seq(b, l, c) =_{\text{df}} \textbf{if } c = 0 \textbf{ then } empty$$
$$\textbf{else } seq(b, l \ominus 1, c-1) \cap \langle b[l \ominus 1] \rangle$$

where the circled operations are taken modulo N. Note that if $c \neq 0$,

$$first(seq(b, l, c)) = b[l \ominus c]$$

and

$$rest(seq(b, l, c)) = seq(b, l, c-1)$$

The definition of the abstract sequence in terms of its concrete representation may now be given:

$$sequence =_{\text{df}} seq(buffer, lastpointer, count)$$

Less formally, this may be written

$$\begin{aligned} sequence =_{\text{df}} \langle\, & buffer[lastpointer \ominus count], \\ & buffer[lastpointer \ominus count \oplus 1], \\ & \ldots, \\ & buffer[lastpointer \ominus 1] \rangle \end{aligned}$$

Another way of conveying this information would be by an example and a picture, which would be even less formal.

The invariant for the monitor is:

$$0 \leqslant count \leqslant N \wedge 0 \leqslant lastpointer \leqslant N-1$$

There are two reasons for waiting, which must be represented by condition variables:

$$nonempty: condition;$$

means that the count is greater than 0, and

nonfull: *condition*;

means that the count is less than *N*.

With this constructive approach to the design (Dijkstra 1968a), it is relatively easy to code the monitor without error.

```
bounded buffer : monitor
  begin buffer : array 0 .. N − 1 of portion;
    last pointer : 0 .. N − 1;
    count : 0 .. N;
    nonempty, nonfull : condition;
    procedure append(x : portion);
      begin if count = N then nonfull . wait;
        note 0 ⩽ count < N;
        buffer[lastpointer] := x;
        lastpointer := lastpointer ⊕ 1;
        count := count + 1;
        nonempty . signal
      end append;
    procedure remove(result x : portion);
      begin if count = 0 then nonempty . wait;
        note 0 < count ⩽ N;
        x := buffer[lastpointer ⊖ count]; count := count − 1;
        nonfull . signal
      end remove;
    count := 0; lastpointer := 0;
  end bounded buffer;
```

A formal proof of the correctness of this monitor with respect to the stated abstraction and invariant can be given if desired by techniques described in Chapter 8. However, these techniques seem not capable of dealing with subsequent examples of this paper.

Single-buffered input and output may be regarded as a special case of the bounded buffer with $N = 1$. In this case, the array can be replaced by a single variable, the *lastpointer* is redundant, and we get:

```
iostream : monitor
  begin buffer : portion;
    count : 0 .. 1;
    nonempty, nonfull : condition;
    procedure append(x : portion);
      begin if count = 1 then nonfull . wait;
        buffer := x;
        count := 1;
        nonempty . signal
      end append;
```

```
    procedure remove(result x: portion);
      begin if count = 0 then nonempty.wait;
        x := buffer;
        count := 0;
        nonfull.signal
      end remove;
    count := 0;
  end iostream;
```

If physical output is carried out by a separate special-purpose channel, then the interrupt from the channel should simulate a call of *iostream.remove(x)*; and similarly for physical input, simulating a call of *iostream.append(x)*.

12.5 Scheduled waits

Up to this point, we have assumed that when more than one program is waiting for the same condition, a signal will cause the longest waiting program to be resumed. This is a good simple scheduling strategy, which precludes indefinite overtaking of a waiting process.

However, in the design of an operating system, there are many cases when such simple scheduling on the basis of first-come–first-served is not adequate. In order to give a closer control over scheduling strategy, we introduce a further feature of a conditional wait, which makes it possible to specify as a parameter of the wait some indication of the priority of the waiting program, e.g.:

busy.wait(p);

When the condition is signalled, it is the program that specified the lowest value of p that is resumed. In using this facility, the designer of a monitor must take care to avoid the risk of indefinite overtaking; and often it is advisable to make priority a nondecreasing function of the time at which the wait commences.

This introduction of a 'scheduled wait' concedes to the temptation to make the condition concept more elaborate. The main justifications are:

(1) It has no effect whatsoever on the *logic* of a program, or on the formal proof rules. Any program which works without a scheduled wait will work with it, but possibly with better timing characteristics.
(2) The automatic ordering of the queue of waiting processes is a simple fast-scheduling technique, except when the queue is exceptionally long – and when it is, central processor time is not the major bottleneck.
(3) The maximum amount of storage required is one word per process. Without such a built-in scheduling method, each monitor may have to

allocate storage proportional to the number of its customers; the alternative of dynamic storage allocation in small chunks is unattractive at the low level of an operating system where monitors are found.

I shall yield to one further temptation, to introduce a Boolean function of conditions:

condname . queue

which yields the value *true* if anyone is waiting on *condname* and *false* otherwise. This can obviously be easily implemented by a couple of instructions, and affords valuable information which could otherwise be obtained only at the expense of extra storage, time, and trouble.

A trivially simple example is an *alarmclock* monitor, which enables a calling program to delay itself for a stated number *n* of time units, or *ticks*. There are two entries:

procedure *wakeme*(*n* : *integer*)
procedure *tick*;

The second of these is invoked by hardware (e.g. an interrupt) at regular intervals, say ten times per second. Local variables are

now : *integer*;

which records the current time (initially zero) and

wakeup : *condition*;

on which sleeping programs wait. But the *alarmsetting* at which these programs will be aroused is known at the time when they start the wait; and this can be used to determine the correct sequence of waking up.

```
alarmclock : monitor
  begin now : integer;
    wakeup : condition;
    procedure wakeme(n : integer);
      begin alarmsetting : integer;
        alarmsetting := now + n;
        while now < alarmsetting do wakeup . wait(alarmsetting);
        wakeup . signal;
        comment In case the next process is due to wake up at the
        same time;
      end;
    procedure tick;
      begin now := now + 1;
        wakeup . signal
      end;
    now := 0
  end alarmclock
```

In the program given above, the next candidate for wakening is actually woken at every tick of the clock. This will not matter if the frequency of ticking is low enough, and the overhead of an accepted signal is not too high.

I am grateful to A. Ballard and J. Horning for posing this problem.

12.6 Further examples

In proposing a new feature for a high-level language it is very difficult to make a convincing case that the feature will be both easy to use efficiently and easy to implement efficiently. Quality of implementation can be proved by a single good example, but ease and efficiency of use require a great number of realistic examples; otherwise it can appear that the new feature has been specially designed to suit the examples, or vice versa. This section contains a number of additional examples of solutions of familiar problems. Further examples may be found in Chapter 10.

12.6.1 Buffer allocation

The bounded buffer described in Section 12.4 was designed to be suitable only for sequences, with small portions, for example, message queues. If the buffers contain high-volume information (for example, files for pseudo off-line input and output), the bounded buffer may still be used to store the *addresses* of the buffers which are being used to hold the information. In this way, the producer can be filling one buffer while the consumer is emptying another buffer of the same sequence. But this requires an allocator for dynamic acquisition and relinquishment of *buffer addresses.* These may be declared as a type

type *bufferaddress* = 1 .. *B*;

where *B* is the number of buffers available for allocation.

The buffer allocator has two entries:

procedure *acquire*(**result** *b* : *bufferaddress*);

which delivers a free *bufferaddress b*; and

procedure *release*(*b* : *bufferaddress*);

which returns a *buffer address* when it is no longer required. In order to keep a record of free buffer addresses the monitor will need:

freepool : **powerset** *bufferaddress*;

which uses the Pascal powerset facility to define a variable whose values range over all sets of buffer addresses, from the empty set to the set containing all buffer addresses. It should be implemented as a *bitmap* of B consecutive bits, where the ith bit is 1 if and only if i is in the set. There is only one condition variable needed:

nonempty : *condition*

which means that *freepool* ≠ *empty*. The code for the allocator is:

```
bufferallocator : monitor
  begin freepool : powerset bufferaddress;
    nonempty : condition;
    procedure acquire (result b : bufferaddress);
      begin if freepool = empty then nonempty . wait;
        b := first(freepool);
        comment Any one would do;
        freepool := freepool − {b};
        comment Set subtraction;
      end acquire;
    procedure release(b : bufferaddress);
      begin freepool := freepool − {b};
        nonempty . signal
      end release;
    freepool := all buffer addresses
  end buffer allocator
```

The action of a producer and consumer may be summarized:

```
producer : begin b : bufferaddress; ...
             while not finished do
               begin bufferallocator . acquire(b);
                 ...fill buffer b...;
                 bounded buffer . append(b)
               end;...
           end producer;

consumer : begin b : bufferaddress;...
             while not finished do
               begin bounded buffer . remove(b);
                 ...empty buffer b...;
                 buffer allocator . release(b)
               end;...
           end consumer;
```

This buffer allocator would appear to be usable to share the buffers among several streams, each with its own producer and its own consumer, and its own instance of a bounded buffer monitor. Unfortunately, when the streams operate at widely varying speeds, and when the freepool is empty, the scheduling algorithm can exhibit persistent undesirable behaviour. If two producers are competing for each buffer as it becomes free, a first-come–first-served discipline of allocation will ensure (apparently fairly) that each gets alternate buffers; and they will consequently begin to produce at equal speeds. But if one consumer is a 1000 lines/min printer and the other is a 10 lines/min teletype, the faster consumer will be eventually reduced to the speed of the slower, since it cannot forever go faster than its producer. At this stage nearly all buffers will belong to the slower stream, so the situation could take a long time to clear.

A solution to this is to use a scheduled wait, to ensure that in heavy load conditions the available buffers will be shared reasonably fairly between the streams that are competing for them. Of course, inactive streams need not be considered, and streams for which the consumer is currently faster than the producer will never ask for more than two buffers anyway. In order to achieve fairness in allocation, it is sufficient to allocate a newly freed buffer to that one among the competing producers whose stream currently owns fewest buffers. Thus the system will seek a point as far away from the undesirable extreme as possible.

For this reason, the entries to the allocator should indicate for what stream the buffer is to be (or has been) used, and the allocator must keep a count of the current allocation to each stream in an array:

count : **array** *stream* **of** *integer*;

The new version of the allocator is:

```
bufferallocator : monitor
  begin freepool : powerset bufferaddress;
    nonempty : condition
    count : array stream of integer;
    procedure acquire(result b : bufferaddress; s : stream);
      begin if freepool = empty then nonempty . wait(count[s]);
        count[s] := count[s] + 1;
        b := first(freepool);
        freepool := freepool − {b}
      end acquire;
    procedure release(b : bufferaddress; s : stream)
      begin count[s] := count[s] − 1;
        freepool := freepool − [b];
        nonempty . signal
      end
    freepool := all bufferaddresses;
    for s : stream do count[s] := 0
  end bufferallocator
```

Of course, if a consumer stops altogether, perhaps owing to mechanical failure, the producer must also be halted before it has acquired too many buffers, even if no one else currently wants them. This can perhaps be most easily accomplished by appropriate fixing of the size of the bounded buffer for that stream and/or by ensuring that at least two buffers are reserved for each stream, even when inactive. It is an interesting comment on dynamic resource allocation that, as soon as resources are heavily loaded, the system must be designed to fall back toward a more static regime.

I am grateful to E. W. Dijkstra (1972a) for pointing out this problem and its solution.

12.6.2 Disk head scheduler

On a moving-head disk, the time taken to move the heads increases monotonically with the distance travelled. If several programs wish to move the heads, the average waiting time can be reduced by selecting, first, the program which wishes to move them the shortest distance. But unfortunately this policy is subject to an instability, since a program wishing to access a cylinder at one edge of the disk can be indefinitely overtaken by programs operating at the other edge or the middle.

A solution to this is to minimize the frequency of change of direction of movement of the heads. At any time, the heads are kept moving in a given direction, and they service the program requesting the nearest cylinder in that direction. If there is no such request, the direction changes, and the heads make another sweep across the surface of the disk. This may be called the 'elevator' algorithm, since it simulates the behaviour of a lift in a multi-storey building.

There are two entries to a disk head scheduler:

(1) *request*(*dest* : *cylinder*);

where

type *cylinder* = 0 .. *cylmax*;

which is entered by a program just *before* issuing the instruction to move the heads to cylinder *dest*.

(2) *release*;

which is entered by a program when it has made all the transfers it needs on the current cylinder.

The local data of the monitor must include a record of the current head position, *headpos*, the current direction of *sweep*, and whether the disk is *busy*:

```
    headpos : cylinder;
    direction : (up, down);
    busy : Boolean
```

We need two conditions, one for requests waiting for an *upsweep* and the other for requests waiting for a *downsweep*:

```
    upsweep, downsweep : condition
```

```
diskhead : monitor
  begin headpos : cylinder;
    direction : (up, down);
    busy : Boolean;
    upsweep, downsweep : condition;
    procedure request(dest : cylinder);
      begin if busy then
        {if headpos < dest ∨ headpos = dest ∧ direction = up
         then upsweep . wait(dest)
         else downsweep . wait(cylmax-dest)};
      busy := true; headpos := dest
      end request;
    procedure release;
      begin busy := false;
        if direction = up then
          {if upsweep. queue then upsweep. signal
                              else {direction := down;
                                    downsweep. signal}}
        else if downsweep. queue then downsweep. signal
                                 else {direction := up;
                                       upsweep. signal}
      end release;
      headpos := 0; direction := up; busy := false
  end diskhead;
```

12.6.3 Readers and writers

As a more significant example, we take a problem which arises in on-line real-time applications such as airspace control. Suppose that each aircraft is represented by a record, and that this record is kept up to date by a number of 'writer' processes and accessed by a number of 'reader' processes. Any number of 'reader' processes may simultaneously access the same record, but obviously any process which is updating (writing) the individual components of the record must have exclusive access to it, or chaos will ensue. Thus we need a class of monitors; an instance of this class local to *each* individual aircraft record will enforce the required discipline for that record. If there are many aircraft, there is a strong motivation for minimizing local data of the monitor; and if each read or write operation is brief, we should also minimize the time taken by each monitor entry.

When many readers are interested in a single aircraft record, there is a danger that a writer will be indefinitely prevented from keeping that record up to date. We therefore decide that a new reader should not be permitted to start if there is a writer waiting. Similarly, to avoid the danger of indefinite exclusion of readers, all readers waiting at the end of a write should have priority over the next writer. Note that this is a very different scheduling rule from that propounded in Courtois *et al.* (1971), and does not seem to require such subtlety in implementation. Nevertheless, it may be more suited to this kind of application, where it is better to read stale information than to wait indefinitely!

The monitor obviously requires four local procedures:

startread	entered by reader who wishes to read.
endread	entered by reader who has finished reading.
startwrite	entered by writer who wishes to write.
endwrite	entered by writer who has finished writing.

We need to keep a count of the number of users who are reading, so that the last reader to finish will known this fact:

readercount : *integer*

We also need a *Boolean* to indicate that someone is actually writing:

busy : *Boolean*;

We introduce separate conditions for readers and writers to wait on:

OKtoread, *OKtowrite* : *condition*;

The following annotation is relevant:

$$OKtoread =_{\mathrm{df}} \neg\, busy$$
$$OKtowrite = \neg\, busy \wedge readercount = 0$$
$$invariant : busy \Rightarrow readercount = 0$$

class *readers and writers* : **monitor**
  begin *readercount* : *integer*;
    busy : *Boolean*;
    OKtoread, *OKtowrite* : *condition*;
    procedure *startread*;
      begin if *busy* ∨ *OKtowrite*. *queue* **then** *OKtoread*. *wait*;
        readercount := *readercount* + 1;
        OKtoread. *signal*;
        comment *Once one reader can start, they all can*;
      end *startread*;

```
    procedure endread;
      begin readercount := readercount − 1;
        if readercount = 0 then OKtowrite.signal
      end endread;
    procedure startwrite;
      begin
        if readercount ≠ 0 ∨ busy then OKtowrite.wait
        busy := true
      end startwrite;
    procedure endwrite;
      begin busy := false;
        if OKtoread.queue then OKtoread.signal
                          else OKtowrite.signal
      end endwrite;
    readercount := 0;
    busy := false;
  end readers and writers;
```

I am grateful to Dave Gorman for assisting in the discovery of this solution.

12.7 Conclusion

This paper suggests that an appropriate structure for a module of an operating system, which schedules resources for parallel user processes, is very similar to that of a data representation used by a sequential program. However, in the case of monitors, the bodies of the procedure must be protected against re-entrance by being implemented as critical regions. The textual grouping of critical regions together with the data which they update seems much superior to critical regions scattered through the user program, as described in Dijkstra (1968b) and Hoare ([22]). It also corresponds to the traditional practice of the writers of operating-system supervisors. It can be recommended without reservation.

However, it is much more difficult to be confident about the condition concept as a synchronizing primitive. The synchronizing facility which is easiest to use is probably the conditional *wait* (Brinch Hansen 1972a; Hoare [22]).

$$wait(B);$$

where B is a general Boolean expression (it causes the given process to wait until B becomes true); but this may be too inefficient for general use in operating systems, because its implementation requires re-evaluation of the expression B after every exit from a procedure of the monitor. The condition variable gives the programmer better control over efficiency and over scheduling; it was designed to be very primitive, and to have a simple proof rule. But perhaps some other compromise between convenience and efficiency might be better. The question whether the signal should always be the last operation of a monitor procedure is still open. These problems will be studied in the design and implementation of a pilot project operating system, currently enjoying the support of the Science Research Council of Great Britain.

Another question which will be studied will be that of the disjointness of monitors: Is it possible to design a separate isolated monitor for each kind of resource, so that it will make sensible scheduling decisions for that resource, using only the minimal information about the utilization of that resource, and using no information about the utilization of any resource administered by other monitors? In principle, it would seem that, when more knowledge of the status of the entire system is available, it should be easier to take decisions nearer to optimality. Furthermore, in principle, independent scheduling of different kinds of resource can lead to deadly embrace. These considerations would lead to the design of a traditional 'monolithic' monitor, maintaining large system tables, all of which can be accessed and updated by any of the procedures of the monitor.

There is no *a priori* reason why the attempt to split the functions of an operating system into a number of isolated disjoint monitors should succeed. It can be made to succeed only by discovering and implementing good scheduling algorithms in each monitor. In order to avoid undesirable interactions between the separate scheduling algorithms, it appears necessary to observe the following principles:

(1) Never seek to make an optimal decision; merely seek to avoid persistently pessimal decisions.
(2) Do not seek to present the user with a virtual machine which is better than the actual hardware; merely seek to pass on the speed, size, and flat unopiniated structure of a simple hardware design.
(3) Use pre-emptive techniques in preference to nonpre-emptive ones where possible.
(4) Use 'grain of time' (Dijkstra, 1972b) methods to secure independence of scheduling strategies.
(5) Keep a low variance (as well as a low mean) on waiting times.
(6) Avoid fixed priorities; instead, try to ensure that every program in the system makes reasonably steady progress. In particular, avoid indefinite overtaking.
(7) Ensure that when demand for resources outstrips the supply (i.e. in overload conditions), the behaviour of the scheduler is satisfactory (i.e. thrashing is avoided).
(8) Make rules for the correct and sensible use of monitor calls, and assume

that user programs will obey them. Any checking which is necessary should be done not by a central shared monitor, but rather by an algorithm (called the *user envelope*) which is local to each process executing a user program. This algorithm should be implemented at least partially in the hardware (e.g. base and range registers, address translation mechanisms, capabilities, etc.).

It is the possibility of constructing separate monitors for different purposes, and of separating the scheduling decisions embodied in monitors from the checking embodied in user envelopes, that may justify a hope that monitors are an appropriate concept for the structuring of an operating system.

12.8 Acknowledgements

The development of the monitor concept is due to frequent discussions and communications with E. W. Dijkstra and P. Brinch-Hansen. A monitor corresponds to the 'secretary' described in Dijkstra (1972b), and is also described in Brinch Hansen (1972b; 1973).

Acknowledgement is also due to the support of IFIP WG.2.3, which provides a meeting place at which these and many other ideas have been germinated, fostered, and tested.

THIRTEEN

Hints on programming-language design

This paper originated from Hoare's keynote address at the ACM SIGPLAN conference in Boston, October 1973 (although it did not appear in the proceedings, it was distributed at the conference). It was subsequently printed as a Stanford Artificial Intelligence Memo (AIM-224, STAN-CS-73-403) in December of that year. The version printed here was published as [43].

Hoare was active in committees working on the design and control of programming languages over many years: he made many contributions to the *ALGOL Bulletin* (e.g. [13]), was a member of IFIP's WG 2.1 (1962–74) and even chaired the ECMA TC10 group working on the standardization of PL/I. This paper is perhaps the most rounded of his published comments on language-design philosophy. The earlier [25] makes more pointed references (including a very positive one to APL); [40] and [57] make further points.

This paper must clearly be read in the context of its date of composition (1973). The relative weight of comment on debugging and reasoning about programs clearly changed as a result of his own later research. Also, a richer notion of types would be appropriate today. But the sound advice in this paper transcends any minor aspects in which it might be considered to be out of date. (Many versions exist of the story about the Mariner I Venus probe. All of them blame software; they differ as to the precise details.)

Subsequent to this publication, Hoare and Wirth consulted for SRI on their 'Yellow' language response to the 'Tinman' requirements. Their consistent advice to simplify even this language was unheeded – but the final Ada language (the 'Green' proposal) was even more baroque.

Abstract

This paper presents the view that a programming language is a tool that should assist the programmer in the most difficult aspects of his art, namely program design, documentation, and debugging. It discusses the objective criteria for evaluating a language design,

C. A. R. Hoare, Hints on programming language design. In C. Bunyan (ed.) *Computer Systems Reliability*, State of the Art Report Vol. 20, pp. 505–34. Reprinted with permission.

and illustrates them by application to language features of both high-level languages and machine-code programming. It concludes with an annotated reading list, recommended for all intending language designers.

13.1 Introduction

I would like in this paper to present a philosophy of the design and evaluation of programming languages that I have adopted and developed over a number of years, namely that the primary purpose of a programming language is to help the programmer in the practice of his art. I do not wish to deny that there are many other desirable properties of a programming language: for example, machine independence, stability of specification, use of familiar notations, a large and useful library, existing popularity, or sponsorship by a rich and powerful organization. These aspects are often dominant in the choice of a programming language by its users, but I wish to argue that they ought not to be. I shall therefore express myself strongly. I fear that each reader will find some of my points wildly controversial; I expect he will find other points that are obvious and even boring; I hope that he will find a few points that are new and worth pursuing.

My approach is first to isolate the most difficult aspects of the programmer's task, and state in general terms how a programming-language design can assist in meeting these difficulties. I discuss a number of goals, which have been followed in the past by language designers, and which I regard as comparatively irrelevant or even illusory. I then turn to particular aspects of familiar high-level programming languages, and explain why they are in some respects much better than machine-code programming, and in certain cases worse. Finally, I draw a distinction between language-feature design and the design of complete languages.

13.2 Principles

If a programming language is regarded as a tool to aid the programmer, it should give him the greatest assistance in the most difficult aspects of his art, namely program design, documentation, and debugging.

(1) *Program design.* The first, and very difficult, aspect of design is deciding what the program is to do, and formulating this as a clear, precise, and acceptable specification. Often just as difficult is deciding how to do it: how to divide a complex task into simpler subtasks, and to specify the

purpose of each part, and define clear, precise, and efficient interfaces between them. A good programming language should give assistance in expressing not only how the program is to run, but what it is intended to accomplish; and it should enable this to be expressed at various levels, from the overall strategy to the details of coding and data representation. It should assist in establishing and enforcing conventions and disciplines that will ensure harmonious co-operation of the parts of a large program when they are developed separately and finally assembled together.

(2) *Programming documentation.* The purpose of program documentation is to explain to a human reader the way in which a program works so that it can be successfully adapted after it goes into service, to meet the changing requirements of its users, or to improve it in the light of increased knowledge, or just to remove latent errors and oversights. The view that documentation is something that is added to a program after it has been commissioned seems to be wrong in principle and counter-productive in practice. Instead, documentation must be regarded as an integral part of the process of design and coding. A good programming language will encourage and assist the programmer to write clear self-documenting code, and even perhaps to develop and display a pleasant style of writing. The readability of programs is immeasurably more important than their writeability.

(3) *Program debugging.* Program debugging can often be the most tiresome, expensive, and unpredictable phase of program development, particularly at the stage of assembling subprograms written by many programmers over a long period. The best way to reduce these problems is by successful initial design of the program, and by careful documentation during the construction of code. But even the best-designed and best-documented programs will contain errors and inadequacies, which the computer itself can help to eliminate. A good programming language will give maximum assistance in this. Firstly, the notations should be designed to reduce as far as possible the scope for coding error; or at least to guarantee that such errors can be detected by a compiler, before the program even begins to run. Certain programming errors cannot always be detected in this way, and must be cheaply detectable at run time; in no case can they be allowed to give rise to machine- or implementation-dependent effects, which are inexplicable in terms of the language itself. This is a criterion to which I give the name *security*. Of course, the compiler itself must be utterly reliable, so that its user has complete confidence that any unexpected effect was occasioned by his own program. And the compiler must be compact and fast, so that there is no appreciable delay or cost involved in correcting a program in source code and resubmitting for another run; and the object code too should be fast and efficient, so that extra instructions can be inserted even in large and time-consuming programs in order to help detect their errors or inefficiencies.

A necessary condition for the achievement of any of these objectives is the utmost simplicity in the design of the language. Without simplicity, even the language designer himself cannot evaluate the consequences of his design decisions. Without simplicity, the compiler writer cannot achieve even reliability, and certainly cannot construct compact, fast, and efficient compilers. But the main beneficiary of simplicity is the user of the language. In all spheres of human intellectual and practical activity, from carpentry to golf, from sculpture to space travel, the true craftsman is the one who thoroughly understands his tools. And this applies to programmers too. A programmer who fully understands his language can tackle more complex tasks, and complete them more quickly and more satisfactorily, than if he did not. In fact, a programmer's need for an understanding of his language is so great that it is almost impossible to persuade him to change to a new one. No matter what the deficiencies of his current language, he has learned to live with them; he has learned how to mitigate their effects by discipline and documentation, and even to take advantage of them in ways that would be impossible in a new and cleaner language which avoids the deficiency.

It therefore seems especially necessary in the design of a new programming language, intended to attract programmers away from their current high-level language, to pursue the goal of simplicity to an extreme, so that a programmer can readily learn and remember all its features, can select the best facility for each of his purposes, can fully understand the effects and consequences of each decision, and can then concentrate the major part of his intellectual effort on understanding his problem and his programs rather than his tool.

A high standard of simplicity is set by machine or assembly code programming for a small computer. Such a machine has an extremely uniform structure, for example a main store consisting of 2^m words numbered consecutively from zero up, a few registers, and a simple synchronous standard interface for communication with and control of peripheral equipment. There is a small range of instructions, each of which has a uniform format; and the effect of each instruction is simple, affecting at most one register and one location of store or one peripheral. Even more important, this effect can be described and understood quite independently of every other instruction in the repertoire. And finally, the programmer has an immediate feedback on the compactness and efficiency of his code. Enthusiasts for high-level languages are often surprised at the complexity of the problems that have been tackled with such simple tools.

On larger modern computers, with complex instruction repertoires and even more complex operating systems, it is especially desirable that a high-level language design should aim at the simplicity and clear modular description of the best hardware designs. But the only widely used languages that approach this ideal are FORTRAN, LISP, and ALGOL 60, and a few languages developed from them. I fear that most more modern programming languages are getting even more complicated; and it is particularly irritating when their proponents claim that future hardware designs should be oriented towards the implementation of this complexity.

13.3 Discussion

The previous two sections have argued that the objective criteria for good language design may be summarized in five catch phrases: simplicity, security, fast translation, efficient object code, and readability. However desirable these may seem, many language designers have adopted alternative principles that belittle the importance of some or all of these criteria, perhaps those that their own languages have failed to achieve.

13.3.1 Simplicity

Some language designers have replaced the objective of simplicity by that of modularity, by which they mean that a programmer who cannot understand the whole of his language can get by with a limited understanding of only part of it. For programs that work as the programmer intended this may be feasible; but if his program does not work, and accidentally invokes some feature of the language that he does not know, he will get into serious trouble. If he is lucky the implementation will detect his mistake, but he will not be able to understand the diagnostic message. Otherwise, he is even more helpless. If to the complexity of his language is added the complexity of its implementation, the complexity of its operating environment, and even the complexity of institutional standards for the use of the language, it is not surprising that when faced with a complex programming task so many programmers are overwhelmed.

Another replacement of simplicity as an objective has been orthogonality of design. An example of orthogonality is the provision of complex integers, on the argument that we need reals and integers and complex reals, so why not complex integers? In the early days of hardware design, some very ingenious but arbitrary features turned up in order codes as a result of orthogonal combinations of the function bits of an instruction, on the grounds that some clever programmer would find a use for them; and some clever programmer always did. Hardware designers have now learned more sense; but language designers are clever programmers and have not.

The principles of modularity, or orthogonality, insofar as they contribute to overall simplicity, are an excellent means to an end; but as a substitute for simplicity they are very questionable. Since in practice they have proved to be a technically more difficult achievement than simplicity, it is foolish to adopt them as primary objectives.

13.3.2 Security

The objective of security has also been widely ignored; it is believed instead that coding errors should be removed by the programmer with the assistance of a so-called *checkout* compiler. But this approach has several practical disadvantages. For example, the checkout compiler and the standard compiler are often not equally reliable. Even if they are, it is impossible to guarantee that they will give the same results, especially on a subtly incorrect program; and, when they do not, there is nothing to help the programmer find the mistake. For a large and complex program the extra inefficiency of the debugging runs may be serious; and even on small programs the cost of loading a large debugging system can be high. You should always pity the fate of the programmer whose task is so difficult that his program will not fit into the computer together with your sophisticated debugging package. Finally, it is absurd to make elaborate security checks on debugging runs, when no trust is put in the results, and then remove them in production runs, when an erroneous result could be expensive or disastrous. What would we think of a sailing enthusiast who wears his life-jacket when training on dry land but takes it off as soon as he goes to sea? Fortunately, with a secure language, the security is equally tight for production and for debugging.

13.3.3 Fast translation

In the early days of high-level languages it was openly stated that speed of compilation was of minor importance, because programs would be compiled only once and then executed many times. After a while it was realized that the reverse was often true, that a program would be compiled frequently while it was being debugged; but instead of constructing a fast translator, language designers turned to independent compilation, which permits a programmer to avoid recompiling those parts of his program that he has not changed since the last time. But this is a poor substitute for fast compilation, and has many practical disadvantages. Often it encourages or even forces a programmer to split a large program into modules that are too small to express properly the structure of his problem. It entails the use of wide interfaces and cumbersome and expensive parameter lists at inappropriate places. And even worse, it prevents the compiler from adequately checking the validity of these interfaces. It requires additional file space to store bulky intermediate code, in addition to source code, which must, of course, never be thrown away. It discourages the programmer from making changes to his data structure or representation, since this would involve a heavy burden of recompilation. And finally the linkage editor is often cumbersome to invoke and expensive to execute. And it is all so unnecessary, if the compiler for a good language can work faster than the linkage editor anyway.

If you want to make a fast compiler even faster, I can suggest three techniques, which have all the benefits of independent compilation and none of the disadvantages.

(1) *Prescan.* The slowest part of a modern fast compiler is the lexical scan, which inputs individual characters, assembles them into words or numbers, identifies basic symbols, removes spaces, and separates the comments. If the source text of the program can be stored in a compact form in which this character handling does not have to be repeated, compilation time may be halved, with the added advantage that the original source program may still be listed (with suitably elegant indentation); and so the amount of file storage is reduced by a factor considerably greater than two. A similar technique was used by the PACT I assembler for the IBM 701.

(2) *Precompile.* This is a directive that can be given to the compiler after submitting *any* initial segment of a large program. It causes the compiler to make a complete dump of its workspace, including dictionary and object code, in a specified user file. When the user wishes to add to his program and run it, he directs the compiler to recover the dump and proceed. When his additions are adequately tested, a further precompile instruction can be given. If the programmer needs to modify a precompiled procedure, he can just redeclare it in the block containing his main program, and normal ALGOL-like scope rules will do the rest. An occasional complete recompilation will consolidate the changes after they have been fully tested. The technique of precompilation is effective only on single-pass compilers; it was successfully incorporated in the Elliott ALGOL programming system.

(3) *Dump.* This is an instruction that can be called by the user program during execution, and causes a complete binary dump of its code and workspace into a named user file. The dump can be restored and restarted at the instruction following the dump by an instruction to the operating system. If all necessary data input and initialization is carried out before the dump, the time spent on this as well as recompilation time can be saved. This provides a simple and effective way of achieving the FORTRAN effect of block data, and was successfully incorporated in the implementation of Elliott ALGOL.

The one remaining use of independent compilation is to link a high-level language with machine code. But even here independent compilation is the wrong technique, involving all the inefficiency of procedure call and all the complexity of parameter access at just the point where it hurts most. A far better solution is to allow machine code instructions to be inserted in-line within a high-level language program, as was done in Elliott ALGOL; or, better, provide a macro facility for machine code, as in PL/360.

Independent compilation is a solution to yesterday's problems; today it has grown into a problem in its own right. The wise designer will prefer to avoid rather than solve such problems.

13.3.4 Efficient object code

There is another argument, which is all too prevalent among enthusiastic language designers, that efficiency of object code is no longer important; that the speed and capacity of computers is increasing and their price is coming down; and that the programming-language designer might as well take advantage of this. This is an argument that would be quite acceptable if used to justify an efficiency loss of ten or twenty percent, or even thirty and forty percent. But all too frequently it is used to justify an efficiency loss of a factor of two, or ten, or even more; and worse, the overhead is not only in time taken but in space occupied by the running program. In no other engineering discipline would such avoidable overhead be tolerated, and it should not be in programming-language design, for the following reasons:

(1) The magnitude of the tasks we wish computers to perform is growing faster than the cost-effectiveness of the hardware.
(2) However cheap and fast a computer is, it will be cheaper and faster to use it more efficiently.
(3) In the future we must hope that hardware designers will pay increasing attention to reliability rather than to speed and cost.
(4) The speed, cost, and reliability of peripheral equipment are not improving at the same rate as those of processors.
(5) If anyone is to be allowed to introduce inefficiency it should be the user programmer, not the language designer. The user programmer can take advantage of this freedom to write better-structured and clearer programs, and should not have to expend extra effort to obscure the structure and write less clear programs just to regain the efficiency that has been so arrogantly pre-empted by the language designer.

There is a widespread myth that a language designer can afford to ignore machine efficiency, because it can be regained when required by the use of a sophisticated optimizing compiler. This is false: there is nothing that the good engineer can afford to ignore. The only language that has been optimized with general success is FORTRAN, which was very specifically designed for that very purpose. But even in FORTRAN, optimization has grave disadvantages:

(1) An optimizing compiler is usually large, slow, unreliable, and late.
(2) Even with a reliable compiler, there is no guarantee than an optimized program will have the same results as a normally compiled one.
(3) A small change to an optimized program may switch off optimization with an upredictable and unacceptable loss of efficiency.
(4) The most subtle danger is that optimization tends to remove from the programmer his fundamental control over and responsibility for the quality of his programs.

The solution to these problems is to produce a language for which a simple straightforward 'non-pessimizing' compiler will produce straightforward object programs of acceptable compactness and efficiency: similar to those produced by a resolutely non-clever (but also non-stupid) machine-code programmer. Make sure that the language is sufficiently expressive to enable most other optimizations to be made in the language itself; and finally, make the language so simple, clear, regular, and free from side-effects that a general machine-independent optimizer can simply translate an inefficient program into a more efficient one with guaranteed identical effects, and expressed in the same source language. The fact that the user can inspect the results of optimization in his own language mitigates many of the defects listed above.

13.3.5 Readability

The objective of readability by human beings has sometimes been denied in favour of readability by a machine; and sometimes even been denied in favour of abbreviation of writing, achieved by a wealth of default conventions and implicit assumptions. It is of course possible for a compiler or service program to expand the abbreviations, fill in the defaults, and make explicit the assumptions. But, in practice, experience shows that it is very unlikely that the output of a computer will ever be more readable than its input, except in such trivial but important aspects as improved indentation. Since in principle programs should be read by others, or re-read by their authors, *before* being submitted to the computer, it would be wise for the programming language designer to concentrate on the easier task of designing a readable language to begin with.

13.4 Comment conventions

If the purpose of a programming language is to assist in the documentation of programs, the design of a superb comment convention is obviously our most important concern. In low-level programming, the greater part of the space on each line is devoted to comment. A comment is always terminated by an end-of-line, and starts either in a fixed column or with a special symbol allocated for this purpose:

LDA X [THIS IS A COMMENT

The introduction of free format into high-level languages prevents the use of the former method; but it is surprising that few languages have adopted the latter. ALGOL 60 has two comment conventions. One is to enclose the text of a comment between the basic word **comment** and a semicolon:

comment this is a comment;

This has several disadvantages over the low-level convention:

(1) The basic word **comment** is too long. It occupies space that would be better occupied by the text of the comment, and is particularly discouraging to short comments.
(2) The comment can appear only after a **begin** or a semicolon, although it would sometimes be more relevant elsewhere.
(3) If the semicolon at the end is accidentally omitted, the compiler will without warning ignore the next following statement.
(4) One cannot put program text within a comment, since a comment must not contain a semicolon.

The second comment convention of ALGOL 60 permits a comment between an **end** and the next following semicolon, **end**, or **else**. This has proved most unfortunate, since omission of a semicolon has frequently led to the compiler ignoring the next following statement:

... **end** this is a mistake $A[i] := x$;

The FORTRAN comment convention defines as comment the whole of a line containing a C in the first column.

C THIS IS A COMMENT

Its main disadvantages are that is does not permit comments on the same line as the code to which they refer, and that it discourages the use of short comments. An unfortunate consequence is that a well-annotated FORTRAN program occupies many pages, even though the greater part of each page is blank. This in itself makes the program unnecessarily difficult to read and understand.

The comment convention of COBOL suffers from the same disadvantages as that of FORTRAN, since it insists that commentary should be in a separate paragraph.

More recently designed languages have introduced special bracketing symbols (e.g. /* and */) to enclose comments, which can therefore be placed anywhere in the program text where they are relevant:

/* THIS IS A COMMENT */

But there still remains the awkward problem of omitting or mispunching one of the comment brackets. In some languages, this will cause omission of statements between two comments; in others it may cause the whole of the rest of the program to be ignored. Neither of these disasters are likely to occur in low-level programs, where the end-of-line terminates a comment.

13.5 Syntax

Another aspect of programming-language design that is often considered trivial or arbritrary is its syntax. But this is also a mistake: the designer should select and observe the best possible syntactic framework for his language, for two important practical reasons:

(1) In a modern fast compiler a significant time can be taken in the assembly of characters into meaningful symbols (identifiers, numbers, and basic words) and in checking the context-free structure of the program.

(2) When a program contains a syntactic error it is important that the compiler should be able to pinpoint the error accurately, to diagnose its cause, recover from it, and continue checking the rest of the program. Recall the first American space probe to Venus, reportedly lost because FORTRAN cannot recognize a missing comma in a *DO* statement. In FORTRAN the statement:

$$DO\ 17\ I = 1\ 10$$

looks to the compiler like an assignment to a (probably undeclared) variable *DO17I:*

$$DO17I = 110.$$

In low-level programming, the use of fixed field format neatly solves both problems. The position and length of each meaningful symbol is known, and it can be copied and compared as a whole without even examining the individual characters; and if one field contains an error it can be immediately pinpointed, and checking can be resumed at the very next field.

Fortunately, free-format techniques have been discovered that solve the problems nearly as neatly as fixed format. The use of a finite-state machine to define the assembly of characters into symbols, and one of the more restrictive forms of context-free grammars (e.g. precedence or topdown or both) to define the structure of a program: these must be recommended to every language designer. It is certainly possible for a machine to analyse more complex grammars, but there is every indication that the human programmer will find greater difficulty, particularly if an error is present or even only suspected. If a compiler cannot diagnose the syntax of an individual statement until it reaches the end of the program, what hope has a poor human?

As an example of what happens when a language departs from the best-known technology, that of context-free syntax, consider the case of the labelled END. This is a convention whereby any identifier between an END and its semicolon automatically signals the end of the procedure with that name, and of any enclosed program structure even if it has no END of its own. At first sight this is a harmless notational convenience, which Peter Landin might call 'syntactic sugar'; but in practice the consequences are disastrous. If the programmer accidentally omits an END *anywhere* in his program, it will automatically and without warning be inserted just before the next following labelled END, which is very unlikely to be where it was wanted. Landin's phrase for this would be 'syntactic rat poison'. Wise programmers have therefore learned to avoid the labelled END, which is a great pity, since if the labelled END had been used merely to *check* the correctness of the nesting of statements it would have been very useful, and permitted earlier and cleaner error recovery, as well as remaining within the disciplines of context-free languages. Here is a classic example of a language feature that combines danger to the programmer with difficulty for the implementor. It is all too easy to reconcile criteria of demerit.

13.6 Arithmetic expressions

A major feature of FORTRAN, which gives it the name FORmula TRANslator, is the introduction of the arithmetic expression. ALGOL 60 extends this idea by the introduction of a conditional expression. Why is this such an advance over assembly code? The traditional answer is that it appeals to the programmer's familiarity with mathematical notation. But this only leads to the more fundamental question, why is the notation of arithmetic expressions of such benefit to the mathematician? The reason seems to be quite subtle and fundamental. It embodies the principles of structuring, which underlie all our attempts to master a complex problem or control a complex situation by analysing it into simpler subproblems, with clean and narrow interfaces between them.

Consider an arithmetic expression of the form

$$E + F$$

where E and F may themselves be simple or complex arithmetic expressions.

(1) The meaning of this whole expression can be understood wholly in terms of an understanding of the meanings of E and F;
(2) the purpose of each part consists solely in its contribution to the purpose of the whole;
(3) the meaning of the two parts can be understood wholly indepen-dendently of each other;
(4) if E or F is itself an arithmetic expression, the same structuring principle can be applied to the analysis of the parts as is applied to the understanding of the whole;
(5) the interface between the parts is clear, narrow, and well controlled: in this case just a single number; and, finally,
(6) the separation of the parts and their relation to the whole is clearly apparent from their written form.

These seem to be six fundamental principles of structuring: transparency of meaning and purpose; independence of parts; recursive application; narrow interfaces; and manifestness of structure. In the case of arithmetic expressions these six principles are reconciled and achieved together with very high efficiency of implementation. But the applicability of the arithmetic expression is seriously limited by the extreme narrowness of the interface. Often the programmer wishes to deal with much larger data structures, for example vectors or matrices or lists; and languages such as APL and LISP have permitted the use of expressions with these structures as operands and results. This seems to be an excellent direction of advance in programming-language design, particularly for special-purpose languages. But the advance is not purchased without some penalty in efficiency and programmer control. The very reason why arithmetic expressions can be evaluated with such efficiency is that the operands and results of each subexpression are sufficiently small to be held in a high-speed register, or stored and recovered from a main-store location by a single instruction. When the operands are too large, and especially when they might be partially or wholly stored on backing store, it becomes much more efficient to use updating operations, since then the space occupied by one of the operands can be used to hold the result. It would therefore seem advisable to introduce special notations into a language to denote such operations as adding one matrix to another, appending one list to another, or making a new entry in a file; for example:

$A. + B$	instead of $A := A + B$ if and A and B are matrices
L1.append($L2$)	if $L1$ and $L2$ are lists.
F. output(x)	if F is a file.

Another efficiency problem that arises from the attempt of a language to provide large data structures and built-in operations on them is that the implementation must select a particular machine representation for the data, and use it uniformly, even in cases where other representations might be considerably more efficient. For example, the APL representation is fine for small matrices, but is very inappropriate or even impossible for large and sparse ones. The LISP representation of lists is very efficient for data held wholly in main store, but becomes inefficient when the lists are so long that they must be held on backing store, particularly disks and tapes. Often the efficiency of a representation depends on the relative frequency of various forms of operation, and therefore the representation should be different in different programs, or even be changed from one phase of a program to another.

A solution to this problem is to design a general-purpose language that provides the programmer with the tools to design and implement his own representation for data and code the operations upon it. This is the main justification for the design of 'extensible' languages, which so many designers have aimed at, with rather great lack of success. In order to succeed, it will be necessary to recognize the following:

(1) The need for an exceptionally efficient base language in order to define the extensions.
(2) The avoidance of any form of syntactic extension to the language. All that is needed is to extend the meaning of the existing operators of the language, an idea that was called *overloading* by McCarthy.
(3) The complete avoidance of any form of automatic type transfer, coercion, or default convention, other than those implemented as an extension by the programmer himself.

I fear that most designers of extensible languages have spurned the technical simplifications that make them feasible.

13.7 Program structures

However far the use of expressions and functional notations may be extended, a programmer will eventually require the capability of updating his environment. Sometimes this will be because he wants to perform input and output, sometimes because it is more efficient to store the results of a computation so that the stored value can be used rather than recomputed at a later time, and sometimes because it is a natural way of representing his problem (for example, in the case of discrete-event simulation or the monitoring and control of some real-world process).

Thus it is necessary to depart from the welcome simplicity of the mathematical expression, but to attempt to preserve as far as possible the structuring principles that it embodies. Fortunately, ALGOL 60 (in its compound, conditional, **for**, and **procedure** statements) has shown the way in which this can be done. The advantages of the use of these program structures is becoming apparent even to programmers using languages that do not provide the notations to express them.

The introduction of program structures into a language not only helps the programmer but also does not injure the efficiency of an implementation. Indeed, the avoidance of wild jumping will be of positive benefit on machines with slave stores or paging hardware; and if a compiler makes any attempt at optimization, the clear indication of the control structure of a program can only simplify this task.

There is one case where ALGOL 60 does not provide an appropriate structure, and that is when a selection must be made from more than two alternatives in accordance with some integer value. In this case, the programmer must declare a switch, specifying a list of labels, and then jump to the *i*th label in this list.

```
        switch SS:= L1, L2, L3;
          ⋮
        go to SS[i];
    L1:   Q1; go to L;
    L2:   Q2; go to L;
    L3:   Q3;
     L:
```

Unfortunately the introduction of the switch as a nameable entity is not only an extra complexity in the language and implementation but also gives plenty of scope for tricky programming and even trickier errors, particularly when jumping to some common continuation point on completion of the alternative action.

The first language designers to deal with the problem of the switch proposed to generalize it by providing the concept of the label array, into which the programmer could store label values. This has some peculiarly unpleasant consequences in addition to the disadvantages of the switch. Firstly, it obscures the program, so that its control structure is not apparent from the form of the program but can only be determined by a run-time trace. And, secondly, the programmer is given the power to jump back into the middle of a block he has already exited from, with unpredictable consequences unless a run-time check is inserted. In ALGOL 60 the scope rules make this error detectable at compile time.

The way to avoid all these problems is a very simple extension to the ALGOL 60 conditional notation, a construction that I have called the **case** construction. In this notation, the example of the switch shown above would take the form:

case i **of**
{Q_1,
Q_2,
Q_3};

This was my first programming-language invention, of which I am still most proud, since it appears to bear no trace of compensating disadvantage.

13.8 Variables

One of the most powerful and most dangerous aspects of machine-code programming is that each individual instruction of the code can change the content of any register or store location and alter the condition of any peripheral: it can even change its neighbouring instructions or itself. Worse still, the identity of the location changed is not always apparent from the written form of the instruction; it cannot be determined until run time, when the values of base registers, index registers, and indirect addresses are known. This does not matter if the program is correct, but if there is the slightest error, even only in a single bit, there is no limit to the damage that may be done, and no limit to the difficulty of tracing the cause of the damage. In summary, the interface between every two consecutive instructions in a machine-code program consists of the state of the entire machine: registers, main store, backing stores, and all peripheral equipment.

In a high-level language, the programmer is deprived of the dangerous power to update his own program while it is running. Even more valuable, he has the power to split his machine into a number of separate variables, arrays, files, etc.; when he wishes to update any of these he must quote its name explicitly on the left of the assignment, so that the identity of the part of the machine subject to change is immediately apparent; and, finally, a high-level language can guarantee that all variables are disjoint, and that updating any one of them cannot possibly have any effect on any other.

Unfortunately, many of these advantages are not maintained in the design of procedures and parameters in ALGOL 60 and other languages. But instead of mending these minor faults, many language designers have preferred to extend them throughout the whole language by introducing the concept of reference, pointer, or indirect address into the language as an assignable item of data. This immediately gives rise in a high-level language to one of the most notorious confusions of machine code, namely that between an address and its contents. Some languages attempt to solve this by even more confusing automatic coercion rules. Worst still, an indirect assignment through a pointer, just as in machine code, can update any store location whatsoever, and the damage is no longer confined to the variable explicitly named as the target of assignment. For example, in ALGOL 68, the assignment:

$$x := y$$

always changes x, but the assignment:

$$x := y + 1;$$

may, if x is a reference variable, change any other variable (of appropriate type) in the whole machine. One variable it can *never* change is x! Unlike all other values (integers, strings, arrays, files, etc.) references have no meaning independent of a particular run of a program. They cannot be input as data, and they cannot be output as results. If either data or references to data have to be stored on files or backing stores, the problems are immense. And on many machines they have a surprising overhead on performance, for example they will clog up instruction pipelines, data lookahead, slave stores, and even paging systems. References are like jumps, leading wildly from one part of a data structure to another. Their introduction into high-level languages has been a step backward from which we may never recover.

13.9 Block structure

In addition to the advantages of disjoint named variables, high-level languages provide the programmer with a powerful tool for achieving even greater security, namely the scope and locality associated with block structure. In FORTRAN or ALGOL 60, if the programmer needs a variable for the purposes of a particular part of his program, he can declare it locally to that part of the program. This enables the programmer to make manifest in the structure of his program the close association between the variable and the code that uses it; and he can be absolutely confident that no other part of the program, whether written by himself or another, can ever interfere with, or even look at, the variable without his written permission, i.e. unless he passes it as a parameter to a particular named procedure. The use of locality also greatly reduces the width of the interfaces between parts of the program; the fact that programmers no longer need to tell each other the names of their working variables is only one of the beneficial consequences.

Like all the best programming-language features, the locality and scope rules of ALGOL 60 are not only of great assistance to the programmer in the decomposition of his task and the implementation of its subtasks; they also permit economy in the use of machine resources, for example main store. The fact that a group of variables is required for purposes local only to part of a program means that their values will usually be relevant only while that part of the program is being executed. It is therefore possible to re-allocate to other purposes the storage assigned to these variables as soon as they are no longer required. Since the blocks of a program in ALGOL 60 are always completed in the exact reverse of the order in which they were entered, the dynamic re-allocation of storage can be accomplished by stack techniques, with small overhead of time and space, or none at all in the case of blocks that are not procedure bodies, for which the administration can be done at compile time. Finally, the programmer is encouraged to declare at the same time those variables that will be used together, and these will be allocated in contiguous locations, which will increase the efficiency of slave storage and paging techniques.

It is worthy of note that the economy of dynamic reallocation is achieved without any risk that the programmer will accidentally refer to a variable that has been re-allocated, and this is guaranteed by a compile-time and not a run-time check. All these advantages are achieved in ALGOL 60 by the close correspondence between the statically visible scope of a variable in a source program and the dynamic lifetime of its storage when the program is run. A language designer should therefore be extremely reluctant to break this correspondence, which can easily be done, for example, by the introduction of references, which may point to variables of an exited block. The rules of ALGOL 68, designed to detect such so-called 'dangling references' at compile time, are both complicated and ineffective; and PL/I does not bother at all.

13.10 Procedures and parameters

According to current theories of structured programming, every large-scale programming project involves the design, use, and implementation of a special-purpose programming language, with its own data concepts and primitive operations, specifically oriented to that particular project. The procedure and parameter are the major tools provided for this purpose by high-level languages since FORTRAN. In itself, this affords all the major advantages claimed for extensible languages. Furthermore, in its implementation as a closed subroutine, the procedure can achieve very great economies of storage at run time. For these reasons, the language designer should give the greatest attention to this feature of this language. Procedure calls and parameter passing should produce very compact code. Lengthy preludes and postludes must be avoided. The effect of the procedure on its parameters should be clearly manifest from its syntactic form, and should be simple to understand and resistant to error. And, finally, since the procedure interface is so often the interface between major parts of a program, the correctness of its use should be subjected to the most rigorous compile-time check.

The chief defects of the FORTRAN parameter mechanism are:

(1) It fails to give a notational distinction at the call side between parameters that convey values into a procedure, those that convey values out of a procedure, and those that do both. This negates many of the advantages that the assignment statement has over machine-code programming.
(2) The shibboleth of the independent compilation prohibits compile-time checks on parameter passing, just where interface errors are most likely, most disastrous, and most difficult to debug.
(3) The ability to define side-effects of function calls negates many of the advantages of arithmetic expressions.

At least FORTRAN permits efficient implementation, unless a misguided but all too frequent attempt is made to permit a mixture of languages across the procedure interface. A subroutine that does not know whether it is being called from ALGOL or from FORTRAN has a hard life.

ALGOL 60 perpetuates all these disadvantages, but not the advantage. The difficulty of compile-time parameter checking is due to the absence of parameter specifications. Even if an implementation insists on full specification (and most do) the programmer has no way of specifying the parameters of a formal procedure parameter. This is one of the excuses for the inefficiency of many ALGOL implementations. The one great advance of ALGOL 60 is the value parameter, which is immeasurably superior to the dummy parameter of FORTRAN and PL/I. What a shame that the name parameter is the default!

But perhaps the most subtle defect of the ALGOL 60 parameter is that the user is permitted to pass the same variable twice as an actual parameter corresponding to two distinct formal parameters. This immediately violates the principles of disjointness, and can lead to many curious, unexpected effects. For example, if a procedure:

$$\textit{matrix multiply}\ (A, B, C)$$

is intended to have the effect:

$$A := B \times C$$

it would seem reasonable to square A by:

$$\textit{matrix multiply}\ (A, A, A)$$

This error is prohibited in standard FORTRAN, but few programmers realize it, and it is rarely enforced by a compile-time or run-time check. No wonder the procedure interface is the one on which run-time debugging aids have to concentrate.

13.11 Types

Among the most trivial but tiresome errors of low-level programming are type errors, for example using a fixed-point operation to add floating-point numbers, using an address as an integer or vice versa, or forgetting the position of a field in a data structure. The effects of such errors, although fully explicable in terms of bit patterns and machine operations, are so totally unrelated to the concept in terms of which the programmer is thinking that the detection and correction of such errors can be exceptionally tedious. The trouble is that the hardware of the computer is far too tolerant and forgiving. It is willing to accept almost any sequence of instructions and make sense of them at its own level. That is the secret of the power, flexibility, and simplicity, and even reliability, of computer hardware, and should therefore be cherished.

But it is also one of the main reasons why we turn to high-level languages, which can eliminate the risk of such error by a compile-time check. The programmer declares the type of each variable, and the compiler can work out the type of each result; it therefore always knows what type of machine-code instruction to generate. In cases where there is no meaningful operation (for example, the addition of an integer and a Boolean) the compiler can inform the programmer of his mistake, which is far better than having to chase its curious consequences after the program has run.

However, not all language designers would agree. Some languages, by complex rules of automatic type transfers and coercions, prefer the dangerous tolerance of machine code, but with the following added disadvantages:

(1) The result will often be 'nearly' right, so that the programmer has less warning of his error.
(2) The inefficiency of the conversion is often a shock.
(3) The language is much complicated by the rules.
(4) The introduction of genuine language extensibility is made much more difficult.

Apart from the elimination of the risk of error, the concept of type is of vital assistance in the design and documentation phases of program development. The design of abstract and concrete data structure is one of the first tools for refining our understanding of problems, and for defining the common interfaces between the parts of a large program. The declaration of the name and structure or range of values of each variable is a most important aspect of clear programming, and the formal description of the relationship of each variable to other program variables is a most important part of its annotation; and finally an informal description of the purpose of each variable and its manner of use is a most important part of program documentation. In fact, I believe a language should enable the programmer to declare the units in which his numbers are expressed, so that a compiler can check that he is not confusing radians and degrees, adding height to weights, or comparing metres with yards.

Again not all language designers would agree. Many languages do not require the programmer to declare his variables at all. Instead they define complex default rules, which the compiler must apply to undeclared variables. But this can only encourage sloppy program design and documentation, and nullify many of the advantages of block structure and type checking; the default rules soon get so complex that they are very likely to give results not expected by the programmer, and as ludicrously or subtly inappropriate to his intentions as a machine-code program that contains a type error.

Of course, wise programmers have learned that it is worthwhile to expend the effort to avoid these dangers. They eagerly scan the compiler listings to ensure that every variable has been declared, and that all the characteristics assigned to it by default are acceptable. What a pity that the designers of these languages take such trouble to give such trouble to their users and themselves.

13.12 Language-feature design

This paper has given many practical hints on how *not* to design a programming language. It has even suggested that many recent languages have followed these hints. But there are very few positive hints on what to put into your next language design. Nearly everything I have ever published is full of positive and practical suggestions for programming language features, notations, and implementation methods; furthermore, for the last ten years, I have tried to pursue the same objectives in language design that I have expounded here; and I have tried to make my proposals as convincing as I could. And yet I have never designed a programming language, only programming language features. It is my belief that these two design activities should be more clearly separated in the future.

(1) The designer of a new feature should concentrate on one feature at a time. If necessary, he should design it in the context of some well-known programming language that he likes. He should make sure that his feature

mitigates some disadvantage or remedies some incompleteness of the language without compromising any of its existing merits. He should show how the feature can be simply and efficiently implemented. He should write a section of a user manual, explaining clearly with examples how the feature is intended to be used. He should check carefully that there are no traps lurking for the unwary user, which cannot be checked at compile time. He should write a number of example programs, evaluating all the consequences of using the feature, in comparison with its many alternatives. And finally, if a simple proof rule can be given for the feature, this would be the final accolade.

(2) The language designer should be familiar with many alternative features designed by others, and should have excellent judgement in choosing the best and rejecting any that are mutually inconsistent. He must be capable of reconciling, by good engineering design, any remaining minor inconsistencies or overlaps between separately designed features. He must have a clear idea of the scope and purpose and range of application of his new language, and how far it should go in size and complexity. He should have the resources to implement the language on one or more machines, to write user manuals, introductory texts, advanced texts; he should construct auxiliary programming aids and library programs and procedures; and, finally, he should have the political will and resources to sell and distribute the language to its intended range of customers. One thing he should not do is to include untried ideas of his own. His task is consolidation, not innovation.

13.13 Conclusion

A final hint: listen carefully to what language users say they want, until you have an understanding of what they *really* want. Then find some way of achieving the latter at a small fraction of the cost of the former. This is the test of success in language design, and of progress in programming methodology. Perhaps these two are the same subject anyway.

13.14 Appendix: annotated reading list

Naur, P. (1960)
The more I ponder the principles of language design, and the techniques that put them into practice, the more is my amazement at and admiration of ALGOL 60. Here is a language so far ahead of its time that it was not only an improvement on its predecessors but also on nearly all its successors.

Of particular interest are its introduction of all the main program-structuring concepts and the simplicity and clarity of its description, rarely equalled and never surpassed. Consider especially the avoidance of abbreviation in the syntax names and equations and the inclusion of examples in every section.

Knuth, D. E. (1967)
Most of these troublespots have been eliminated in the widely used subsets of the language. When you can design a language with so few troublespots, you can be proud. The real remaining troublespot is the declining quality of implementations.

Wirth, N. and Hoare C. A. R. [9]
This language is widely known as ALGOL W. It remedies many of the defects of ALGOL 60 and includes many of the good features of FORTRAN IV and LISP. Its introduction of references avoids most of the defects described above under 'Variables'. It has been extremely well implemented on the IBM 360, and has a small and scattered band of devoted followers.

Wirth, N. (1968)
This introduces the benefits of program structures to low-level programming for the IBM/360. It was hastily designed and implemented as a tool for implementing ALGOL W; it excited more interest than ALGOL W, and has been widely imitated on other machines.

Wirth, N. (1971c)
Pascal was designed to combine the machine-independence of ALGOL W with the efficiency and control of PL/360. New features are the simple but powerful and efficient type definition capabilities, including sets, and a very clean treatment of files. When used to write its own translator, it achieves a remarkable combination of clarity of structure and detail together with high efficiency in producing good object code.

Dahl, O.-J., *et al.* (1972)
This expounds a systematic approach to the design, development, and documentation of computer programs. The last section is an excellent introduction to Simula 67 and the ideas that underlie it.

McCarthy, J. (1960)
This paper describes a beautifully simple and powerful fully functional language for symbol manipulation. It introduces the scan–mark garbage-collection technique, which makes such languages feasible. LISP has some good interactive implementations, widely used in artificial intelligence projects. It has also been extended in many ways, some good and some bad, some local and some short-lived.

ASA Standard FORTRAN (1964)
This language had the right objectives. It introduces the array, the arithmetic expression, and the procedure. The parameter mechanism is very efficient, and potentially secure. It has some very efficient implementations for numerical applications. When used outside this field it is little more helpful or machine-independent than assembly code, and can be remarkably inefficient. Its input–output is cumbersome, prone to error, and surprisingly inefficient. The standardizers have maintained the horrors of early implementations (the equivalence algorithm, second-level definition) but, in resolutely setting their face against the 'advance' of language-design technology, have saved it from many later horrors.

ASA Standard COBOL (1968)
Describes a language suitable for simple applications in business data processing. It contains good data structuring capability but poor facilities for abstraction. It aimed at readability but unfortunately achieved only prolixity; it aimed to provide a complete programming tool, in a way few languages have since. It is poor for variable format processing. The primacy of the character data item makes it rather inefficient on modern machines; and the methods provided to regain efficiency (e.g. SYNCHRONIZED) often introduce machine-dependency and insecurity.

FOURTEEN

Recursive data structures

This chapter is most readily seen as belonging to Hoare's work on language design. By this stage his thoughts were strongly influenced by the ability to reason about programs. The paper in [8] can be seen as a precursor to that published here: it was a warning about the evolving design of ALGOL 68. The difficulties of proving facts about programs which make use of general pointers are under-stated in point 9 of the case against 'general pointers'. Just like jump statements, they should be the concern of machine code generated by a (trusted) compiler rather than expressions about which proofs can be safely constructed.

The paper recognizes the need for recursive data structures to represent objects such as symbolic expressions. The traditional approach to the definition of such arbitrarily sized objects is to make pointers explicit. Hoare proposes that the recursive types are described as such and offers elegant notation for analysing the cases involved.

The paper thus offers a safer language: it 'extend(s) as far as possible the range of errors that can no longer be made.' But it also goes further by explaining how Burstall's 'structural induction' idea can be used in proofs. There is also a clear link to the proof methods of Chapter 8 both in the use of invariants and in the concept of representations. (Here the term 'abstraction function' is used for the relation between representation and abstraction.) The ideas of Rod Burstall, described in this paper, have been incorporated (in untyped form) in experimental pattern-matching versions of LISP, and more recently in ML and Miranda.

This paper also includes extensive discussion of implementation techniques for the proposed language features and discusses the use of programmer-supplied 'memo functions'. The paper was submitted in April 1974, revised in July and published ([51]) in June 1975. The text was available in October 1973 as Stanford Technical Report STAN-CS-73-400.

Abstract

The power and convenience of a programming language may be enhanced for certain applications by permitting tree-like data structures to be defined by recursion. This

C. A. R. Hoare, Recursive data structures, *Int. J. Computer and Information Sciences,* **4**(2), 105–32 (June 1975). This paper is republished by kind permission of Plenum Publishing Corporation.

paper suggests a pleasing notation by which such structures can be declared and processed; it gives the axioms which specify their properties, and suggests an efficient implementation method. It shows how a recursive data structure may be used to represent another data type, for example, a set. It then discusses two ways in which significant gains in efficiency can be made by selective updating of structures, and gives the relevant proof rules and hints for implementation. The examples show that a certain range of applications in symbol manipulation can be efficiently programmed without introducing the low-level concept of a reference into a high-level programming language.

14.1 Introduction

In a language such as ALGOL 68 (van Wijngaarden 1969) PL/I (PL/I Language Specifications) or Simula 67 (Birthwhistle *et al.* 1973) a central role is played by the concept of a reference or *pointer*. In Simula 67 these are used for data structuring and for dynamic storage allocation. In ALGOL 68, they are also used in the treatment of ordinary variables, result parameters, and in indirect addressing; and in PL/I they are also used for value ('dummy') parameters, and even for buffered input/output. However, there are many reasons to believe that the introduction of references into a high-level language is a seriously retrograde step, for the following reasons.

(1) It reintroduces the same unpleasant confusion between addresses and their contents which afflicts machine-code programmers.
(2) In ALGOL 68, confusion is doubly confounded by complex coercion and balancing rules.
(3) In PL/I the explicit allocation and deallocation of storage afford unbounded scope for complexity and error.
(4) The variables subject to change by a program statement are no longer manifest from the form of the statement. For example, if x and y are reference variables,

$$x := y,$$

obviously changes the value of x, but a statement in ALGOL 68 like

$$x := y + 1;$$

may change the value of a, or b, or any other variable of appropriate type: One variable it cannot possibly change is x!
(5) It is possible to use a reference value pointing to an area of local workspace which has been de-allocated. In PL/I this can cause disaster without warning; in ALGOL 68 certain rather complex rules ensure that the danger can sometimes (but not always) be averted by a compile-time check. This is known as the problem of the 'dangling reference'.
(6) In contrast to values of all normal types (integers, reals, arrays, strings,

files, etc.), the value of a reference can never be input to a program, nor can it be output from it (except possibly in a total post mortem dump). In fact, a reference has no independent meaning, and can be interpreted only in terms of the entire machine state at a particular time in a particular run of a particular program.

(7) The use of references reduces the efficiency of execution on machines with instruction lookahead, data pre-fetch, pipelines, slave stores, or paging systems, counteracting all these laudable attempts by hardware to make a machine seem faster or larger than it really is.

(8) When data are to be held permanently or temporarily on backing store (e.g., files on tape or disk), the use of references can create almost insuperable difficulties to implementor, user, or both, especially when the references point between one level of store and another.

(9) Proof methods for dealing with a language that permits general pointers are significantly more complicated, in some cases, even when the pointers are not used.

(10) The use of scan–mark garbage collection, especially with compaction, introduces a large and uncontrollable overhead at unpredictable places in the execution of the program, and reference counts can be even more costly.

An early warning of some of the dangers of referencing may be found in Hoare ([8]).

There appears to be a close analogy between references in data and jumps in a program. A jump is a powerful multipurpose tool, present in the object code produced by compilers for conventional machines. But it is also an undisciplined feature, which can be used to create wide interfaces between parts of a program which appear to be disjoint. That is why a high-level programming language like ALGOL 60 has introduced a range of program structures such as compound statements, conditional statements, **while** statements, **procedure** statements, and recursion to replace many of the uses of the machine-code jump. Indeed, perhaps the only remaining purpose of the jump in a high-level language is to indicate irreparable breakdown in the structure of a program. Similarly, if references have any role in data structuring, it may be a purely destructive one.

It would therefore seem highly desirable to attempt to classify all those special purposes to which references may be put, and to replace them in a high-level language by several more structured principles and notations, each of them avoiding at least some of the problems listed above. In this task, it is encouraging that ALGOL 60 (Naur 1960) has already isolated three such uses, namely parameters, variable-length arrays, and procedure workspace. Furthermore, ALGOL (Chapter 3) and Pascal (Wirth 1971c) have introduced references as representations of many–one relationships in a relational network, and have done so in a manner which mitigates some of the disadvantages listed above. For certain kinds of graph manipulation these are an excellent tool; the proposals expounded in this paper are not intended to supplant them, but rather to suggest a simpler tool which is more suitable when the graphs take the special form of trees.

One of the main reasons for using stored machine addresses is that the amount of storage that will be required by an item of data is not known to the compiler. In this paper we will consider a class of data structures for which the amount of storage required can actually vary during the lifetime of the data, and we will show that it can be satisfactorily accommodated in a high-level language using solely high-level problem-oriented concepts, and without the introduction of references.

14.2 Concepts and notations

The method of specifying the set of values of a data space by recursion has long been familiar to modern logicians (Kleene 1952). For example, the propositions treated in conventional propositional calculus may be defined by the following four rules:

A1 All *proposition* letters are *propositions*.
A2 If p is a *proposition,* then so is $\neg p$.
A3 If p and q are *propositions*, then so are $(p \wedge q)$ and $(p \vee q)$.
A4 All *propositions* can be obtained from *proposition* letters by a finite number of applications of the above rules.

When the set of propositions as defined above is treated as an object of mathematical study, it is known as a *generalized arithmetic,* and an additional axiom is postulated:

A5 Two *propositions* are equal only if they have been obtained by the same rule from equal components.

Exactly the same idea is familiar to programmers in the use of the BNF notation for the definition of programming language grammars. For example, propositions could be defined:

$$
\begin{aligned}
\langle \textit{proposition} \rangle ::= {} & \langle \textit{proposition letter} \rangle \mid \\
& \neg \langle \textit{proposition} \rangle \mid \\
& (\langle \textit{proposition} \rangle \wedge \langle \textit{proposition} \rangle) \mid \\
& (\langle \textit{proposition} \rangle \wedge \langle \textit{proposition} \rangle) \mid \\
\langle \textit{proposition letter} \rangle ::= {} & \langle \textit{letter} \rangle
\end{aligned}
$$

Both these methods of defining data not only specify the abstract structure of the data; they also state how any value can be represented as a linear stream of characters, for example

$$(P \wedge (\neg P \vee Q))$$

However, we wish to put aside issues of the external appearance of the data, and concentrate on its abstract structural properties. This abstraction is familiar to an algebraist (Cohn 1965), who calls the resulting data space a *word algebra* on a given finite set of generators. A generator is a function which maps its parameter(s) onto the larger structure of which they are immediate components. A generator with no parameters is known as a constant. In the case of propositions, four generators are required:

(1) *prop*: *letter* → *proposition*; which converts any letter into a *proposition* letter (logicians often use a different type font for this).
(2) *neg: proposition* → *proposition;* which constructs the negation of its argument.
(3) *conj* (Chapter 3) *disj: proposition* × *proposition* → *proposition*; which takes two arguments and whose result is their conjunction or disjunction, repectively.

In symbol manipulation programs, it is common to deal with variables, parameters, and functions whose values range over data spaces such as logical propositions. In a language like Pascal, which permits and encourages the programmer to define and use his own data types, it seems reasonable to permit him to use recursive definitions when necessary. A possible notation for such a type definition was suggested by Knuth (1973); it is a mixture of BNF (the | symbol) and the Pascal definition of a type by enumeration, for example:

type *proposition*
= (*prop*(*letter*)| *neg*(*proposition*)|
conj, disj (*proposition, proposition*));

It is assumed that the type '*letter*' is defined elsewhere, for example, as a subrange of characters

type *letter* = 'A' .. 'Z'

The effect of this type definition is threefold: (1) it introduces the name of the type; (2) it introduces the names of its generators; these must be unique throughout the scope of the type; (3) it gives the number and type(s) of the argument(s) of the generators (if any).

In more complicated examples, mutually recursive type definitions may be required. Type definitions of this sort were suggested by McCarthy (1963a).

A type is intended to be used to declare variables, parameters (and functions) ranging over the type, e.g.,

$$P1,\ P2 : proposition;$$

and the generators can be used to define values of the type; e.g., the sequence of instructions

$$\begin{aligned} &P1 := prop('P');\\ &P2 := neg(P1);\\ &P2 := disj(P2,\ prop('Q'));\\ &P2 := conj(P1,\ P2); \end{aligned}$$

would leave as the value of *P2* a proposition which would normally be written

$$P \wedge (\neg P \vee Q))$$

In most languages with references and types, recursive type definitions are permitted only if the recursive components of each structure are declared as references. This seems to be a low-level machine-oriented restriction; after all, we do not insist that recursive calls of a procedure should be signalled by such special notations. It is true that a recursive data structure which is held in a conventionally addressed main store will usually be represented by means of machine addresses, but it seems a good idea that the programmer should be encouraged to ignore the machine-oriented details of the representation (just as he ignores details of the implementation of integers and of recursive procedures), and should concentrate on the more pleasant abstract properties of the structure. The implementor should also have the freedom to use a different representation, for example, when the data are held on a backing store. Thus the programmer may, if he wishes, imagine a machine which allocates a fixed amount of space to hold the current value of a variable of recursive type, and if it is called upon to fit in a larger value, it adopts the same expedient that we do with pencil and paper – it merely writes smaller!

In defining operations on a data structure, it is usually necessary to enquire which of the various forms the structure takes, and what are its components. For this, I propose an elegant notation which has been suggested in Burstall 1969 and implemented as a 'pattern-matching' extension of LISP (McBride *et al.* 1970). Consider, for example, a function intended to count the number of ∧ symbols contained in a proposition. Like many functions operating on recursively defined data, it will be recursive:

```
function andcount (p:proposition): integer;
   andcount:= cases p of
              (prop(c) → 0
               neg(q) → andcount(q)
               conj(q, r) → andcount(q) + andcount(r) + 1 |
               disj(q, r) → andcount(q) + andcount(r));
```

Line 1 declares *andcount* to be an integer-valued function of one proposition, known as *p* in the body of the function.

Line 2 states that the result of *andcount* is assigned by computing the following expression. This is a '**case** expression' whose effect will depend on the value of *p*.

Line 3 states that if the value of *p* is a *proposition letter c*, the result is zero.

Line 4 states that if the value of *p* is a negation, let *q* be the negated *proposition* and the result is found by computing the *andcount* of *q*.

Line 5 states that if the value of *p* is a conjunction, let *q* and *r* be the names of its components, and the result is one more than the sum of the *andcounts* for *q* and *r*.

Note that the identifiers *c*, *q*, and *r* are like formal parameters: They are declared by appearing in the parameter list to the left of the arrow, and their scope is confined to the right-hand side of the arrow, only as far as the vertical bar. Their types are determined by the types given in the declaration of the corresponding generator, e.g., *c* is a letter, and *q* and *r* are propositions. We shall insist, for the time being, that the programmer shall *not* make assignments to these variables.

In this example the cases are listed in the same sequence as the generators were declared; however, a programming language could permit the order to be varied without danger of ambiguity.

The language features described above are capable of expressing all the functional aspects of LISP, and many of the procedure aspects as well. For example, the list structure of LISP *S*-expressions can be defined:

type *list* = (*unit* (*identifier*)| *cons* (*list, list*))

where the type identifier is assumed to be defined elsewhere. The function *cons* is defined as part of this declaration. The other LISP basic functions can be programmed:

```
function car (l: list): list;
   car:= cases l of (unit (id) → error |
                     cons (left, right) → left);
function cdr (l: list): list; ... similar ...
function atom (l: list): Boolean;
   atom:= cases l of (unit (any) → true | cons (x, y) → false);
function equals (l1, l2): Boolean;
equals:= cases l1 of
        (unit (id1) → cases l2 of (unit (id2) → id1 = id2 |
                                   cons (x, y) → false)|
        cons (x1, y1) → cases l2 of (unit (id2) → false |
                                     cons (x2, y2) → equals (x1, y1) ∧
                                                     equals (x2, y2)));
```

Here, *error* is assumed to trigger the standard diagnostic mechanism. In practice, the **cases** notation will often be found more convenient, clear, and less prone to error than the functions *car*, *cdr*, and *atom* (although the disadvantages of LISP can often be mitigated by good layout).
For example, the familiar *append* function may be written

function *append* (*l1, l2*: *list*): *list;*
  append:= **cases** *l1* **of**
    (*unit* (*id*) → **if** *id* = *NIL* **then** *l2* **else** *error* |
    cons (*first, rest*) → *cons* (*first, append* (*rest, l2*)));

Just as LISP can be embedded in any language which permits recursive data structures, so can all recursive data structures be represented as LISP lists, and processed by LISP functions. For example;

$$conj('P', disj(neg('P'), 'Q'))$$

can be represented (in *S*-expression form)

$$(CONJ\ P(DISJ(NEG\ P)Q))$$

An *andcount* function for propositions represented in this way would be

$$\begin{aligned} andcount := (&atom(l) \to 0,\\ &car(l) = 'NEG \to andcount(cadr(l)),\\ &car(l) = 'CONJ \to andcount(cadr(l))\\ &\qquad\qquad + andcount(caddr(l)) + 1,\\ &car(l) = 'DISJ \to andcount(cadr(l))\\ &\qquad\qquad + andcount(caddr(l)));\end{aligned}$$

Note that the arrows in this program are LISP conditionals.

This example illustrates some of the advantages of the type declaration for recursive data structures:

(1) The check against the error of applying the function to a structure that is *not* a proposition can be made more rigorous, and can occur at compile time rather than run time.
(2) It is easier to check that all cases have been dealt with.
(3) The formal parameters seem to be more readable and perspicuous than the abbreviations *car, cadr, caddr,* etc.

In the next section it will be shown how a compiler can sometimes take advantage of the extra information supplied by a type declaration to secure more compact representations and more efficient code than is usually achieved in LISP.

To summarize the notation conventions introduced in this section, here are the syntax specifications of recursive type declarations and **case** expressions:

⟨*type declaration*⟩ ::= **type**⟨*type identifier*⟩ = (⟨*generator list*⟩)
⟨*generator list*⟩ ::= ⟨*generator*⟩ | ⟨*generator*⟩⟨*or symbol*⟩⟨*generator list*⟩
⟨*or symbol*⟩ ::= | (*i.e., vertical stroke*)
⟨*generator*⟩ ::= ⟨*generator identifier*⟩ | ⟨*generator identifier*⟩(⟨*type list*⟩)
⟨**type** *list*⟩ ::= ⟨*type*⟩ | ⟨*type*⟩, ⟨*type list*⟩
⟨*case expression*⟩ ::= **cases** ⟨*expression*⟩ **of** (⟨*case list*⟩)
⟨*case list*⟩ ::= ⟨*case clause*⟩ | ⟨*case clause*⟩⟨*or symbol*⟩⟨*case list*⟩
⟨*case clause*⟩ ::= ⟨*pattern*⟩ → ⟨*expression*⟩
⟨*pattern*⟩ ::= ⟨*generator identifier*⟩(⟨*formal parameter list*⟩)|
⟨*generator identifier*⟩
⟨*formal parameter list*⟩ ::= ⟨*formal parameter*⟩|
⟨*formal parameter*⟩, ⟨*formal parameter list*⟩
⟨*formal parameter*⟩ ::= ⟨*identifier*⟩

14.3 Implementation

The normal method of representing a recursive data structure for processing in the main store of a computer is as a *tree,* using machine addresses to link the *nodes,* and a small integer, called a *tag,* in each node (or equivalently with the address) to indicate which of the generators was used to define this node. Each node contains as components the values of the arguments of the generator, which may be themselves addresses of other nodes, or may be just simple values.

For example, in the case of a proposition, the name of the generator is represented by an integer between 0 and 3. If the node is a proposition letter (tag 0), this will be followed immediately by a representation of the letter. If it is a negation, the tag 1 is followed by the address of the negated proposition. In the remaining two cases, the code 2 or 3 is followed by a pair of locations, pointing to the components of the conjunction or disjunction. Thus the value

$$(P \wedge (\neg P \vee Q))$$

as constructed above would be represented as in Fig. 14.1. Of course, this example is untypically simple. A picture of a more realistic proposition would explain why the programmer may prefer not to think in terms of references.

On many machines it will be possible to pack the tag in with one of the components of the node, or pack two addresses in a single word, thereby saving a word of storage on that node. It can be seen that when nodes have more than two components it is possible to use less space than the standard LISP representation for the same information.

The call of a (nonconstant) generator involves the dynamic acquisition of

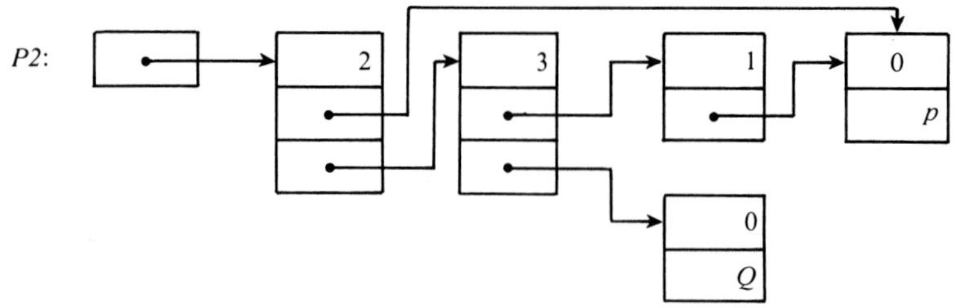

Figure 14.1

a few words of contiguous main storage, and planting in them the values of its simple parameters and the addresses of its recursive parameters. The value returned by the generator is the address of the new node. There is no need to make a fresh copy of the recursive components, since it is quite permissible for two separate variables to 'share' the same components, as was shown in Fig. 14.1, and more so in Fig. 14.2. It can be seen that *P1* has value $Q \wedge (\neg P \vee Q)$ and *P2* and *P3* have the same value, $P \wedge (\neg P \vee Q)$. However, this shared use of storage is entirely invisible to the programmer, who has no means of finding out whether it has occurred or not. The test of equality on recursive data structures is like the *EQUAL* function of LISP rather than the *EQ* primitive, in that it tests equality of content rather than equality of address (although the obvious short cut should be taken when the addresses are found to be equal). Furthermore, the prohibition on the selective updating of components of a structure prevents the programmer

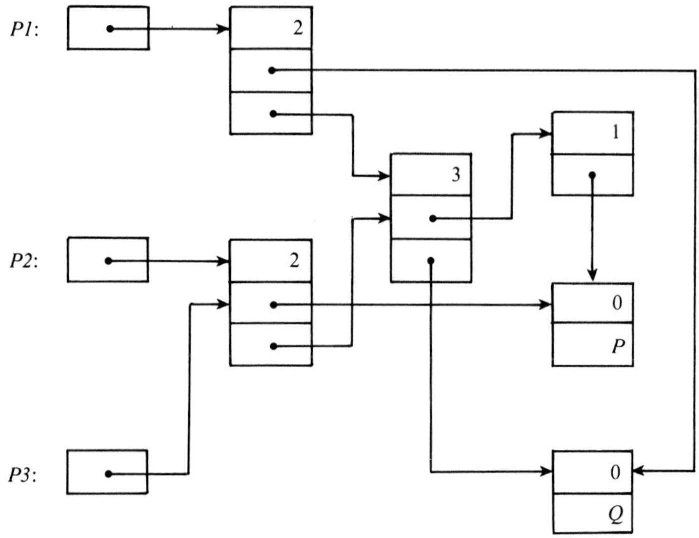

Figure 14.2

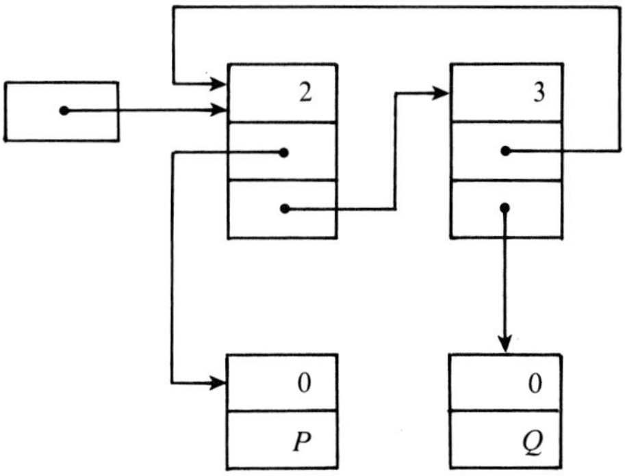

Figure 14.3

from changing a node on one tree and testing to see whether the change has affected the other. The same restriction also prevents the establishment of cyclic structures, such as that of Fig. 14.3.

Such a structure would appear to have the 'infinite' value

$$(P \wedge (P \wedge (P \wedge \cdots \vee Q)) \vee Q)$$

and this would fail to satisfy the axiom of finite generation. Thus the prohibition on selective updating seems to be a vital means of preserving the integrity of recursive data structures, as well as permitting a more economical 'shared' representation. The mathematical properties of structures with cycles are explored in Scott (1971).

This shared subtree representation using addresses is not the only possible representation of recursive data structures. If the structure is to be held on backing store, it can be converted to a linear stream, replacing every address by the stream representing the tree to which it points. In this representation, the example $P \wedge (\neg P \vee Q)$ would appear

2	0	P	3	1	0	P	0	Q

This, of course, will require copies to be taken of all shared branches, thereby usually occupying more space; but the elimination of addresses will tend to compensate for this. Of course, on re-input of the structure, it would be advisable to re-establish as much sharing as possible; before acquiring a new node to accommodate given values, if a node containing these values is already present in store, it can be used instead. Indeed, the re-use of existing storage in this way may be adopted as a general policy, which can be effective in certain kinds of application (for example, it makes test of equality very cheap); in any case, it is entirely invisible as far as the logic of the program is concerned. In a conventional non-associative store a hashing technique is recommended for finding a node with given contents;

hence in LISP it is known as 'the hashing *cons*.' (Anderson 1973). It is also used in SNOBOL (Chapter 3).

If sharing is used, it is no longer possible to reclaim all the storage allocated to a variable on exit from the block in which the variable was declared, since its components may also be components of the value of some variable global to that block. In order to reclaim storage when it runs out (and it soon will), it is necessary to use a scan–mark garbage collector, invented by McCarthy (1960) for this purpose. This will be more complicated than the standard LISP garbage collector, since it will have to deal in blocks of different size, and it will have to know the type of each node and the relative position of each address within it. In many applications, the sizes of the nodes do not vary too wildly, so the problem of fragmentation should not be significant, except in the case of arrays, which may be treated separately. The cost per node of garbage collection should be no greater than in LISP, and if nodes are larger than two components, some saving in time may be possible.

The **case** expression can be compiled into highly efficient code. The value being considered may be loaded into an index register. The tag is then used to do an indexed jump leading to the portion of object code dealing with that particular case. There is no need to check the range of the index; it is logically impossible for it to be wrong! If there are more than two alternatives, this could be more compact and efficient than a sequence of tests. The left-hand side of the arrow generates no code at all. In compiling the right-hand side, the formal parameters of this case can be accessed by means of a single 'reverse' indexed instruction (Ross 1961) requiring a single store access. In accessing the third or subsequent component of a node, this will be more compact and efficient than the LISP use of *cadr, caddr,* etc.

With reasonable co-operation from the programmer, this implementation would seem to offer a significant improvement on the efficiency of compiled LISP, perhaps even a factor of two in space–time cost for suitable applications. But even more significant may be the fact that normal operations on numbers, characters, bits, etc., can be carried out with direct machine code instructions, without a preliminary run-time type check, and without any risk of obtaining absurdly wrong results. Of course, in an interpretive implementation, this comparison does not hold, and LISP retains certain advantages of simplicity and flexibility.

14.4 Axioms

The axioms for a recursive data type are closely modelled on the corresponding informal definition of the type as given in the axioms A1–A5 at the beginning of Section 14.2. Note that the fourth axiom is expressed quite informally; in its normal formalization it appears as a principle of 'structural induction' (Burstall 1969). Consider any predicate $\mathscr{P}(q)$, which we wish to prove true of all propositions q, i.e., we wish to prove

$$\forall q\text{: } proposition.\ \mathscr{P}(q)$$

The principle of structural induction states that this can be established by proving the theorem for all the ways in which a proposition q can be generated, and furthermore in these proofs $\mathscr{P}$ may be assumed true of all propositional *components* of q. This may be expressed in the proof rule:

A4′
$$\frac{\begin{array}{l}\forall\text{: } letter.\mathscr{P}(prop(c))\\ \forall p\text{: } proposition.\ \mathscr{P}(p) \Rightarrow \mathscr{P}(neg(p))\\ \forall p, q\text{: } proposition.\ \mathscr{P}(p) \wedge \mathscr{P}(q) \Rightarrow \mathscr{P}(conj(p, q)) \wedge \mathscr{P}(disj(p, q))\end{array}}{\forall q\text{: } proposition.\ \mathscr{P}(q)}$$

The first three lines of this rule are the antecedents, and the last line is the conclusion of the deduction.

The fifth axiom, dealing with equality, is most easily formalized by giving axioms defining the meaning of the **cases** expression.

For propositions the axiom takes the form:

A5
$$\begin{array}{l}\textbf{cases}\ prop(d)\ \textbf{of}\ (\ldots \mid prop(c) \rightarrow e \mid \ldots) = e^{c}_{d}\\ \wedge\ \textbf{cases}\ neg(p)\ \textbf{of}\ (\cdots \mid neg(q) \rightarrow e \mid \cdots) = e^{q}_{p}\\ \wedge\ \textbf{cases}\ conj(p, q)\ \textbf{of}\ (\cdots \mid conj(r, s) \rightarrow e \mid \cdots) = e^{r,s}_{p,q}\\ \wedge\ \textbf{cases}\ disj(p, q)\ \textbf{of}\ (\cdots \mid disj(r, s) \rightarrow e \mid \cdots) = e^{r,s}_{p,q}\end{array}$$

where e^{x}_{y} means the expression formed from e by replacing all free occurrences of the variable x by the expression y (with appropriate modifications of bound variables when necessary).

The question now arises, are these axioms sufficiently powerful to prove everything we need to know about recursive data structures? Of course, this question is not precise enough to permit a definitive answer, but our confidence in the power of the axioms can be established by showing their close analogy with the Peano axioms for natural numbers, which have been found adequate for all practical purposes of arithmetic. They, too, can be defined as recursive data structures:

type *NN* = (*zero*, *succ*(*NN*));

and the **cases** notation permits the traditional method of defining recursive functions; for example

```
function plus (m, n: NN): NN;
  plus:= cases n of (zero → m | succ(p) → succ(plus(m, p)));
```

The axioms for natural numbers defined as a recursive data structure are as follows:

N1 Zero is an *NN*.
N2 If n is an *NN*, so is $succ(n)$.

N3
$$\frac{\mathscr{P}(zero) \qquad \forall n\colon NN.\,\mathscr{P}(n) \Rightarrow \mathscr{P}(succ(n))}{\forall n\colon NN.\ \mathscr{P}(n)}$$

N4 $\textbf{cases}\ zero\ \textbf{of}\ (zero \to e \mid succ(n) \to f) = e$
$\wedge\, \textbf{cases}\ succ(m)\ \textbf{of}\ (zero \to e \mid succ(n) \to f) = f^n_m$

Axioms N1 and N2 are the same as Peano's. Axiom N3 is the principle of mathematical induction. From Axiom N4 we can readily prove the remaining two Peano axioms:

(1) $succ(n) \neq zero$.
Proof by contradiction: Assume $succ(n) = zero$. Hence

$$\begin{aligned} &\textbf{cases}\ succ(n)\ \textbf{of}\ (zero \to true \mid succ(n) \to false)\\ &= \textbf{cases}\ zero\ \textbf{of}\ (zero \to true \mid succ(n) \to false)\\ &\therefore\ false = true\ \text{(by Axiom N4)}\end{aligned}$$

(2) $succ(m) = succ(n) \Rightarrow m = n$.
Proof: Assume the antecedent. hence

$$\begin{aligned} &\textbf{cases}\ succ(m)\ \textbf{of}\ (zero \to zero \mid succ(m) \to m)\\ &= \textbf{cases}\ succ(n)\ \textbf{of}\ (zero \to zero \mid succ(m) \to m)\\ &\therefore\ m^m_m = m^m_n,\ \text{i.e. } m = n\ \text{(by Axiom N4)}\end{aligned}$$

It is worthy of note that when none of the generators have parameters, the recursive data structure reduces to a PASCAL type definition by enumeration, and the axioms still remain valid. For example, the Boolean type may be defined by

$$\textbf{type}\ Boolean = (true \mid false);$$

and the axioms are as follows:

B1 *True* and *false* are *Booleans*.

B2
$$\frac{\mathscr{P}(true) \qquad \mathscr{P}(false)}{\forall b\colon Boolean.\ \mathscr{P}(b)}$$

B3 $\textbf{cases}\ true\ \textbf{of}\ (true \to e \mid false \to f) = e$
$\textbf{cases}\ false\ \textbf{of}\ (true \to e \mid false \to f) = f$

If desired, the notation '**if** *B* **then** *e* **else** *f*' may be regarded as an abbreviation for '**cases** *B* **of** $(true \to e \mid false \to f)$.'

14.5 Classes

Many interesting and useful algebras are not word algebras – for example, finite sets and finite mappings (e.g., sparse arrays). However, they can be represented as *subsets* of a word algebra, consisting of elements satisfying some additional property known as an *invariant* for that type. A type which is a subset of word algebra will be called a *class*. In order to ensure that each newly generated value of the type will actually satisfy the invariant, the programmer must have the ability to specify (1) the initial value of any declared variable of the class, and (2) the function(s) which are to be used to generate all other values of the class. A programming language can dictate (and its compiler can check) that the actual generators for the recursive class are never used outside the bodies of these function(s). In this way, by proving that the results of these functions satisfy the invariant (whenever their parameters satisfy it), it is possible to guarantee that all values ever generated will be within the desired subset. This idea was expounded in Chapter 8.

As an example, consider the representation of a set of integers. For this purpose we shall use a single-chained list of integers, which possesses the additional invariant property of being sorted. Of course, a binary search tree would be a more efficient representation in most cases. However, for purposes of exposition, the chained list is a simpler representation; a binary tree can be implemented by the same methods as an exercise by the interested reader. The operations required for a set are (say) insertion of a possibly new element, deletion of a possibly present element, and a test of membership of a possible element. A suggested form for the class declaration is

```
(1) class intset ⊂ (empty | list(intset, integer));
(2) begin function insertion (s: intset, i: integer): intset;
      insertion := cases s of
                    (empty → list(empty, i)|
                    list(rest, j) → if i = j then s
                                    else if i > j then list(insertion(rest, i), j)
                                    else list(s, i));
      function deletion(s: intset, i: integer): intset;
        deletion := cases s of
                     (empty → empty |
                     list(rest, j) → if i = j then rest
                                     else if i > j then list(deletion
                                                             (rest, i), j)
                                     else s);
```

```
        function has(s: intset, i: integer): intset;
          has:= cases s of
                 (empty → false |
                 list(rest, j) → if i = j then true
                                 else if i > j then has(rest, i)
                                 else false);
(3)     intset:= empty
      end intset;
```

Notes

(1) Introduces the class name *intset*, and delares that it will be a subset of the recursive type with generators *empty* and *list*. The scope of these generator names is confined to this class declaration.

(2) The body of the class declaration, as in Chapter 8, has the form of a block, in which are declared those procedures and functions which are to be used by the programmer on values of the class, namely the functions *insertion, deletion* and *has*.

(3) The body of the block specifies the initial value of all declared variables of the class. The name of the class itself is used for this purpose.

It is the intention that a class can be used in the same way as a type, for example:

declaration	
(including initialization to *empty*):	R, S: *intset*;
assignment:	R:= *insertion*$(S, 37)$
	S:= R; R:= *deletion*$(R, 56)$;
test:	**if** *has*$(R, 37)$ **then** ...

As suggested in Chapter 8, the criterion of correctness of a class can be expressed in terms of an *invariant* and an *abstraction function.*

The abstraction function $\mathscr{A}$ which maps each list onto the set which it represents can be defined by recursion:

$$\begin{aligned}\mathscr{A}(l\text{: } intset) =_{\text{df}} \ & \textbf{cases } l \textbf{ of}\\ & (empty \to null\ set \mid\\ & list(l1, i) \to \{i\} \cup \mathscr{A}(l1));\end{aligned}$$

and the invariant can be expressed

$$\begin{aligned}sorted(l\text{: } intset) =_{\text{df}} \ & \textbf{cases } l \textbf{ of}\\ & (empty \to true \mid\\ & list(l1, i) \to i = min(\mathscr{A}(l)) \wedge i \notin \mathscr{A}(l1))\end{aligned}$$

The criterion of correctness of the insertion function can now be formally expressed in the notation of Chapter 8.

$$sorted(s)\{\text{body of } insertion\}sorted(insertion) \wedge \mathscr{A}(insertion) = \{i\} \cup \mathscr{A}(s)$$

Since *insertion* is a recursive function, the proof of this will require assumption of the correctness of the recursive call, namely '*insertion*(*rest*, *i*)'. This hypothesis may be expressed as

$$[sorted(rest) \Rightarrow\ ]sorted(insertion(rest, i)) \\ \wedge \mathscr{A}(insertion(rest, i)) = \{i\} \cup \mathscr{A}(rest)$$

in which the antecedent is true for all *intsets*, and may be omitted. Using the rule of assignment and distributing function application through the cases, we obtain the following lemma:

$$\begin{aligned}
&sorted(s) \Rightarrow \textbf{cases } s \textbf{ of} \\
&\qquad (empty \rightarrow sorted(list(empty, i)) \wedge \mathscr{A}(list(empty, i)) \\
&\qquad\qquad = \{i\} \cup \mathscr{A}(s) && (1) \\
&\qquad list(rest, j) \rightarrow \textbf{if } i = j \textbf{ then } sorted(s) \wedge \mathscr{A}(s) = \{i\} \cup \mathscr{A}(s) && (2) \\
&\qquad\qquad \textbf{else if } i > j \textbf{ then} \\
&\qquad\qquad\qquad sorted(list(insertion(rest, i), j)) && (3) \\
&\qquad\qquad \rightarrow \wedge \mathscr{A}(list(insertion(rest, i), j)) \\
&\qquad\qquad\qquad = \{i\} \cup \mathscr{A}(s) && (4) \\
&\qquad\qquad \textbf{else } sorted(list(s, i)) \wedge \mathscr{A}(list(s, i)) \\
&\qquad\qquad\qquad = \{i\} \cup \mathscr{A}(s)) && (5)
\end{aligned}$$

Each case can be readily proved from the definition of $\mathscr{A}$ and *sorted;* no further inductions are required.

The proofs for *deletion* and *has* are rather similar.

14.6 Memo functions

In this section, we shall explore a particular case of selective updating of components of a recursive data structure, which enables the programmer to secure the advantages of the memo function advocated by Michie (1967) Consider the old example of differentiation of symbolic expressions. The simplest implementation is to define expressions as a type:

type *expression* = (*constant*(*real*)| *variable*(*identifier*)|
  minus(*expression*)|
  sum, product, quotient(*expression, expression*));

and define the derivative with respect to *t* as follows:

```
function dbydt(e: expression): expression;
        dbydt:= cases e of
                (constant(any) → constant(0)|
                variable(x) → if x = 't' then constant (1)
                                             else constant (0)
                minus(u) → minus(dbydt(u))|
                sum(u, v) → sum(dbydt(u), dbydt(v)) |
                product(u, v) → sum(product(u, dbydt(v)),
                   product(v, dbydt(u)))
                   quotient(u, v) →
                      quotient(sum(dbydt(u);
                         product(minus(e), dbydt(v))), v));
```

Using these declarations we may write:

```
position, speed, acceleration: expression;
position:= quotient(constant(3), variable('t'));
speed:= dbydt(position);
acceleration:= dbydt(speed).
```

But this implementation can involve heavy penalties in both space and time:

(1) A large amount of space will be wasted in storing expressions of the form

$$e+0, \quad e\times 1, \quad e\times 0, \quad \text{etc.}$$

This may be mitigated by declaring expressions as a **class**, in which the generation of such redundant expressions is inhibited, by the use of programmed functions.

(2) If an expression is to be differentiated repeatedly with respect to *t*, much time and space can be spent on recomputing the derivatives of the subexpressions; this time could be saved if the previously computed derivative were stored as a third component of each node representing a sum, a product, or a quotient. The value of this component (known as a *memo* component) starts off as 'unknown', but when the derivative of this subexpression is computed, it is stored here; and if the derivative is required again, the stored value is used instead of being recomputed.

For the sake of simplicity, in the following program the functions perform only the most trival of simplifications. In a serious symbol manipulation program, all these functions would be more complicated. The algorithm is based on a program using references which was described in Hoare ([11]).

```
class expression ⊂ (variable (identifier)| constant (real)| mi (expression)|
                    su, pr, qu(expression, expression,
                    (unknown | known (expression))));

(1)  begin constant zero = constant (0), one = constant (1);
       function sum(left, right: expression): expression;
         sum:= if left = zero then right else if right = zero then left
                 else su(left, right, unknown);
       function minus(e: expression): expression;
         minus:= cases e of(constant(x) → constant(− x)|
(2)                  mi(f) → f | else mi(e));
       function product(left, right: expression): expression;
         product:= if left = zero ∨ right = one then left
                     else if right = zero ∨ left = one then right
                     else pr(left, right, unknown);
       function quotient(left, right: expression): expression;
         quotient:= if left = zero ∨ right = one then left
                      else qu(left, right, unknown);
       function dbydt(e: expression): expression;
         cases e of
         (variable(x) → dbydt:= if x = 't' then one else zero |
         constant(any) → dbydt:= zero |
         mi(u) → dbydt:= minus(dbydt(u))|
         su(u, v, deriv) → cases deriv of
                           (known(f) → f|
                           unknown → {dbydt:= sum(dbydt(u), dbydt(v));
(3, 4)                                deriv:= known(dbydt)})|
         pr(u, v, deriv) → cases deriv of
                           (known(f) → f|
                           unknown →
                             {dbydt:= sum(product(u, dbydt(v)),
                                          product(v, dbydt(u)));
                             deriv:= known(dbydt)})|
         qu(u, v, deriv) → cases deriv of
                           (known(f) → f|
                           unknown →
                             {dbydt:= quotient(sum(dbydt(u),
                                      product minus(e)dbydt(v)))v);
                                      deriv:= known(dbydt)}));
       expression:= zero
     end expression;
```

Notes

(1) The Pascal *constant* declaration can be used here to save space and time and trouble.

(2) It seems a convenience to write **else** to stand for all the cases not explicitly mentioned.
(3) It is also convenient to use the name of a function as a variable inside its body (except, of course, when it has actual parameters).
(4) The notation { } is used for **begin end.**

The correctness of this class obviously depends on the preservation of the invariant that if *e* has the form *su*, *pr*, or *qu*, then its memo component either contains the value *unknown* or *known*(*dbydt*(*e*)); or, more formally,

$$\forall e, u, v, d\text{: } expression.\ e = su(u, v, known(d)) \vee e = pr(u, v, known(d)) \vee e = qu(u, v, known(d)) \Rightarrow d = dbydt(e))$$

The proof of this invariant is wholly trivial.

More substantially, it will also be necessary to prove

$$dbydt(e) = de/dt$$

Note that the abstraction function for the class must not mention the memo component. It is this that makes the existence of the third component logically invisible to the user of the class, although one hopes that he notices the gain in efficiency. Furthermore, the invariant which describes the value of the memo component must not mention any variable subject to change by the program.

It is noteworthy that the use of selective updating immediately permits establishment of cyclic structures, but because of its logical invisibility, this does not seem to matter. For example, after a series of assignments like those shown earlier, a diagram of the stored structures will be as shown in Fig. 14.4.

The use of memo components does not invalidate the sharing of subtrees, again because of the invisibility of the updating. Indeed, its main benefits are directly due to the preservation of sharing, and can be increased by increasing the amount of sharing. If the memo function method is widely used, it becomes very attractive to choose the 'hashing' technique of storage allocation; for example, it would save two words of storage in Fig. 14.4. However, in the use of this technique, it would be necessary to ignore the contents of the memo component, so that if a newly generated expression were identical to one in which the memo component was already known, they would still be correctly identified, and the derivative of the newly generated expression would be available 'for free'. For this reason, it would seem to be a good idea for a programming language to insist that a programmer single out a memo component by a special form of declaration, say by prefixing it by the word *memo*. A similar method has been used successfully in some large theorem-proving systems (Waldinger and Levitt, 1973).

The language feature defined here places on the programmer the respon-

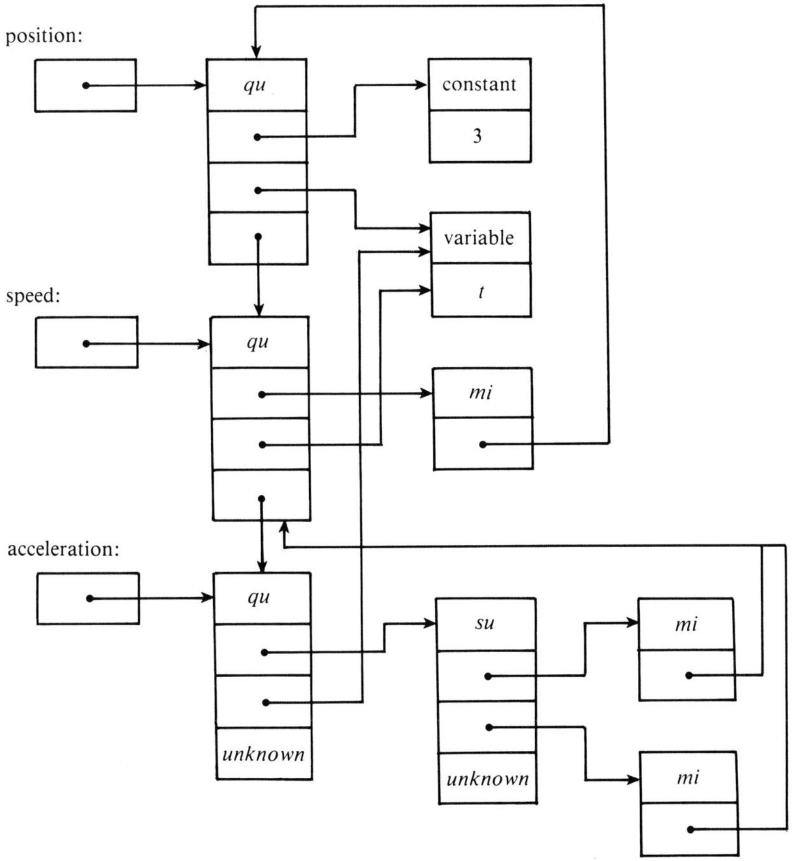

Figure 14.4. Position = $3/t$. Speed = $-$position$/t = -3/t^2$.

$$\text{Acceleration} = \frac{(-\text{speed}) + (-\text{speed})}{t} = \frac{3/t^2 + 3/t^2}{t} = \frac{6}{t^3}$$

sibility for correct maintenance of a memo component, and it helps him in this only by supplying an appropriate proof method. This has the advantage that the programmer can readily control the nature and amount of information to be memorized. For example, if partial derivatives are required with respect to exactly three variables, three memo components can be declared. If the identity of the controlled variable is not known in advance, it can also be stored in a memo component, so that repeated differentiation with respect to the same variable will always be efficient, although when a different variable is used, the memory is overwritten. Or the programmer can maintain a small list of such variable/value pairs, choosing to 'forget' certain of them when the list gets too long. Finally, he can choose which nodes will have memo components and which will not. This gives the programmer much better control of efficiency in time and storage than the automatic technique suggested in Michie (1967), although at a cost of requiring correct programming. Since run-time efficiency is the sole objective of the memo technique, perhaps this is not too high a price.

The implementation of this memo technique perhaps constitutes one of the better-disciplined uses of the controversial LISP functions *RPLACA* and *RPLACD* (Anderson 1973).

14.7 Nonshared representations

In the previous sections we have given examples for which an implementation using shared substructures would give significant savings in storage space and time. However, the use of automatic storage sharing has some significant penalties which will be particularly acute in cases where little advantage can be taken of sharing:

(1) When the result of a function is the same as its argument except at a single node, a new copy must be made of that node and *all* nodes through which it was accessed.
(2) Storage which goes out of use, either because of updating or because of block exit, cannot be immediately reclaimed for other uses.
(3) The programmer tends to lose control of the efficiency of use of one of his most precious assets, main storage.
(4) The programmer has no control over addressing vagrancy, which is necessary for successful use of paging systems or backing stores.
(5) The time spent in scan–mark garbage collection can be the heaviest single cost in the execution of an efficiently compiled program.

Some of these disadvantages could be mitigated by a run-time reference count, which can distinguish between shared and nonshared nodes. However, the storage and continual testing and updating of reference counts can involve even worse overheads.

Consider, for example, a program operating on *intsets* (as defined in Section 14.5) which only ever needs one such set; or if it needs several, it only ever updates the sets by assignments of the form

$$S1 := insertion(S1, 57);$$
$$\text{or } S2 := deletion(S2, 93);$$

and never performs a 'cross-assignment' of the form

$$S1 := S2;$$
$$\text{or } S2 := insertion(S1, 57).$$

In such a program, the two sets would never in practice come to share any subcomponent. Even if the program did make an occasional cross-assignment, the sharing patterns would be dissipated rapidly by subsequent updating of either set.

If it is known that there is no sharing, the programmer can minimize penalty (1) by selective updating of components of his structure through procedures operating directly upon the structure, rather than functions producing potentially large structured values. As suggested in Chapter 8, we shall declare **procedure**s local to the class:

procedure *insert*(*i*: integer);
procedure *remove* (*i*: integer);

These procedures are regarded as being 'components' of every variable of the class, and can be invoked by naming the variable followed by the procedure call (separated by a dot):

S1.insert(57);
S2.remove(93);

which are intended to be equivalent to the updating assignments

S1:= *insertion*(*S1*, 57);
S2:= *deletion*(*S2*, 93).

As in Chapter 8, the bodies of these procedures are permitted to update the components of the structure to which they are local, but any other access or updating should be prohibited.

Penalty (2) can be avoided by reclaiming all space allocated to a variable of recursive type on exit from the block to which it is local, or on overwriting its previous value by assignment. This will involve searching down all chains of pointers that are accessible from the variable, in a manner similar to the scan phase of a conventional garbage collector.

On a paged machine, which offers a large virtual address space, there is an even easier and more effective method for dealing with block exit. On declaration of a variable of recursive type, a certain proportion of the remaining *virtual address* space is allocated to that variable on the stack. Any actual storage required by that variable as it grows will be allocated from that virtual area. On exit from the block the normal contraction of the stack will recover the virtual addresses, and the actual storage allocated will disappear automatically.

Penalty (3) is overcome because the amount of storage used is exactly equal at all times to the amount required to represent the structure which the programmer has himself built up.

Penalty (4) is mitigated by the storage allocation strategy described above, whereby all storage allocated to a given structure will be contiguous, and so the following of chains of pointers within the same structure (the usual case) will not require excessive numbers of pages in main store.

Penalty (5) is reduced, since marking and collecting are avoided, and time taken to recover storage is proportional to the amount of storage recovered. This time can be further reduced by compiling the code for scanning each type of structure directly from the type declaration. Furthermore, on a paged machine, the overhead on block exit is zero.

In writing procedures to operate on a recursive data structure, it is sometimes necessary to refer to the anonymous variable to which the procedure is currently being applied. For this purpose, we borrow a notation from Simula 67, which uses the form

this *classname*

where classname is the name of the class. The class declaration for a procedural version of *intset* might be written as follows:

```
class intset ⊂ (empty | list(intset, integer)); comment intset is represented
                                                  as a subset of this word
                                                  algebra
  begin procedure insert(i: integer);
    cases this intset of
      (empty → this intset:= list(empty, i)|
      list(rest, j) → if i > j then rest.insert(i)
                   else if j < i then this intset:= list(this intset, i));   (i)
      procedure remove(i: integer);
      cases this intset of
        (empty → do nothing |
        list(rest, j) → if i = j then this intset:= rest
                     else if i > j then rest.delete(i));                     (ii)
      function has(i: integer): Boolean;
      cases this interest of
        (empty → has:= false |
        list(rest, j) → if i = j then has:= true
                     else if i > j then has:= rest.has(i)
                     else has:= false);
      this intset:= empty
  end intset.
```

In principle, to prevent accidental introduction of sharing, it is necessary to make a fresh copy of every actual parameter to a generator; for example on the line marked (i) above,

list(**this** *intset*,*i*)

should cause a fresh copy of **this** *intset* to be made, and its address to be planted as the first component of the new link. Then the address of the new link is assigned back to **this** *intset*, thereby triggering a garbage collection scan of the overwritten value. But this would be atrociously inefficient. We must therefore postulate a compiler which can detect the fact that the variable occurs exactly once on each side of the assignment, and therefore that the copying and the garbage collection can both be inhibited.

A similar optimization is also needed on the line marked (ii), where a component value is being assigned. In this case, a compiler could detect that only a single link of the chain becomes free as the result of the assignment, and can plant in the object code an explicit instruction to return this link only to the free list. These two optimizations are effectively a compile-time garbage collection by reference count (Darlington and Burstall 1973).

A final optimization is to note that the recursive calls of the three procedures all occur at the end of the execution of the bodies, and that the recursion can therefore be replaced by an iteration, which includes appropriate updating of the parameters (including the parameter before the dot).

After these optimizations are made, the program for the body of the procedure insert might be expressed as follows:

```
begin ptr: ref intset;
  ptr:= address of (this intset);
  repeat: cases ptr of
           (empty → {store[ptr]:= list(empty, i); goto exit}|
            list(rest,j) → if i > j then
                              {ptr:= address of(rest); goto repeat}
                         else if j < i then {store[ptr]:= list(store[ptr], i);
                                             goto exit});
exit: end insert;
```

Here, *ptr* points to the address of the intset variable which is to be updated, and *store*[*ptr*] is the contents of the address. (The reader will undoubtedly be confused by the fact that these contents will usually also be an address.) This type of pointer has quite a different purpose from the pointers that are used to glue together the components of a recursive data structure. However, the notations introduced above to express this new purpose are as inelegant as the jumps which have crept into the program, and I would not recommend them for a high-level language, in spite of the fact that the optimized program may be orders of magnitude more efficient.

The importance of avoiding copying suggests the introduction of a multiple assignment statement, of the form

$$(a, b, c) := (e, f, g);$$

which assigns to variables a, b, c the values of the expressions e, f, g, respectively, the assignments *all* taking place *after* evaluation of the expressions. Now if the left-hand variables are pointers, each of which occurs only once (in whole or in part) on the right-hand side, all copying and run-time garbage collection can be inhibited. A special case of this is the form

$$(a, b) := (b, a);$$

which can be implemented as a simple exchange of pointers, and perhaps deserves a special notation:

$$a :=: b;$$

All the optimizations described above (and more) have been implemented in a system which automatically improves programs (Darlington and Burstall 1973). In fact, even the transition between the functional and the procedure form has been automated. However, there are some disadvantages in placing such heavy reliance on optimization. For example, an apparently small change to the program (e.g., moving a statement from before to after a recursive procedure call) may have a totally disproportionate effect on efficiency. Thus, either the programmer has to understand the optimization algorithm, or he will lose control and responsibility for the efficiency of his program. This is particularly serious when efficiency is the main reason for introducing selective updating anyway. Finally, an optimizing compiler is often large, slow, unreliable, and late.

An ideal solution would be to find an elegant and convenient notational convention to express the three special cases which are susceptible to optimization, and then encourage the programmer to use them. But I have not been able to find an acceptable proposal.

A second solution is to design a low-level language capable of expressing the optimized versions, and to use an optimizer to translate between the two levels, and output the result in the lower-level language for the inspection and/or approval of the original programmer. But this is rather too reminiscent of the assembly code output by current FORTRAN translators.

Meanwhile, the only solution (certainly when none of the ideas has been embodied in an implemented programming language) is to use the abstractions as an aid to reliable program design and documentation (and even proof). The programmer can then manually translate his abstract program into some lower-level language with explicit pointers, using systematic correctness-preserving techniques. This is, of course, the method recommended in structured programming (Dijkstra 1972c).

14.8 Conclusion

This paper has described a number of old programming techniques and new notations to express them. The notations are intended to be suitable as the basis of a special-purpose language for symbol manipulation, or as an extension to a high-level, general-purpose language like ALGOL 60 or Pascal. The objective has been to isolate a number of useful and efficient simple cases of the use of references, which are susceptible to simple proof techniques, and to formalize the syntactic conventions that guarantee their validity. There still remains an unsolved problem connected with achievement of the highest efficiency in elective updating.

A referee has kindly pointed out that the language features proposed here avoid some of the additional problems which have introduced complexity into the definition, implementation, and use of ALGOL 68:

(1) The alternative generators provide a facility analogous to the UNION of modes in ALGOL 68; however, each alternative has an explicit name, and the compiler does not have to rely on context to determine which alternative is being created. Thus there is no need for the ALGOL 68 restrictions on 'related modes'.
(2) The **case** approach to discrimination permits an efficient implementation with a small integer tag. The conformity clause of ALGOL 68, which provides the analogous facility, allows any two values to be compared for mode, thereby requiring a unique global integer to be allocated to each mode, and stored with each instance of that mode.
(3) In the current proposal, the question whether two separate but similar declarations declare the 'same' type is wholly irrelevant to the language and to the programs expressed in it. After all, no one enquires whether two separate but similar procedure declarations declare the 'same' procedure. However, in ALGOL 68 this is a serious and complicated question.

14.9 Acknowledgements

I am grateful to D. B. Anderson, H. J. Enea, M. Sintzoff, and the referees for helpful comments on previous drafts of this paper.

FIFTEEN

Parallel programming: an axiomatic approach

The aspiration to extend the axiomatic approach to parallel programming was already present in drafts of Chapter 4; some axioms are given in [22]. This chapter presents a more extensive set than there. It also provides a key link between Hoare's attempts to find ways of constraining shared-variable parallelism and his adoption of communication-based parallelism. Apart from a number of interesting insights, this paper presents a shared-variable parallel program for the prime number sieve (cf. Chapter 9). This problem has also become a classic which has stimulated other researchers including Jones (1983).

The paper was submitted in April 1974, revised in June of the same year and published ([52]) in 1975.

Abstract

This paper develops some ideas expounded in (Hoare [22]. It distinguishes a number of ways of using parallelism, including disjoint processes, competition, co-operation, and communication. In each case an axiomatic proof rule is given.

15.1 Introduction

A previous paper (Hoare [22]) summarizes the objectives and criteria for the design of a parallel programming feature for a high-level programming language. It gives an axiomatic proof rule which is suitable for disjoint and competing processes, but seems to be inadequate for co-operating processes. Its proposal of the 'conditional critical region' also

C. A. R. Hoare, Parallel programming: an axiomatic approach, Reprinted with permission from: *Computer Languages,* **1** (2), 151–60 (1975).

seems to be inferior to the more structured concept of the class (Chapter 8) or monitor (Hoare ([42]); Brinch Hansen 1973). This paper introduces a slightly stronger proof rule, suitable for co-operating and even communicating processes. It suggests that the declaration is a better way of dealing with competition than the resource.

15.2 Concepts and notations

We shall use the notation ([22])

$$Q_1 \parallel Q_2$$

to denote a parallel program consisting of two processes Q_1 and Q_2 which are intended to be executed 'in parallel'. The program $Q_1 \parallel Q_2$ is defined to terminate only if and when both Q_1 and Q_2 have terminated.

The notation

$$P\,\{Q\}\,R$$

asserts that if a propositional formula P is true of the program variables before starting execution of the program statement Q, then the propositional formula R will be true on termination of Q, if it ever terminates. If not, $P\,\{Q\}\,R$ is vacuously true.

The notation

$$Q_1 \subseteq Q_2$$

asserts that the program statements Q_1 and Q_2 have identical effects under all circumstances on all program variables, provided that Q_1 terminates. The notation $Q_1 \equiv Q_2$ means $Q_1 \subseteq Q_2 \wedge Q_2 \subseteq Q_1$, i.e., if either of them terminates, so does the other, and then they have identical effects. The theory and logic of the $\subseteq$ relation are taken from Scott (1970).

The notation

$$\frac{A B}{C}$$

denotes a proof rule which permits the deduction of C whenever theorems of the form A and B have been deduced.

The notations for assignment ($x := e$) and composition of statements ($Q_1; Q_2$) have the same meaning as in ALGOL 60, but side-effects of function evaluation are excluded.

As examples of proof rules whose validity follows fairly directly from these definitions we give:

$$\frac{P\,\{Q_1\}\,S \quad S\,\{Q_2\}\,R}{P\,\{Q_1;\,Q_2\}\,R} \qquad \text{(Rule of Composition)}$$

$$\frac{Q_1 \subseteq Q_2 \quad P\,\{Q_2\}\,R}{P\,\{Q_1\}\,R} \qquad \text{(Rule of Containment)}$$

We will use the word *process* to denote a part of a program intended to be executed in parallel with some other part; and use the phrase *parallel program* to denote a program which contains or consists of two or more processes. In this paper we will talk in terms of only two processes; however, all results generalize readily to more than two.

15.3 Disjoint processes

Our initial method of investigation will be to enquire under what circumstances the execution of the parallel program $Q_1 \parallel Q_2$ can be guaranteed to be equivalent to the sequential program $Q_1; Q_2$. Preferably these circumstances should be checkable by a purely syntactic method, so that the checks can be carried out by a compiler for a high-level language.

The most obvious case where parallel and serial execution are equivalent is when two processes operate on disjoint data spaces, in the same way as jobs submitted by separate users to a multiprogramming system. Within a single program, it is permissible to allow each process to access values of common data, provided none of them update them. In order to ensure that this can be checked at compile time, it is necessary to design a language with the decent property that the set of variables subject to change in any part of the program is determinable merely by scanning that part. Of course, assignment to a component of a structured variable must be regarded as changing the whole variable, and variables assigned in conditionals are regarded as changed, whether that branch of the conditional is executed or not.

Given a suitable syntactic definition of disjointness, we can formulate the proof rule for parallel programs in the same way as that for sequential ones:

$$\frac{P\,\{Q_1\}\,S \quad S\,\{Q_2\}\,R}{P\,\{Q_1 \parallel Q_2\}\,R} \qquad \text{(Asymmetric Parallel Rule)}$$

provided that Q_1 and Q_2 are disjoint.

The proof of this (if proof it needs) may be based on the commutativity of the basic units of action performed in the execution of Q_1 and Q_2. Consider an arbitrary assignment $x_1 := e_1$ contained in Q_1 and an arbitrary assignment $x_2 := e_2$ contained in Q_2. Since Q_1 and Q_2 are disjoint, e_2 does not contain x_1 and e_1 does not contain x_2. The values of expressions are independent of the values of the variables they do not contain, and consequently they are unaffected by assignment to those variables. It follows that:

$$(x_1 := e_1;\ x_2 := e_2) \equiv (x_2 := e_2;\ x_1 := e_1),$$

i.e., these two assignment statements commute.

Consider now any interleaving of units of action of Q_1 and Q_2. If any action of Q_2 precedes any action of Q_1, the commutativity principle (together with substitution of equivalents) may be used to change their order, without changing the total effect. Provided both Q_1 and Q_2 terminate, this interchange may be repeated until all actions of Q_1 precede all actions of Q_2. But this extreme case is just the effect of executing the whole of Q_1 followed by the whole of Q_2. If one or both of Q_1 and Q_2 fails to terminate, then both $Q_1; Q_2$ and $Q_1 \parallel Q_2$ equally fail to terminate.

Thus we have proved that

$$Q_1 \parallel Q_2 \equiv Q_1; Q_2$$

and consequently their correctness may be proved by the same proof rule.

Of course, this justification is still very informal, since it is based on the assumption that parallel execution is equivalent to an arbitrary interleaving of 'units of action'. It assumes, for example, that two 'simultaneous' accesses of the same variable will not interfere with each other, as they might if one access got hold of half the variable and the other got hold of the other half. Such ridiculous effects are in practice excluded by the hardware of the computer or store. On a multiprocessor installation the design of the store module ensures that two accesses to the same (in practice, even neighbouring) variables will exclude each other in time, so that even if requests arrive 'simultaneously', one of them will be completed before the other starts. This concept of exclusion, together with commutativity, will assume greater importance in what follows.

In [22] the proof rule for disjoint processes was given in the more symmetric form:

$$\frac{P_1\ \{Q_1\}\ R_1 \qquad P_2\ \{Q_2\}\ R_2}{P_1 \wedge P_2\ \{Q_1 \parallel Q_2\}\ R_1 \wedge R_2} \quad \text{(Symmetric Parallel Rule)}$$

provided that P_1, Q_1, R_1 are disjoint from P_2, Q_2, R_2. This proof rule may be simpler to use for systematic or automatic program construction than the asymmetric rule given above, in cases where the desired result of a program is of the form $R_1 \wedge R_2$, and the program is not intended to change any variable common to R_1 and R_2. The symmetric form of the rule can be derived from the asymmetric form, by showing that every proof using the former could also have the latter. Assume $P_1\ \{Q_1\}\ R_1$ and $P_2\ \{Q_2\}\ R_2$ have been proved. The disjointness of R_1 and Q_2 and the disjointness of P_2 and

Q_1 ensure the truth of $P_2 \{Q_1\} P_2$ and $R_1 \{Q_2\} R_1$; hence

$$P_1 \wedge P_2 \{Q_1\} R_1 \wedge P_2$$

and

$$R_1 \wedge P_2 \{Q_2\} R_1 \wedge R_2.$$

One application of the asymmetric parallel rule gives

$$P_1 \wedge P_2 \{Q_1 \parallel Q_2\} R_1 \wedge R_2$$

which is the same conclusion as the symmetric rule.

In [22] it was shown that disjoint parallelism permits the programmer to specify an overlap between input/output operations and computation, which is probably the main benefit which parallelism can offer the applications programmer. In contrast to other language proposals, it does so in a secure way, giving the user absolute compile-time protection against time-dependent errors.

15.4 Competing processes

We shall now explore a number of reasons why the rule of disjointness may be found unacceptably restrictive, and show in each case how the restriction can be safely overcome.

One important reason may be that the two processes each require occasional access to some limited resource such as a line printer or an on-line device for communication with the programmer or user. In fact, even main store for temporary working variables may be a limited resource, since each word of main store can be allocated as local workspace to only one process at a time, but may be re-allocated (when that process has finished with it) to some other process that needs it.

The normal mechanism in a sequential programming language for making a temporary claim on storage during execution of a block of program is the *declaration*. One of the great advantages of the declaration is that the scope of use of a variable is made manifest to the reader and writer; and furthermore, the compiler can make a compile-time check that the variable is never used at a time when it is not allocated. This suggests that the declaration would be a very suitable notation by which a parallel process may express the acquisition and relinquishment of other resources, such as line printers. After all, a line printer may be regarded as a data structure (largely implemented in hardware) on which certain operations (e.g. print a line) are defined to be available to the programmer. More accurately, the concept of a line printer may be regarded as a type or class of variable, new instances of which can be 'created' (i.e. claimed) and named by means of declaration, e.g., using the notation of Pascal (Wirth 1971c):

begin *managementreport*: *lineprinter*; ... .

The individual operations on this variable may be denoted by the notations of Chapter 8:

managementreport.output(*itemline*);

which is called from within the block in which the *managementreport* is declared, and which has the effect of outputting the value of *itemline* to the line printer allocated to *managementreport*.

This proposal has a number of related advantages:

(1) The normal scope rules ensure that no programmer will use a resource without claiming it,
(2) or forget to release it when he has finished with it.
(3) The same proof rule for declarations (given in Hoare [17]) may be used for parallel processes.
(4) The programmer may abstract from the number of items of resource actually available.
(5) If the implementer has available several disjoint items of a resource (e.g. two line printers), they may be allocated simultaneously to several processes within the same program.

These last three advantages are not achieved by the proposal in [22],

There are also two disadvantages:

(1) Resource constraints may cause deadlock, which an implementation should try to avoid by compile-time and/or run-time techniques ([22], Dijkstra 1968b). This proposal gives no means by which a programmer can assist in this.
(2) The scope rules for blocks ensure that resources are released in exactly the reverse order to that in which they are acquired. It is sometimes possible to secure greater efficiency by relaxing this constraint.

Both these disadvantages may reduce the amount of parallelism achievable in circumstances where the demand on resources is close to the limit of their availability. But of course they can never affect the logical correctness of the programs.

It is noteworthy that the validity of sharing a resource between two processes, provided that they are not using it at the same time, also depends on the principle of commutativity of units of action. In this case, the entire block within which a resource is claimed and used must be regarded as a single unit of action, and must not be interleaved with execution of any other block to which the same resource is allocated. The programmer presumably does not mind which of these two blocks is executed first; for example, he does not mind which of the two files is output first on the line printer, because he is interested in them only after they have been separated by the operator. Thus as far as he is concerned, the two blocks commute as units of action; of course, he could not tolerate arbitrary interleaving of lines from the two files.

15.5 Co-operating processes

Hitherto, parallel programming has been confined to disjoint and competing processes, which can be guaranteed by a compile-time check to operate on disjoint data spaces. The reason for insisting on disjointness is that this is an easy way for the compiler to check that the units of action of each process will commute. In the next two sections we shall investigate the effects of relaxing this restriction, at the cost of placing upon the programmer the responsibility of proving that the units of action commute. Processes which update one or more common variables by commutative operations are said to *co-operate.*

One consequence of the commutativity requirement is that neither process can access the *value* of the shared variable, because this value will in general depend on whether it is taken before or after updating by the other process. Furthermore, updating of a shared variable must be regarded as a single unit of action, which occurs either wholly before or wholly after any other such updating. For these reasons, the use of normal assignment for updating a variable seems a bit misleading, and it seems better to introduce the kind of notation used in Hoare ([30]), for example:

$$n{:}{+}\,1 \qquad \text{in place of} \qquad n := n + 1.$$

One useful commutative operation which may be invoked on a shared set is that which adds members to that set, i.e. set union:

$$s{:}\cup t \qquad (\text{i.e. } s := s \cup t),$$

since evidently $s{:}\cup t; s{:}\cup t' \equiv s{:}\cup t'; s{:}\cup t$ for all values of t and t'. A similar commutative operation is set subtraction, which removes any elements of t from s:

$$s{:}-\,t.$$

As an example of the use of this, consider the prime-finding algorithm known as the sieve of Eratosthenes. An abstract parallel version of this algorithm may be written using traditional set notations:

sieve:= $\{i \mid 2 \leqslant i \leqslant N\}$;
p1:= 2; *p2*:= 3;
while $p1^2 \leqslant N$ **do**
  begin {remove multiples of (*p1*)||remove multiples of (*p2*)};
    if $p2^2 < N$ **then** *p1*:= $min\{i \mid i > p2 \wedge i \in sieve\}$
        else *p1*:= *p2*;
    if $p1^2 < N$ **then** *p2*:= $min\{i \mid i > p1 \wedge i \in sieve\}$
  end;

The validity of the parallelism can be assured if the only operation on the sieve performed by the re-entrant procedure 'remove multiples of (*p*)' is set subtraction:

procedure *remove multiples of* (*p*: 2..*N*);
  begin *i*: 2..*N*;
    for *i*:= p^2 **step** *p* **until** *N* **do** *sieve*:– {*i*}
  end;

Of course, when a variable is a large data structure, as in the example given above, the apparently atomic operations upon it may in practice require many actual atomic machine operations. In this case an implementation must ensure that these machine operations are not interleaved with some other operation on that same variable. A part of a program which must not be interleaved with itself or with some other part is known as a critical region (Dijkstra 1968b). The notational structure suggested in Chapter 8 seems to be a good one for specifying updating operations on variables, whether they are shared or not; and the proof rules in the two cases are identical. The need to set up an exclusion mechanism for a shared variable supports the suggestion of Brinch Hansen (1973) that the possibility of sharing should be mentioned when the variable is declared.

It is worthy of note that the validity of a parallel algorithm depends only on the fact that the *abstract* operations on the structured variable commute. The actual effects on the concrete representation of that variable may possibly depend on the order of execution, and therefore be non-deterministic. In some sense, the operation of separating two files of line-printer paper is an abstraction function, i.e., a many–one function mapping an ordered pair onto a set. Abstraction may prove to be a very important method of controlling the complexity of parallel algorithms.

In [22] it was suggested that operations on a shared variable *s* should be expressed by the notation

with *s* **do** *Q*,

where *Q* was to be implemented as a critical region, so that its execution would exclude in time the execution of any other critical region with the same variable s. But the present proposal is distinctly superior:

(1) It uses the same notations and proof rules as sequential programs.
(2) It recognizes the important rôle of abstraction.
(3) The intended effect of the operation as a *unit* of action is made more explicit by the notation.
(4) The scope rules make deadlock logically impossible.

Finally, the proof rule given in [22] is quite inadequate to prove co-operation in achieving any goal (other than preservation of an invariant, which was true to start with!).

A useful special case of co-operation between parallel processes which satisfies the commutativity principle is the use of the 'memo function' suggested by Michie (1967). Suppose there are certain values which may or may not be needed by either or both processes, and each value requires some lengthy calculation to determine. It would be wasteful to compute all the values in advance, because it is not known in advance which of them will be needed. However, if the calculation is invoked from one of the co-operating processes, it would be wasteful to throw the result away, because it might well be needed by the other process. Consequently, it may pay to allocate a variable (e.g. an array A) in advance to hold the values in question, and set it initially to some null value. The function which computes the desired result is now adapted to first look at the relevant element of A. If this is not null, the function immediately returns the value it finds without further computation. If not, the function computes the result and stores it in the variable. The proof of the correctness of such a technique is based on the invariance of some such assertion as:

$$\forall i(A[i] \neq \mathbf{null} \Rightarrow A[i] = f(i)),$$

where A is the array (possibly sparse) in which the results are stored, and f is the desired function. The updating of the array A must be a single unit of action; the calculation of the function f may, of course, be re-entrant.

15.6 Communicating programs

The commutativity principle, which lies at the basis of the treatment of the preceding sections, effectively precludes all possibility of communication between processes, for the following reason. The method that was used in Section 15.3 to prove

$$Q_1 \parallel Q_2 \equiv Q_1; Q_2$$

can also be used to prove

$$Q_1 \parallel Q_2 \equiv Q_2 \parallel Q_1.$$

It follows that a legitimate implementation of 'parallelism' would be to execute the whole of Q_1 and then the whole of Q_2, or to do exactly the reverse. But if there were any communication between Q_1 and Q_2, this would not be possible, since it would violate the commonsense principle that a communication cannot be received before it has been sent.

In order to permit communication between Q_1 and Q_2 it is necessary to relax the principle of commutativity in such a way that complete execution of Q_2 before starting Q_1 is no longer possible. Consider an arbitrary unit of action q_1 of Q_1, and an arbitrary unit of action q_2 of Q_2. We say that q_1 and q_2 *semicommute* if:

$$q_2;\, q_1 \subseteq q_1;\, q_2.$$

If all q_1 and q_2 semicommute, we say that Q_1 and Q_2 are *communicating* processes, and that Q_1 is the producer process, and Q_2 is the consumer (Dijkstra 1968b).

The effect of semicommutivity is that some interleavings of units of action may be undefined; but moving actions of Q_2 *after* actions of Q_1 will never give a different result or make the interleaving less well-defined; consequently the execution of the whole of Q_1 before starting Q_2 is still a feasible implementation, in fact the one that is most defined:

$$Q_1 \,\|\, Q_2 \subseteq Q_1;\, Q_2.$$

Thus it is still justified to use the same proof rule for parallel as for sequential programs.

If assertional proof methods are used to define a programming-language feature, it is reasonable to place upon an implementor the injunction to bring a program to a successful conclusion whenever it is logically feasible to do so (or there is a good engineering reason not to, e.g., integer overflow). Of course it is not logically possible to terminate a program of which *false* is provably true on termination. In the case of communicating programs, termination can be achieved by simply delaying an action of Q_2 where necessary until Q_1 has performed such actions as make it defined, which will always occur provided Q_1; Q_2 terminates.

The paradigm cases of semicommutative operations are input and output of items to a sequence. Output of an item x to sequence s will be denoted:

$$s.output(x);$$

it is equivalent to

$$s := s^\frown\langle x\rangle;$$

where $^\frown$ is the symbol of concatenation, and $\langle x\rangle$ is the sequence whose only item is x. This operation appends the item x to the end of the sequence and is always defined. Input of the first item from a sequence s to the variable y

will be denoted:

$$s.input(y)$$

which is equivalent to a unit of action consisting of two operations:

$$y := first(s); \qquad s := rest(s);$$

where *first* maps a sequence onto its first item and *rest* maps a sequence onto a shorter sequence, namely the sequence with its first item removed. The removal of an item from an empty sequence is obviously undefined; on a non-empty sequence it is always defined. A sequence to which an item has just been output is never empty. Hence

$$s.input(y); s.output(x) \subseteq s.output(x); s.input(y)$$

i.e., these operations semicommute. Consequently a sequence may be used to communicate between two processes, provided that the first performs only output and the second performs only input. If the second process tries to input too much, their parallel execution does not terminate, but neither does their sequential execution. Processes communicating by means of a sequence were called coroutines by Conway (1963), who pointed out the equivalence between sequential and parallel execution.

In practice, for reasons of economy, the potentially infinite sequence used for communication is often replaced by a bounded buffer, with sufficient space to accommodate only a few items. In this case, the operation of output will have to be delayed when the buffer is full, until input has created space for a new item. Furthermore, the program may fail to terminate if the number of items output exceeds the the number of items input by more than the size of the buffer. And finally, since either process may have to wait for the other, purely sequential execution is in general no longer possible, because it does not terminate if the *total* length of the output sequence is larger than the buffer (which it usually is). Thus the parallel program is actually more defined than the corresponding sequential one, which may seem to invalidate our proof methods.

The solution to this problem is to consider the relationship between the abstract program using an unbounded sequence and the concrete program using a bounded buffer representation for the sequence. In this case, the concrete program is the same as the abstract one in all respects except that it contains an operation of concrete output (to the buffer) whenever the abstract program contains abstract output (to the sequence), and similarly for input. Concrete output always has the same effect as abstract output when it is defined, but is sometimes undefined (when the buffer is full), i.e.:

$$\text{concrete output} \subseteq \text{abstract output}.$$

The replacement of an operation by a less well-defined one can never change the result of a program (by the principle of continuity (Scott 1970)), so the concrete program is still contained in the abstract one

$$\text{concrete} \subseteq \text{abstract}.$$

This justifies the use of the same proof rule for the concrete as for the abstract program. The abstract sequence plays the role of the 'mythical' variables used by Clint (1973); here again, abstraction proves to be a vital programming tool.

In order to implement a concrete data representation for a variable which is being used to communicate between processes, it is necessary to have some facility for causing a process to 'wait' when it is about to perform an operation which is undefined on the abstract data or impossible on its current representation. Furthermore, there must be some method for 'signalling' to wake up a waiting process. One method of achieving this is the condition variable described in Hoare ([42]). Of course, if either process of the concrete program can wait for the other, it is possible for the program to reach deadlock, when both processes are waiting. In this case it is not reasonable to ask the implementor to find a way out of the deadlock, since it would involve a combinatorial investigation, where each trial could involve backtracking the program to an earlier point in its execution. It is therefore the programmer's responsibility to avoid deadlock. The assertional proof methods given here cannot be used to prove absence of deadlock, which is a form of nontermination peculiar to parallel programs.

A natural generalization of one-way communication is two-way communication, whereby one process Q_1 uses a variable s_1 to communicate to Q_2, and Q_2 uses a variable s_2 to communicate with Q_1. Communication is achieved, as before, by semicommutative operations. It is now impossible to execute Q_1 and Q_2 sequentially in either order; and it is plain that the proof rule should be symmetric. Furthermore, the correctness of Q_1 may depend on some property S_2 of s_2 which Q_2 must make true, and similarly, Q_2 may need to assume some property S_1 of s_1 which Q_1 must make true. Hence we derive the rule:

$$\frac{P_1 \wedge S_2 \{Q_1\}\ S_1 \wedge R_1 \quad P_2 \wedge S_1 \{Q_2\}\ S_2 \wedge R_2}{P_1 \wedge P_2 \{Q_1 \parallel Q_2\}\ R_1 \wedge R_2}$$

(Rule of Two-way Communication)

where P_1, Q_1, R_1, S_1 are disjoint from P_2, Q_2, R_2, S_2 except for variables s_1, s_2, which are subject only to semicommutative operations in Q_1 and Q_2 as explained above; and P_1, S_1, R_2 may contain s_1 (but not s_2) and P_2, S_2, R_1 may contain s_2 (but not s_1). The informal proof of this is also complex. The complexity of the rule and its proof suggests that two-way communication is likely to be a more problematic programming method than one-way. Also, the problems of possible deadlock are much more severe.

15.7 Summary

This paper explores the conditions under which the introduction of parallelism (concurrency) in a program does not increase the complexity of the program, as judged by the ease of proving its correctness. These conditions are formulated as syntactic rules, which can in principle be enforced by compile-time checks. The basis rule is that of disjointness, which states that any nonlocal variable updated by any parallel process must not be accessed by any other parallel process. Under this condition, the effect of a parallel program is the same as if its constituent processes had been executed sequentially; the proof rule is therefore also the same.

The remainder of the paper examines the conditions under which the strict rule of disjointness can be relaxed. Three cases are distinguished:

(1) Competing processes, which require exclusive use of some global resource during certain phases of their execution.
(2) Co-operating processes, each of which makes its contribution to the construction of some final desired result.
(3) Communicating processes, which transmit information to each other at intermediate stages in their progress.

For competing processes, it is suggested that an ALGOL 60 style of declaration provides a suitable notation and proof rule. For co-operating processes it is shown that their correctness depends on a proof of the commutativity of the updating operations on the shared data; and for communicating processes it is shown that a weaker form of commutativity (semicommutativity) is required. These last two conditions cannot be checked at compile time.

SIXTEEN

Communicating sequential processes

E. W. Dijkstra, in his Foreword to [94] writes:

> When concurrency confronted the computing community about a quarter of a century ago, it caused an endless confusion,... The disentanglement of that confusion required the hard work of a mature and devoted scientist who, with luck, would clarify the situation. Tony Hoare has devoted a major part of his scientific endeavours to that challenge, and we have every reason to be grateful for that.

CSP is the culmination of his language design work to harness parallelism. Monitors (cf. Chapter 12) had shown that the confusion coming from shared store could be avoided but the problems caused by the need to suspend an execution which could not complete still betray machine-level origins such as interrupts. The boldest step in the design of CSP is to base the whole interaction between processes on unbuffered communication. Add to this a clear approach to nondeterminacy (though some would argue with the treatment of 'fairness') and a clear notation and the result is a language which dramatically simplifies the problem of constructing (correct) parallel systems. Hoare had liked the communicating process model of concurrency since 1967–68 when he left Elliott. His first attempt to describe a guarded-command type of construct was disliked by Edsger W. Dijkstra because of the cumbersome notation. Hoare's study of Simula put him onto the track which led to Monitors and Pascal-Plus.

Hoare's ideas on parallelism had been evolving since he presented [58] at the 1975 Marktoberdorf Summer School. In discussions there, Dijkstra again objected to the cumbersome notations and the semantics based on complex nested copying. In addition, Hoare recalls that his teaching at Belfast showed him that students kept confusing input/output with parameter passing. A Science Research Council Senior Fellowship in 1976–77 gave him the chance to work on the details of the CSP paper which was submitted in March 1977, revised in August of the same year and published ([66]) in August 1978. This

---

C. A. R. Hoare; Communicating sequential processes, *Comm. ACM* **21**(8), 666–77 (1978).

is one of the most widely cited papers on parallelism and it has been reprinted several times.

This paper did not, of course, solve all of the problems. It concedes that

'The most serious [problem] is that it fails to suggest any proof method to assist in the development and verification of correct programs.' But the work on both models and proof rules was already underway before actual publication and soon led to a large body of research material, the easiest access to which is certainly Hoare's book [94].

The CSP language itself also evolved and, amongst other derivatives Occam™ (see Jones 1987) is particularly important. This language is one fruit of Hoare's collaboration with INMOS. The development of the related transputer chip is another major development. Hoare had expected even in 1976 that such machine architectures would come quickly.

Abstract

This paper suggests that input and output are basic primitives of programming and that parallel composition of communicating sequential processes is a fundamental program structuring method. When combined with a development of Dijkstra's guarded command, these concepts are surprisingly versatile. Their use is illustrated by sample solutions of a variety of familiar programming exercises.

16.1 Introduction

Among the primitive concepts of computer programming, and of the high-level languages in which programs are expressed, the action of assignment is familiar and well understood. In fact, any change of the internal state of a machine executing a program can be modelled as an assignment of a new value to some variable part of that machine. However, the operations of input and output, which affect the external environment of a machine, are not nearly so well understood. They are often added to a programming language only as an afterthought.

Among the structuring methods for computer programs, three basic constructs have received widespread recognition and use: A repetitive construct (e.g. the **while** loop), an alternative construct (e.g. the conditional **if**..**then**..**else**), and normal sequential program composition (often denoted by a semicolon). Less agreement has been reached about the design of other important program structures, and many suggestions have been made. Subroutines (FORTRAN), procedures (ALGOL 60 (Naur 1960)), entries (PL/I), coroutines (UNIX (Thompson 1976)), classes (Simula 67 (Dahl *et al.* 1967)), processes and monitors (Concurrent Pascal (Brinch Hansen 1975)), clusters (CLU (Liskov 1974)), forms (ALPHARD (Wulf *et al.* 1976)), actors (Atkinson and Hewitt 1976).

The traditional stored-program digital computer has been designed primarily for deterministic execution of a single sequential program. Where the desire for greater speed has led to the introduction of parallelism, every attempt has been made to disguise this fact from the programmer, either by hardware itself (as in the multiple function units of CDC 6600) or by the software (as in an I/O control package, or a multiprogrammed operating system). However, developments of processor technology suggest that a multiprocessor machine, constructed from a number of similar self-contained processors (each with its own store), may become more powerful, capacious, reliable, and economical than a machine which is disguised as a monoprocessor.

In order to use such a machine effectively on a single task, the component processors must be able to communicate and to synchronize with each other. Many methods of achieving this have been proposed. A widely adopted method of communication is by inspection and updating of a common store (as in ALGOL 68 (van Wijngaarden 1969), PL/I, and many machine codes). However, this can create severe problems in the construction of correct programs and it may lead to expense (e.g. crossbar switches) and unreliability (e.g. glitches) in some technologies of hardware implementation. A greater variety of methods has been proposed for synchronization: semaphores (Dijkstra 1968b), events (PL/I), conditional critical regions (Hoare [22]), monitors and queues (Concurrent Pascal (Brinch Hansen 1975)), and path expressions. Most of these are demonstrably adequate for their purpose, but there is no widely recognized criterion for choosing between them.

This paper makes an ambitious attempt to find a single simple solution to all these problems. The essential proposals are:

(1) Dijkstra's guarded commands (1975a) are adopted (with a slight change of notation) as sequential control structures, and as the sole means of introducing and controlling nondeterminism.

(2) A parallel command, based on Dijkstra's *parbegin* (1968b), specifies concurrent execution of its constituent sequential commands (processes). All the processes start simultaneously, and the parallel command ends only when they are all finished. They may not communicate with each other by updating global variables.

(3) Simple forms of input and output command are introduced. They are used for communication between concurrent processes.

(4) Such communication occurs when one process names another as destination for output *and* the second process names the first as source for input. In this case, the value to be output is copied from the first process to the second. There is *no* automatic buffering: In general, an input or output command is delayed until the other process is ready with the corresponding output or input. Such delay is invisible to the delayed process.

(5) Input commands may appear in guards. A guarded command with an input guard is selected for execution only if and when the source named in the input command is ready to execute the corresponding output command. If several input guards of a set of alternatives have ready destinations, only one is selected and the others have *no* effect; but the choice between them is arbitrary. In an efficient implementation, an output command which has been ready for a long time should be favoured; but the definition of a language cannot specify this since the relative speed of execution of the processes is undefined.
(6) A repetitive command may have input guards. If all the sources named by them have terminated, then the repetitive command also terminates.
(7) A simple pattern-matching feature, similar to that of Reynolds (1965), is used to discriminate the structure of an input message, and to access its components in a secure fashion. This feature is used to inhibit input of messages that do not match the specified pattern.

The programs expressed in the proposed language are intended to be implementable both by a conventional machine with a single main store, and by a fixed network of processors connected by input/output channels (although very different optimizations are appropriate in the different cases). It is consequently a rather static language: The text of a program determines a fixed upper bound on the number of processes operating concurrently; there is no recursion and no facility for process-valued variables. In other respects also, the language has been stripped to the barest minimum necessary for explanation of its more novel features.

The concept of a communicating sequential process is shown in Sections 16.3–16.5 to provide a method of expressing solutions to many simple programming exercises which have previously been employed to illustrate the use of various proposed programming-language features. This suggests that the process may constitute a synthesis of a number of familar and new programming ideas. The reader is invited to skip the examples which do not interest him.

However, this paper also ignores many serious problems. The most serious is that it fails to suggest any proof method to assist in the development and verification of correct programs. Secondly, it pays no attention to the problems of efficient implementation, which may be particularly serious on a traditional sequential computer. It is probable that a solution to these problems will require (1) imposition of restrictions in the use of the proposed features; (2) re-introduction of distinctive notations for the most common and useful special cases; (3) development of automatic optimization techniques; and (4) the design of appropriate hardware.

Thus the concepts and notations introduced in this paper (although described in the next section in the form of a programming language fragment) should not be regarded as suitable for use as a programming language, either for abstract or for concrete programming. They are at best only a partial solution to the problems tackled. Further discussion of these and other points will be found in Section 16.7.

16.2 Concepts and notations

The style of the following description is borrowed from ALGOL 60 (Naur, 1960). Types, declarations, and expressions have not been treated; in the examples, a Pascal-like notation (Wirth 1971c) has usually been adopted. The curly braces { } have been introduced into BNF to denote none or more repetitions of the enclosed material. (Sentences in parentheses refer to an implementation: they are not strictly part of a language definition.)

⟨*command*⟩ ::= ⟨*simple command*⟩ | ⟨*structured command*⟩
⟨*simple command*⟩ ::= ⟨*null command*⟩ | ⟨*assignment command*⟩
  | ⟨*input command*⟩ | ⟨*output command*⟩
⟨*structured command*⟩ ::= ⟨*alternative command*⟩
  | ⟨*repetitive command*⟩ | ⟨*parallel command*⟩
⟨*null command*⟩ ::= *skip*
⟨*command list*⟩ ::= {⟨*declaration*⟩; | ⟨*command*⟩;}⟨*command*⟩

A command specifies the behaviour of a device executing the command. It may succeed or fail. Execution of a simple command, if successful, may have an effect on the internal state of the executing device (in the case of assignment), or on its external environment (in the case of output), or on both (in the case of input). Execution of a structured command involves execution of some or all of its constituent commands, and if any of these fail, so does the structured command. (In this case, whenever possible, an implementation should provide some kind of comprehensible error diagnostic message.)

A null command has no effect and never fails.

A command list specifies sequential execution of its constituent commands in the order written. Each declaration introduces a fresh variable with a scope which extends from its declaration to the end of the command list.

16.2.1 Parallel commands

⟨*parallel command*⟩ ::= [⟨*process*⟩{||⟨*process*⟩}]
⟨*process*⟩ ::= ⟨*process label*⟩⟨*command list*⟩
⟨*process label*⟩ ::= ⟨*empty*⟩ | ⟨*identifier*⟩ ::
  | ⟨*identifier*⟩ (⟨*label subscript*⟩{,⟨*label subscript*⟩})::

⟨*label subscript*⟩ ::= ⟨*integer constant*⟩ | ⟨*range*⟩
⟨*integer constant*⟩ ::= ⟨*numeral*⟩ | ⟨*bound variable*⟩
⟨*bound variable*⟩ ::= ⟨*identifier*⟩
⟨*range*⟩ ::= ⟨*bound variable*⟩ : ⟨*lower bound*⟩ .. ⟨*upper bound*⟩
⟨*lower bound*⟩ ::= ⟨*integer constant*⟩
⟨*upper bound*⟩ ::= ⟨*integer constant*⟩

Each process of a parallel command must be *disjoint* from every other process of the command, in the sense that it does not mention any variable which occurs as a target variable (see Sections 6.2.2 and 6.2.3) in any other process.

A process label without subscripts, or one whose label subscripts are all integer constants, serves as a name for the command list to which it is prefixed; its scope extends over the whole of the parallel command. A process whose label subscripts include one or more ranges stands for a series of processes, each with the same label and command list, except that each has a different combination of values substituted for the bound variables. These values range between the lower bound and the upper bound inclusively. For example, $X(i:l..n) :: CL$ stands for

$$X(1) :: CL_1 \| X(2) :: CL_2 \| \ldots \| X(n) :: CL_n$$

where each CL_j is formed from CL by replacing every occurrence of the bound variable i by the numeral j. After all such expansions, each process label in a parallel command must occur only once and the processes must be well formed and disjoint.

A parallel command specifies concurrent execution of its constituent processes. They all start simultaneously and the parallel command terminates successfully only if and when they have all successfully terminated. The relative speed with which they are executed is arbitrary.

Examples

(1) [*cardreader*?*cardimage* || *lineprinter*!*lineimage*]

Performs the two constituent commands in parallel, and terminates only when both operations are complete. The time taken may be as low as the longer of the times taken by each constituent process, i.e. the sum of its computing, waiting, and transfer times.

(2) [*west* :: *DISASSEMBLE* || *X* :: *SQUASH* || *east* :: *ASSEMBLE*]

The three processes have the names *west*, *X*, and *east*. The capitalized words stand for command lists which will be defined in later examples.

(3) [*room* :: *ROOM* || *fork*(*i*:0..4) :: *FORK* || *phil*(*i*:0..4) :: *PHIL*]

There are eleven processes. The behaviour of *room* is specified by the command list *ROOM*. The behaviour of the five processes *fork*(0), *fork*(1), *fork*(2), *fork*(3), *fork*(4), is specified by the command list *FORK*, within which the bound variable *i* indicates the identity of the particular fork. Similar remarks apply to the five processes *PHIL*.

16.2.2 Assignment commands

⟨*assignment command*⟩ ::= ⟨*target variable*⟩ := ⟨*expression*⟩
⟨*expression*⟩ ::= ⟨*simple expression*⟩ | ⟨*structured expression*⟩
⟨*structured expression*⟩ ::= ⟨*constructor*⟩ (⟨*expression list*⟩)
⟨*constructor*⟩ ::= ⟨*identifier*⟩ | ⟨*empty*⟩
⟨*expression list*⟩ ::= ⟨*empty*⟩ | ⟨*expression*⟩{,⟨*expression*⟩}
⟨*target variable*⟩ ::= ⟨*simple variable*⟩ | ⟨*structured target*⟩
⟨*structured target*⟩ ::= ⟨*constructor*⟩ (⟨*target variable list*⟩)
⟨*target variable list*⟩ ::= ⟨*empty*⟩ | ⟨*target variable*⟩
    {,⟨*target variable*⟩}

An expression denotes a value which is computed by an executing device by application of its constituent operators to the specified operands. The value of an expression is undefined if any of these operations are undefined. The value denoted by a simple expression may be simple or structured. The value denoted by a structured expression is structured; its constructor is that of the expression, and its components are the list of values denoted by the constituent expressions of the expression list.

An assignment command specifies evaluation of its expression, and assignment of the denoted value to the target variable. A simple target variable may have assigned to it a simple or a structured value. A structured target variable may have assigned to it a structured value, with the same constructor. The effect of such assignment is to assign to each constituent simpler variable of the structured target the value of the corresponding component of the structured value. Consequently, the value denoted by the target variable, if evaluated *after* a successful assignment, is the same as the value denoted by the expression, as evaluated *before* the assignment.

An assignment fails if the value of its expression is undefined, or if that value does not *match* the target variable, in the following sense: A *simple* target variable matches any value of its type. A *structured* target variable matches a structured value, provided that: (1) they have the same constructor, (2) the target variable list is the same length as the list of components of the value, (3) each target variable of the list matches the corresponding component of the value list. A structured value with no components is known as a 'signal'.

Examples

(1) $x := x + 1$	the value of x after the assignment is the same as the value of $x + 1$ before.

(2) $(x, y) := (y, x)$	exchanges the value of x and y.
(3) $x := cons(left, right)$	constructs a structured value and assigns it to x.
(4) $cons(left, right) := x$	fails if x does not have the form $cons(y, x)$; but if it does, then y is assigned to *left*, and z is assigned to *right*.
(5) $insert(n) := insert(2 * x + 1)$	equivalent to $n := 2 * x + 1$.
(6) $c := P(\,)$	assigns to c a 'signal' with constructor P, and no components.
(7) $P(\,) := c$	fails if the value of c is not $P()$; otherwise has no effect.
(8) $insert(n) := has(n)$	fails, due to mismatch.

Note: Successful execution of both (3) and (4) ensures the truth of the postcondition $x = cons(left, right)$; but (3) does so by changing x and (4) does so by changing left and right. Example (4) will fail if there is *no* value of left and right which satisfies the postcondition.

16.2.3 Input and output commands

⟨*input command*⟩ ::= ⟨*source*⟩?⟨*target variable*⟩
⟨*output command*⟩ ::= ⟨*destination*⟩!⟨*expression*⟩
⟨*source*⟩ ::= ⟨*process name*⟩
⟨*destination*⟩ ::= ⟨*process name*⟩
⟨*process name*⟩ ::= ⟨*identifier*⟩ | ⟨*identifier*⟩(⟨*subscripts*⟩)
⟨*subscripts*⟩ ::= ⟨*integer expression*⟩{,⟨*integer expression*⟩}

Input and output commands specify communication between two concurrently operating sequential processes. Such a process may be implemented in hardware as a special-purpose device (e.g. cardreader or line printer), or its behaviour may be specified by one of the constituent processes of a parallel command. Communication occurs between two processes of a parallel command whenever (1) an input command in one process specifies as its source the process name of the other process; (2) an output command in the other process specifies as its destination the process name of the first process; and (3) the target variable of the input command matches the value denoted by the expression of the output command. On these conditions, the input and output commands are said to *correspond*. Commands which correspond are executed simultaneously, and their combined effect is to assign the value of the expression of the output command to the target variable of the input command.

An input command fails if its source is terminated. An output command fails if its destination is terminated or if its expression is undefined.

(The requirement of synchronization of input and output commands means that an implementation will have to delay whichever of the two commands happens to be ready first. The delay is ended when the corresponding command in the other process is also ready, or when the other process terminates. In the latter case the first command fails. It is also possible that the delay will never be ended, for example, if a group of processes are attempting communication but none of their input and output commands correspond with each other. This form of failure is known as a deadlock.)

Examples

(1) *cardreader*?*cardimage* — from *cardreader*, read a card and assign its value (an array of characters) to the variable *cardimage*.

(2) *lineprinter*!*lineimage* — to *lineprinter*, send the value of *lineimage* for printing.

(3) $X?(x, y)$ — from process named X, input a pair of values and assign them to x and y.

(4) $DIV!(3 * a + b, 13)$ — to process DIV, output the two specified values.

Note: If a process named DIV issues command (3), and a process named X issues command (4), these are executed simultaneously, and have the same effect as the assignment: $(x, y) := (3 * a + b, 13)$ $(\equiv x := 3 * a + b; y := 13)$.

(5) *console*$(i)?c$ — from the ith element of an array of consoles, input a value and assign it to c.

(6) *console*$(j - 1)!$"A" — to the $(j - 1)$th console, output character "A".

(7) $X(i)?V(\ )$ — from the ith of an array of processes X, input a signal $V(\ )$; refuse to input any other signal.

(8) *sem*!$P(\ )$ — to *sem* output a signal $P(\ )$.

16.2.4 Alternative and repetitive commands

⟨repetitive command⟩ ::= ∗*⟨alternative command⟩*
⟨alternative command⟩ ::= [*⟨guarded command⟩*
  { □*⟨guarded command⟩*}]
⟨guarded command⟩ ::= *⟨guard⟩* → *⟨command list⟩*
  | (*⟨range⟩*{,*⟨range⟩*})*⟨guard⟩* → *⟨command list⟩*
⟨guard⟩ ::= *⟨guard list⟩* | *⟨guard list⟩*;*⟨input command⟩*
  | *⟨input command⟩*
  ⟨guard list⟩ ::= *⟨guard element⟩*{;*⟨guard element⟩*}
⟨guard element⟩ ::= *⟨Boolean expression⟩* | *⟨declaration⟩*

A guarded command with one or more ranges stands for a series of guarded commands, each with the same guard and command list, except that each has a different combination of values substituted for the bound variables. The values range between the lower bound and upper bound inclusive. For example, $(i:1\,..\,n)G \rightarrow CL$ stands for

$$G_1 \rightarrow CL_1 \square G_2 \rightarrow CL_2 \square \ldots \square G_n \rightarrow CL_n$$

where each $G_j \rightarrow CL_j$ is formed from $G \rightarrow CL$ by replacing every occurrence of the bound variable i by the numeral j.

A guarded command is executed only if and when the execution of its guard does not fail. First its guard is executed and then its command list. A guard is executed by execution of its constituent elements from left to right. A Boolean expression is evaluated: If it denotes *false*, the guard fails, but an expression that denotes *true* has no effect. A declaration introduces a fresh variable with a scope that extends from the declaration to the end of the guarded command. An input command at the end of a guard is executed only if and when a corresponding output command is executed. (An implementation may test whether a guard fails simply by trying to execute it, and discontinuing execution if and when it fails. This is valid because such a discontinued execution has no effect on the state of the executing device.)

An alternative command specifies execution of exactly one of its constituent guarded commands. Consequently, if all guards fail, the alternative command fails. Otherwise an arbitrary one with successfully executable guard is selected and executed. (An implementation should take advantage of its freedom of selection to ensure efficient execution and good response. For example, when input commands appear as guards, the command which corresponds to the earliest ready and matching output command should in general be preferred; and certainly, no executable and ready output command should be passed over unreasonably often.)

A repetitive command specifies as many iterations as possible of its constituent alternative command. Consequently, when all guards fail, the repetitive command terminates with no effect. Otherwise, the alternative command is executed once and then the whole repetitive command is executed again. (Consider a repetitive command when all its true guard lists end in an input guard. Such a command may have to be delayed until either (1) an output command corresponding to one of the input guards becomes ready, or (2) all the sources named by the input guards have terminated. In case (2), the repetitive command terminates. If neither event ever occurs, the process fails (in deadlock).)

Examples

(1) $[x \geqslant y \rightarrow m := x \,\square\, y \geqslant x \rightarrow m := y]$

If $x \geqslant y$, assign x to m; if $y \geqslant x$ assign y to m; if both $x \geqslant y$ and $y \geqslant x$, either assignment can be executed.

(2) $i := 0; *[i < size;\ content(i) \neq n \rightarrow i := i + 1]$

The repetitive command scans the elements content(i), for $i = 0, 1, \ldots,$ until either $i \geqslant size$, or a value equal to n is found.

(3) $*[c : character;\ west!c \rightarrow east!c]$

This reads all the characters output by *west*, and outputs them one by one to *east*. The repetition terminates when the process *west* terminates.

(4) $*[(i : 1\,..\,10) continue(i);\ console(i)?c \rightarrow X!(i, c);\ console(i)!ack(\,);$
$continue(i) := (c \neq sign\ off)]$

This command inputs repeatedly from any of ten consoles, provided that the corresponding element of the Boolean array *continue* is *true*. The bound variable i identifies the originating console. Its value, together with the character just input, is output to X, and an acknowledgment signal is sent back to the originating console. If the character indicated 'sign off', *continue*(i) is set *false*, to prevent further input from that console. The repetitive command terminates when all ten elements of *continue* are *false*. (An implementation should ensure that no console which is ready to provide input will be ignored unreasonably often.)

(5) $*[n{:}integer;\ X?insert(n) \rightarrow INSERT$
$\square\, n{:}\ integer;\ X?has(n) \rightarrow SEARCH;\ X!(i < size)$
$]$

(Here, and elsewhere, capitalized words *INSERT* and *SEARCH* stand as abbreviations for program text defined separately.)

On each iteration this command accepts from X *either* (a) a request to *insert*(n), (followed by *INSERT*) *or* (b) a question *has*(n), to which it outputs an answer back to X. The choice between (a) and (b) is made by the next output command in X. The repetitive command terminates when X does. If X sends a non-matching message, deadlock will result.

(6) $*[X?V(\,) \rightarrow val := val + 1$
$\quad \square\, val > 0;\ Y?P(\,) \rightarrow val := val - 1$
$\quad]$

On each iteration, accept *either* a $V(\,)$ signal from X and increment *val*, *or* a $P(\,)$ from Y, and decrement *val*. But the second alternative cannot be selected unless *val* is positive (after which *val* will remain invariantly nonnegative). (When $val > 0$, the choice depends on the relative speeds of X and Y, and is not determined.) The repetitive command will terminate when both X and Y are terminated, or when X is terminated and $val \leqslant 0$.

16.3 Coroutines

In parallel programming coroutines appear as a more fundamental program structure than subroutines, which can be regarded as a special case (treated in the next section).

16.3.1 Copy

Problem: Write a process X to copy characters output by process *west* to process *east*.

Solution

$X :: *[c : character;\ west?c \rightarrow east!c]$

Notes
(1) When *west* terminates, the input *west*?*c* will fail, causing termination of the repetitive command, and of process X. Any subsequent input command from *east* will fail.
(2) Process X acts as a single-character buffer between *west* and *east*. It permits *west* to work on production of the next character, before *east* is ready to input the previous one.

16.3.2 Squash

Problem: Adapt the previous program to replace every pair of consecutive asterisks '**' by an upward arrow '↑'. Assume that the final character input is not an asterisk.

Solution

```
X :: *[c: character; west?c →
   [c ≠ asterisk → east?c
   ▯c = asterisk → west?c;
      [c ≠ asterisk → east!asterisk; east!c
      ▯c = asterisk → east!upward arrow
   ]] ]
```

Notes

(1) Since *west* does not end with asterisk, the second *west?c* will not fail.

(2) As an exercise, adapt this process to deal sensibly with input which ends with an odd number of asterisks.

16.3.3 Disassemble

Problem: To read cards from a cardfile and output to process *X* the stream of characters they contain. An extra space should be inserted at the end of each card.

Solution

```
*[cardimage:(1..80)character; cardfile?cardimage →
   i: integer; i:= 1;
   *[i ⩽ 80 → X!cardimage(i); i:= i + 1]
   X!space
```

Notes

(1) '(1..80)*character*' declares an array of 80 characters, with subscripts ranging between 1 and 80.

(2) The repetitive command terminates when the cardfile process terminates.

16.3.4 Assemble

Problem: To read a stream of characters from process *X* and print them in lines of 125 characters on a lineprinter. The last line should be completed with spaces if necessary.

Solution

```
lineimage:(1..125)character;
integer; i:= 1;
*[c: character; X?c →
   lineimage(i):= c;
```

```
    [i ⩽ 124 → i := i + 1
    ▯i = 125 → lineprinter!lineimage; i := 1
  ]  ];
  [i = 1 → skip
  ▯i > 1 → * [i ⩽ 125 → lineimage(i) := space; i := i + 1];
    lineprinter!lineimage
  ]
```

Note
When *X* terminates, so will the first repetitive command of this process. The last line will then be printed, if it has any characters.

16.3.5 Reformat

Problem: Read a sequence of cards of 80 characters each, and print the characters on a line printer at 125 characters per line. Every card should be followed by an extra space, and last line should be completed with space if necessary.

Solution

[*west* :: *DISASSEMBLE* || *X* :: *COPY* || *east* :: *ASSEMBLE*]

Notes
(1) The capitalized names stand for program text defined in previous sections.
(2) The parallel command is designed to terminate after the card file has terminated.
(3) This elementary problem is difficult to solve elegantly without coroutines.

16.3.6 Conway's problem (1963)

Problem: Adapt the above program to replace every pair of consecutive asterisks by an upward arrow.

Solution

[*west* :: *DISASSEMBLE* || *X* :: *SQUASH* || east :: *ASSEMBLE*]

16.4 Subroutines and data representations

A conventional nonrecursive subroutine can be readily implemented as a coroutine, provided that (1) its parameters are called 'by value' and 'by result', and (2) it is disjoint from its calling program. Like a FORTRAN subroutine, a coroutine may retain the values of local variables (*own* variables, in ALGOL terms) and it may use input commands to achieve the effect of 'multiple entry points' in a safer way than PL/I. Thus a coroutine can be used like a Simula class instance as a concrete representation for abstract data.

A coroutine acting as a subroutine is a process operating concurrently with its user process in a parallel command: $[subr :: SUBROUTINE \,\|\, X :: USER]$. The *SUBROUTINE* will contain (or consist of) a repetitive command: $*[X?(value\ params) \rightarrow \ldots;\ X!(result\ params)]$, where '...' computes the results from the values input. The subroutine will terminate when its user does. The *USER* will call the subroutine by a pair of commands:

$$subr!(arguments); \ldots; subr?(results).$$

Any commands between these two will be executed concurrently with the subroutine.

A multiple-entry subroutine, acting as a representation for data (Chapter 8), will also contain a repetitive command which represents each entry by an alternative input to a structured target with the entry name as constructor. For example,

$*[X?entry1(value\ params) \rightarrow \ldots$
$\square X?entry2(value\ params) \rightarrow \ldots$
$]$

The calling process *X* will determine which of the alternatives is activated on each repetition. When *X* terminates, so does this repetitive command. A similar technique in the user program can achieve the effect of multiple exits.

A recursive subroutine can be simulated by an array of processes, one for each level of recursion. The user process is level zero. Each activation communicates its parameters and results with its predecessor and calls its successor if necessary:

$$[recsub(0) :: USER \,\|\, recsub(i{:}\ 1..reclimit) :: RECSUB].$$

The user will call the first element of

$$recsub : recsub(1)!(arguments); \ldots; recsub(1)?(results);.$$

The imposition of a fixed upper bound on recursion depth is necessitated by the 'static' design of the language.

This clumsy simulation of recursion would be even more clumsy for a mutually recursive algorithm. It would not be recommended for conventional programming; it may be more suitable for an array of microprocessors for which the fixed upper bound is also realistic.

In this section, we assume each subroutine is used only by a *single* user process (which may, of course, itself contain parallel commands).

16.4.1 Function: division with remainder

Problem: Construct a process to represent a function-type subroutine, which accepts a positive dividend and divisor, and returns their integer quotient and remainder. Efficiency is of no concern.

Solution

```
[DIV :: *[x, y : integer; X?(x, y) →
    quot, rem: integer; quot := 0; rem := x;
    *[rem ⩾ y → rem := rem − y; quot := quot + 1];
    X!(quot, rem)
    ]
|| X :: USER
]
```

16.4.2 Recursion: factorial

Problem: Compute a factorial by the recursive method, to a given limit.

Solution

```
[fac(i: 1..limit) ::
*[n: integer; fac(i − 1)?n →
    [n = 0 → fac(i − 1)!]
    ▯n > 0 → fac(i + 1)!n − 1,
       r: integer, fac(i + 1)?r, fac(i − 1)!(n * r)
    ]]
|| fac(0) :: USER
]
```

Note
This unrealistic example introduces the technique of the 'iterative array' which will be used to better effect in later examples.

16.4.3 Data representation: small set of integers (see also Chapter 8)

Problem: To represent a set of not more than 100 integers as a process, S, which accepts two kinds of instruction from its calling process X: (1) $S!insert(n)$, insert the integer n in the set, and (2) $S!has(n)$; ...; $S?b$, b is set *true* if *n* is in the set, and *false* otherwise. The initial value of the set is *empty*.

Solution

```
S::
content: (0..99)integer; size: integer; size := 0;
*[n: integer; X?has(n) → SEARCH; X!(i < size)
▯n: integer; X?insert(n) → SEARCH;
   [i < size → skip
   ▯i = size; size < 100 →
      content(size) := n; size := size + 1
] ]
```

where *SEARCH* is an abbreviation for:

```
i: integer; i := 0;
*[i < size; content(i) ≠ n → i := i + 1]
```

Notes

(1) The alternative command with guard '*size* < 100' will fail if an attempt is made to insert more than 100 elements.

(2) The activity of insertion will in general take place concurrently with the calling process. However, any subsequent instruction to *S* will be delayed until the previous insertion is complete.

16.4.4 Scanning a set

Problem: Extend the solution to 16.4.3 by providing a fast method for scanning all members of the set without changing the value of the set. The user program will contain a repetitive command of the form:

```
  S!scan( ); more: Boolean; more := true;
*[more; x: integer; S?next(x) → ... deal with x...
▯more; S?noneleft( ) → more := false
]
```

where *S*!*scan*( ) sets the representation into a scanning mode. The repetitive command serves as a **for** statement, inputting the successive members of *x* from the set and inspecting them until finally the representation sends a signal that there are no members left. The body of the repetitive command is *not* permitted to communicate with *S* in any way.

Solution: Add a third guarded command to the outer repetitive command of *S*:

```
...□X?scan( ) → i: integer; i := 0;
                *[i < size → X!next(content(i)); i := i + 1];
                X!noneleft( )
```

16.4.5 Recursive data representation: Small set of integers

Problem: Same as above, but an array of processes is to be used to achieve a high degree of parallelism. Each process should contain at most one number. When it contains no number, it should answer *false* to all inquiries about membership. On the first insertion, it changes to a second phase of behaviour, in which it deals with instructions from its predecessor, passing some of them on to its successor. The calling process will be named $S(0)$. For efficiency, the set should be sorted, i.e. the ith process should contain the ith largest number.

Solution:

```
S(i:1..100) ::

*[n: integer; S(i – 1)?has(n) → S(0)!false
□n: integer; S(i – 1)?insert(n) →
   *[m: integer; S(i – 1)?has(m) →
      [m ≤ n → S(0)!(m = n)
      □m > n → S(i + 1)!has(m)
      ]
   □m: integer; S(i – 1)?insert(m) →
      [m < n → S(i + 1)!insert(n); n := m
      □m = n → skip
      □m > n → S(i + 1)!insert(m)
] ] ]
```

Notes

(1) The user process $S(0)$ inquires whether n is a member by the commands $S(1)!has(n);\ldots;[(i:1..100)S(i)?b \rightarrow skip]$. The appropriate process will respond to the input command by the output command in line 2 or line 5. This trick avoids passing the answer back 'up the chain'.
(2) Many insertion operations can proceed in parallel, yet any subsequent '*has*' operation will be performed correctly.
(3) All repetitive commands and all processes of the array will terminate after the user process $S(0)$ terminates

16.4.6 Multiple exits: Remove the least member

Exercise: Extend the above solution to respond to a command to yield the least member of the set and to remove it from the set. The user program will invoke the facility by a pair of commands:

$S(1)!least(\ );\ [x\colon integer: S(1)?x \rightarrow \ldots \text{deal with } x \ldots$
$\quad \square S(1)?noneleft(\ ) \rightarrow \ldots$
$\quad]$

or, if he wishes to scan and empty the set, he may write:

$S(1)!least(\ )\colon more\colon Boolean;\ more := true;$
$\quad *[more;\ x\colon integer;\ S(1)?x \rightarrow \ldots \text{deal with } x \ldots;\ S(1)!least(\ )$
$\quad \square more;\ S(1)?noneleft(\ ) \rightarrow more := false$
$\quad]$

Hint: Introduce a Boolean variable, b, initialized to *true*, and prefix this to all the guards of the inner loop. After responding to a $!least(\ )$ command from its predecessor, each process returns its contained value n, asks its successor for its least, and stores the response in n. But if the successor returns '*noneleft*( )', b is set false and the inner loop terminates. The process therefore returns to its initial state (solution due to David Gries).

16.5 Monitors and scheduling

This section shows how a monitor can be regarded as a single process which communicates with more than one user process. However, each user process must have a different name (e.g. *producer*, *consumer*) or a different subscript (e.g. $X(i)$) and each communication with a user must identify its source or destination uniquely.

Consequently, when a monitor is prepared to communicate with *any* of its user processes (i.e. whichever of them calls first) it will use a guarded command with a range. For example:

$$*[(i\colon 1..100)X(i)?(\text{value parameters}) \rightarrow \ldots;\ X(i)!(\text{results})].$$

Here, the bound variable i is used to send the results back to the calling process. If the monitor is not prepared to accept input from some particular user (e.g. $X(j)$) on a given occasion, the input command may be preceded by a Boolean guard. For example, two successive inputs from the same process are inhibited by $j = 0;\quad *[(i\colon 1..100)i \neq j;\ X(i)?(\text{values}) \rightarrow \ldots; j := i]$. Any attempted output from $X(j)$ will be delayed until a subsequent iteration, after the output of some process $X(i)$ has been accepted and dealt with.

Similarly, conditions can be used to delay acceptance of inputs which would violate scheduling constraints – postponing them until some later occasion when some other process has brought the monitor into a state in which the input can validly be accepted. This technique is similar to a conditional critical region (Chapter 8) and it obviates the need for special synchronizing variables such as events, queues, or conditions. However, the absence of these special facilities certainly makes it more difficult or less efficient to solve problems involving priorities – for example, the scheduling of head movement on a disk.

16.5.1 Bounded buffer

Problem: Construct a buffering process X to smooth variations in the speed of output of portions by a producer process and input by a consumer process. The consumer contains pairs of commands $X!more(\ ); X?p$, and the producer contains commands of the form $X!p$. The buffer should contain up to ten portions.

Solution

```
X::
buffer: (0..9) portion;
in, out: integer; in := 0; out := 0;
comment 0 ≤ out ≤ in ≤ out + 10;
  *[in < out + 10; producer?buffer(in mod 10) → in := in + 1
  ▯out < in; consumer?more( ) → consumer!buffer(out mod 10);
     out := out + 1
  ]
```

Notes

(1) When $out < in < out + 10$, the selection of the alternative in the repetitive command will depend on whether the producer produces before the consumer consumes, or vice versa.
(2) When $out = in$, the buffer is empty and the second alternative cannot be selected even if the consumer is ready with its command $X!more(\ )$. However, after the producer has produced its next portion, the consumer's request can be granted on the next iteration.
(3) Similar remarks apply to the producer, when $in = out + 10$.
(4) X is designed to terminate when $out = in$ and the producer has terminated.

16.5.2 Integer semaphore

Problem: To implement an integer semaphore, S, shared among an array $X(i{:}\ 1..100)$ of client processes. Each process may increment the semaphore by $S!V(\ )$ or decrement it by $S!P(\ )$, but the latter command must be delayed if the value of the semaphore is not positive.

Solution

```
S:: val: integer; val:= 0;
  *[(i: 1..100)X(i)? V( ) → val:= val + 1
  □(i: 1..100)val > 0; X(i)? P( ) → val:= val − 1
  ]
```

Notes

(1) In this process, no use is made of knowledge of the subscript i of the calling process.

(2) The semaphore terminates only when all hundred processes of the process array X have terminated.

16.5.3 Dining philosophers

(Problem due to E. W. Dijkstra)

Problem: Five philosophers spend their lives thinking and eating. The philosophers share a common dining room where there is a circular table surrounded by five chairs, each belonging to one philosopher. In the centre of the table there is a large bowl of spaghetti, and the table is laid with five forks (see Fig. 16.1). On feeling hungry, a philosopher enters the dining room, sits in his own chair, and picks up the fork on the left of his place. Unfortunately, the spaghetti is so tangled that he needs to pick up and use the fork on his right as well. When he has finished, he puts down both forks, and leaves the room. The room should keep a count of the number of philosophers in it.

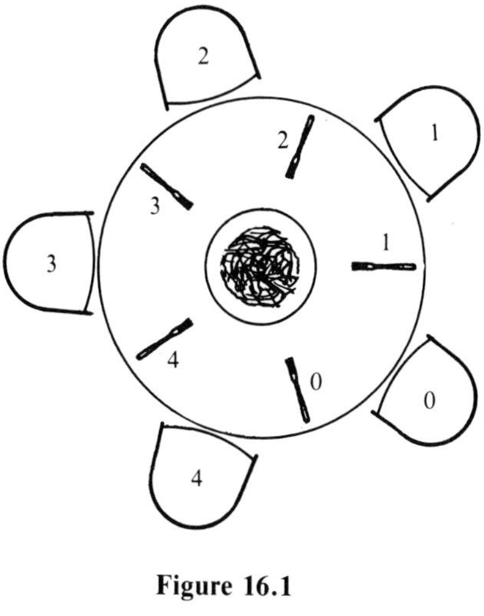

Figure 16.1

Solution: The behaviour of the *i*th philosopher may be described as follows:

```
PHIL = *[... during ith lifetime ... →
        THINK;
        room!enter( );
        fork(i)!pickup( ); fork((i + 1)mod 5)!pickup( );
        EAT;
        fork(i)!putdown( ); fork((i + 1)mod 5)!putdown( );
        room!exit( )
        ]
```

The fate of the *i*th fork is to be picked up and put down by a philosopher sitting on either side of it:

```
FORK =
  *[phil(i)?pickup( ) → phil(i)?putdown( )
  □phil((i − 1)mod 5)?pickup( ) → phil((i − 1)mod 5)?putdown( )
  ]
```

The story of the room may be simply told:

```
ROOM = occupancy: integer; occupancy := 0;
  *[(i: 0..4)phil(i)?enter( ) → occupancy := occupancy + 1
  □(i: 0..4)phil(i)?exit( ) → occupancy := occupancy − 1
  ]
```

All these components operate in parallel:

```
[room :: ROOM || fork(i: 0..4) :: FORK || phil(i: 0 :: PHIL].
```

Notes

(1) The solution given above does not prevent all five philosophers from entering the room, each picking up his left fork and starving to death because he cannot pick up his right fork.

(2) *Exercise*: Adapt the above program to avert this sad possibility. *Hint*: Prevent more than four philosophers from entering the room. (Solution due to E. W. Dijkstra.)

16.6 Miscellaneous

This section contains further examples of the use of communicating sequential processes for the solution of some less familiar problems; a parallel version of the sieve of Eratosthenes, and the design of an iterative array. The proposed solutions are even more speculative than those of the previous sections, and in the second example, even the question of termination is ignored.

16.6.1 Prime numbers: the Sieve of Eratosthenes (McIlroy 1968)

Problem: To print in ascending order all primes less than 10 000. Use an array of processes, *SIEVE*, in which each process inputs a prime from its predecessor and prints it. The process then inputs an ascending stream of numbers from its predecessor and passes them on to its successor, suppressing any that are multiples of the original prime.

Solution

```
SIEVE(i: 1..100) ::
  p. mp: integer;
  SIEVE(i − 1)?p;
  print!p;
  mp := p; comment mp is a multiple of p;
*[m: integer, SIEVE(i − 1)?m →
      *[m > mp → mp := mp + p];
      [m = mp → skip
      ▯m < mp → SIEVE(i + 1)?m
] ]
|| SIEVE(0) :: print!2; n: integer; n := 3;
      *[n < 10000 → SIEVE(1)!n; n := n + 2]
|| SIEVE(101) :: *[n: integer; SIEVE(100?n → print!n]
|| print :: *[(i: 0..101)n: integer; SIEVE(i)?n → ...]
```

Notes

(1) This beautiful solution was contributed by David Gries.

(2) It is algorithmically similar to the program developed in (Dijkstra 1972c, pp. 27–32).

16.6.2 An iterative array: matrix multiplication

Problem: A square matrix A of order 3 is given. Three streams are to be input, each stream representing a column of an array IN. Three streams are to be output, each representing a column of the product matrix $IN \times A$. After an initial delay, the results are to be produced at the same rate as the input is consumed. Consequently, a high degree of parallelism is required. The solution should take the form shown in Fig. 16.2. Each of the nine nonborder nodes inputs a vector component from the west and a partial sum from the north. Each node outputs the vector component to its east, and an updated partial sum to the south. The input data is produced by the west border nodes, and the desired results are consumed by south border nodes. The north border is a constant source of zeros and the east border is

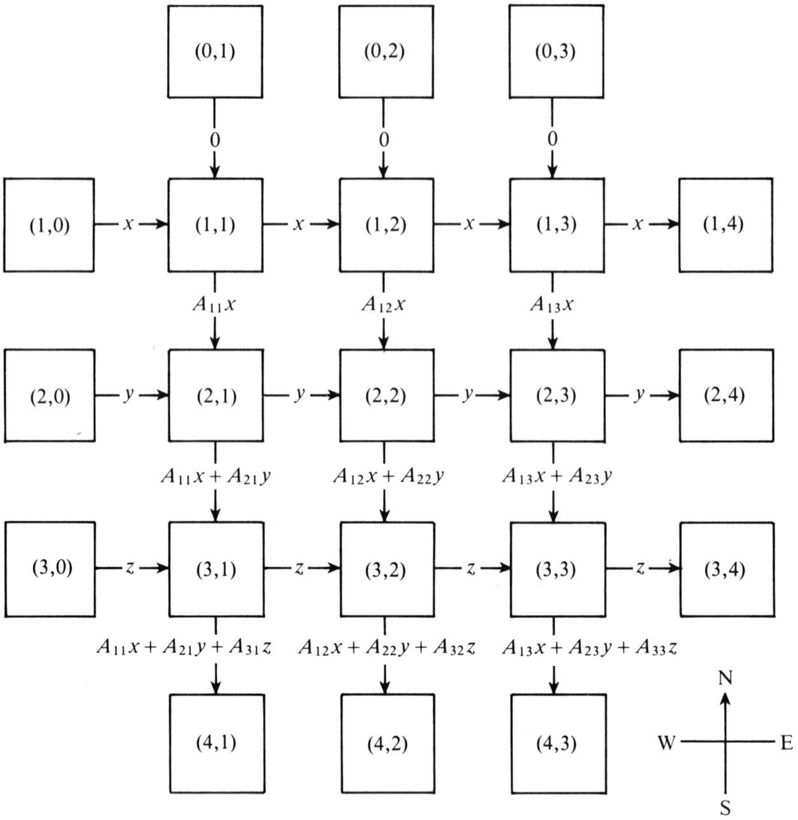

Figure 16.2

just a sink. No provision need be made for termination nor for changing the values of the array A.

Solution: There are twenty-one nodes, in five groups, comprising the central square and the four borders:

$M(i{:}\,1..3, 0) :: WEST$
$\| M(0, j{:}\,1..3) :: NORTH$
$\| M(i{:}\,1..3, 4) :: EAST$
$\| M(4, j{:}\,1..3) :: SOUTH$
$\| M(i{:}\,1..3, j{:}\,1..3) :: CENTRE$

The *WEST* and *SOUTH* borders are processes of the user program; the remaining processes are:

$NORTH = *[true \rightarrow M(1, j)!0]$
$EAST = *[x: real; M(i, 3)?x \rightarrow skip]$
$CENTRE = *[x: real; M(i, j-1)?x \rightarrow$
$\quad M(i, j+1)!x; sum: real;$
$\quad M(i-1, j)?sum; M(i+1, j)!(A(i, j) * x + sum)$
]

16.7 Discussion

A design for a programming language must necessarily involve a number of decisions which seem to be fairly arbitrary. The discussion of this section is intended to explain some of the underlying motivation and to mention some unresolved questions.

16.7.1 Notations

I have chosen single-character notations (e.g. !, ?) to express the primitive concepts, rather than the more traditional boldface or underlined English words. As a result, the examples have an APL-like brevity, which some readers find distasteful. My excuse is that (in contrast to APL) there are only a very few primitive concepts and that it is standard practice of mathematics (and also good coding practice) to denote common primitive concepts by brief notations (e.g. $+$, $\times$). When read aloud, these are replaced by words (e.g. plus, times).

Some readers have suggested the use of assignment notation for input and output:

⟨*target variable*⟩ := ⟨*source*⟩
⟨*destination*⟩ := ⟨*expression*⟩

I find this suggestion misleading: it is better to regard input and output as distinct primitives, justifying distinct notations.

I have used the same pair of brackets ([...]) to bracket all program structures, instead of the more familiar variety of brackets (**if**..**fi**, **begin**..**end**, **case**..**esac**, etc.). In this I follow normal mathematical practice, but I must also confess to a distaste for the pronunciation of words like **fi**, **od**, or **esac**.

I am dissatisfied with the fact that my notation gives the same syntax for a structured expression and a subscripted variable. Perhaps tags should be distinguished from other identifiers by a special symbol (say #).

I was tempted to introduce an abbreviation for combined declaration and input, e.g. $X?(n: integer)$ for $n: integer; X?n$.

16.7.2 Explicit naming

My design insists that every input or output command must name its source or destination explicitly. This makes it inconvenient to write a library of processes which can be included in subsequent programs, independent of the process names used in that program. A partial solution to this problem is to allow one process (the *main* process) of a parallel command to have an empty label, and to allow the other processes in the command to use the empty process name as source or destination of input or output.

For construction of large programs, some more general technique will also be necessary. This should at least permit substitution of program text for names defined elsewhere – a technique which has been used informally throughout this paper. The COBOL *COPY* verb also permits a substitution for formal parameters within the copied text. But whatever facility is introduced, I would recommend the following principle: Every program, after assembly with its library routines, should be printable as a text expressed wholly in the language, and it is this printed text which should describe the execution of the program, independent of which parts were drawn from a library.

Since I did not intend to design a complete language, I have ignored the problem of libraries in order to concentrate on the essential semantic concepts of the program which is actually executed.

16.7.3 Port names

An alternative to explicit naming of source and destination would be to name a *port* through which communication is to take place. The port names would be local to the processes, and the manner in which pairs of ports are to be connected by channels could be declared in the head of a parallel command.

This is an attractive alternative which could be designed to introduce a useful degree of syntactically checkable redundancy. But it is semantically equivalent to the present proposal, provided that each port is connected to exactly one other port in another process. In this case each channel can be identified with a tag, together with the name of the process at the other end. Since I wish to concentrate on semantics, I preferred in this paper to use the simplest and most direct notation, and to avoid raising questions about the possibility of connecting more than two ports by a single channel.

16.7.4 Automatic buffering

As an alternative to synchronization of input and output, it is often proposed that an outputting process should be allowed to proceed even when the inputting process is not yet ready to accept the output. An implementation would be expected automatically to interpose a chain of buffers to hold output messages that have not yet been input.

I have deliberately rejected this alternative, for two reasons: (1) It is less realistic to implement in multiple disjoint processors, and (2) when buffering is required on a particular channel, it can readily be specified using the given primitives. Of course, it could be argued equally well that synchronization can be specified when required by using a pair of buffered input and output commands.

16.7.5 Unbounded process activation

The notation for an array of processes permits the same program text (like an ALGOL recursive procedure) to have many simultaneous 'activations'; however, the exact number must be specified in advance. In a conventional single-processor implementation, this can lead to inconvenience and wastefulness, similar to the fixed-length array of FORTRAN. It would therefore be attractive to allow a process array with no *a priori* bound on the number of elements; and to specify that the exact number of elements required for a particular execution of the program should be determined dynamically, like the maximum depth of recursion of an ALGOL procedure or the number of iterations of a repetitive command.

However, it is a good principle that every actual run of a program with unbounded arrays should be identical to the run of some program with all its arrays bounded in advance. Thus the unbounded program should be defined as the 'limit' (in some sense) of a series of bounded programs with increasing bounds. I have chosen to concentrate on the semantics of the bounded case – which is necessary anyway and which is more realistic for implementation on multiple microprocessors.

16.7.6 Fairness

Consider the parallel command:

```
[X:: Y!stop( ) || Y:: continue: Boolean; continue := true;
     *[continue; X?stop( ) → continue := false
       ▯continue → n := n + 1
       ]
].
```

If the implementation always prefers the second alternative in the repetitive command of *Y*, it is said to be *unfair*, because although the output command in *X* could have been executed on an infinite number of occasions, it is in fact always passed over.

The question arises: Should a programming language definition specify that an implementation must be *fair*? Here, I am fairly sure that the answer is 'no'. Otherwise, the implementation would be obliged to successfully complete the example program shown above, in spite of the fact that its nondeterminism is unbounded. I would therefore suggest that it is the programmer's responsibility to prove that his program terminates correctly – without relying on the assumption of fairness in the implementation. Thus the program shown above is incorrect, since its termination cannot be proved.

Nevertheless, I suggest that an efficient implementation should try to be reasonably fair and should ensure that an output command is not delayed unreasonably often after it first becomes executable. But a proof of correctness must not rely on this property of an efficient implementation. Consider the following analogy with a sequential program: An efficient implementation of an alternative command tends to favour the alternative which can be most efficiently executed, but the programmer must ensure that the logical correctness of his program does not depend on this property of his implementation.

This method of avoiding the problem of fairness does not apply to programs such as operating systems which are intended to run forever, because in this case termination proofs are not relevant. But I wonder whether it is ever advisable to write or to execute such programs. Even an operating system should be designed to bring itself to an orderly conclusion reasonably soon after it inputs a message instructing it to do so. Otherwise, the *only* way to stop it is to 'crash' it.

16.7.7 Functional coroutines

It is interesting to compare the processes described here with those proposed in Kahn (1974); the differences are most striking. There, coroutines are strictly deterministic: No choice is given between alternative sources of input. The output commands are automatically buffered to any required degree. The output of one process can be automatically fanned out to any number of processes (including itself!) which can consume it at differing rates. Finally, the processes there are designed to run forever, whereas my proposed parallel command is normally intended to terminate. The design in Kahn (1974) is based on an elegant theory which permits proof of the properties of programs. These differences are not accidental – they seem to be natural consequences of the difference between the more abstract applicative (or functional) approach to programming and the more machine-oriented imperative (or procedural) approach, which is taken by communicating sequential processes.

16.7.8 Output guards

Since input commands may appear in guards, it seems more symmetric to permit output commands as well. This would allow an obvious and useful simplification in some of the example programs, for example, in the bounded buffer (Section 16.5.1). Perhaps a more convincing reason would be to ensure that the externally visible effect and behaviour of every parallel command can be modelled by some sequential command. In order to model the parallel command

$Z :: [X!2 \parallel Y!3]$

we need to be able to write the sequential alternative command:

$Z :: [X!2 \rightarrow Y!3 \,\square\, Y!3 \rightarrow X!2]$

Note that this *cannot* be done by the command

$Z :: [\mathit{true} \rightarrow X!2;\ Y!3 \,\square\, \mathit{true} \rightarrow Y!3;\ X!2]$

which can fail if the process Z happens to choose the first alternative, but the processes Y and X are synchronized with each other in such a way that Y must input from Z before X does, e.g.

$Y :: Z?y;\ X!\mathit{go}(\,)$
$\parallel X :: Y?\mathit{go}(\,);\ Z?x$

16.7.9 Restriction: Repetitive command with input guard

In proposing an unfamiliar programming-language feature, it seems wiser at first to specify a highly restrictive version rather than to propose extensions – especially when the language feature claims to be primitive. For example, it is clear that the multidimensional process array is not primitive, since it can readily be constructed in a language which permits only single-dimensional arrays. But I have a rather more serious misgiving about the repetitive command with input guards.

The automatic termination of a repetitive command on termination of the sources of all its input guards is an extremely powerful and convenient feature but it also involves some subtlety of specification to ensure that it is implementable; and it is certainly not primitive, since the required effect can be achieved (with considerable inconvenience) by explicit exchange of '*end*( )' signals. For example, the subroutine $DIV(4.1)$ could be rewritten:

$[DIV :: \mathit{continue}\text{: Boolean};\ \mathit{continue} := \mathit{true};$
$*[\mathit{continue};\ X?\mathit{end}(\,) \rightarrow \mathit{continue} := \mathit{false}$
$\square\,\mathit{continue};\ x, y\text{: integer};\ X?(x, y) \rightarrow \ldots;\ X!(\mathit{quot}, \mathit{rem})$

```
|| X:: USER PROG; Div!end( )
  ]
```

Other examples would be even more inconvenient.

But the dangers of convenient facilities are notorious. For example the repetitive commands with input guards may tempt the programmer to write them without making adequate plans for their termination; and if it turns out that the automatic termination is unsatisfactory, reprogramming for explicit termination will involve severe changes, affecting even the interfaces between the processes.

16.8 Conclusion

This paper has suggested that input, output, and concurrency should be regarded as primitives of programming, which underlie many familiar and less familiar programming concepts. However, it would be unjustified to conclude that these primitives can wholly replace the other concepts in a programming language. Where a more elaborate construction (such as a procedure or monitor) is frequently useful, has properties which are more simply provable, and can be implemented more efficiently than the general case, there is a strong reason for including in a programming language a special notation for that construction. The fact that the construction can be defined in terms of simpler underlying primitives is a useful guarantee that its inclusion is logically consistent with the remainder of the language.

16.9 Acknowledgements

The research reported in this paper has been encouraged and supported by a Senior Fellowship of the Science Research Council of Great Britain. The technical inspiration was due to Edsger W. Dijkstra (1975b), and the paper has been improved in presentation and content by valuable and painstaking advice from D. Gries, D. Q. M. Fay, E. W. Dijkstra, N. Wirth, R. Milne, M. K. Harper, and its referees. The role of IFIP W.G.2.3 as a forum for presentation and discussion is acknowledged with pleasure and gratitude.

SEVENTEEN

A calculus of total correctness for communicating sequential processes

The period after the publication of the CSP paper (cf. Chapter 16) saw exciting developments in the theory of parallelism. This period coincided with Hoare's move to Oxford, where he worked with colleagues who were keen to assist in the mathematical foundations of programming. The Programming Research Group had been the birthplace of Denotational Semantics; its first Professor, Christopher Strachey, had formed a unique collaboration with Dana Scott, who was still in Oxford on Hoare's arrival. Joe Stoy, who wrote the definitive book on denotational semantics (Stoy 1977), had held the PRG together during the interregnum. Perhaps most importantly, Hoare now acquired a succession of mathematically sophisticated Ph.D. students (such as John Kennaway, Bill Roscoe and Steve Brookes).

This paper provides a proof theory for reasoning about process expressions. Although it does not refer to [66] (i.e. Chapter 16), the constructs used to build the process expressions are strongly related. The processes are proved to satisfy assertions on the messages which pass along the channels and their 'ready sets'. The proof system given here is not complete in two senses: there are things one cannot express in the channel assertions and some (true) assertions can be neither proved nor disproved. This paper, then, must be seen as a step towards more powerful theories of communicating processes. Other papers were to bring channels into a more central position (e.g. [75]) or to introduce 'refusal sets' (cf. [90]). The problem, uncovered in the current chapter, of hiding infinite communication complicates much of the work on reasoning about processes. The assertions here avoid any mention of the internal state of a process. For the buffer-like examples considered, this works well. Other classes of specification would be hampered by this restriction.

This paper was first drafted as a Programming Research Group monograph

C. A. R. Hoare, A calculus of total correctness for communicating processes, *The Science of Computer Programming,* **1** (1–2), 49–72 (October 1981). This paper is republished by kind permission of Elsevier Science Publishers BV.

(No. 23) in 1981; it was submitted for publication in July 1981 and published in ([76]) in the same year.

Abstract

A process communicates with its environment and with other processes by synchronized output and input on named channels. The current state of a process is defined by the sequences of messages which have passed along each of the channels, and by the sets of messages that may next be passed on each channel. A process satisfies an assertion if the assertion is at all times true of all possible states of the process. We present a calculus for proving that a process satisfies the assertion describing its intended behaviour. The following constructs are axiomatized: output; input; simple recursion; disjoint parallelism; channel renaming, connection and hiding; process chaining; nondeterminism; conditional; alternation; and mutual recursion. The calculus is illustrated by proof of a number of simple buffering protocols.

17.1 Assertions

A process communicates with its environment by sending and receiving messages on named channels (Fig. 17.1(a)). The names of these channels constitute the *alphabet* of the process. A process may be constructed from a group of subprocesses, intercommunicating on a network of named channels (Fig. 17.1(b, c)). A message output by one process along a channel is received instantaneously by all other processes connected by that channel, provided that all these processes are simultaneously prepared to input that message.

On each named channel, it is possible to keep a record of all messages passing along it. (For simplicity, we ignore direction of communication: if desired, this could be recorded as part of each message.) At any given moment, the record of all messages that have passed so far on a channel c is a finite sequence, which will be denoted by the variable $c.past$. At the very beginning, the value of $c.past$ (for each channel c) is the empty sequence $\langle\,\rangle$. During the evolution of a process, whenever a message m is communicated on channel c, the value of $c.past$ is extended on the right by m, and the new value is $(c.past\langle m\rangle)$.

At any given moment, the set of messages which a process is prepared to communicate on channel c is denoted by the variable $c.ready$. When the process is not prepared to communicate at all on channel c, the value of $c.ready$ is the empty set $\emptyset$. When a process is prepared to *input* on channel c, the value of $c.ready$ is the set M of all possible messages for that channel. When a process is prepared to *output* some message value m (selected from M), then the value of $c.ready$ is the unit set $\{m\}$, which has m as its only member.

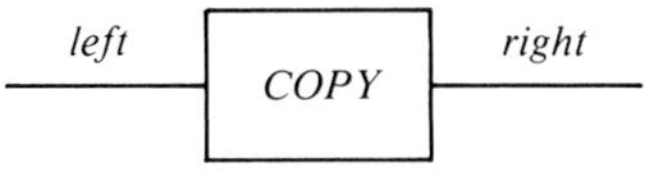

(a) A process with alphabet {*left*, *right*}.

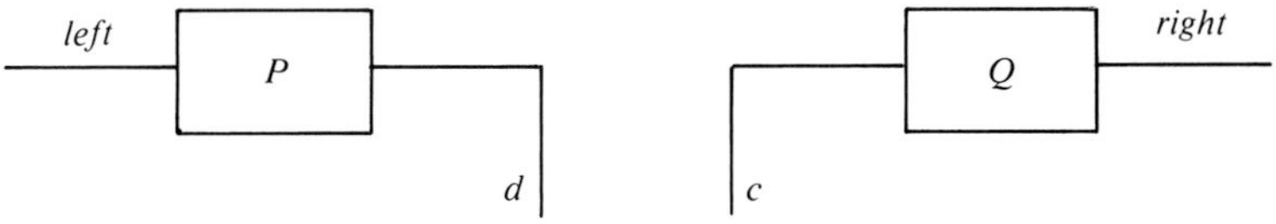

(b) A process ($P \,|||\, Q$) with alphabet {*left*, *c*, *d*, *right*}.

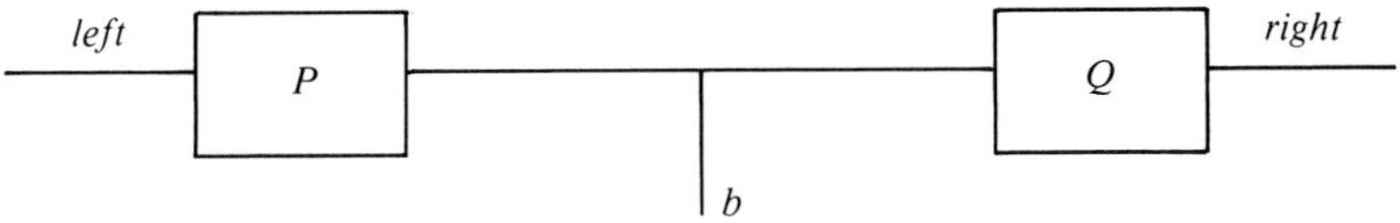

(c) The process ($b = (c \leftrightarrow d)$ **in** B) with alphabet {*left*, *b*, *right*}.

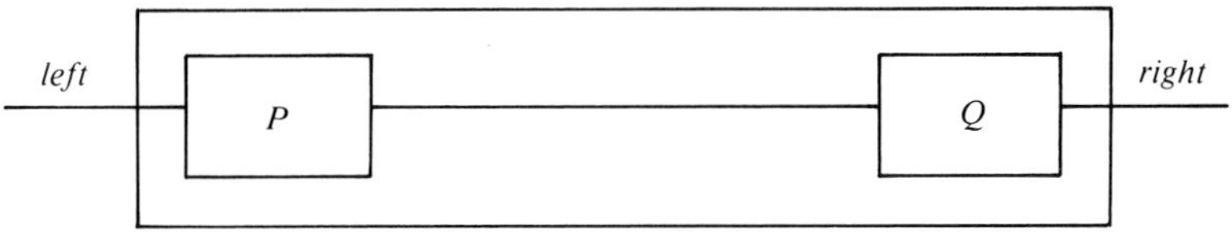

(d) The process (**chan** b **in** C) with alphabet {*left*, *right*}.

Figure 17.1

Variables of the form *c.past*, *c.ready* are known as channel variables. Since we do not wish to be concerned with the internal states and transitions of a process, we shall identify the current externally observable state of a process with the current values of its channel variables.

An *assertion* with a given alphabet is a normal sentence of logic and mathematics, which may contain free channel variables of the form *c.past* and *c.ready*, where *c* is a channel name in the alphabet of the assertion. The assertion describes certain possible states of some process at certain moments of time. For example, the following are assertions, with informal explanations of their meaning:

(1) $left.past = right.past$. 'The sequence of messages which has passed so far along the left channel is the same as the sequence that has passed along the right channel';
(2) $left.ready = M$. 'The left channel is ready for input of any message in the set M';
(3) $right.past < left.past$. 'The messages passed on the right channel form a proper initial subsequence of the messages that have passed on the left';
(4) $right.ready = \{first(left.past - right.past)\}$. 'The right channel is ready for output of the earliest message on the left which has not yet been transmitted on the right'.

Assertions may be readily combined by the familiar connectives of logic. For example, we define for future use the assertion:

$$BUFF =_{df} left.past = right.past \wedge left.ready = M$$
$$\vee\ right.past < left.past \wedge right.ready = \{first(left.past - right.past)\}.$$

This assertion describes all possible states of a buffering process (or transparent communications protocol), which outputs on its right channel the same sequence of messages which it inputs from the left, though possibly after some delay. When $left.past = right.past$, the process has an empty buffer, and it must then be prepared to input any message from the left. In the alternative case, the buffer is nonempty; it contains the sequence $(left.past - right.past)$ of messages which are awaiting output on the right; and now the buffering process must be prepared to output the first element of this buffer. The assertion *BUFF* does not say whether or not input on the left is possible when the buffer is nonempty; and thus it does not specify any particular bound on the size of the buffer.

Let P be a process and let R be an assertion with the same alphabet as P. Then P is said to *satisfy* R if at *all* times during any possible evolution of P (before and after each communication) the assertion R correctly describes the observable state of P, i.e., the sequences of messages that have passed along its named channels, and the sets of messages that are ready to be communicated on the very next step. This relation between processes and assertions is abbreviated:

$$P \textbf{ sat } R.$$

For example any process P which is to serve as a buffer or transparent communications protocol must satisfy the assertion *BUFF*. There are many processes that do so – for example, a bounded buffer of any finite size or even an unbounded buffer; examples will be given later.

It follows from the intended interpretation of the relation *satisfies* that the following properties should be true for all processes P, and all predicates, R, S:

H1 P **sat** $TRUE$.

$TRUE$ is a predicate which is always true of everything; it must therefore always be true of the behaviour of every process.

H2 $\neg(P\ \textbf{sat}\ FALSE)$.

$FALSE$ is the predicate that is always false of anything; it cannot therefore correctly describe the behaviour of any process.

H3 $$\frac{R \Rightarrow S}{(P\ \textbf{sat}\ R) \Rightarrow (P\ \textbf{sat}\ S)}.$$

If $(R \Rightarrow S)$ is a theorem, every state in which R is true is also a state in which S is true. If all states of P are correctly described by R, they must also be correctly described by S, and hence $((P\ \textbf{sat}\ R) \Rightarrow (P\ \textbf{sat}\ S))$ is also true. H3 is a useful proof rule, known as the 'rule of consequence'.

Corollary

$$\frac{R \equiv S}{(P\ \textbf{sat}\ R) \equiv (P\ \text{sat}\ S)}.$$

H4 If n is *not* a channel variable, and does *not* occur in P:

$$(\forall n : N . P\ \textbf{sat}\ R(n)) \equiv (P\ \textbf{sat}(\forall n : N . R(n))).$$

If, for each n in some set N, P satisfies $R(n)$, then each state of P is correctly described by $R(n)$, for all n in N. The converse implications follows from (H3), and $\forall$-introduction.

Corollary

$$(P\ \textbf{sat}\ R) \wedge (P\ \textbf{sat}\ S) \equiv (P\ \textbf{sat}(R \wedge S)).$$

These four conditions are rather similar to the healthiness conditions introduced by Dijkstra (1975a) to check the validity of each clause in the definition of his weakest precondition for sequential programming. Unfortunately, our calculus is not strong enough to *prove* healthiness in all cases; so we have to introduce the conditions as independent axioms, which must at least be *consistent* with the other proof rules of the calculus.

Let R be an assertion not containing the variable n; then we define $R \upharpoonright n$ (R restricted to n) as the assertion satisfied by a process which behaves as described by R for at least $n-1$ steps, i.e., at least until the total number of communications on all channels reaches n. Let $\{a, \ldots, z\}$ be the alphabet of R. Let $※ s$ stand for the length of the sequence s. Then we can define:

$$R \upharpoonright n =_{\text{df}} (※\, a.past + \cdots + ※\, z.past \geqslant n) \vee R.$$

Example

$$BUFF \upharpoonright n =_{\mathrm{df}} (\divideontimes\, left.past + \divideontimes\, right.past \geqslant n) \vee BUFF.$$

Theorem 17.1

For any assertion R:
(a) $R \upharpoonright 0$ is a theorem,
(b) $(\forall n\colon NAT. R \upharpoonright n) \equiv R$.

Proof $c.past$ is a finite sequence for each channel c. So $\divideontimes\, c.past$ is a natural number. R does not contain n, so

$$\begin{aligned}(\forall n{:}NAT. R \upharpoonright n) &\equiv (\forall n.NAT.\, \divideontimes\, a.past + \cdots + \divideontimes\, z.past \geqslant n) \vee R \\ &\equiv R.\end{aligned}$$

Let R be an assertion possibly containing a variable x, and let e be an expression of the same type as x. Then we define $R[e/x]$ as the assertion formed from R by substituting e for every free occurrence of x. (If any free variable of e would thereby become bound to a bound variable in R, the collision must be averted by systematic change of the offending bound variable). For example, we define

$$\begin{aligned}BUFF' &=_{\mathrm{df}} (BUFF \upharpoonright (n+1))[\langle x\rangle left.past / left.past],\\ BUFF'' &=_{\mathrm{df}} BUFF'[\langle x\rangle right.past / right.past].\end{aligned}$$

After performing the substitutions, $BUFF''$ expands to

$$\begin{aligned}&\divideontimes\, \langle x\rangle left.past + \divideontimes\, \langle x\rangle right.past \geqslant n+1\\ &\quad \vee \langle x\rangle left.past = \langle x\rangle right.past \wedge left.ready = M\\ &\quad \vee \langle x\rangle right.past < \langle x\rangle left.past\\ &\qquad \wedge right.ready = \{first(\langle x\rangle left.past - \langle x\rangle right.past)\}.\end{aligned}$$

The following theorem is typical of the lengthy but shallow truths required in proofs of correctness of programs:

Theorem 17.2

$$BUFF \upharpoonright n \Rightarrow (\forall x\colon M. BUFF'').$$

Proof Each clause of the left-hand side implies the corresponding clause on the right-hand side.

Let R be an assertion with alphabet $\{a \ldots z\}$. We introduce the convention that

$$R[\langle\rangle / past]$$

is the result of substituting the empty sequence $\langle\rangle$ for *every* occurrence of *any* of the channel variables $a.past, \ldots, z.past$. For example

$$\begin{aligned}BUFF[\langle\rangle / past] \equiv (&\langle\rangle = \langle\rangle \wedge left.ready = M\\ &\vee \langle\rangle < \langle\rangle \wedge \cdots \qquad)\end{aligned}$$

which is equivalent to '$left.ready = M$'. If P **sat** R, then $R[\langle\rangle/past]$ describes all the possible states of P at its very beginning, before it has engaged in communication on any of its channels. These states are defined in terms of $a.ready, \ldots, z.ready$, which specify the sets of communications for which P should be ready on its very first step. Thus if any process is to satisfy the assertion *BUFF*, it must at the beginning be ready to input on its left channel any value in the set M.

By a similar convention

$$R[\emptyset/ready]$$

is the result of substituting the empty set $\emptyset$ for *every* occurrence of *any* of the channel variables $a.ready, \ldots, z.ready$. For example

$$\begin{aligned} BUFF[\emptyset/ready] \equiv (&left.past = right.past \wedge \emptyset = M \\ &\vee right.past < left.past \wedge \emptyset = \{\cdots\}) \end{aligned}$$

which is always false. If P **sat** R, then $R[\langle\rangle/past]$ describes all possible states of P in which it is not ready for communication along *any* of its channels. These states are known as *deadlock* states; and it is usually desired to prove that they cannot occur. The states are defined in terms of the variables $a.past, \ldots, z.past$; and therefore we only need to prove that $R[\emptyset/ready]$ is false for *all* values of these variables. For example, any process that satisfies *BUFF* can never deadlock (unless the set M of all possible messages is empty – a possibility which we can realistically ignore).

As a final convention, we allow successive substitutions to be separated by commas; for example

$$R[\langle\rangle/past, \emptyset/ready] = (R[\langle\rangle/past])[\emptyset/ready].$$

One of the simplest processes with alphabet A is the process $STOP_A$ which is already deadlocked at its start. Clearly, it is never ready to do anything, so $c.ready = \emptyset$ for all c in A. Furthermore, the sequence of messages transmitted along each channel remains forever empty, i.e. $c.past = \langle\rangle$. In summary, the process $STOP_A$ has only this single state; consequently, it satisfies an assertion R if and only if R correctly describes its only state, i.e. if R is true when all the variables of the form $c.ready$ take the value $\emptyset$, and all the variables of the form $c.past$ take the value $\langle\rangle$. This informal reasoning justifies the axiom

$$(STOP_A \textbf{ sat } R) \equiv R[\emptyset/ready, \langle\rangle/past].$$

Examples The following are theorems:

$$STOP_A \textbf{ sat } (c.ready \neq \{x\} \wedge \text{※}\, c.past \neq 3),$$
$$\neg(STOP_{LR} \textbf{ sat } BUFF)$$

where $LR = \{left, right\}$.

$STOP_A$ is rather a useless process; it has been introduced here only to provide a simple example of an axiom, and how it can be informally justified.

17.2 Processes and proof rules

In the remainder of this paper, we introduce a number of programming constructs suitable for the programming of communicating processes. Each construct is given a syntax, and an informal explanation of its semantics. The semantics is formalized by an axiom or proof rule which is illustrated by application to some simple example. Treatment of each example is spread over several consecutive subsections.

17.2.1 Output

Let P be a process; let c be a channel name in the alphabet of P; and let e be an expression (*not* containing channel variables). Then we use the notation

$$(c!e \rightarrow P)$$

to denote the process which first outputs the value of e on channel c and then behaves like P. In its initial state, when the past of all its channels is empty, this process is prepared to communicate the value of e on channel c, so that $c.ready = \{e\}$. It is not prepared to communicate on any other channel, so initially $d.ready = \emptyset$ for all channels d other than c. An assertion R is true of this initial state if and only if it is true when the channel variables of R take their initial values, as described above. This may be expressed by substituting these values in R, giving

$$R[\langle\rangle / past,\ \{e\}/c.ready, \emptyset/\langle ready\rangle]$$

(The use of the expression e to stand for its value is justified only in a programming notation which excludes assignment of new values to variables occurring in e.)

The subsequent states of $(c!e \rightarrow P)$ are very similar to the states of P; the only difference is in the value of $c.past$. If in a state of P $c.past$ has value s, then in the corresponding state of $(c!e \rightarrow P)$, $c.past$ has the value $\langle e\rangle s$. In order to prove

$$(c!e \rightarrow P) \textbf{ sat } R$$

it is the process P that must ensure, not that its *own* states satisfy R, but rather that the corresponding states of $(c!e \rightarrow P)$ are correctly described by R. In other words, R must be true when the value of $c.past$ is replaced by

$(\langle e \rangle c.past)$; or more formally:

$$P \textbf{ sat } (R[\langle e \rangle c.past / c.past]).$$

To prove that all states of a process are correctly described by R, it is sufficient to prove that the initial state satisfies R, and that the subsequent states do so too. The preceding paragraphs deal with these two cases; putting them together we get the rule:

$$((c!e \to P) \textbf{ sat } R) \equiv (R[\langle\rangle / past, \{e\}/c.ready, \emptyset / ready] \\ \wedge P \textbf{ sat}(R[\langle e \rangle c.past / c.past]))$$

Example

$((right!\ x \to p) \textbf{ sat } BUFF') \equiv S \wedge (p \textbf{ sat } BUFF'[\langle x \rangle\ right.past / right.past])$

where $S =_{df} BUFF'[\langle\rangle / past, \{x\}/right.ready, \emptyset / ready]$.

On performing the substitutions, S expands to

$$※\langle x \rangle + ※\langle\rangle \geqslant n+1 \\ \vee \langle x \rangle = \langle\rangle \wedge \emptyset = M \\ \vee \langle\rangle < \langle x \rangle \wedge \{x\} = \{first(\langle x \rangle = \langle\rangle)\}.$$

The last clause makes S a trivial theorem.

Theorem 17.3 $((right!\ x \to p) \textbf{ sat } BUFF') \equiv (p \textbf{ sat } BUFF'')$.

Proof The theorem S can be omitted from a conjunction, and the definition of $BUFF''$ is used.

The axiom for output has the same apparent 'backwards' quality as the axiom for assignment in sequential programming. Readers who have become familiar with the latter may note that the command $(c!e \to P)$ has the same apparent effect on *c.past* as the command

$$(P;\ c.past := \langle e \rangle c.past)$$

provided that P contains no assignment to variables of e. Thus the second term of the axiom of output is derivable from the axiom of assignment.

17.2.2 Input

Let $P(x)$ be a process whose behaviour (but not alphabet) possibly depends on the value of the free variable x. Let c be a channel in the alphabet of $P(x)$, and let M be a finite set of message values which can be communicated on channel c. Then

$$(c?x : M \to P(x))$$

is the process which is initially prepared to input on channel c any value in the set M. The newly input value is given the local name x, and the process subsequently behaves like $P(x)$. The variable x is regarded as a bound variable, so

$$(c?x:\mathrm{M} \rightarrow P(x))$$

is the same process as

$$(c?y:M \rightarrow P(y)).$$

Example

$$COPYSTEP =_{\mathrm{df}} (left?x:M \rightarrow (right!x \rightarrow p)).$$

COPYSTEP first inputs a value from the left, then outputs this same value to the right, and then behaves like p.

The input command is similar to the output command except in two respects. Firstly, the initial value of $c.ready$ is not just a single value, but the whole of the set M. Secondly, the subsequent behaviour $P(x)$ may depend on the input value x, which is not known in advance; and therefore $P(x)$ must be proved to meet its specification for *all* values of x ranging over the set M. This reasoning informally justifies the axiom:

Let R be an assertion *not* containing x:

$$((c!x:M \rightarrow P(x)) \textbf{ sat } R) \equiv (R[\langle\rangle/past, M/c.ready, \emptyset/ready] \\ \wedge \forall x:M.(P(x) \textbf{ sat } R[\langle x\rangle c.past/c.past])).$$

Example

$$(COPYSTEP \textbf{ sat } (BUFF \restriction n+1)) \equiv S \wedge (\forall x:M.(right!x \rightarrow p) \textbf{ sat } BUFF')$$

where

$$S =_{\mathrm{df}} (BUFF \restriction n+1)[\langle\ \rangle/past,\ M/left.ready,\ \emptyset/ready] \\ \equiv (\text{※}\langle\rangle + \text{※}\langle\rangle \geqslant n+1) \vee (\langle\rangle = \langle\rangle \wedge M = M) \vee (\langle\rangle < \langle\rangle \wedge \cdots).$$

The second clause makes S a theorem.

Theorem 17.4

$$(COPYSTEP \textbf{ sat } (BUFF \restriction n+1)) \equiv (p \textbf{ sat}(\forall x:M.BUFF'')).$$

Proof Theorem 17.3, definition of *BUFF*′ and H4.

17.2.3 Recursion

Let p be a variable standing for a process with a given alphabet. Let $F(p)$ be the description of a process (with the same alphabet) containing none or more occurrences of the variable p. Then

$$\mu p.F(p)$$

is the recursively defined process, which starts off behaving like $F(p)$, and on encountering an occurrence of p, behaves like $(\mu p.F(p))$ again.

Example $COPY =_{\mathrm{df}} \mu p.(left?x : M \rightarrow (right!x \rightarrow p))$.

The process *COPY* is an infinitely repeating cycle, each iteration of which inputs a message from the left and outputs the same message to the right.

A recursively defined process is intended to be a 'fixed point' of its defining function F, i.e.,

$$\mu p.F(p) = F(\mu p.F(p)). \tag{1}$$

Let R be an assertion, and suppose for an arbitrary process p we can prove

$$(p \textbf{ sat } (R \upharpoonright N)) \Rightarrow (F(p) \textbf{ sat } R \upharpoonright (n+1)) \quad \text{for all } n. \tag{2}$$

From Theorem 17.1(a) and H1 it follows that

$$(\mu p.F(p)) \textbf{ sat } (R \upharpoonright 0).$$

By substituting $\mu p.F(p)$ for p in (2) and using (1) we get

$$(\mu p.F(p) \textbf{ sat } R \upharpoonright n) \Rightarrow (\mu p.F(p) \textbf{ sat } R \upharpoonright (n+1))$$

By the obvious induction on n we get

$$\forall n.(\mu p.F(p) \textbf{ sat } (R \upharpoonright n)).$$

By H4 and Theorem 17.1(b), we conclude

$$(\mu p.\mathrm{F}(p)) \textbf{ sat } R.$$

This reasoning serves as an informal justification of the following proof rule:

$$\frac{(p \textbf{ sat}(R \upharpoonright n)) \Rightarrow (F(p) \textbf{ sat } (R \upharpoonright n+1))}{\mu p.F(p) \textbf{ sat } R}$$

Theorem 17.5

$$COPY \textbf{ sat } BUFF.$$

Proof By the rule given above, it is sufficient to prove

$$(p \textbf{ sat } (BUFF \upharpoonright n)) \Rightarrow (COPYSTEP \textbf{ sat } (BUFF \upharpoonright n+1)).$$

By Theorem 17.4, this is equivalent to

$$(p \textbf{ sat } BUFF \upharpoonright n) \Rightarrow (p \textbf{ sat } (\forall x\colon M.BUFF''))$$

which follows from Theorem 17.2 by H3.

Now at last we see the motivation for the choice of assertions used in the previous examples. Of course, a proof would normally be presented in the reverse order, with proof requirements for the component processes being derived by formal manipulation from the proof requirement of the whole process. The reader is invited to use this top-down method to prove the obvious fact

$$(\mu p.(b!0 \rightarrow p)) \textbf{ sat } (b.ready \neq \emptyset).$$

17.2.4 Channel renaming

Let P be a process, with channel c in its alphabet, and let d be a channel name *not* in its alphabet. Then $P[d/c]$ is taken to denote a process that behaves just like P, except that

c is removed from its alphabet,
d is included in its alphabet,
whenever P would have used channel c for input or output,
$P[d/c]$ uses d instead.

$P[d/c]$ can clearly be derived from the definition of the process P by replacing each occurrence of the name c by an occurrence of d.

Example

$$COPY[d/right] = \mu p.(left?x: M \rightarrow (d!x \rightarrow p)).$$

A similar transformation may be made to any assertion satisfied by P, in accordance with the following convention:

$$R[d/c] =_{\text{df}} R[d.past/c.past,\ d.ready/c.ready].$$

The appropriate axiom is quite obvious:

$$(P[d/c] \textbf{ sat } R[d/c]) \equiv (P \textbf{ sat } R).$$

17.2.5 Disjoint parallelism

Let P and Q be processes with disjoint alphabets. Since they have no channel name in common, they are unconnected, and therefore cannot communicate or interact with each other in any way. The notation $(P \,|||\, Q)$ denotes a process which behaves like P and Q evolving in parallel; its alphabet is clearly the union of the alphabets of P and Q. Channel renaming can be used when needed to achieve disjointness of alphabets.

Example

$$PROT =_{df} (COPY[d/right]) \,|||\, (COPY[c/left]).$$

This combination is illustrated in Fig. 17.1(b).

The states of $(P \,|||\, Q)$ correspond to elements of the Cartesian product space of the set of states of P and the set of states of Q. If P satisfies S, then S has the same alphabet as P; it therefore correctly describes the current values of those channels in the state of $(P \,|||\, Q)$ which are in the alphabet of P; and hence

$$(P \,|||\, Q) \textbf{ sat } S.$$

Similarly, if Q **sat** T it follows that

$$(P \,|||\, Q) \textbf{ sat } T.$$

Hence by H4 (corollary), we justify the proof rule

$$\frac{(P \textbf{ sat } S) \wedge (Q \textbf{ sat } T)}{(P \,|||\, Q) \textbf{ sat } (S \wedge T)}$$

Example Let

$$BUFF(c, d) =_{df} BUFF[d/right] \wedge BUFF[c/left].$$

Theorem 17.6

$$PROT \textbf{ sat } BUFF(c, d).$$

Proof Immediate from Theorem 17.5 and the proof rules for renaming and disjoint parallelism.

17.2.6 Channel connection

Let P be a process with channels c and d in its alphabet. We may wish to connect together these two channels, so that messages passed on either of them are simultaneously passed on the other. For technical reasons, we give a new name b to the newly connected channel, and eliminate the names c and d from the alphabet of P. The process resulting from this connection and renaming will be denoted

$$(b = c \leftrightarrow d \textbf{ in } P)$$

Example

$$PROTOC =_{df} (b = c \leftrightarrow d \textbf{ in } PROT).$$

This is illustrated in Fig. 17.1(c).

When two channels c and d are connected, a message can be passed on the connecting channel b if and only if both of the connected channels are ready for that communication; so at all times:

$$b.ready = (c.ready \cap d.ready).$$

As a consequence, whenever c is ready for output and d for input, $d.ready$ is the universal set M, and the connected channel b is ready for output of the same value as c. Similar remarks apply when d is ready for output and c for input. When both c and d are ready for input, so is b. When either of c or d is unready then so is b. There remains the case that both c and d are ready for output, and the readiness of b depends on whether the values output are the same. This case is not very useful, and should probably be excluded in a practical programming notation.

Each message transmitted on either of the connected channels c and d is instantaneously passed by the connecting channel b to the other one. The sequences of messages so transmitted must therefore always be the same

$$b.past = c.past = d.past.$$

It is the duty of an implementation of the connection operator to ensure that b.ready and $b.past$ have the right values, as described in the above paragraphs. The programmer can just assume that this has been done. Thus we derive the proof rule

$$\frac{P \textbf{ sat } R}{(b = c \leftrightarrow d \textbf{ in } P) \textbf{ sat } (b.ready = c.ready \cap d.ready \\ \wedge\, b.past = c.past = d.past \wedge R)}.$$

Unfortunately, the assertion in the consequent of this rule contains the channel names c and d, which are not supposed to be in the alphabet of the process concerned. This problem is easily solved by the valid technique of weakening the consequent H3; it is easy to check that the following proof rule is a logical consequence of the one justified above.

$$\frac{P \textbf{ sat } R}{(b = c \leftrightarrow d \textbf{ in } P) \textbf{ sat } (\exists x, y.b.ready = x \cap y \\ \wedge\, R[b.past/c.past,\ b.past/d.past, \\ x/c.ready,\ y/d.ready])}.$$

Theorem 17.7

$$PROTOC \textbf{ sat } \exists x, y.(b.ready = x \cap y \wedge BB)$$

where

$$BB =_{\text{df}} BUFF(c, d)[b.past/c.past,\ b.past/d.past,\ x/c.ready,\ y/d.ready].$$

Proof Immediate from Theorem 17.6.
Here is BB written out in full:

$$\begin{aligned}&(\mathit{left.past} = \mathit{b.past} \wedge \mathit{left.ready} = M\\ &\quad \vee \mathit{b.past} < \mathit{left.past} \wedge y = \{\mathit{first}(\mathit{left.\ past} - b.\mathrm{past})\})\\ &\wedge (\mathit{b.past} = \mathit{right.past} \wedge x = M\\ &\qquad \vee \mathit{right.past} < \mathit{b.past} \wedge \mathit{right.ready} = \{\mathit{first}(\mathit{b.past} - \mathit{right.past})\}).\end{aligned}$$

17.2.7 Hiding

Let P be a process with channel b in its alphabet. Suppose that b is a channel which connects two or more component subprocesses of P, as described in the previous section. Since b is still in the alphabet of P, it can still be used for communication with the environment of P. Indeed, no communication can take place on channel b without the knowledge and consent of the environment. However, in the design of any mechanism, we usually wish to conceal its internal workings from its environment; and this is especially important for electronic devices, which can work millions of times faster than the environment. We therefore wish to hide from the environment of P all communications passing between subprocesses of P along channel b. Each such communication is intended to occur automatically and instantaneously as soon as all the processes connected by the channel are ready for it. And, of course, channel b must be removed from the alphabet of P. The required effect is denoted:

$$(\mathbf{chan}\ b\ \mathbf{in}\ P)$$

which declares the name b as a local channel in P. As with other local variables, we postulate,

$$(\mathbf{chan}\ b\ \mathbf{in}\ P) = (\mathbf{chan}\ c\ \mathbf{in}\ P[c/b])$$

where c is not in the alphabet of P.

Example

$$\mathit{PROTOCOL} =_{\mathrm{df}} (\mathbf{chan}\ b\ \mathbf{in}\ \mathit{PROTOC}).$$

In this example, the channel b connects the two parallel subprocesses of the process *PROTOC*. One of the processes acts like a trivial transmitter of a protocol, and the other as a trivial receiver. The channel b serves as the transmission line between them. The user of the mechanism is not concerned with the nature, number, or content of the messages passing along the transmission line, which are therefore concealed from him, as shown in Fig. 17.1(d).

A state of the process (**chan** b **in** P) is said to be *stable* if there is no further possibility of communication on channel b, i.e.

$$b.ready = \emptyset.$$

In an unstable state, when communication is possible on channel b, we want that communication to take place invisibly at high speed; and this will bring the process to a new and usually different state. Of course, if one of the other channels is ready at the same time as b, and the environment is prepared to communicate on that channel, the external communication can occur instead – but this cannot be relied upon. If the environment is *not* prepared to communicate on any of the other ready channels, we insist that a ready internal communication must sooner or later occur – and preferably sooner. Thus the unstable states are evanescent, and cannot be relied upon; in specifying the externally visible behaviour of processes, it seems sensible to ignore them. In other words we choose to interpret

$$P \textbf{ sat } R$$

as a claim that R is true of all *stable* states of P.

For each stable state of (**chan** b **in** P), there exists a state of P in which $b.ready = \emptyset$ and in which $b.past$ has some value of no further interest. This informal reasoning suggests a proof rule

$$\frac{(P \textbf{ sat } R)}{(\textbf{chan } b \textbf{ in } P) \textbf{ sat } (\exists b.past.R[\emptyset/b.ready])}.$$

(Here we have quantified over a channel variable as if it were an ordinary variable. The meaning is the same as if an ordinary variable s had been substituted, i.e.

$$\exists s.R[s/b.past, \emptyset/b.ready].)$$

Unfortunately this proof rule leads to a contradiction. Consider the process

$$P =_{\text{df}} \mu p.b!0 \rightarrow p.$$

P outputs an unbounded sequence of zeros on channel b, and is always prepared to output another; we can prove

$$P \textbf{ sat } (b.ready \neq \emptyset).$$

From this, using the incorrect rule given above, we deduce

$$(\textbf{chan } b \textbf{ in } P) \textbf{ sat } \exists b.past.((b.ready \neq \emptyset)[\emptyset/b.ready]).$$

The assertion here reduces to $\emptyset \neq \emptyset$, which violates the condition H2 (counterexample due to W. A. Roscoe).

The trouble here is that we have tried to hide an *infinite* sequence of internal communications, with disastrous consequences for our theory. The consequences in practice could be equally unfortunate, because the resulting process might expend all its energies on internal communication, and never pay any further attention to its environment. This phenomenon is known as 'livelock' or 'infinite chatter', and there are sound theoretical and practical reasons for requiring a programmer to prove it cannot occur. A simple way of doing this is to prove that the number of messages which can be passed along the hidden channel b is bounded by some total function f of the state of the other non-hidden channels:

$$\text{※}\, b.past \leqslant f(c.past, \ldots, z.past)$$

where $c, \ldots, z$ are all the other channels in the alphabet of the process.

Summarizing the discussion above, we formulate the proof rule:

$$\frac{P\ \mathbf{sat}(R \wedge (\text{※}\, b.past \leqslant f(c.past, \ldots, z.past)))}{(\mathbf{chan}\ b\ \mathbf{in}\ P)\ \mathbf{sat}\ (\exists b.past. R[\emptyset / b.ready])}.$$

Theorem 17.8 $PROTOCOL$ **sat** $(\exists b.past, x, y. (\emptyset = x \cap y \wedge BB))$

Proof $BB \Rightarrow (BB \wedge \text{※}\, b.past \leqslant \text{※}\, left.past)$.

The conclusion follows from Theorem 17.7 and H3.

We are at last ready to prove

Theorem 17.9 $PROTOCOL$ **sat** $BUFF$

Proof We prove the assertion of Theorem 17.8 implies $BUFF$. Expanding the assertion BB we get four cases:

$$\begin{aligned}
&left.past = b.past = right.past \wedge left.ready = x = M \\
\vee\ &right.past < b.past = left.past \wedge \\
&right.ready = \{first(b.past - right.past)\} \wedge \cdots \\
\vee\ &right.past = b.past < left.past \wedge x = M \wedge y = \{\cdots\} \\
\vee\ &right.past < b.past < left.past \wedge \\
&right.ready = first(b.past - right.past) \wedge y = \cdots
\end{aligned}$$

where irrelevant phrases are replaced by ellipses.

The first two clauses obviously imply the corresponding clauses of $BUFF$. The third clause describes an unstable state, and contradicts the term $(\emptyset = x \cap y)$; this case is therefore eliminated. The fourth clause also implies the corresponding clause of $BUFF$, using transitivity of $<$ and the fact that

$$r < b < l \Rightarrow first(b - r) = first(l - r).$$

17.2.8 Process chaining

The connection of processes in a series by their right and left channels is such a useful operation that it deserves a special notation:

$$(P\langle\equiv\rangle Q) =_{\text{df}} \textbf{chan } b \textbf{ in } (b = c \leftrightarrow d \textbf{ in } ((P[d/right])|||(Q[c/left])))$$

where b, c, d are fresh channel names.

Example

$$PROTOCOL = (COPY\langle\equiv\rangle COPY).$$

Unfortunately, the proof rule for this defined construct is hardly simpler than its definition. Let s, x, and y be fresh variables. Let

$$S' = S[s/right.past][x/right.ready], \qquad T' = T[s/left.past][y/left.ready].$$

Let f be a total function of pairs of sequences.

$$\frac{P \textbf{ sat } S,\ Q \textbf{ sat } T,\quad S' \wedge T' \Rightarrow s \leqslant f(left.past, right.past)}{(P\langle\equiv\rangle Q) \textbf{ sat } (\exists s, x, y.(x \cap y = \emptyset \wedge S' \wedge T'))}.$$

Theorem 17.10

If P **sat** $BUFF$ and Q **sat** $BUFF$, then $(P\langle\equiv\rangle Q)$ **sat** $BUFF$.

Proof Essentially the same as given for Theorem 17.9.

Corollaries

$$(PROTOCOL\langle\equiv\rangle COPY) \textbf{ sat } BUFF,$$
$$(PROTOCOL\langle\equiv\rangle PROTOCOL) \textbf{ sat } BUFF,$$

etc.

17.2.9 Nondeterministic union

Let P and Q be process descriptions with the same alphabet. Then the notation

$$(P \textbf{ or } Q)$$

stands for a process that behaves either like P or like Q. The choice between the alternatives is left completely unspecified, and may be made arbitrarily as the process (P **or** Q) evolves, or may be fixed by its implementor before the start. The choice cannot be influenced by the environment of the process, and is undetectable at the time it is made – though it may be deducible from the subsequent behaviour of the process.

Example

$$(PROTOCOL \textbf{ or } COPY).$$

This behaves either like a two-place buffer or a one-place buffer, the choice being unspecified and unknown. If, during the life of this process, the length of *left.past* ever exceeds the length of *right.past* by two, then we can deduce that the choice has fallen on *PROTOCOL*.

If we want to be sure that $(P \textbf{ or } Q)$ satisfies R, since we do not know which of P or Q will be selected, we had better prove that they both satisfy R:

$$(P \textbf{ or } Q) \textbf{ sat } R \equiv (P \textbf{ sat } R) \wedge (Q \textbf{ sat } R).$$

Theorem 17.11

$$(\mathit{PROTOCOL} \textbf{ or } \mathit{COPY}) \textbf{ sat } \mathit{BUFF}.$$

Proof From Theorems 17.9 and 17.5.

17.2.10 Conditional

Let e be a Boolean-valued expression *not* containing any channel variables. Let P and Q be processes with the same alphabet. Then the process

$$\textbf{if } e \textbf{ then } P \textbf{ else } Q$$

is one that behaves like P if e evaluates to *true*, or behaves like Q if e evaluates to *false*. The proof rule is correspondingly simple:

$$((\textbf{if } e \textbf{ then } P \textbf{ else } Q) \textbf{ sat } R)$$
$$\equiv \textbf{if } e \textbf{ then } (P \textbf{ sat } R) \textbf{ else } (Q \textbf{ sat } R).$$

An example will be given in Section 17.2.12.

17.2.11 Alternation

Let $P(x)$ and $Q(y)$ be processes whose behaviour possibly depends on the values of the free variables x and y respectively; but all of them have the same alphabet. Let c and d be *distinct* channel names in this alphabet. Let M be the set of messages that can be communicated on c, and let N be the set for d. Then the notation

$$(c?x: M \rightarrow P(x) \square\, d?y: N \rightarrow Q(y))$$

denotes a process which behaves as follows. Initially, it is prepared to input *either* on channel c *or* on channel d; in the first case its subsequent behaviour is defined by $P(x)$, where x stands for the value input on c; and in the second case, its subsequent behaviour is defined by $Q(y)$, where y is the value input on d. Only one of the two inputs can take place; but in contrast to nondeterministic union, the choice can be influenced by the other processes connected to the channels c and d. If the process (or processes) connected to one of them remains forever unprepared for communication, then communication can still occur, but only on the other channel. But if all the processes connected to each of the channels become ready for communication, then it is nondeterministic on which channel the communication will take place. An efficient implementation should select the first to become ready; but such considerations of efficiency rightly cannot be formalized in a calculus of correctness; and a programmer clearly must not rely on them, since he has delegated to the implementor all control over the relative speeds of the processes.

Example

$$MERGESTEP =_{\text{df}} (left1?x : M \to right!(1, x) \to p \\ \qquad \Box\, left2?x : M \to right!(2, x) \to p).$$

This process has alphabet $\{left1, left2, right\}$. It inputs a message x on either *left1* or *left2*, tags it with a 1 or 2 to indicate its source, and outputs the tagged message on the right, after which it behaves like p.

In the initial state of a process described using $\Box$, both the channels involved are ready for input, and all the other channels are unready. Each subsequent state corresponds either to a state of $P(x)$ or to a state of $Q(y)$; and *both* cases must be proved correct. The proof rule is therefore modelled on that for simple input.

If c and d are distinct channel names

$$(c?x : M \to P(x) \,\Box\, d?y : N \to Q(y)) \textbf{ sat } R \\ \equiv R[\langle\rangle/past, M/c.ready, N/d.ready, \emptyset/ready] \\ \wedge \forall x : M.P(x) \textbf{ sat } R[\langle x\rangle c.past/c.past] \\ \wedge \forall y : N.Q(y) \textbf{ sat } R[\langle y\rangle d.past/d.past].$$

Example Let $sel(n, s)$ be a sequence formed from s by selecting only those items tagged with n, and then removing the tags; or, more formally

$$sel(n, s) = \textbf{if } s = \langle\rangle \textbf{ then } \langle\rangle \\ \textbf{else if } first(s) = (n, x) \textbf{ then } \langle x\rangle\, sel(n, \text{rest}(s)) \\ \textbf{else } sel(n, rest(s)).$$

Let

$$MERGED =_{\text{df}} sel(1, right.past) \leqslant left1.past \\ \wedge\, sel(2, right.past) \leqslant left2.past \\ \wedge\, (left1.ready = left2.ready = M \vee right.ready \neq \emptyset).$$

Theorem 17.12

$$
\begin{aligned}
&\mathit{MERGESTEP}\ \mathbf{sat}\ (\mathit{MERGED} \upharpoonright n+1) \\
&\equiv \forall x{:}\, M.(\mathit{right}!(1,x) \to p)\ \mathbf{sat}\ (\mathit{MERGED} \upharpoonright n+1) \\
&\qquad\qquad [\langle x\rangle \mathit{left1.past} / \mathit{left1.past}] \\
&\wedge\ \forall x{:}\, M.(\mathit{right}!(2,x) \to p)\ \mathbf{sat}\ (\mathit{MERGED} \upharpoonright n+1) \\
&\qquad\qquad [\langle x\rangle \mathit{left2.past} / \mathit{left2.past}].
\end{aligned}
$$

Proof The omitted terms are trivial theorems.

The reader may care to complete the proof that

$$(\mu p.\mathit{MERGESTEP})\ \mathbf{sat}\ \mathit{MERGED}.$$

The notation and proof rule for alternation can clearly be adapted for more than two alternatives; and since $(c!e \to P)$ is the same as $(c?x{:}\{e\} \to P)$, output can be readily substituted for input.

17.2.12 General recursion

The method of defining processes by recursion can be generalized to allow mutual recursion. A set of processes defined by mutual recursion constitute a solution to a set of simultaneous fixed point equations, just as $\mu p.F(p)$ is a solution for p in the single equation

$$p =_{\mathrm{df}} F(p).$$

A pair of mutually recursive equations take the form

$$p =_{\mathrm{df}} F(p, q), \qquad q =_{\mathrm{df}} G(p, q)$$

where $F(p, q)$ and $G(p, q)$ are process descriptions, which in general contain the process variables p and q.

The method of mutual recursion generalizes even further to infinite sets of simultaneous equations, one for each member s in some counting set S:

$$p(s) = F(p, s) \qquad \text{for all } s \text{ in } S.$$

The solutions to all these simultaneous equations constitute an array p, with an element $p(s)$ for each s in S. This array of processes is denoted by the formula

$$\mu p(s{:}\, S).\, F(p, s).$$

However, it is often clearer to write the definitions in the equational form shown above.

Example

Let M^* be the set of all finite sequences of elements of M.

Let
$$IN =_{\text{df}} (left?x: M \rightarrow p(\langle x \rangle)).$$

Let
$$\begin{aligned} INOROUT =_{\text{df}} (&left?x: M \rightarrow p(s\langle x \rangle) \\ &\square\; right!first(s) \rightarrow p(rest(s)) \\ &). \end{aligned}$$

Let
$$STEP =_{\text{df}} \textbf{if } s = \langle\, \rangle \textbf{ then } IN \textbf{ else } INOROUT.$$

Let
$$B =_{\text{df}} \mu p(s: M^*).STEP.$$

The same definition can be written out more clearly in the form of an equation in B:

$$\begin{aligned} B(s) =_{\text{df}} \textbf{if } s = \langle\, \rangle \textbf{then } & left?x: M \rightarrow B(\langle x \rangle) \\ \textbf{else } & (left?\ x: M \rightarrow B(s\langle x \rangle) \\ & \square\; right!\ first(s) \rightarrow B(rest(s)) \\ &). \end{aligned}$$

for all s in M^*

For each s in M^*, $B(s)$ behaves like an unbounded buffer with current content s. If s is empty, $B(s)$ is prepared only to input on the left any value x in M, and then behave like $B(\langle x \rangle)$, that is, like a buffer containing only the value x. But if s is nonempty, $B(s)$ is prepared:

either (1) to input a new element x, which is appended to the stored buffer, so that its subsequent behaviour is $B(s\langle x \rangle)$,
or (2) to output the first element of its buffer, which is then removed, so that its subsequent behaviour is $B(rest(s))$.

The proof rule for generalized recursion is similar to that for simple recursion, except that the formulae are quantified over all s in the counting set S.

$$\frac{(\forall s: S.p(s) \textbf{ sat } (R(s) \restriction n) \Rightarrow \forall s: S.F(p, s) \textbf{ sat } (R(s) \restriction n+1))}{\forall s: S((\mu p(s: S) F(p, s))(s)) \textbf{ sat } R(s)}.$$

Example

Let us define

$$BUFF(s) =_{\text{df}} BUFF[(s\ left.past)/left.past].$$

$BUFF(s)$ describes the behaviour of a buffer that has input the sequence s, but not yet output it. $BUFF(s)$ therefore should describe the future behaviour of the process $B(s)$, as stated in the following theorem:

Theorem 17.13

$$\forall s : S.B(s)\ \mathbf{sat}\ BUFF(s).$$

Proof By the rule of recursion, we can assume

$$\forall s : M^*.\ p(s)\ \mathbf{sat}\ (BUFF(s) \upharpoonright n) \tag{0}$$

and must prove

$$STEP\ \mathbf{sat}\ (BUFF(s) \upharpoonright n+1) \qquad \text{for } s \in M^*$$

which by the conditional rule, splits in two:

$$s = \langle\rangle \Rightarrow IN\ \mathbf{sat}\ (BUFF(s) \upharpoonright n+1) \tag{1}$$

and

$$s \neq \langle\rangle \Rightarrow INOROUT\ \mathbf{sat}\ (BUFF(s) \upharpoonright n+1). \tag{2}$$

For (1), we assume $s = \langle\rangle$ and need to prove

$$(BUFF(s) \upharpoonright n+1)[\langle\rangle/past, M/left.ready,\ \emptyset/ready] \tag{1a}$$

$$\wedge\ p(\langle x\rangle)\ \mathbf{sat}\ (BUFF(s) \upharpoonright n+1)[\langle x\rangle left.past/left.past] \qquad \text{for all } x. \tag{1b}$$

(1a) is a trivial theorem, and the assertion of (1b) is equivalent to

$$BUFF[s\langle x\rangle left.past/left.past] \upharpoonright n$$

which by definition is $BUFF(s\langle x\rangle) \upharpoonright n$. So (1b) follows directly from the assumption (0) and the condition $s = \langle\rangle$.

For (2) we assume $s \neq \langle\rangle$ and need to prove

$$(BUFF(s) \upharpoonright n+1)[\langle\rangle/past,\ M/left.ready,\ \{first(s)\}/right.ready,\ \emptyset/ready] \tag{2a}$$

$$\wedge\ \forall x : M.p(s\langle x\rangle)\ \mathbf{sat}\ (BUFF(s) \upharpoonright n+1)[\langle x\rangle left.past/left.past] \tag{2b}$$

$$\wedge\ p(rest(x))\ \mathbf{sat}\ (BUFF(s) \upharpoonright n+1)[\langle first(s)\rangle right.past/right.past]. \tag{2c}$$

(2a) is a trivial theorem. The assertion of (2b) is equivalent to $BUFF(s\langle x\rangle) \upharpoonright n$, and the assertion of (2c) is equivalent to $BUFF(rest(s)) \upharpoonright n$; so both (2b) and (2c) follow from the assumption (0).

To check the above claims of trivial theoremhood or equivalence, it is necessary only to expand the abbreviations. For example

$$\begin{aligned}
&(BUFF(s) \upharpoonright n+1)[\langle first(s)\rangle right.past/right.past] \\
&\quad \equiv \#\, left.past + \#(\langle first(s)\rangle right.past) \geqslant n+1 \\
&\qquad \vee (s\ left.past) = \langle first(s)\rangle right.past \wedge left.ready = M \\
&\qquad \vee \langle first(s)\rangle right.past < (s\ left.past) \\
&\qquad\quad \wedge right.ready = \{first/((s\ left.past) - \langle first(s)\rangle right.past)\},
\end{aligned}$$

$$\begin{aligned}
&BUFF(rest(s)) \upharpoonright n \\
&\quad \equiv \text{※}\, left.past + \text{※}\, right.past \geqslant n \\
&\qquad \vee (rest(s)left.past) = right.past \wedge left.ready = M \\
&\qquad \vee right.past < (rest(s)left.past) \\
&\qquad\quad \wedge right.ready = \{first((rest(s)left.past) - right.past)\}.
\end{aligned}$$

When $s \neq \langle\rangle$, these are clearly equivalent, clause by clause.

Theorem 17.14

$$B(\langle\rangle)\ \mathbf{sat}\ BUFF.$$

Proof Put $s = \langle\rangle$ in Theorem 17.13.

17.3 Discussion

The proof methods described in this paper can be used to establish many useful properties of a process that are expressible as assertions about values of its channel variables. Such properties include:

(1) *Absence of deadlock*. If P **sat** R, then the assertion

$$\neg R[\emptyset/ready]$$

describes all those values of $a.past, \ldots, z.$past that do *not* lead to deadlock. If this is a theorem, deadlock can never occur.

(2) *Termination*. If P **sat** R, and if we can prove

$$R \Rightarrow \text{※}\, a.past + \cdots + \text{※}\, z.past \leqslant n$$

then we can be sure that P terminates in at most n steps.

(3) *Fairness*. A process P is said to be *fair* with respect to a channel c if it cannot indefinitely often service the other channels and neglect to service c. Thus any buffer is fair to its left channel and any finite bounded buffer is fair to its right channel. This condition may be formulated

$$BUFF_n \equiv BUFF \wedge \text{※}\,(left.past - right.past) \leqslant n.$$

To prove that P is a bounded buffer, we need to prove

$$\exists n(P\ \mathbf{sat}\ BUFF_n).$$

Note this is quite different from

$$P\ \mathbf{sat}\ (\exists n.BUFF_n)$$

since $\exists n BUFF_n$ is equivalent to *BUFF*, which is satisfied by an infinite buffer.

However, there are some properties of a process which are impossible to formulate in our calculus. For example, it is impossible to state or prove that *P* is a nondeterministic process. Indeed for any assertion *R*, if *P* **sat** *R* is proved, then there exists a *deterministic* process *Q* that also satisfies *R*. In particular, it is not possible to force an implementation to delay making a non-deterministic choice until after the start of the process, or indeed to force a choice before the start. The time at which nondeterminism is resolved is taken to be wholly invisible, and wholly irrelevant to the logical correctness of a process.

We make no claim that the calculus presented here is complete, in the sense that every proposition or its negation is provable. For example it does not seem possible to prove:

$$\textbf{chan } b \textbf{ in } (a!0 \to (\mu p.b!0 \to p))\textbf{sat}(a.past \in \{0\}^*)$$

or its negation. It is much more important that the calculus should be *consistent* in the sense that it should not permit proof of some proposition together with its negation. The easiest way to prove consistency is to construct a mathematical model of the set of all processes, and to prove that all the axioms of the calculus are truths about the model and that the proof rules preserve this validity. Suitable models may perhaps be found in Brinch Hansen (1975) or Campbell and Haberman (1974).

It is also desirable to be able to prove simple algebraic identities among processes, for example

$$(P\langle\equiv\rangle(Q1 \textbf{ or } Q2)) = ((P\langle\equiv\rangle Q1) \textbf{ or } (P\langle\equiv\rangle Q2)),$$
$$((right!\,e \to P)\langle\equiv\rangle(left?x : M \to Q)) = (P\langle\equiv\rangle Q[e/x]).$$

Such identities might be readily proved in a suitable model.

A final advantage of the construction of a model is that it may give better confidence that the notation introduced for the programming of processes can actually be implemented in a realistic and efficient manner. But mathematical model-building could be a rather arbitrary game, unless the model can be shown to satisfy some fairly simple proof rules, which can be used in correctness proofs of useful programs. It is hoped that our calculus will serve that purpose, although its application to large programs will not be as simple as one might hope.

The set of programming constructs which we have axiomatized is fairly extensive. Notable omissions are sequential composition, local variables, and assignment. There is reason to suppose that the treatment of these constructs will present some difficulty.

This paper has proved that five different processes satisfy the specification

BUFF:

$$\begin{array}{l} COPY, \\ PROTOCOL, \\ (PROTOCOL \langle \equiv \rangle COPY), \\ (PROTOCOL \textbf{ or } COPY), \\ B(\langle\, \rangle). \end{array}$$

Here are two more such processes:

$$C(\langle\, \rangle) \tag{1}$$

where $C =_{\mathrm{df}} \mu p(s : M^*)$ **if** $s = \langle\, \rangle$ **then** IN **else** $(INOROUT$ **or** $OUT)$

where $OUT =_{\mathrm{df}} (right!first(x) \rightarrow p(rest(s)))$,

$$\mu p.(left?x : M \rightarrow (p \langle \equiv \rangle (right!x \rightarrow COPY))). \tag{2}$$

In example (1), the depth of buffering may change dynamically (for example, according to fluctuating availability of storage). Example (2) is an unbounded buffer like $B(\langle\, \rangle)$. Both examples may be proved by methods described here.

17.4 Acknowledgement

This paper has greatly benefited from the advice and inspiration of visitors and students at the Programming Research Group, particularly Rick Hehner, Zhou Chao Chen, Steve Brookes, Bill Roscoe and Cliff Jones.

EIGHTEEN

Programming is an engineering profession

This chapter resulted from a collection of material from various occasional articles. It was put together as a sort of prospectus for an M.Sc. course at Oxford University which aimed to attract programmers from industry. The text of this chapter is a version of the PRG-27 Oxford monograph published in May 1982; a shorter version of the paper is available in [83]; the same text is published under a different title in [89].

In earlier times and in less advanced societies, the welfare of a community depended heavily on the skill and dedication of its craftsmen – the millers, blacksmiths, spinners, weavers, joiners, thatchers, cobblers and tailors. A craftsman possesses skills, not shared by his clients, which he has acquired by long and ill-paid apprenticeship to a master of his craft. He learns exclusively by imitation, practice, experience and by trial and error. He knows nothing of the scientific basis of his techniques, nothing of geometry or even of drawing, nothing of mathematics, or even of arithmetic. He cannot explain how or why he does what he does, and yet he works effectively, by himself or in a small team, and can usually complete the tasks he undertakes in a predictable time scale and at a fixed cost, and with results that are predictably satisfactory to his clients.

The programmer of today shares many of the attributes of the craftsman. He learns his craft by a short but highly paid apprenticeship in an existing programming team, engaged in some on-going project; and he develops his skills by experience rather than by reading books or journals. He knows nothing of the logical and mathematical foundations of his profession. He does not like to explain or document his activities. Yet he works effectively, by himself or in small teams, and he sometimes manages to complete the

C. A. R. Hoare, Programming is an engineering profession. In P. J. L. Wallis (ed.), *Software Engineering*, State of the Art Report Volume 11, No. 3, pp. 77–84. Reprinted with permission.

tasks he undertakes at the predicted time within the predicted costs, and to the satisfaction of his client.

In primitive societies of long ago we hear of another class of specialist on whom the welfare of the community depended. Like the craftsman, he is dedicated to his task; like the craftsman he is regarded with respect, perhaps even tinged with awe, by his many satisfied clients. There are several names given to such a man – a seer, a soothsayer, a sorcerer or wizard, a witch doctor or high priest. I shall just call him a high priest.

There are many differences between the craftsman and the high priest. One of the most striking is that the high priest is the custodian of a weighty set of sacred books, or magician's manuals, which he alone is capable of reading. When he is consulted by his client with some new problem, he refers to his sacred books to see whether he can find some spell or incantation which has proved efficacious in the past; and having found it, he tells his client to copy it carefully and use it in accordance with a set of elaborate instructions. If the slightest mistake is made in copying or in following the instructions, the spell may turn to a curse, and bring misfortune to the client. The client has no hope of understanding the nature of the error or why it has evoked the wrath of his deity – the high priest himself has no inner understanding of the ways of his god. The best the client can hope for is to go right back to the beginning, and start the spell again; and if this does not work, he goes back to the high priest for a new spell.

And that is another feature of the priesthood – when something goes wrong, as it quite often does, it somehow always turns out to be the ignorance or stupidity or impurity or wickedness of the client; it is never the fault of the high priest or his god. It is notable that when the harvest fails, it is the high priest who sacrifices the king, never the other way round.

Programmers of the present day share many of the attributes of the high priest. We have many names – coder, systems analyst, computer scientist, informatician, chief programmer: I shall just use the word 'programmer' to stand for them all. Our altars are hidden from the profane, each in its own superbly air-conditioned holy of holies, ministered to night and day by a devoted team of acolytes, and regarded by the general public with mixed feelings of fear and awe, appropriate for their condition of powerless dependence.

An even more striking analogy is the increasing dominance of our sacred books – the basic software manuals for our languages and operating systems which have become essential to our every approach to the computer. Only 30 years ago our computers' valves and tanks and wires filled the walls and shelves of a large room, which the programmer would enter, carrying in his pocket his programming manual – a piece of folded cardboard known as the 'facts card'. Now the situation is reversed: the programmer enters a large room whose walls and shelves are filled with software manuals: but in case he wants some urgent calculations he carries in his pocket – a computer.

18.1 The rise of engineering

In recent centuries with the advance of technology, we have seen the emergence of a new class of specialist – the professional engineer. The most striking characteristic of an engineer is the manner in which he qualifies for entry into his profession: not only does he work out the long apprenticeship of the craftsman, not only does he undergo the brief graduation of initiation ceremonies of the high priest, but both of these are preceded by many years of formal study in schools and in universities. His education covers a wide range of topics, including the mathematical foundations of the differential calculus, the derivation and solution of complex equations, the physical principles underlying the science of materials, as well as the specific technicalities of a particular branch of his subject, and a large catalogue of known design methods and specific practical techniques. However, this is only a start: during his professional career the engineer will expect to continue his education, to expand his skills, and to keep pace with technological progress by coninued study of new books and learned journals, and attendance of specialist orientation courses. The older crafstmen will complain that the engineer already knows far more than he needs for the day-to-day practice of his profession; but his colleagues and clients will realize that the weight of background learning develops his good judgement and increases his competence and authority at all times; even if a recondite scrap of knowledge is used only once in his career, then the learning has paid for itself many times over.

We would like to claim that computer programming has transcended its origins as a craft, has avoided the temptation to form itself into a priesthood, and can now be regarded as a fully fledged engineering profession. Certainly, we have some right to this claim. Through our professional Societies we have formulated a code of professional ethics and a structure and syllabus of professional examinations. We discharge our duty to the community by giving evidence to government commissions on social consequences of computing, on privacy, on employment. Because of the great demand for our services, our clients and employers are willing to offer us professional salaries, and it is hardly likely we shall refuse them.

But more than this is needed for true professional status. What is the great body of professional knowledge common to all educated programmers? Where are the reference libraries of standard works on known general methods and specific techniques and algorithms oriented to particular applications and requirements? What are the theoretical, mathematical or physical principles which underlie the daily practice of the programmer? Until recently, these questions had no answer. Now the answers are beginning to emerge. We can point to the ACM curriculum for the study of computer science at university as a corpus of common knowledge for the programmer, though the proportion of computer science graduates in the programming profession is still low. Don Knuth's books (1973) on the art of computer programming form an excellent encyclopaedia of known techniques – but only three volumes have so far appeared, and how many programmers consult even those? And finally, we have only recently come to a realization of the mathematical and logical basis of computer programming: we can now begin to construct program specifications with the same accuracy as an engineer can survey a site for a bridge or road, and on this basis we can now construct programs proved to meet their specification with as much certainty as the engineer assures us his bridge will not fall down. Introduction of these techniques promises to transform the arcane and error-prone craft of computer programming to meet the highest standards of a modern engineering profession.

Let me expand on the nature and consequences of this discovery. It is like the Greek discovery of axiomatic geometry as the basis of the measurement of land, map-making, and its later use in plans and elevations for the design and construction of buildings and bridges. It is like the discovery of the Newtonian laws of motion and the differential calculus as the basis of astronomy as well as more mundane tasks like the navigation of ships and the direction of artillery fire. It is like the discovery of stress analysis as the basis for the reliable and economic construction of steel frame buildings, bridges, and oil platforms.

This is just analogy. The analogy between programming and more traditional engineering disciplines is a very fruitful one, and it has been the basis of many theoretical and practical advantages to our profession. But analogies are dangerous, especially if they are applied without consideration of the underlying reality. I would therefore like to concentrate attention on three points where the analogy breaks down:

(1) The difference in methods by which we achieve reliability.
(2) Our difficulty in establishing structural isolation of parts of a large program.
(3) Our need for improved intellectual and mechanical tools.

18.2 Reliability

In principle, we should find it much easier than other professional engineers to achieve the highest standards of quality, accuracy and predictability of time scale and cost because the raw materials with which we work are much simpler, more plentiful, and much more reliable. Our raw materials are the binary digits in the stores and registers, disks and tapes of our computers. Our problem is that we have too many of them rather than too few. These bits are manipulated exactly in accordance with our instructions, at a rate of millions of operations per second for many weeks or months without mistake. When the hardware does go wrong it is the engineer, not the programmer, who is called upon to mend it.

That is why computer programming should be the most reliable of all professional disciplines. We do not have to worry about problems of faulty castings, defective components, careless labourers, storms, earthquakes or other natural hazards: we are not concerned with friction or wear or metal fatigue. Our only problems are those we make for ourselves and our colleagues by our over-ambition or carelessness, by our failure to recognize the mathematical and theoretical foundations of programming, and our failure to base our professional practice upon them.

Yet in some ways the engineers have an advantage over us. Because they are dealing with continuously varying quantities like distance, temperature, and voltage, it is possible for them to increase confidence in the reliability of an engineering product by testing it at the extremes of its intended operating range, for example, by exposure to heat and cold, or by voltage margins. We do the same in program testing, but in our case it is futile. Firstly we have to deal with impossibly many more variables and secondly these variables take discrete values, for which interpolation and extrapolation are wholly invalid. The fact that a program works for value zero and value 65 535 gives no confidence that it will work for any of the values in between, unless this fact is proved by logical reasoning based on the very text of the program itself. But if this logical reasoning is correct, then there was no need for the test in the first place. That is why it is an essential prerequisite to the improvement of our professional practices that we learn to reason effectively about our programs, to prove their correctness before we write them, so that we know that they will not only pass all their tests, but will go on working correctly forever after.

18.3 Structure

Traditional engineers have a further advantage over programmers: when they split a complex design into a number of component parts, to be designed independently of each other, they can take advantage of the spatial separation of the parts to ensure that there can be no unexpected interaction effects. If the parts are wholly unconnected, this is very easy to check by simple visual inspection. Thus when we turn our car to the left, we may be very confident that this will have no direct effect on the cigarette-lighter, the rear mirror, or the carburettor. When such interaction effects do occur, they are recognized as the most difficult to trace and eliminate.

But in the programming of conventional computers, there is no similar concept of spatial separation. Any instruction in a binary computer program can modify any location in the store of the computer including those that contain instructions. And if this happens incorrectly only once in a thousand million instructions executed, the consequences of the whole program will be totally unpredictable and uncontrollable. There is no hope that a prior visual inspection of the binary content of store will enable us to check that such interaction cannot occur, or to find the cause of its occurrence afterwards. There is no structure or isolation of components in a binary computer program, other than that which has been carefully designed into it from the start, and maintained by the most rigorous discipline throughout implementation.

In spite of this, the programmer is often asked to include some feature into his program as an afterthought: and the only quick way to do this is to insert new instructions which cross all the boundaries between the carefully isolated components and violate all the structural assumptions on which the original design was based. It would be repugnant to an engineer to introduce direct cross-coupling effects between the steering and carburettor of a motor car, or the tape decks and floating-point unit of a computer. A programmer is all too willing to do his best and his profession gets a bad name when unpredicted side-effects occur.

A partial solution to this problem lies in the use of a high-level language like ALGOL 60 with secure rules governing the scope, locality, and types of variable. In such a language the programmer can declare the structure of his program and data, stating which groups of variables are to be accessed or changed by which parts of his program. An automatic compiler can then check that the appropriate disciplines have been observed throughout the whole of a large program, and can therefore give the same confidence to the programmer as the engineer gains by spatial separation of his components. Further confidence can be gained by running the program on a machine like the Burroughs 5500 which makes similar checks while the program is running. In better established engineering disciplines, the observance of such elementary safety precautions has long been enforced by legislation. It is the law that dictates the measures that prevent unwanted interaction effects between an industrial machine and the body of its operator.

18.4 Tools of the trade

This brings me to the final disadvantage suffered by the programmer, the poor quality of the tools of his trade. I refer to his programming languages, operating systems, utility programs, library subroutines, all of which are supplied in profusion by the manufacturer of his computer. Many of these are so complicated that mastery of them absorbs all his intellectual efforts, leaving him little energy to apply to his client's original problem. Some operating systems are so poorly designed that they require 20 reissues (or 'releases') spread over a decade, before the original design faults have been rendered tolerable. They are so unreliable that each issue has a thousand faults corrected by the next issue, which introduces a thousand new faults of its own. When finally the agony of reissues comes to an end, instead of rejoicing, the poor programmer is cajoled or forced to accept an early issue of some 'new' product. Such complexity, unreliability, and instability of basic tools were doubtless endured by engineers of each newly emergent discipline: but gradually the engineers developed better toolkits for their own use. That is a task which still faces the programming profession today, the design of programming tools which are reliable, stable, convenient and, above all, simple to understand, control, and use.

A crude measure of the simplicity of an engineering tool is the length of the manual required to give a full and complete account of how to use it and avoid misusing it. At present our software manuals are both voluminous and inadequate. I believe that a solution to our problems can be sought in the design of software which can be completely described by shorter manuals. If an electronic engineer finds a method of satisfying with 20 components a need which has hitherto required 30, the value of his discovery is immediately recognized and is often highly rewarded by fame or by money. When a software engineer designs a product that can be fully defined in 20 pages of manual, when the rival product has been inadequately defined in 100, his achievement is just as great, and possibly more beneficial, for he has achieved an economy in our scarcest resource – not silicon or even gold, but our own precious human intellect.

18.5 How do we get there from here?

My description of the professional achievement of programmers of the future may seem to be nothing but an academic dream – a pleasant one for our clients, but perhaps something more like a nightmare for us. However are we going to make such a fantastic improvement in our working methods? We are like the barber-surgeons of earlier ages, who prided themselves on the sharpness of their knives, and the speed with which they could dispatch their duties, either of shaving a beard or amputating a limb. Imagine the dismay with which they greeted the academic who told them that the practice of surgery should be based on a long and detailed study of human anatomy, on familiarity with surgical procedures pioneered by great doctors of the past and that it should be carried out only in a strictly controlled 'bug-free' environment, far removed from the hair and dust of the normal barber's shop. Even if they accepted the validity and necessity for these improvements, how would they ever achieve them? How could all those hairdressers be re-educated in the essential foundations of surgery? Clearly, a two-week course in Structured Surgery is all that we can readily afford. But more is needed, much more.

First we need good books which can be studied by programmers and programming teams to familiarize themselves with the concepts of mathematical proof, and show how proof methods may be applied to the everyday practice of program specification, design, and implementation. Such books are beginning to appear in the publishers' lists, one of which is (Gries 1978).

We also need a journal in which practising programmers can read the results of current research to keep themselves up to date with the most effective technology. A new journal of this kind, entitled *The Science of Computer Programming*, has just been founded.

Most of the books and articles on programming methods are of necessity illustrated only by small examples. Indeed, many of the programming methods advocated by the authors have never yet been applied to large programs. This is not a defect of their research, it is necessity. All advances in engineering are tested first on small-scale models, in wave tanks, or in wind tunnels. Without models, the research would be prohibitively expensive, and progress would be correspondingly slow.

Nevertheless, I believe that the time has come to attempt to scale up the use of formal mathematical methods to industrial application. This can best be achieved by collaborative development projects between a university or polytechnic and an industrial company or software house. Such a project might be an entirely new program, or it might be a restructuring or redesign of some existing software product in current use, perhaps one which has lost its original structure as a result of constant amendment and enhancement. The great advantage of these joint projects is that they bring home to academic researchers some of the exigencies of working on much larger programs: and they give a practical training in formal methods to larger numbers of experienced programmers in industry. This is technology transfer in its best sense – a transfer of benefits in both directions.

18.6 Education

As I have emphasized already, the major factor in the wider propagation of professional methods is education, an education which conveys a broad and deep understanding of theoretical principles as well as their practical application, an education such as can be offered by our universities and polytechnics. Lecturers and professors regard it as their duty and privilege to keep abreast with the latest developments in their subjects, and to adapt, improve and expand their courses to pass on their understanding to their students. Many entrants to computer science courses have acquired a familiarity with the basic mechanics of programming at their schools: and at university they are ready to absorb the underlying mathematical principles, which will help them to control the complexity of their designs and the reliability of their implementations.

Over the next decades, while the graduates of computer science courses are entering their profession, we will have an extremely awkward period, in which almost none of the senior professionals and managers will have any knowledge or understanding of the new methods, while those whom they recruit will seem to them to be talking academic gibberish. This could be a grave hindrance to the development of our profession. Furthermore, it would be a terrible wasted opportunity, because one of the major benefits of the technique of mathematical abstraction is that it enables a chief programmer or manager to exert real technical control over his teams, without delving into the morass of technical detail with which his programmers are often tempted to overwhelm him.

The solution to this problem is for the ambitious senior programmers of the present day to make the effort now to gain the necessary mastery of the subject, and so ensure that they will become in future the effective chief programmers, technical managers, and technical directors of their companies and institutions.

One way of acquiring a professional reorientation of this kind is to take a specialist postgraduate post-experience course in a new and important subject. Thus an electronic engineer might now be going back to university to study VLSI design: or an industrial chemist might be taking a Master's course in polymer science or genetic engineering, offered by some forward-looking university or polytechnic. I believe that ambitious programmers should not be reluctant to follow the example of the well-established engineering disciplines. That is why at Oxford University we have instituted a new MSc course in computation, devoted primarily to the objective of improving programming methods and ensuring their wider application. A similar course is offered at the Wang Institute in the USA.

18.7 Conclusion

In 1828, on the occasion of the grant of Royal Charter to the Institution of Civil Engineers, Thomas Tredgold defined civil engineering as 'the art of directing the great sources of power in Nature for the use and convenience of man'. Many branches of engineering have been established since that date. They have all been concerned with the capture, storage and transformation of energy, or with the processing, shaping and assembly of materials. Computer programmers work with neither energy nor materials, but with a more intangible concept. We are concerned with the capture, storage, and processing of information. When the nature of our activities is more widely understood, both within our profession and outside, then we shall be deservedly recognized and respected as a branch of engineering. And I believe that in our branch of engineering, above all others, the academic ideals of rigour and elegance will pay the highest dividends in practical terms of reducing costs, increasing performance, and in directing the great sources of computational power on the surface of a silicon chip to the use and convenience of man.

> It has long been my personal view that the separation of practical and theoretical work is artificial and injurious. Much of the practical work done in computing, both in software and in hardware design, is unsound and clumsy because the people who do it do not have any clear understanding of the fundamental principles underlying their work. Most of the abstract mathematical and theoretical work is sterile because it has no point of contact with real computing. One of the central aims of the Programming Research Group as a teaching and research group has been to set up an atmosphere in which this separation cannot happen ...
>
> Christopher Strachey (1974)

NINETEEN

A couple of novelties in the propositional calculus

This paper was submitted on 31 March 1983 and published in 1985 as [93]. The inspiration was due to conversations with Bill Craig. The *negmajority* operator was inspired by the predicative semantics of CSP's $\square$ operator. The infix notation of the conditional was perhaps a response to Dijkstra's criticism of the asymmetry of the more traditional guarded-command notation. The relation between *negmajority* and the more familiar *majority* operator was pointed out by Edsger Dijkstra.

Abstract

It is often convenient to regard a dyadic operator as a 'curried' monadic operator, in order to facilitate expression of its algebraic properties. Similarly, a triadic operator can be curried to give a dyadic one; and when the resulting operator is expressed in infix form, its algebraic properties may be surprisingly elegant. This paper gives two amusing examples, which were prompted by a study of the logical foundations of computer programming.

19.1 The conditional

The *conditional* can be defined as a ternary operator of the propositional calculus:

$$P \lhd Q \rhd R =_{\text{df}} P \wedge Q \vee \bar{Q} \wedge R \; (= (P \vee \bar{Q}) \wedge (Q \vee R)).$$

It should be read: '*P* **if** *Q* **else** *R*'. A computer programmer may be familiar

C. A. R. Hoare, A couple of novelties in the propositional calculus, *Zeitschr. f. Math. Logik und Grundlagen d. Math.*, **31**(2), 173–8 (1985). This paper is republished by kind permission of Zeitschr. f. Math. Logik und Grundlagen d. Math.

with this operator expressed in a variety of notations:

if Q **then** P **else** R	(ALGOL 60)
$(COND(Q, P)(T, R))$	(LISP)
$(Q \rightarrow P, R)$	(Semantics)
if $Q \rightarrow P \,\square\, \neg Q \rightarrow R$ **fi**	(E. W. Dijkstra).

Mathematicians often use conditional definitions

$$X =_{\text{df}} \begin{cases} P & \text{if } Q, \\ R & \text{otherwise.} \end{cases}$$

But I much prefer a notation which allows $\triangleleft Q \triangleright$ to be treated as a binary operator written in infix form, since then its algebraic properties may be elegantly expressed as follows:

(1) $\triangleleft Q \triangleright$ is idempotent,
(2) $\triangleleft Q \triangleright$ is associative,
(3) $\triangleleft Q \triangleright$ distributes through $\triangleleft R \triangleright$ (in both directions).

All truth functions can be defined in terms of the conditional, together with the two truth constants *true* and *false*:

(4) $P \wedge Q = P \triangleleft Q \triangleright Q \qquad (= P \triangleleft Q \triangleright \mathit{false})$.
(5) $P \vee Q = P \triangleleft P \triangleright Q \qquad (= \mathit{true} \triangleleft P \triangleright Q)$,
(6) $\bar{Q} = \mathit{false} \triangleleft Q \triangleright \mathit{true}$.

The following identities are useful for the simplification of conditional propositions:

(7) $\mathit{true} \triangleleft Q \triangleright \mathit{false} = Q$,
(8) $P \triangleleft Q \triangleright (R \triangleleft Q \triangleright S) = P \triangleleft Q \triangleright S$,
(9) $P \triangleleft (Q \triangleleft R \triangleright S) \triangleright T = (P \triangleleft Q \triangleright T) \triangleleft R \triangleright (P \triangleleft S \triangleright T)$,
(10) $P \triangleleft \mathit{false} \triangleright Q = P$,
(11) $P \triangleleft \mathit{false} \triangleright Q = Q$.

The last two laws by themselves enable a conditional expression to be computed as a truth function of its arguments. Thus the familiar method of truth tables can be used to detect whether any proposition function expressed in terms of conditionals is a tautology.

A more interesting question is: 'Are the laws (1)–(11) sufficient to prove that all tautologies are uniformly true?' Since $\wedge$, $\vee$, and negation can be eliminated by (4)–(6), we can confine attention to propositions expressed wholly in terms of conditionals and the truth constants. In fact, such propositions can be reduced to a nice (but lengthy) normal form. In preparation, here are some long but useful lemmas:

(12) $(P \triangleleft Q \triangleright R) \triangleleft S \triangleright (T \triangleleft Q \triangleright U)$

$$= (P \triangleleft S \triangleright T) \triangleleft Q \triangleright (R \triangleleft S \triangleright U).$$

Proof

$$\begin{aligned}\text{L.h.s.} &= (P \lhd S \rhd (T \lhd Q \rhd U)) \lhd Q \rhd (R \lhd S \rhd (T \lhd Q \rhd U)) && \text{by (3)}\\ &= ((P \lhd S \rhd T) \lhd Q \rhd (\ldots)) \lhd Q \rhd ((\ldots) \lhd Q \rhd (R \lhd S \rhd U)) && \text{by (3)}\\ &= \text{r.h.s.} \quad \text{by (2) and (8).}\end{aligned}$$

The structure of this theorem can be more clearly displayed in two dimensions:

$$\left\{\begin{matrix} P \\ \lhd Q \rhd \\ R \end{matrix}\right\} \lhd S \rhd \left\{\begin{matrix} T \\ \lhd Q \rhd \\ U \end{matrix}\right\} = \left\{\begin{matrix} (P \lhd S \rhd T) \\ \lhd Q \rhd \\ (R \lhd S \rhd U) \end{matrix}\right\}.$$

The next theorem is similarly displayed:

$$(13)\quad \left\{\begin{matrix} R11 \\ \lhd R21 \rhd \\ R31 \end{matrix}\right\} \lhd Q \rhd \left\{\begin{matrix} R12 \\ \lhd R22 \rhd \\ R32 \end{matrix}\right\} = \left\{\begin{matrix} (R11 \lhd Q \rhd R12 \\ \lhd\ R21 \lhd Q \rhd R22 \rhd \\ (R31 \lhd Q \rhd R32 \end{matrix}\right\}.$$

Proof

$$\begin{aligned}\text{R.h.s.} &= ((R11 \lhd Q \rhd R12) \lhd \mathrm{R21} \rhd (R31 \lhd Q \rhd R32))\\ &\quad \lhd Q \rhd ((R11 \lhd Q \rhd R12) \lhd R22 \rhd (R31 \lhd Q \rhd R32)) && \text{by (9)}\\ &= ((R11 \lhd R21 \rhd R31) \lhd Q \rhd (\ldots))\\ &\qquad \lhd Q \rhd ((\ldots) \lhd Q \rhd (R12 \lhd R22 \rhd R32)) && \text{by (12)}\\ &= \text{l.h.s.} \quad \text{by (2) and (8).}\end{aligned}$$

Lemma Let Q be a proposition letter, and let R be a formula expressed solely in terms of conditionals and truth constants. Then R can be expanded by laws (1)–(11) (and substitution of equals) to the form $R1 \lhd Q \rhd R2$, where $R1$ and $R2$ do not contain Q; nor do they contain any proposition letter except those which were originally in R.

Proof (by cases).

(a) If R does not contain Q, then $R = R \lhd Q \rhd R$ by (1).
(b) If R is just Q, then $R = \mathit{true} \lhd Q \rhd \mathit{false}$ by (7).
(c) If R is of the form $R1 \lhd R2 \rhd R3$, we apply this procedure recursively to the three components $R1, R2, R3$ to get

$$\begin{aligned}R &= (R11 \lhd Q \rhd R12) \lhd R21 \lhd Q \rhd R22 \rhd (R31 \lhd Q \rhd R32)\\ &= (R11 \lhd R21 \rhd R31) \lhd Q \rhd (R12 \lhd R22 \rhd R32) \text{ by (13).}\end{aligned}$$

This satisfies the requirements of the lemma.

To reduce a formula R to normal form, it is necessary first to choose an ordering

$$(Q_1, Q_2, \ldots, Q_n)$$

which includes all proposition letters Q_i in R. Then R can be reduced by the lemma to

$$R = R1 \lhd Q_1 \rhd R2.$$

Applying the lemma again to $R1$ and $R2$ (w.r.t. Q_2)

$$R = (R11 \lhd Q_2 \rhd R21) \lhd Q_1 \rhd (R21 \lhd Q_2 \rhd R22).$$

Proceeding recursively with $(Q_3, \ldots, Q_n)$ we eventually obtain a form in which all the propositional variables Q_i appear as conditional operators $\lhd Q_i \rhd$. Each $\lhd Q_i \rhd$ will appear 2^i times; and if $i \neq n$ the dominant operator on its left and on its right will be $\lhd Q_{i+1} \rhd$. The only remaining operands will be expressed in terms of $\lhd\, true \rhd$, $\lhd\, false \rhd$, *true*, and *false*. All of these can be reduced to truth constants by laws (10) and (11). This gives the required normal form.

Examples Let the list of variables be (P, Q).

(1) $true \rightarrow (true \lhd Q \rhd true) \lhd P \rhd (true \lhd Q \rhd true)$.

(2) $P \rightarrow true \lhd P \rhd false$
$\rightarrow (true \lhd Q \rhd true) \lhd P \rhd (false \lhd Q \rhd false)$.

(3) $P \vee \bar{Q} \rightarrow P \lhd P \rhd (false \lhd Q \rhd true)$
$\rightarrow (true \lhd P \rhd false) \lhd true \lhd P \rhd false \rhd (false \lhd Q \rhd true)$
$\lhd P \rhd (false \lhd Q \rhd true)$
$\rightarrow true \lhd P \rhd (false \lhd Q \rhd true)$
$\rightarrow (true \lhd Q \rhd true) \lhd P \rhd (false \lhd Q \rhd true)$.

The normal form is clearly equivalent to a truth table expressed as a binary tree. For each assignation of truth values to the variables $Q_1, Q_2, \ldots, Q_n$, it is possible to look up the truth value of the normal form by a binary search, choosing the left operand of $\lhd Q_i \rhd$ if Q_i is true, and the right operand if it is false. The final selected operand of Q_n is the truth value of the formula. Clearly a formula is a tautology if and only if all these ultimate operands are true. Similarly, two propositional formulae are equivalent if and only if they reduce to the same normal form with respect to the same list of proposition letters.

19.2 Negmajority

The *negmajority* of three operands is defined as the truth value given by the majority of their votes, except that the vote of the middle operand is negated:

$$P[Q]R =_{\text{df}} P \wedge \bar{Q} \vee \bar{Q} \wedge R \vee R \wedge P \; (= (P \vee \bar{Q}) \wedge (\bar{Q} \vee R) \wedge (R \vee P)).$$

Again, regarding $[Q]$ as an infix operator, its algebraic properties can be elegantly expressed:

(1) $[Q]$ is idempotent,
(2) $[Q]$ is commutative,
(3) $[Q]$ is associative,
(4) $[Q]$ distributes through $[R]$.

All truth functions can be defined in terms of the negmajority operator:

(5) $P \wedge Q = P[\mathit{true}]Q$,
(6) $P \vee Q = P[\mathit{false}]Q$,
(7) $\bar{P} = \mathit{false}[P]\mathit{true}$.

In view of (5) and (6), each of the laws (1), (2) and (3) express two familiar truths of the propositional calculus, and law (4) summarizes no less than four distribution laws.

The following law, together with (1) and (2), permits the truth value of $P[Q]R$ to be computed from the truth values of its three operands:

(8) $P[Q]Q = P$.

Proof At least two of the operands of $P[Q]R$ must have the same truth value. If it is the outer pair, that value (by (1)) is the result; otherwise the third operand gives the result (by (8), and if necessary, (2)).

The following law expresses the 'skew symmetry' of the operator:

(9) $P[Q]R = R[\bar{P}]\bar{Q}$.

We also have an astonishing analogue of law (9) for the conditional operator:

(10) $P[Q[R]S]T = (P[Q]T)[\bar{R}](P[S]T)$.

The question again arises, are these laws adequate to prove all tautologies in the propositional calculus? Again, the answer is affirmative; but this time we shall prove it by establishing the familiar laws which enable every formula to be reduced to the conjunctive or disjunctive normal form.

The first proved law expresses both of de Morgan's laws:

(11) $\overline{P[Q]R} = \bar{P}[\bar{Q}]\bar{R}$.

Proof L.h.s. $= \mathit{false}[P[Q]R]\mathit{true}$ by (7)
$= (\mathit{false}[P]\mathit{true})[\bar{Q}](\mathit{false}[R]\mathit{true})$ by (10)
$=$ r.h.s. by (7).

(12) $\overline{\mathit{true}} = \mathit{false}$.

Proof L.h.s. $= \mathit{false}[\mathit{true}]\mathit{true}$ by (7)
$=$ r.h.s. by (8).

(13) $\overline{\mathit{false}} = \mathit{true}$.

Proof L.h.s. $= \mathit{false}[\mathit{false}]\ \mathit{true}$ by (7)
$= \mathit{true}[\mathit{false}]\mathit{false}$ by (2)
$=$ r.h.s. by (8).

(14) $\bar{\bar{P}} = P$.

Proof L.h.s. $= \mathit{false}[\bar{P}]\mathit{true}$ by (7)
$= \mathit{false}[\bar{P}]\ \overline{\mathit{false}}$ by (13)
$= P[\mathit{false}]\mathit{false}$ by (9)
$=$ r.h.s. by (8).

(15) $P \wedge \bar{P} = \mathit{false}$.

Proof L.h.s. $= P[\overline{\overline{\mathit{true}}}]\ \bar{P}$ by (5), (14)
$= \overline{\mathit{true}}[P]P$ by (9)
$=$ r.h.s. by (8), (12).

(16) $P \vee \bar{P} = \mathit{true}$.

Proof L.h.s. $= P[\overline{\overline{\mathit{false}}}]\bar{P}$ by (6), (14)
$= \overline{\mathit{false}}\ [P]P$ by (9)
$=$ r.h.s. by (8), (13).

(17) $(P[S]R)[Q](P[\bar{S}]R) = P[Q]R$.

Proof L.h.s. $= P[S[\bar{Q}]\bar{S}]R$ by (10)
$= P[Q[S]S]R$ by (9)
$= P[Q]R$ by (8).

(18) $(P[\bar{S}]\bar{Q})[S](\bar{Q}[\bar{S}]R)[S](P[\bar{S}]R) = P[Q]R$.

Proof L.h.s $= ((S[Q]P)[S](S[Q]R))[S](P[\bar{S}]R)$ by (9), (2)
$= (S[Q](P[S]R))[S](P[\bar{S}]R)$ by (4)
$= (S[S](P[\bar{S}]R))[\bar{Q}]((P[S]R)[S](P[\bar{S}]R))$ by (4)
$= (P[\bar{S}]R)[Q](P[S]R)$ by (8), (2), (17)
$= P[Q]R$ by (2), (17).

Corollaries

$$P[Q]R = P \wedge Q \vee \bar{Q} \wedge R \vee P \wedge R$$
$$= (P \vee \bar{Q}) \wedge (\bar{Q} \vee R) \wedge (P \wedge R).$$

Proof Substitute *true* or *false* for A in (18) and use (5), (6), (12), (13).

Now the reduction of an expression to normal form is simple: Replace all occurrences of $P[Q]R$ by its equivalent in terms of $\wedge$, $\vee$ and negation, using one of the corollaries of theorem (18); and then use the proven properties of $\wedge$, $\vee$, and negation to reduce the formula to conjunctive or disjunctive normal form. Of course, such a reduction is not recommended in practice;

but its possibility shows that laws (1)–(10) (together with substitution of equals) are sufficient to prove all equivalences in the propositional calculus.

19.3 Conclusion

If this brief note has any merit, it can only be because the infix notations lend a measure of elegance to the formulation of the laws and theorems. Are there any other triadic operators which have nice properties when expressed in infix form?

Take any pair of dyadic truth functions (say $\equiv$ and $\not\equiv$) which share a number of nice algebraic properties. Define

$$P\,\{true\}\,R =_{\mathrm{df}} (P \equiv R), \qquad P\,\{false\}\,R =_{\mathrm{df}} (P \not\equiv R).$$

Then $\{Q\}$ will share the same algebraic properties. It is simple fun to discover a set of laws that make the operator expressively complete and logically complete (if indeed it is so). I wonder how often such operators will obey an 'unnesting law' such as (9) for the conditional or (10) for the negmajority.

TWENTY

Programs are predicates

Hoare was elected a Fellow of the Royal Society in 1982. Within a week of his election, he was invited, together with Atiyah and Shepherdson, to organize a Symposium on Mathematical Logic and Programming Languages. This event took place in 1984 (see [95] for proceedings). This paper ([96]) represents his personal contribution to the scientific programme.

Rick Hehner had first suggested the idea of viewing programs as predicates whilst he was on an extended visit to Oxford. It is interesting to contrast the approach here where a program P is translated into a predicate R with that in Chapter 16 where one proves $P\,\mathbf{sat}\,R$. The step made here foreshadows the development of algebraic laws as in [102].

The translation into a (single) predicate is interesting and gives great simplification especially to theoretical investigations. For practical specifications, however, it is often more convenient to use predicate pairs where a precondition records the applicable domain separately from the postcondition. This separation results in calculation methods which are helpful in program design and development.

Abstract

A computer program is identified with the strongest predicate describing every relevant observation that can be made of the behaviour of a computer executing that program. A programming language is a subset of logical and mathematical notations, which is so restricted that products in the language can be automatically implemented on a computer. The notations enjoy a number of elegant algebraic properties, which can be used for optimizing program efficiency.

A specification is a predicate describing all permitted observations of a program, and it may be expressed with greatest clarity by taking advantage of the whole language of logic and mathematics. A program P meets its specification S iff

$$\models P \Rightarrow S.$$

The proof of this implication may use all the classical methods of mathematics and logic.

C. A. R. Hoare, Programs are predicates, In C. A. R. Hoare and J. C. Shepherdson (eds.), *Mathematical Logic and Programming Languages*, Prentice-Hall International, pp. 141–54 (1985). This paper is also republished by kind permission of The Royal Society, since it originally appeared in their *Philosophical Transactions*.

These points are illustrated by design of a small language that includes assignments, conditionals, nondeterminism, recursion, input, output, and concurrency.

20.1 Introduction

It is the aim of the natural scientist to discover mathematical theories, formally expressed as predicates describing the relevant observations that can be made of some physical system. A physical system is fully defined by the strongest predicate that describes it. Such predicates contain free variables, standing for values determined by observation, for example a for acceleration, v for velocity, t for time, etc.

The aim of an engineer is complementary to that of the scientist. He starts with a specification, formally expressible as a predicate describing the desired observable behaviour of a system or product not yet in existence. Then, with a limited set of tools and materials, within a limited time scale and budget, he must design and construct a product that meets that specification. The product is fully defined by the strongest specification that it meets.

For example, an electronic amplifier may be required to amplify its input voltage by a factor of ten. However, a condition of its correct working is that the input voltage must be held in the range 0 to 1 V. Furthermore, a margin of error of up to 1 V is allowed on the output. This informal specification may be formalized as a predicate, with free variables:

V_i, standing for the ith observed input voltage;
$\tilde{V}_i$, standing for the ith observed output voltage.

Then the specification is

$$\forall i.(i \leqslant j \Rightarrow 0 \leqslant V_i \leqslant 1) \Rightarrow |\tilde{V}_j - 10 \times V_j| \leqslant 1.$$

Table 20.1(a), and (b) shows the first six observations made of two different amplifiers. The first observation of each amplifier shows it working with perfect accuracy at the midpoint of its range. The second observation is only just within the margin of tolerance. On the third observation the amplifier reveals its 'nondeterminism': it does not always give the same output voltage for the same input voltage. On the fourth observation something goes wrong. For 4(a) it is the amplifier that has gone wrong, because the 5 V output is outside the permitted margin of error. Even if every subsequent observation is satisfactory, this product has not met its specification, and should be returned to its maker. For 4(b), it is the observer who is at fault in supplying an excessive input of 1.3 V. As a result, the amplifier breaks, and its subsequent behaviour is entirely

Table 20.1 Observations made of two different amplifiers

Observation number	(*a*)		(*b*)	
	V	$\tilde{V}$	V	$\tilde{V}$
1	0.5	5	0.5	5
2	0.4	5	0.4	5
3	0.5	4	0.5	4
4	0.3	5	1.3	13
5	0.6	6	0.6	6
6	0.7	7	0.7	997

unconstrained: no matter what it does, it continues to meet its original specification. So on the sixth observation, it is the observer who returns to his Maker.

The serious point of this example is to illustrate the usefulness of material implication in a specification. The consequent of the implication describes the desired relation between the inputs and the outputs of the system. The antecedent describes the assumptions that must be satisfied by the inputs of the system for it to continue working. If the assumptions are falsified, the product may break, and its subsequent (but not its previous) behaviour may be wholly arbitrary. Even if it seems to work for a while, it is completely worthless, unreliable, and even dangerous.

A computer programmer is an engineer whose main materials are the notations and structures of his programming language. A program is a detailed specification of the behaviour of a computer executing that program. Consequently, a program can be identified abstractly with a predicate describing all relevant observations that may be made of this behaviour. This identification assigns a meaning to the program (Floyd 1967), and a semantics to the programming language in which it is expressed.

These philosophical remarks lead to the main thesis of this paper, namely that programs are predicates. However, the converse claim would be incorrect, because any predicate that is wholly unsatisfiable (for example the predicate *false*) cannot correspond to a program. If it did, the behaviour of a computer executing that program would be wholly unobservable! Consequently, every observation of that behaviour would satisfy every specification! A product that satisfies every need is known as a *miracle*. Since such a product is also in principle unobservable, philosophical considerations lead us to suppose that it does not exist. Certainly any notation in which such a miracle could be expressed would not be an implementable programming language. There are also obvious practical reasons for ensuring that all predicates expressible as programs are in some sense computable, and can be computed at a cost that is controllable by the programmer and acceptable to his client.

The design of a programming notation requires a preliminary selection of what are the relevant observable phenomena, and a choice of free variables to denote them. A meaning must then be given to the primitive components of the language, and to the operators that compose programs from smaller subprograms. Ideally, these operators should have pleasant algebraic properties, which permit proof of the identity of two programs whenever they are indistinguishable by observation. The achievement of these ideals is far from easy: so the language introduced in the next section for illustrative purposes has been kept very simple. It includes nondeterminism, output, input, recursion, concurrency, assignment, and conditional.

20.2 A simple programming language

The first and simplest predicate that is expressible in our simple programming language is the predicate *true*. This predicate is satisfied by *all* observations. If this is the *strongest* specification of a product, then there is no constraint whatever on the behaviour or misbehaviour of the product. The only customer who is certain to be satisfied with this product is one who would be satisfied by *anything*. Thus the program *true* is the most useless of all products, just as a tautology is the most useless of scientific theories.

Now the most useless of computer programs is one that immediately goes into an infinite loop or recursion. Such a program is clearly broken or unstable, and can satisfy only the most undemanding customer. Thus we identify the infinitely looping program with the predicate *true*. This may be a controversial decision; but in practice the ascription of a meaning to a divergent program is arbitrary, because no programmer will ever deliberately want to write a program that runs any risk of looping forever.

20.2.1 Non-determinism

The first and simplest operator of our programming language is disjunction. If P and Q are programs, the program $(P \vee Q)$ behaves either like P or like Q. There is no way of controlling or predicting the choice between P and Q; the choice is arbitrary or non-deterministic. All that is known is that each observation of $(P \vee Q)$ must be an observation of the behaviour of P or of Q or of both.

The algebraic properties of disjunction are very familiar: it is idempotent, symmetric, associative, etc. Furthermore, it is *distributive* (through disjunction) and *strict* in the sense that

$$P \vee \mathit{true} = \mathit{true} \vee P = \mathit{true}.$$

This means that if either P or Q may break then so may $(P \vee Q)$. To an engineer, a product that *may* break is as bad as one that *does*, because you can never rely on it.

20.2.2 Processes

Now we must be more specific about the nature of the objects described by programs in our simple language. These objects are called *processes*; a process should be regarded as a 'black box' connected to its environment by two wires. One of the wires is used for input of discrete messages, and the other for output (Fig. 20.1). A process engages in an unbounded sequence of communications, each of which is either an input from the input wire or an output to the output wire (but not both). If the environment is not ready for the communication, the process waits for it to become so, and vice versa. There is no 'buffer' in the wire; the act of communication requires simultaneous synchronized participation of both the sender and the receiver.

We postulate that the passing of a message on either wire is an observable aspect of the behaviour of the process. Imagine that there is a tape recorder attached to each of the wires, recording each message as it passes, but not recording the length of the gaps between the messages. At any moment, we can observe the current content of each of the two tapes. We introduce the free variable 'in' to stand for the current content of the tape recorder on the input wire, and *out* to stand for the sequence of messages recorded from the output wire.

We also postulate that the internal state of a process cannot be directly observed: the black box has no openable lid. However, we assume that we can observe, by a green light perhaps, whether the process is working properly. This will be indicated by the value of a free Boolean variable *stable*, which takes as value either *true* or *false*. If ever *stable* goes *false*, the machine is broken, and anything may happen (beware!).

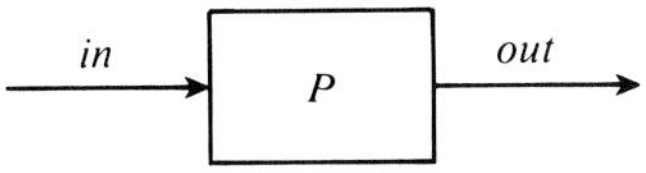

Figure 20.1 A process.

20.2.3 Specifications

To formulate specifications, we need some notations to describe sequences of messages:

$\langle\ \rangle$ is the empty sequence, containing no messages. This is the value of both variables *in* and *out* if they are observed at the very start of the process;
$|s|$ is the length of s.

If s is a sequence other than $\langle\ \rangle$,

s_0 is the first message of s,
s' is the result of removing the first message of s,
$s^\dagger$ is the result of removing the last message of s (truncation).

If s and t are sequences,

$s^\frown t$ is the result of concatenating s and t in this order.
$s \leqslant t =_{\text{df}} \exists u \,.\, s^\frown u = t$, i.e. s is an initial segment of t.

This is clearly a partial order with bottom $\langle\ \rangle$.

Using these notations, we can describe the behaviour of certain simple processes. For example, a process that just copies messages from its input to its output is always stable, and every observation of it shows the output sequence either exactly equal to the input sequence or one shorter:

$$COPY =_{\text{df}} stable \wedge (out = in \vee out = in^\dagger).$$

This copying process must always output each message immediately after inputting it. A more general buffering process relaxes this constraint. For example, a double buffer may be specified:

$$BUFF2 =_{\text{df}} stable \wedge out \in \{in, in^\dagger, in^{\dagger\dagger}\}.$$

An unbounded buffer ensures that the output is always a copy of some initial segment of the input sequence

$$BUFF =_{\text{df}} stable \wedge out \leqslant in.$$

Thus we see how predicates with free variables *in*, *out* and *stable* (together with conventional mathematical notations) can effectively describe and specify the behaviour of processes. But *none* of these notations can feature in our simple programming language; nor can they be included in any other programming language, since they can be used to express unsatisfiable predicates, such as

$$in \leqslant out \wedge out \leqslant in \wedge in \neq out$$

or unimplementable predicates like

$$stable \wedge |in| \geqslant 3,$$

which requires a process to input three messages before it starts! Our programming language must therefore be restricted to notations defined in the remaining paragraphs of this section. The restrictions will also ensure that no process can ever stop, so it will be impossible to implement the specification: $stable \wedge |in| + |out| \leqslant k$.

20.2.4 Output

Let P be a predicate exactly describing the behaviour of a process, and let e be a term composed of (say) constants, variables, and a fixed selection of primitive recursive functions. We introduce the notation

$$!e \rightarrow P$$

to describe the process that first outputs the value of e on its output wire, and then behaves as described by P.

The very first observation of the behaviour of $(!e \rightarrow P)$ is that it is stable and that the sequences of input and output messages are both empty. In every subsequent observation, the output sequence is non-empty, and its first message has value e. Furthermore, on removing the first message from the output sequence, the resulting observation will be an observation of the behaviour of P. These remarks explain the definition:

$$\begin{aligned} !e \rightarrow P(in, out, stable) =_{\mathrm{df}} & \; out = in = \langle\ \rangle \wedge stable \\ & \vee out \neq \langle\ \rangle \leqslant out_0 = e \wedge P(in, out', stable). \end{aligned}$$

This operator is distributive but not strict:

$$!e \rightarrow (P \vee Q) = (!e \rightarrow P) \vee (!e \rightarrow Q).$$

As an example, we give

$$\begin{aligned} (!x \rightarrow COPY) = & ((in = out = \langle\ \rangle \wedge stable) \\ & \vee (out \neq \langle\ \rangle \wedge out_0 = x \\ & \wedge stable \wedge out' \in \{in, in^{\dagger}\})). \end{aligned}$$

Notice how the output has introduced the free variable x into the formula.

20.2.5 Input

Let $P(x)$ be a predicate (possibly containing the variable x among its free variables) that describes exactly the behaviour of a process as a function of the initial value of x. Then we introduce the notation

$$?x \rightarrow P(x)$$

to describe the process that first inputs a value of its input wire, and then behaves like $P(v)$, where v is the value it has just input.

The initial observation of the behaviour of $(?x \rightarrow P(x))$ is exactly the same as that of a process that starts with an output. In every subsequent observation, the input sequence is nonempty. Furthermore, on removing the first message from the input sequence, the resulting observation will be an observation of $P(in_0)$, i.e. the process that results from setting the initial value of x to in_0. These remarks explain the definition:

$$?x \rightarrow P(x, in, out, stable) =_{\text{df}} ((out = in = \langle\ \rangle \wedge stable) \\ \vee (in \neq \langle\ \rangle \wedge P(in_0, in', out, stable))).$$

This operator is distributive, and binds the variable specified:

$$(?x \rightarrow (P(x) \vee Q(x))) = ((?x \rightarrow P(x)) \vee (?x \rightarrow Q(x)))$$
$$(?x \rightarrow P(x)) = (?y \rightarrow P(y)) \text{ when } x \text{ is not free in } P(y) \\ \text{and } y \text{ is not free in } P(x).$$

As an example we give

$$\begin{aligned}(?x \rightarrow (!x \rightarrow COPY)) &= ((in = out = \langle\ \rangle \wedge stable) \\ &\quad \vee in \neq \langle\ \rangle \wedge (in' = out = \langle\ \rangle \wedge stable \\ &\qquad \vee (out \neq \langle\ \rangle \wedge out_0 = in_0 \\ &\qquad \wedge stable \wedge out' \in \{in', in'^{\dagger}\}))) \\ &= stable \wedge (in = out = \langle\ \rangle \\ &\qquad \vee |in| = 1 \wedge out = \langle\ \rangle \\ &\qquad \vee out_0 = in_0 \wedge out' \in \{in', in'^{\dagger}\}) \\ &= COPY.\end{aligned}$$

Note how the input has eliminated the free variable x from the formula. Note also that *COPY* is the solution for ξ in the equation

$$\xi = (?x \rightarrow (!x \rightarrow \xi)).$$

20.2.6 Recursion

Let ξ be a variable standing for an unknown process. Let $P(\xi)$ be a formula containing ξ, but otherwise containing only the notations of our simple programming language: disjunction, output, input, and the constant *true*. Consider now the equation

$$\xi = P(\xi).$$

This may be taken as a recursive definition of a process with name ξ and body $P(\xi)$. Every time ξ is encountered in the body, it stands for another copy of the whole body $P(\xi)$. The predicate that is the weakest solution to this equation will be denoted

$$\mu\xi \,.\, P(\xi).$$

But does such a solution exist? D. S. Scott has shown how to answer this question. Consider the sequence of predicates

$$true, P(true), P(P(true)), \ldots, P^n(true), \ldots$$

and define

$$\mu\xi \,.\, P(\xi) =_{\text{df}} \forall n \geqslant 0 \,.\, P^n(true).$$

The fact that this is the weakest solution to the equation given above depends on the fact that $P(\xi)$ is a *continuous* function of ξ, in the sense that it distributes over the universal quantification of descending chains of predicate, i.e.

$$P(\forall n \geqslant 0 \,.\, Q_n) = \forall n \geqslant 0 \,.\, P(Q_n) \quad \text{whenever} \quad \vDash Q_{n+1} \Rightarrow Q_n \quad \text{for all } n.$$

The continuity of all programs expressed in our simple language is assured by the fact that each operator of the language is continuous, and the composition of continuous operators is also continuous. We therefore have good reason to insist that all future operators introduced into the language must also be continuous.

The simplest example of recursion is the infinite loop

$$\mu\xi \,.\, \xi = \forall n \geqslant 0 \,.\, true = true.$$

A more interesting example is the program that copies messages from its input to its output

$$\mu\xi \,.\, (?x \rightarrow !x \rightarrow \xi) = \forall n \geqslant 0 \,.\, P_n,$$

where $P_0 = true$
and $P_{n+1} = (?x \rightarrow !x \rightarrow P_n)$.

The first few terms of the series are

$$\begin{aligned} P_1 = (&in = out = \langle\,\rangle \wedge stable \\ &\vee in \neq \langle\,\rangle \wedge (in' = out = \langle\,\rangle \wedge stable \\ &\qquad\qquad \vee out \neq \langle\,\rangle \wedge out_0 = in_0 \wedge true)), \\ P_2 = (&in = out = \langle\,\rangle \wedge stable \\ &\vee in' = out = \langle\,\rangle \wedge stable \\ &\vee in' = out' = \langle\,\rangle \wedge in_0 = out_0 \wedge stable \\ &\vee in'' = out' = \langle\,\rangle \wedge in_0 = out_0 \wedge stable \\ &\vee in'' = out'' = \langle\,\rangle \wedge in_0 = out_0 \wedge (in')_0 = (out')_0). \end{aligned}$$

In general, P_n describes the first $2n$ communications of a process that correctly copies the first n messages from the input to the output and then breaks. We therefore guess the general form

$$\begin{aligned} P_n = (&|in| + |out| < 2n \Rightarrow \\ &\quad stable \wedge (out = in \vee out = in^{\dagger})) \\ &\wedge (|in| + |out| = 2n \Rightarrow out = in). \end{aligned}$$

Finally, we draw the conclusion (which was obvious all along) that

$$\mu\xi(?x \to !x \to \xi) = \forall n \geqslant 0 \,.\, P_n$$
$$= stable \wedge (out = in \vee out = in^{\dagger})$$
$$= COPY.$$

A simpler way to prove this identity is to show that the predicate *COPY* is a solution to the defining equation of the recursion, i.e.

$$COPY = (?x \to !x \to COPY).$$

The fact that this is the *weakest* solution is a consequence of the fact that it is the *only* solution. A program $P(\xi)$ is said to be *guarded* for ξ if every possible occurrence of ξ is preceded by an input or output operation. Thus

$$(!x \to \xi) \vee (?y \to !x \to \xi) \qquad \text{is guarded,}$$

but $$(!x \to \xi) \vee \xi \qquad \text{is not guarded.}$$

If $P(\xi)$ is guarded for ξ, then the equation

$$\xi = P(\xi)$$

has an unique solution $\mu\xi \,.\, P(\xi)$.

20.2.7 Chain

If P and Q are processes, we define $(P \gg Q)$ as the result of connecting the output wire of P to the input wire of Q (see Fig. 20.2). Communications along this connecting wire cannot be observed from the environment; they occur automatically whenever P is ready to output and Q is ready to input. All communication on the input wire of $(P \gg Q)$ is performed by P and all output to the environment is performed by Q. $(P \gg Q)$ is itself a process, and may be chained to other processes:

$$(P \gg Q) \gg R.$$

A simple example of a chain is formed by two instances of the *COPY*

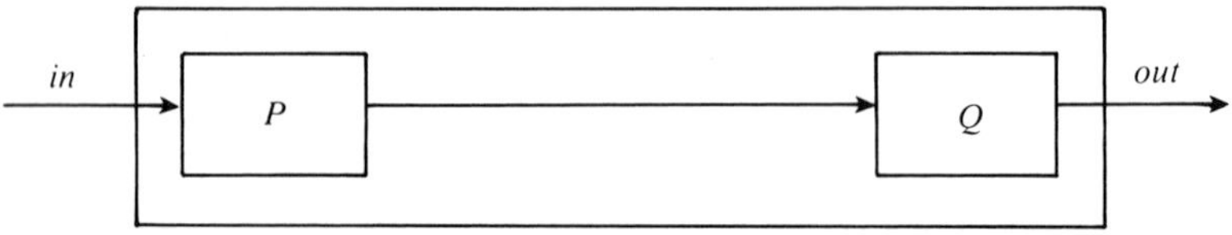

Figure 20.2 A chain.

process connected to each other to make a double buffer:

$$\begin{aligned}(COPY \gg COPY) &= stable \wedge \exists b\,.\, b \in \{in, in^\dagger\} \wedge out \in \{b, b^\dagger\}\\ &= stable \wedge out \in \{in, in^\dagger, in^{\dagger\dagger}\}\\ &=_{\text{df}} BUFF2.\end{aligned}$$

A more spectacular example is a program that implements an unbounded buffer by chaining a recursive instance of itself:

$$\begin{aligned}\mu\xi\,.\,(?x \to (\xi \gg (!x \to COPY)))&\\ &= stable \wedge out \leqslant in\\ &=_{\text{df}} BUFF.\end{aligned}$$

A chain that does nothing but internal communication is just as broken as one that is engaged in an infinite recursion:

$$(\mu\xi\,.\,!0 \to \xi) \gg (\mu\xi\,.\,?x \to \xi) = true.$$

Instead of giving an explicit definition of the chaining operator as a predicate, let us list the algebraic properties we would like it to have. Clearly it should be continuous and distributive; it should also be strict, so that it breaks whenever either of its operands is broken; finally, it should obey the following four laws, which describe the expected behaviour of input and ouput. First, when the left operand outputs and the right operand inputs, both these actions take place simultaneously; the communication cannot be observed, but its effect is to copy the value of the expression from the outputting to the inputting process. These remarks are formalized in the law

$$(!e \to P) \gg (?x \to Q(x)) = P \gg Q(e). \tag{1}$$

If either operand of $\gg$ starts with a communication with the other, but the other starts with an external communication, then the external communication takes place first, and the other process must wait:

$$(?e \to P) \gg (!f \to Q) = !f \to ((!e \to P) \gg Q), \tag{2}$$

$$(?x \to P(x)) \gg (?y \to Q(y)) = ?z \to (P(z) \gg (?y \to Q(y))), \tag{3}$$

where z is chosen not to occur in $Q(y)$. The last of the four laws states that when *both* operands start with an external communication, then either communication may occur first, the choice being nondeterminate:

$$\begin{aligned}(?x \to P(x)) \gg (!f \to Q) = (?z \to (P(z) \gg (!f \to Q)))&\\ \vee (!f \to ((?x \to P(x)) \gg Q))).&\end{aligned} \tag{4}$$

If P and Q are finite in the sense that they contain no recursions, then the collection of laws given is complete, in the sense that $(P \gg Q)$ can be reduced to 'normal' form that does not contain $\gg$. Thus for finite processes, the meaning of the chaining operator (if it has one) is uniquely defined by these laws. The continuity condition for $\gg$ ensures that chaining is uniquely defined for processes containing recursion as well. The proof of this depends on the fact that every process can be expressed as a universal quantification of a descending chain of finite processes. This fact also permits proof of other desirable properties of chaining, for example that it is associative.

The discovery of an explicit definition of the chaining operator is not simple. A first attempt at a definition can be based on the fact that if at any time there exists some sequence b of messages that could have passed on the internal channel, then the current trace of the external channels is a possible observation of the chain. So we make a preliminary definition:

$$P(in, out, stable) \gg_0 Q(in, out, stable)$$
$$=_{\text{df}} \exists b \,.\, P(in, b, stable) \wedge Q(b, out, stable).$$

But $\gg_0$ is neither strict nor continuous, and so cannot be the right definition of $\gg$.

To ensure continuity, we need to describe the conditions under which the chain may break as a result of engaging in an infinite sequence of internal communications, a phenomenon known as *infinite chatter*:

$$CHATTER =_{\text{df}} \forall n \geqslant 0 \,.\, \exists b \,.\, |b| > n \wedge P(in, b, true) \wedge Q(b, out, true).$$

To ensure strictness, we need to identify those cases when the chain diverges as a result of divergence of just one of its operands. These cases are characterized by the fact that *stable* is *false* (in fact this was the main reason why the variable *stable* was introduced into the formal system).

$$UNSTAB1 =_{\text{df}} \exists b \,.\, P(in, b, false) \wedge Q(b, out, true)$$
$$\vee\, P(in, b, true) \wedge Q(b, out, false)).$$

Finally, we need to ensure that once the chain breaks it remains broken forever, i.e. it degenerates to the bottom process *true*. To do this we introduce a modal operator ($\diamond R$) to mean 'there was a time when R was true':

$$\diamond R(in, out, stable) =_{\text{df}}$$
$$\exists a \leqslant in \,.\, \exists b \leqslant out \,.\, R(a, b, stable).$$

At last we can formulate the definition of the chaining operator

$$P \gg Q =_{\text{df}} (P \gg_0 Q \vee \diamond CHATTER \vee \diamond UNSTAB1).$$

That this definition has all the required algebraic properties is only a conjecture: the proof would depend on the fact that the operands of $\gg$ are not arbitrary predicates but are restricted to the notations of our simple programming language.

20.2.8 Assignment

Let x be a list of distinct variables, let e be a list of the same number of expressions, and let $P(x)$ be a program describing the behaviour of a process as a function of the initial values of x. We then define

$$(e \succ x \to P(x)) =_{\text{df}} P(e),$$

i.e. the result of simultaneously substituting each variable in the list x by the corresponding expression in the list e, making sure that free variables of e remain free after the substitution. We assume for simplicity that all expressions of e are defined for all values of the variables they contain, so that if y is a list of distinct fresh variables

$$e \succ x \to P(x) = (\exists y \, . \, y = e \wedge P(y)) = (\forall y \, . \, y = e \Rightarrow P(y)).$$

The predicate $e \succ x \to P(x)$ describes the behaviour of a process that first simultaneously assigns the values of e to the variables of x and then behaves like $P(x)$. The initial assignment is an internal action, and is therefore wholly unobservable. In more conventional programming notation this would be written

$$x := e; \; P(x).$$

A simple example of a program that uses assignment is one that implements a double buffer

$$\begin{aligned} &?x \to \mu\xi \, . \, ((?x \to ?x \to \xi) \vee (?y \to !x \to (y \succ x \to \xi))) \\ &\quad = \mathit{stable} \wedge \mathit{out} \in \{\mathit{in}, \mathit{in}^{\dagger}, \mathit{in}^{\dagger\dagger}\} \\ &\quad = \mathit{BUFF2}. \end{aligned}$$

20.2.9 Conditional

Let b be a propositional formula, i.e. a single expression that for all values of its free variables yields a result that is either true or false. Let P and Q be programs. Define

$$P \lhd b \rhd Q =_{\text{df}} (b \wedge P \vee \bar{b} \wedge Q).$$

This is a process that behaves like P if b is initially true and like Q if b is initially false. The conventional programming notation for a conditional is

if b **then** P **else** Q.

The reason for the infix notation is that this permits elegant expression of algebraic properties such as idempotence, associativity and distributivity,

$$
\begin{aligned}
&\mu\xi\,.\,(?x \to ?y \to \\
&\quad 0, x \succ q, r \to \\
&\quad \mu\psi\,.\,((q+1, r-y \succ q, r \to \psi) \\
&\qquad\qquad \lhd\, r \geqslant y \,\rhd\, (!q \to !r \to \xi)))
\end{aligned}
$$

Figure 20.3 Long division.

```
begin
  ξ: input x; input y;
     q := 0; r := x;
  ψ: if r ⩾ y then begin q := q + 1;
                          r := r − y;
                          goto ψ
                    end
              else begin output q;
                          output r;
                          goto ξ
                    end
end
```

Figure 20.4 Conventional notation.

for example

$$
\begin{aligned}
P \lhd b \rhd (Q \lhd b \rhd R) &= (P \lhd b \rhd Q) \lhd b \rhd R \\
&= P \lhd b \rhd R.
\end{aligned}
$$

A complete set of algebraic laws for $\lhd\, b \,\rhd$ is given in Chapter 19.

A simple example of the use of a conditional is to construct a program (see Figure 20.3) that repeatedly inputs a pair of natural numbers and outputs the quotient and remainder of division of the first by the second. If the divisor is zero, the program breaks. The program uses the simple but slow method of successive subtraction. To emphasize the familiarity of these ideas, Figure 20.4 gives a translation into the notations of a more conventional programming language.

20.2.10 Sequential composition

If P and Q are processes, their sequential composition $(P; Q)$ is a process that behaves like P until P successfully terminates, and then it behaves like Q. If P never terminates successfully, neither does $(P; Q)$. The process that does nothing but terminate successfully will be called *skip*.

Let us give the algebraic laws that we would expect to govern the behaviour of sequential composition. First it must be continuous and distributive and strict in its first argument. Clearly it should be associative and have *skip* as its unit. Finally $(;Q)$, considered as a unary postfix operator, should distribute backward through all other operators of our language (except $\gg$):

$$(!e \rightarrow P); Q = !e \rightarrow (P; Q),$$
$$(?x \rightarrow P(x)); Q = ?z \rightarrow (P(z); Q),$$
$$(e \succ\!\!- x \rightarrow P(x)); Q = e \succ\!\!- z \rightarrow (P(z); Q), \qquad \text{(for } z \text{ not free in } Q)$$
$$(P \lhd b \rhd R); Q = (P; Q) \lhd b \rhd (R; Q).$$

As for $\gg$, we have sufficient laws to eliminate sequential composition from every finite program. The continuity property ensures that the operator is uniquely defined for all programs, provided that it exists. It is quite difficult to formulate the definition in a satisfactory fashion; for further discussion see Hehner (1984). Certainly, successful termination must be an observable event, and the final values of all variables must also be observable.

20.3 Conclusion

This paper has made the claim that a computer program can be identified with the strongest predicate describing all relevant observations that can be made of a computer executing the program. The claim is illustrated by the formal definition of the notations of a very simple programming language. The claim is justified by purely philosophical arguments. A stronger justification would be its promised practical benefits for the specification and development of reliable programs.

Before writing a program, the programmer is recommended to formulate a specification S of what his program is intended to accomplish. S is a description of the observations that are admissible for his program when it is constructed. The major problem in formulating S is to ensure the utmost simplicity and clarity, so that there can remain no doubt that it describes accurately just what is wanted; for if it does not, there is nothing that the mathematician or the programmer can do to remedy the consequences, which may be disastrous. For this reason, there should be no restriction on the range of concepts and notations used to express the specification: the full set of logical and mathematical notations should be available for use in the overriding interests of clarity. If suitable concepts are not yet known, new branches of mathematics must be developed to meet the need.

Once the specification is formulated, the task of the programmer remains to find a predicate P, expressed in the restricted notations of his programming language, such that P logically implies the specification S, i.e.

$$\models P \Rightarrow S.$$

Because of the notational restrictions, and in the pursuit of efficiency, P will in general get much longer and more complicated than S. But in proving the correctness of P, the programmer may use all the familiar techniques and methods of classical mathematics. Consequently, he does not need the cumbersome specialized proof rules that have often been associated with proof-oriented programming language definitions (Chapter 4). Finally, if the specification is not tautologous, the total correctness of the program will be established.

I certainly do not recommend that a large program be proved correct by expanding all the definitions and translating it explicitly into one gigantic predicate. A far more effective technique is to perform the proofs as necessary during the design and construction of the program. This is known as 'top-down programming', and is now described in five steps.

(1) Suppose the original specification is S. The programmer needs the insight to see that the achievement of S will involve completion of (say) two subtasks. He formulates the specification of these subtasks as predicates T and U.

(2) Using only the notations of his programming language he then constructs a framework $P(\xi, \psi)$, containing the names ξ and ψ to stand for the subtask programs that have not yet been written.

(3) He then slots the specifications T and U in place of these two subprograms, and proves that this satisfies the original specification S, i.e.

$$\models P(T, U) \Rightarrow S.$$

Note that $P(T, U)$ is a predicate expressed in a mixture of conventional and programming notations.

(4) He can now safely delegate to others the subtasks of writing programs Q and R, which satisfy the specifications T and U, i.e.

$$\models Q \Rightarrow T$$

and

$$\models R \Rightarrow U.$$

(5) When this is done, he can slot programs Q and R into the original framework P, and he may be sure that the result will meet the original specification S,

$$\models P(Q, R) \Rightarrow S.$$

This assurance is gained not by laborious integration testing after delivery of the components, but by a proof that has been made even before the task of writing the subprograms has started. Since the subprograms have been constructed by use of similar reliable methods, the risk of error should be quite small. And the validity of this method of programming by parts depends only on the fact that all operators of our programming language are monotonic in the sense that they respect implication ordering.

If $\quad S \Rightarrow T$
then $\quad P(S) \Rightarrow P(T)$.

Another effective method of programming is to write first an inefficient program P that meets the specification S. This can be useful as a demonstration or training prototype of the eventual product. Then the algebraic laws can be used to transform P into a more efficient program Q, such that

$$\models Q \Rightarrow P.$$

Clearly Q will meet any specification that P meets. If P is a nondeterministic program, the transformation may use implications as well as equivalences in the pursuit of greater efficiency.

Thus the approach advocated in this paper includes that of the other contributors to this meeting, in that it gives a mathematical model for the notations of a simple executable programming language and uses algebraic laws for optimization. It differs from the other contributions in making three recommendations:

(1) Specifications should *not* be confined to the notations of an executable programming language.

(2) Implication, rather than just equivalence, should be used to prove correctness of programs, and to transform them in the interests of efficiency.

(3) These methods need not be confined to applicative programming languages. They should be extended to conventional procedural languages, which can be efficiently executed on computers of the present day.

I am grateful to: A. J. R. G. Milner (1980) for his pioneering work in the mathematical theory of communicating systems; E. C. R. Hehner (1983) for pointing out that programs are predicates; D. S. Scott (1981) for the domain theory that underlies a proper theory of recursion; S. D. Brookes and A. W. Roscoe (1984) and E.-R. Olderog (1984) for construction of the model on which this exposition is based; E. W. Dijkstra (1976) (p. 217) for his realization of the value of nondeterminacy, and his insistence on total correctness.

TWENTY-ONE

The mathematics of programming

This chapter contains the text of Hoare's 'inaugural' lecture at Oxford (the explanation for the delay from his appointment in 1976 is contained in the paper; Section 5 was not read) given on 17 October 1985 and published as [101]. This talk ran through many 'drafts' including those in the USA, India and Scotland.

This paper makes a fascinating comparison with Chapter 7 because of the emphasis here on a formal approach. Moreover, the concern with mathematical aspects of correctness is no longer expressed in the style of Chapters 4 and 8; the concern here is with algebraic properties. The work on weakest pre-specification can be studied in [99] (which appeared as a Programming Research Group monograph before the referenced publication); the algebraic properties of the occam language are covered in [102].

Mr Vice-Chancellor, Ladies and Gentlemen!

This is my inaugural lecture as Professor of Computation at Oxford University. I was appointed to this post just nine years ago, after the tragically premature death of its brilliant first occupant, Christopher Strachey. Nine years is a long delay for an inaugural lecture; but it has taken all those nine years to introduce an undergraduate curriculum in Computing at Oxford. Although many universities had been producing graduates in this subject for many years before I was appointed here, it is only this week that we welcome to Oxford and to this lecture the first entrants to our new Honour School in Mathematics and Computation.

So it is the new School rather than myself that I wish to inaugurate today. I shall do so by describing some of the research goals pursued by Christopher Strachey and his colleagues and successors in the Programming

C. A. R. Hoare, *The mathematics of programming,* Oxford University Press (1986). An Inaugural Lecture delivered before Oxford University (17 October 1985).

Research Group; for these have also inspired and guided the design of our new School. Our principles may be summarized under four headings.

(1) *Computers are mathematical machines.* Every aspect of their behaviour can be defined with mathematical precision, and every detail can be deduced from this definition with mathematical certainty by the laws of pure logic.
(2) *Computer programs are mathematical expressions.* They describe with unprecedented precision and in every minutest detail the behaviour, intended or unintended, of the computer on which they are executed.
(3) *A programming language is a mathematical theory.* It includes concepts, notations, definitions, axioms and theorems, which help a programmer to develop a program which meets its specification, and to prove that it does so.
(4) *Programming is a mathematical activity.* Like other branches of applied mathematics and engineering, its successful practice requires determined and meticulous application of traditional methods of mathematical understanding, calculation and proof.

These are general philosophical and moral principles, and I hold them to be self-evident – which is just as well, because all the actual evidence is against them. Nothing is really as I have described it, neither computers nor programs nor programming languages nor even programmers.

Digital computers of the present day are very complicated devices and rather poorly defined. As a result, it is usually impractical to reason logically about their behaviour. Sometimes the only way of finding out what they will do is by experiment. Such experiments are certainly not mathematics. Unfortunately, they are not even science, because it is impossible to generalize from their results or to publish them for the benefit of other scientists.

Many computer programs of the present day are of inordinate size – many thousands of pages of closely printed text. Mathematics has no tradition of dealing with expressions on this scale. Normal methods of calculation and proof seem wholly impractical to conduct by hand; and fifteen years of experience suggest that computer assistance can only make matters worse.

Programming languages of the present day are even more complicated than the programs which they are used to write and the computers on which they are intended to run. Valiant research has been directed to formulate mathematical definitions of these standard languages. But the size and complexity of the definitions make it impractical to derive useful theorems, or to prove relevant properties of programs in practice.

Finally, many programmers of the present day have been educated in ignorance or even fear of mathematics. Of course, there are many programmers who are university graduates in pure or applied mathematics.

They may have acquired a good grasp of topology, calculus or group theory. But it never occurs to them to take advantage of their mathematical skills to define a programming problem and search for its solution.

Our present failure to recognize and use mathematics as the basis for a discipline of programming has a number of notorious consequences. They are the same consequences as would result from a similar neglect of mathematics in the drawing of maps, marine navigation, bridge building, air traffic control, or the exploration of space. In the older branches of science and engineering, the relevant physical and mathematical knowledge is embodied in a number of equations, formulae and laws, many of which are simple enough to be taught to children at school. The practising scientist or engineer will be intimately familiar with these laws, and will use them explicitly or even instinctively to find solutions to otherwise intractable problems.

What then are the laws of programming, which help the programmer to control the complexity of his tasks? Many programmers would be hard pressed to name a single law. Those who have suffered from bad programs might claim that programmers are such an undisciplined crew that even if they know any laws, they would instantly violate them.

21.1 Arithmetic

To refute this malicious accusation, I shall now show by example that the laws of programming are as simple and as obvious and as useful as the laws you find in any other branch of mathematics, for example, in elementary arithmetic. Consider multiplication of numbers. Figure 21.1 shows some of the relevant algebraic laws; multiplication is associative, its identity (or unit) is the number 1, it has the number 0 as its zero (or fixed point), and finally, it distributes through addition.

Figure 21.2 gives the defining properties of an ordering relation like comparison of the magnitude of numbers. Such an order is reflexive, antisymmetric and transitive. These laws hold also for a partial ordering such as the inclusion relation between sets.

$$x \times (y \times z) = (x \times y) \times z$$
$$x \times 1 = x = 1 \times x$$
$$x \times 0 = 0 = 0 \times x$$
$$(x + y) \times z = (x \times z) + (y \times z)$$

Figure 21.1 Laws of multiplication.

$$x \subseteq x$$
$$x \subseteq y \land y \subseteq x \Rightarrow x = y$$
$$x \subseteq y \land y \subseteq z \Rightarrow x \subseteq z$$

Figure 21.2 Partial Ordering.

$$(x \cup y) \subseteq z \Leftrightarrow x \subseteq z \land y \subseteq z$$
$$x \cup x = x$$
$$x \cup y = y \cup x$$
$$x \cup (y \cup z) = (x \cup y) \cup z$$
$$x \subseteq y \Leftrightarrow x \cup y = y$$

Figure 21.3 Least upper bound (l.u.b.).

Figure 21.3 describes the properties of the least upper bound or l.u.b. of an ordering, denoted by the traditional cup notation. These laws are equally valid, whether the l.u.b. is the union of two sets or the greater of two numbers. The first law states the fundamental property that the l.u.b. is an upper bound on both its operands, and it is the least of all such bounds. The remaining laws are derived from the fundamental law by the properties of ordering. They state that the l.u.b. operator is idempotent, symmetric and associative. Finally, the partial ordering can itself be defined in terms of l.u.b.

Figure 21.4 shows some additional laws which hold for natural numbers or nonnegative integers. Here, the least upper bound of two numbers is simply the greater of them. If you multiply the greater of x or y by z, you get the same result as multiplying both x and y by z, and then choosing the greater of these products. This fact is clearly and conveniently stated in the laws of distribution of multiplication through the least upper bound. An immediate consequence of these laws is that multiplication is a monotonic operator, in the sense that it preserves the ordering of its operands. If you

$$x \cup y = \text{the greater of } x \text{ and } y$$

$$(x \cup y) \times z = (x \times z) \cup (y \times z)$$
$$z \times (x \cup y) = (z \times x) \cup (z \times y)$$
$$w \subseteq y \land x \subseteq z \Rightarrow w \times x \subseteq y \times z$$

Figure 21.4 Natural numbers.

decrease either factor the product can only decrease too, as stated in the last law of Figure 21.4.

In the arithmetic of natural numbers, multiplication does not in general have an exact inverse. Instead, we commonly use a quotient operator, which approximates the true result from below. It is obtained from normal integer division by just ignoring the remainder. Thus, the result of dividing y by non-zero z is the largest number such that when you multiply it back by z the result still does not exceed y. This fact is clearly stated in the first law of Figure 21.5. The same fact is stated more simply in the second law, which I will call the fundamental law of division.

I must apologize to those members of the audience who are my distinguished colleagues in the Faculty of Mathematics for reminding them of these simple mathematical facts. But the fundamental law of division may be slightly unfamiliar. I invite you to consider the category-theoretic interpretation of a poset, and the relationship of multiplication and division as adjoint functors. Or perhaps there is a connection with Galois connections. If there is, please let me know.

The fundamental law of division is very useful in proving the other properties of this operator. For example, the third law of Figure 21.5 is proved by substituting y divided by z for x in the previous law. The last law states that division by a product is the same as successive division by its two factors. A proof is given in Figure 21.6.

The proof shows that any w which is bounded by the left-hand side of the equation is bounded also by the right-hand side, and vice versa; it follows

$$
\begin{aligned}
&\text{if } z \neq 0,\ y \div z = \max\{x \mid x \times z \subseteq y\}\\
&\quad x \subseteq (y \div z) \Leftrightarrow (x \times z) \subseteq y\\
&\quad (y \div z) \times z \subseteq y\\
&\quad x \div (y \times z) = (x \div z) \div y
\end{aligned}
$$

Figure 21.5 Quotient of natural numbers.

$$
\begin{aligned}
&\text{given } y \neq 0 \text{ and } z \neq 0,\\
w \subseteq x \div (y \times z) &\Leftrightarrow w \times (y \times z) \subseteq x\\
&\Leftrightarrow (w \times y) \times z \subseteq x\\
&\Leftrightarrow w \times y \subseteq x \div z\\
&\Leftrightarrow w \subseteq (x \div z) \div y
\end{aligned}
$$

Figure 21.6 A proof.

by the properties of partial ordering that the two sides are equal. The only laws used in the main part of the proof are the associativity of multiplication and the fundamental law of division, which is used three times to move a divisor from one side of the inequality to the other.

21.2 Programs

That completes my brief review of some of the algebraic laws of elementary arithmetic. I shall now show how computer programs obey very similar algebraic laws – in fact, and hardly by accident, they will turn out to be exactly the same. I shall write programs in a mathematical notation first introduced by Dijkstra. Some of the commands are summarized in Figure 21.7.

The *SKIP* command terminates, but does nothing else. In particular, it leaves the values of all variables unchanged.

The *ABORT* command is at the other extreme. It may do anything whatsoever, or it may fail to do anything whatsoever. In particular, it may fail to terminate. This is the behaviour of a computer that has gone wrong, or a program that has run wild, perhaps by corrupting its own code. *ABORT* is not a command you would ever want to write; in fact, you should take pains to prove that you have not done so by accident. In such proofs and in the general mathematics of programming, the *ABORT* command plays a valuable role. And however much we dislike it, there is ample empirical evidence for its existence.

The sequential composition of two commands x and y is written $(x; y)$. This starts behaving like x. If and when x terminates, y starts in an initial state equal to the final state left by x. Then $(x; y)$ terminates when y terminates, but fails to terminate if either x or y fails to do so.

The basic algebraic laws for sequential composition are given in Figure 21.8. The first law is an associative law, stating that if three commands are combined sequentially, it does not matter in which way they are bracketed. The second law gives *SKIP* as the unit or identity of composition. It states that a command x remains unchanged when it is either followed or preceded by *SKIP*. The third law gives *ABORT* as a zero

SKIP	does nothing, but terminates
ABORT	does anything, and may fail to terminate
$x; y$	does x first; when x terminates it does y

Figure 21.7 Commands.

$$x; (y; z) = (x; y); z$$
$$SKIP; x = x = x; SKIP$$
$$ABORT; x = ABORT = x; ABORT$$

Figure 21.8 Laws for composition.

or fixed point for composition. You cannot program your way out of the mess by preceding it or following it by any other command. Note that these three algebraic laws for composition are exactly the same as those for multiplication of numbers, with merely a change in notation.

The next important feature of programming is the conditional. Let b be a logical expression which in all circumstances evaluates to a logical value *true* or *false*. If x and y are commands, I introduce the notation

$$x \lhd b \rhd y \qquad (x \textbf{ if } b \textbf{ else } y)$$

to denote the conditional command. It is obeyed by first evaluating the logical expression b. If the result is *true*, then the command x is obeyed and y is omitted. If the result is *false*, then y is obeyed and x is omitted. This informal description is summarized in the first law of Figure 21.9.

I now regard the **if** symbol $\lhd$ and the **else** symbol $\rhd$ as brackets surrounding the logical expression b, so that the notation

$$\lhd b \rhd \qquad (\textbf{if } b \textbf{ else})$$

appears as an infix operator between two commands x and y. The reason for this novel notation is that it simplifies expression and use of the relevant algebraic laws. For example, the conditional $\lhd b \rhd$ is idempotent and associative, and it distributes through $\lhd c \rhd$ for any logical expression c. Finally, sequential composition distributes leftward (but not rightward) through a conditional.

Figure 21.10 shows a picture of the conditional as a structured flow chart. Such pictures actually inhibit the use of mathematics in programming, and I

$$(x \lhd true \rhd y) = x = (t \lhd false \rhd x)$$
$$(x \lhd b \rhd x) = x$$
$$x \lhd b \rhd (y \lhd b \rhd z) = (x \lhd b \rhd y) \lhd b \rhd z$$
$$= x \lhd b \rhd z$$
$$x \lhd b \rhd (y \lhd c \rhd z) = (x \lhd b \rhd y) \lhd c \rhd (x \lhd b \rhd z)$$
$$(x \lhd b \rhd y); z = (x; z) \lhd b \rhd (y; z)$$

Figure 21.9 Conditional.

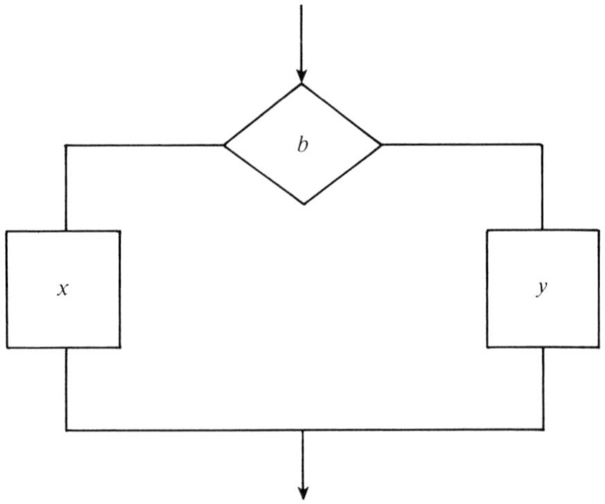

Figure 21.10 Conditional as flow chart.

do not approve of them. They may be useful in first presenting a new idea, and in committing it to memory. Their rôle is similar to that of the picture of an apple or a zebra in a child's alphabet book. But excessive reliance on pictures continued into later life would not be regarded as a good qualification for one seeking a career as a professional author. It is equally inappropriate for a professional programmer. Confucius is often quoted as saying that a picture is worth ten thousand words – so please never draw one that isn't.

Unfortunately, there exist problems which are so widespread and so severe that even flow charts must be recommended and actually welcomed as their solution. Figure 21.11 shows how we have taught a generation of schoolchildren to express the structure of a conditional in BASIC. Programming in BASIC is like doing arithmetic with roman numerals. To start with, for simple tasks like addition and subtraction, roman numerals are much easier than arabic, because you do not first have to learn one hundred

```
410  IF b THEN GOTO 554
411
        :
550  GOTO 593
554
        :
593  REM
```

Figure 21.11 BASIC.

facts about addition and subtraction of the ten digits, and you avoid most of the complications of carry and borrow. Roman numerals have another advantage – they are easier to carve on stone.

The disadvantages of roman numerals become apparent only in more complex tasks such as multiplication, or worse, division. For division of roman numerals, the only known technique is trial and error. You have to guess the solution, test it by multiplying back the divisor and compare the dividend, and make a new guess if the previous one was wrong. This is exactly the way we teach schoolchildren to write and debug their BASIC programs. But compared with BASIC programming, division of roman numerals is quite easy, because the fundamental law of division tells you whether the new guess should be smaller or greater than the last.

Thankfully, arabic numerals have displaced roman ones in our schools, and the effective algorithm for long division has replaced the roman method of trial and error by an orderly process of calculation; when carefully executed, it leads invariably to the correct solution. In cases of doubt, the answer can still be checked by multiplication; but if this discovers an error, you do not try to debug the digits of your answer one by one. You go back over the steps of the calculation, and correct them – or else start again. The long division algorithm was discovered by Briggs, who was appointed the first Savilean Professor of Geometry at Oxford in 1619. It is ironic that as computers have eliminated the need to teach long division in schools, they have replaced it by such stone-age notations as BASIC.

But it is foolish to develop an emotional fixation on mere notation. For each task, a mathematician chooses the most appropriate notation. For chalking up a slate for drinks for my guests after this lecture, I shall use the most primitive notation of all – unary.

IIIII IIII

21.3 Abstraction

I now have great pleasure in introducing the concept of an abstract command. An abstract command is one that specifies general properties of the desired behaviour of a computer, without prescribing exactly how it is to be achieved. We shall see that abstraction is the primary technique whereby the software engineer can control the complexity of his tasks. In conventional engineering, the same rôle is fulfilled by the technique of numerical approximation. Such approximation is often valid for continuous natural phenomena, but not for discrete mathematical activities like programming, where every binary digit is significant, and the smallest change will result in *ABORT*.

$x \cup y$ behaves like x or y

$$
\begin{aligned}
x \cup x &= x \\
x \cup y &= y \cup x \\
x \cup (y \cup z) &= (x \cup y) \cup z \\
x \cup ABORT &= ABORT
\end{aligned}
$$

Figure 21.12 Abstraction.

A simple example of an abstract command is the union or l.u.b. $(x \cup y)$ of two commands x and y, which may themselves be abstract or concrete. The union command may be obeyed by obeying either of its operands. The choice between them is left open, and may be made later by the programmer, by a compiler, or even by some device in a machine while it executes the program.

The properties of the union operator (Fig. 21.12) are exactly what you would expect. A command to do x or x leaves you no choice but to do x. To do x or y gives you the same choice as y or x. And in a choice between three alternatives, it does not matter in what order you choose between one of them and a subsequent choice between the other two. And finally, *ABORT* is the abstract program which allows any behaviour whatsoever. Thus, to allow further choice does not alter the range of options permitted by *ABORT*.

The introduction of abstraction permits the definition of a useful ordering relation between concrete and abstract commands. If y is an abstract command specifying some desired effect, and x is a concrete command which achieves that effect, we say that x satisfies y, and use the familiar notation for a partial order

$$x \subseteq y$$

The command x may also be abstract, in which case the ordering relation means that x is the same as y, or it is more specific, more concrete or more deterministic than y. In either case, x meets the specification y, because every possible execution of x is described and therefore allowed by y. As stated in Fig. 21.13, the satisfaction relation is a partial order, and the abstraction operator is its least upper bound.

Abstract commands may be combined by all the same operators as concrete commands. Figure 21.14 shows that the sequential composition distributes through abstract choice in both directions, in the same way that multiplication distributes through the greater of two numbers. It follows that composition is monotonic in both its operands. In fact, all the operators of a programming language are monotonic in this sense. There are good theoretical reasons for this; and there are also very beneficial

$$
\begin{gathered}
x \subseteq y \Leftrightarrow x \cup y = y \\
x \subseteq x \\
x \subseteq y \wedge y \subseteq x \Rightarrow x = y \\
x \subseteq y \wedge y \subseteq z \Rightarrow x \subseteq z \\
(x \cup y) \subseteq z \Rightarrow x \subseteq z \cup y \subseteq z
\end{gathered}
$$

Figure 21.13 Satisfaction.

$$
\begin{gathered}
(x \cup y); z = (x; z) \cup (y; z) \\
z; (x \cup y) = (z; x) \cup (z; y) \\
w \subseteq y \wedge x \subseteq z \Rightarrow w; x \subseteq y; z
\end{gathered}
$$

Figure 21.14 Sequential composition.

consequences for practical solution of programming problems, as I shall now show.

21.4 Refinement

According to the principles I outlined at the beginning of this lecture, the task of a programmer can be described as a problem in mathematics. We start with an abstract description y of what we want the computer to do, carefully checking that it is an accurate description of the right problem. This is often the most difficult part of our task, and requires the most powerful tools. So in the specification y, we take advantage of the full range of concepts and notations of mathematics, including even concepts which cannot be represented on any computer, and operations which could never be implemented in any programming language.

Turning now to the second part of the programmer's task, we must find some program x which solves the inequation

$$x \subseteq y$$

where y is the specification of the program. Mathematics provides many formulae and methods for the solution of equations and inequations, from linear and quadratic to differential and integral. In all cases, the derivation of a solution may use the full power of mathematics, but the solution itself must be expressed as a formula in some more restricted notation. You cannot use the derivative symbol when asked to differentiate a formula, or an integral sign when asked to integrate. That would be just too easy. And the same is true in programming, where the eventual solution must be expressed in the restricted notations of an implemented concrete programming language.

The most powerful general method of solving a complicated problem is to split it into simpler subproblems, which can then be solved independently. The same method can be applied again to the subproblems until they are simple enough to solve by some other more direct method. In the case of computer programming, this is often called top-down development or stepwise refinement; and it is illustrated in Fig. 21.15. We start with the problem of finding some command x (expressed in a concrete programming language) which meets the specification y (expressed in the abstract language of mathematics). The first step requires the insight to split y into two sequential subproblems, and the skill to specify these as abstract programs v and w. Before proceeding further, we prove the correctness of our design so far by showing that the sequential composition of v and w meets the original specification y, or more formally

$$v; w \subseteq y$$

Now these two subproblems v and w may be solved one after the other or simultaneously, by a single programmer or by two teams of programmers, according to the size of the task. When both subproblems are solved, we will have two commands t and u, expressed in the restricted notations of our chosen programming language, each meeting their respective specifications

$$t \subseteq v$$
$$\text{and } u \subseteq w$$

Now all that remains is to deliver their sequential composition ($t; u$) as a solution to the original problem y. Correctness of the solution has been established not by the traditional laborious and ultimately unsound method of integration testing and debugging after the components have been

Problem:	find x such that $x \subseteq y$	
Step 1:	find v, w such that $v;w \subseteq y$	
Step 2a:	find t such that $t \subseteq v$	
Step 2b:	find u such that $u \subseteq w$	
Step 3:	deliver $t;u$	
Proof:	$t;u \subseteq v; w$	; monotonic, (2)
$\because$	$t;u \subseteq y$	$\subseteq$ transitive, (1)

Figure 21.15 Top-down development.

constructed; but rather by a mathematical proof, which was completed on the very first step, even before their construction began.

The validity of the general method of top-down development depends on monotonicity of the composition operator and transitivity of the abstraction ordering. The method can therefore be applied to any other operator of a concrete programming language. It has been treated at length in many learned articles and books. Such is the simplifying power of mathematics that the whole method can be described, together with a proof of its validity, within the seven short lines of Fig. 21.15.

I have drawn an analogy between multiplication of natural numbers and sequential composition of commands in programming. This analogy extends even to division. As with division of natural numbers, the quotient of two commands is not an exact inverse. However, it is uniquely defined by the same fundamental law, as shown in Fig. 21.16. The quotient of y by z is the most abstract specification of a program x, which, when followed by z, is sure to meet the specification y. As a consequence, the quotient itself, when followed by z, meets the original specification. And finally, when the divisor is the composition of two commands, the quotient may be calculated by successive division by these two commands in the reverse order. Since the composition of commands is not symmetric, the reversal of the order is important here.

In factorization of large numbers, division obviously saves a lot of effort, because you have to guess only one of the factors, and obtain the other one by a mere calculation. The division of commands offers the same advantages in the factorization of programming problems. In the refinement procedure which I have just described, it replaces the guesswork required in discovering two simpler subtasks by the discovery of only the second of them, as shown in Fig. 21.17. Furthermore, the proof obligation in step I has been eliminated. It is replaced by a formal calculation of the weakest specification which must be met by the first operand of the composition. Reduction of guesswork and proof to mere calculation is the way in which a mathematician simplifies his own tasks, as well as those of the user of mathematics – the scientist, the engineer, and now also the programmer.

The quotient operator for commands of a programming language was discovered and explored in a series of research seminars in Oxford in 1985.

$$(x; z) \subseteq y \Leftrightarrow x \subseteq (y \div z)$$
$$(y \div z); z \subseteq y$$
$$x \div (y; z) = (x \div z) \div y$$

Figure 21.16 Quotient of commands.

Problem:	find x such that $x \subseteq y$	
Step 1:	choose suitable w	
Step 2a:	find t such that $t \subseteq y \div w$	
Step 2b:	find u such that $u \subseteq w$	
Step 3:	deliver $t; u$	
Proof:	$t; u \subseteq (y \div w); w$	; monotonic
	$(y \div w); w \subseteq y$	property of $\div$
$\therefore$	$t; u \subseteq y$	$\subseteq$ transitive

Figure 21.17 Development by quotient.

It is a slight generalization of Dijkstra's weakest precondition, which is one of the most effective known methods for the design and development of correct algorithms, as shown in numerous examples by David Gries.

21.5 Program maintenance

In my description of the task of a programmer, I have concentrated on the more glamorous part of that task, that of specifying, designing and writing new programs. But a significant proportion of a programmer's professional life is spent on making changes to old programs. Some of these changes are necessitated by the discovery of errors, and some by changes in the specification of the desired behaviour of the program. The program and the specification are so large that it is not practical to write a new program from scratch; so when only a small part of the specification is changed, it is hoped that only a small part of the program will need changing to meet it.

Of course, such a hope is not always fulfilled. Consider again the analogy of the division of numbers. A small change in the least significant digits of the dividend results in a small change in the least significant digits of the quotient, and can be achieved by a small amount of recalculation. But a small change in the most significant digit of either operand requires the calculation to be started again, and leads to a completely different result. In the case of programs, it is often very difficult to know which small changes in a large specification will require major changes to the code.

It is therefore one of the most important duties of the original programmer to decide which parts of a specification are most likely to be changed, and structure a program design so that a change to one part of the specification requires a change to only one part of the program. The programmer should then document the program with instructions on how

Given:	$f(x) \subseteq g(y)$
Problem:	find x' such that $f(x') \subseteq g(y')$
Case I:	$f = g$
	solve $x' \subseteq y'$
Case 2:	f has approximate inverse f^{-1}
	solve $x' \subseteq f^{-1}(g(y'))$

Figure 21.18 Maintenance.

to carry out the change. This too can be done in a rigorous mathematical fashion (Fig. 21.18). Let y be that part of a complete specification $g(y)$ which is liable to change. Let x be that command in a big program $f(x)$ which is designed to change when y changes. The problem now is to change x to x' so that $f(x')$ meets the changed specification $g(y')$.

The problem of program maintenance is most easily solved when the structure of the program f is the same as the structure of the specification g, because in this case it is sufficient to ensure that the modified component meets the modified specification. But it is not always possible to preserve the structure of a specification in the design of a program. This is because a specification is often most clearly structured with the aid of such logical operators as negation and conjunction, which are not available in an implemented programming language. Nevertheless, mathematics can often help. If the program f has an approximate inverse f^{-1}, defined in the same way as for the quotient, then it is possible to calculate the proof obligation of the modified program as

$$x' \subseteq f^{-1}(g(y'))$$

21.6 Conclusion

Now I must inject a note of realism into my mathematical speculations. On dividing two integers, the result of the division is usually much smaller than both the operands. On dividing one program by another, the result can be larger than both the operands put together, and requires massive simplification before it can be used effectively. It is this problem that discourages the use of mathematics in program design, and presents the challenge for continuing research.

The problem of size of mathematical formulae is exactly the same problem that limits the use of mathematics in other branches of science and engineering. Scientists believe as fervently as I do in the principle that the whole of nature is governed by mathematical laws of great simplicity and elegance; and brilliant scientists have discovered many laws which accurately predict the results of experiments conducted in a rigorously controlled laboratory environment. But when the engineer tries to apply the same laws in practice, the number of uncontrollable variables is so great that a full calculation of the consequences of each design decision is hopelessly impractical. The movement of a tennis ball through the air is doubtless governed by mathematical equations; but the tennis player does not calculate the parameters of his return shot by solving them. The mere thought of doing so would completely spoil his game. Both engineer and sportsman have trained themselves to an almost instinctive feel and understanding for the appropriate action to meet each need.

Experienced programmers have developed a similar intuitive understanding of the behaviour of computer programs, many of which now achieve great sophistication together with high reliability. Nevertheless, I would suggest that the skills of our best programmers will be even more effective when exercised within the framework of an understanding and application of the relevant mathematical principles, with particular emphasis on abstraction. The mathematics has been demonstrated on small examples, as it were in the laboratory. At Oxford, in the Computing Laboratory, we have started a number of collaborative projects to scale up these methods for application in an industrial environment. Preliminary indications are quite promising, both for advances in theory and for benefits in practice.

We are concentrating our attention on the areas of greatest necessity, where lack of mathematical precision leads to the heaviest costs. In particular, I list five such areas: specifications, systems software, standards, silicon structures, and safety.

21.6.1 Specifications

In the initial specification and early design of a large-scale software product, the use of mathematics has been found to clarify design concepts, and enable a wide variety of options to be explored at a time when less successful alternatives can be cheaply discarded. As a result, the final agreed specification may enjoy that simplicity and conceptual integrity which characterizes the highest quality in design. Furthermore, user manuals, tutorials and guides which are based on mathematical specifications can be better structured, more complete and more comprehensible, even to users who have no knowledge of the underlying mathematics. This promises to mitigate the greatest single cause of error, inconvenience and frustration in the use of sophisticated software products – that is, failure to read and understand the user manual.

Effective methods of specification of large programs will be taught and used extensively in our undergraduate courses, particularly in a third-year course on operating systems. They have been explored in a collaborative contract between Oxford University and IBM (UK) Ltd, which is now entering its fifth year. Our research with IBM has concentrated on a widely sold software product known as the Customer Information Control System, or CICS for short. A determined attempt to construct a mathematical model of the existing product brought to light a number of tricky questions, which could not be answered even by those who had designed the programs and implemented them. This discovery gave our industrial collaborators the confidence to submit designs of new products to our analysis. Again, they were astonished by the depth and range of the issues which we were able to bring to light at the earliest stages of design. So eventually they allowed us to show them how to do it; and now they are doing it better than we can.

We have proved that ordinary programmers enjoy learning mathematics, and enjoy applying it. They call for our assistance only when they find problems for which our standard methods seem inadequate. Then we have to conduct a mathematical exploration to discover new methods, or refine, extend and generalize the existing methods. This has been an invaluable stimulus to our more abstract research.

21.6.2 Systems software

The basic systems software of a computer includes such items as an operating system, language compilers, utilities, transaction processing packages and database management systems. These programs are written by large teams of programmers, and they are delivered to thousands or millions of customers, who use them daily, hourly, or even continuously. In the years after delivery of such software, many thousands of errors are discovered by the customers themselves; and each error must be laboriously analysed, corrected and re-tested; and the corrections must be delivered to and installed by every customer in the next release of the software. A reduction in the number of corrections needed would be very cost-effective for the supplier and even more convenient for the customers. No method by itself can guarantee absolute reliability, but in combination with management control, a mathematical approach looks promising because even when mistakes are made, they can be traced to their source, and steps can be taken to ensure they do not happen again.

Methods of reliable program design will be taught throughout our new undergraduate syllabus, but especially in a second-year course in Software Engineering. Research in this area is continuing at Oxford in collaboration with IBM, and with other companies including Racal and British Petroleum. In these research contracts we hope to design and develop computer aids to large-scale program construction. The first such aid, which we have already developed, is a good word processor with an adequate range of mathematical symbols. Next we need a filing system, which will control the many versions of documents and programs produced by large programming teams. And finally, we would like some computer assistance in the calculation of the properties of abstract and concrete programs, and in the manipulation of the large formulae which arise.

21.6.3 Standards

The standardization of languages and interfaces in hardware and in software is a vital precondition for free competition and for propagation of technical advances to large numbers of satisfied customers. The construction of a mathematical specification for these standards offers the same promise of improved quality in design that I have described before; there is also a hope of reducing the ambiguities and misunderstandings which lead to errors and incompatibility in various implementations of the standard, and which have prevented full benefit from being obtained from existing standards.

Mathematical methods for the description of programming language standards appear in our new undergraduate syllabus in the third-year course on denotational semantics. They are based on the pioneering discoveries of Christopher Strachey and Dana Scott at Oxford. They are being applied to the design of new programming languages such as occam and Ada. The occam programming language has been designed by INMOS, the British microprocessor company, and includes the programming concepts which I have used in this lecture. It also includes operators specifying concurrent execution of commands or processes, which communicate with each other by input and output. The language is the basis of the design of the new microprocessor, known as the transputer, which has just been announced by INMOS. The language was used extensively in the design of the transputer itself. It is already being used in space, for programming a collection of computers in a British satellite.

The successful design of occam was inspired and guided by a mathematical study conducted at Oxford. We now have a denotational semantics of the language. We also have a set of algebraic laws, which are being used by INMOS to assist in correct construction of programs and compilers for the language. Occam is the first practical programming language which fulfils its role as a mathematical theory, giving practical assistance to programmers in writing correct programs.

21.6.4 Silicon structures

The advance of technology in very large scale integration (VLSI) now makes it possible to build hardware of a complexity matching that of software. As a result, the number of design errors detected during manufacture and testing of complex devices is also beginning to match that of software. But now each error costs many thousands of dollars to remove; what is worse, by delaying introduction of a new device to the market, a single error can prevent an innovative company from assuming market leadership, or even prejudice its survival. As a result, many products are delivered with known design errors, for which the customer will never obtain correction or restitution. Fortunately, mathematical methods similar to those for sequential programs can be adapted to check logic designs. These methods are especially valuable when the design involves concurrency or parallelism.

At Oxford this subject will appear in our new undergraduate syllabus in the second-year courses on VLSI design and distributed computing. We are also pursuing further research into silicon design, in collaboration with INMOS, GEC, and other companies. Our objective is to continue the mathematical process leading from specification through design right down to a description of the circuits which are implanted into silicon. It appears that the occam language will play a valuable intermediary role in this process. If we can do this efficiently and reliably, we will achieve several orders of magnitude improvement in the cost and performance of special-purpose computing devices. These will be devices which are accurately and completely specified in such a way that their behaviour can be predicted and controlled by logical reasoning.

21.6.5 Safety

Computer programs are increasingly used in systems which are critical to the safety of the general public – control of railway signalling, aero-engines, chemical and nuclear processes. All the engineering techniques used in these systems are subject to the most rigorous analysis and control, often enforced by law. Mathematical methods offer the best hope of extending such control to computer sofware; and when this happens, a computer program could gain a reputation as the most reliable component of any system in which it is embedded.

The production of error-free programs has for over fifteen years been the motivation of my own research. The methods are not easy to apply, and there is very little knowledge of their existence, even among those who need them most. It has been difficult to find industrial collaborators who admit that they need help in safety-critical programming. But every graduate from our new School will know and understand the relevant theory, and will be able to put it into practice.

I started this lecture with a summary of the mathematical principles which underlie the practice of computing, and of the current widespread failure to recognize those principles. I have ended with a description of the ways in which research at Oxford has been directed to bridging the gap between theory and practice, between mathematics and computer applications. Unfortunately, I have not been able to describe all the research in which we are engaged. Even worse, I have failed to give credit to widespread research outside Oxford. And now there is no time to list all my other failures and omissions.

My main hope is that I have conveyed to you some flavour of the kind of mathematics in which we are engaged. I believe that our work is justified not only by its utility, but also by the beauty of the mathematics itself. By explicit appeal to mathematics, even computer programs can share in this beauty. For in the computing profession the greatest benefits in reduction of costs and improvement of quality can be achieved only by conscientious pursuit of the traditional academic virtues of rigour and elegance. I end with a quotation from Christopher Strachey, who wrote in 1974:

> It has long been my personal view that the separation of practical and theoretical work is artificial and injurious. Much of the practical work done in computing, both in software and in hardware design, is unsound and clumsy because the people who do it do not have any clear understanding of the fundamental principles underlying their work. Most of the abstract mathematics and theoretical work is sterile because it has no point of contact with real computing. One of the central aims of the Programming Research Group, as a teaching and research group, has been to set up an atmosphere in which this separation cannot happen ...

Ever since, we have continued to pursue exactly this aim. As a result, my years at Oxford have been the most exciting and scientifically fruitful years of my life. I hope I have conveyed to you some of this excitement, and that you are consoled thereby for the long delay in hearing what I have presumptuously presented as an inaugural lecture.

TWENTY-TWO

An overview of some formal methods for program design

It is fitting that the last reprinted paper should be one of Hoare's more general articles. Throughout his development of important scientific contributions, Hoare has been prepared to take time to communicate the evolution of computing science to a wider audience. The contrast, however, with his first contributions of this sort is marked: here, the reader is plunged straight into an example of a formal development.

This paper was written mainly during Hoare's 1986/87 sabbatical at the University of Texas and published ([112]) in 1987. The motive for writing the article was to counteract the two widely held, and related, beliefs:

(1) That a notation used for specification of requirements should also be executable by computer.
(2) That some single formal notational system should be adequate for all purposes in program design.

If these beliefs can be refuted by an example as simple as greatest common divisor, it must be obvious the the specification of major systems requires the use of notations chosen for specification rather than for implementation.

Abstract

The code of a computer program is a formal text, describing precisely the actions of a computer executing that program. As in other branches of engineering, the progress of its implementation as well as its eventual quality can be promoted by additional design documents, formalized before starting to write the final code. These preliminary documents may be expressed in a variety of notations suitable for different purposes at different stages of a project, from capture of requirements through design and implementation, to delivery and long-term maintenance. These notations are derived from mathematics, and include algebra, logic, functions, and procedures. The connection between the notations is provided by mathematical calculation and proof.

This article introduces and illustrates a selection of formal methods by means of a single recurring example, the design of a program to compute the greatest common divisor of two positive numbers. It is hoped that some of the conclusions drawn from analysis of this simple example will apply with even greater force to software engineering projects on a more realistic scale.

22.1 Requirements

Imagine that a software engineer is called upon to construct a mechanism or subroutine to compute the greatest common divisor z of two positive integers x and y. By an even greater feat of imagination, assume no prior knowledge of the concept of greatest common divisor, or of how to compute it. So the first task is to ensure that the engineer and client have the same understanding of what is required. Let us suppose first that they agree to confine attention to positive whole numbers (excluding zero). The required relationship between the parameters (x, y) and the result (z) may be formalized as follows:

(D1.1) z divides x
(D1.2) z divides y
(D1.3) z is the greatest of the set of numbers satisfying both these conditions
(D1.4) 'p divides q' means 'there exists a positive whole number w such that $pw = q$'
(D1.5) 'p is the greatest member of a set S' means 'p is in S, and no member of S is strictly greater than p'

It is essential that the notations used for formalization of requirements should be mathematically meaningful, but it would be unwise to place any other restriction upon them. Even in this simple example we have used logic, arithmetic, and set theory. An engineer should take advantage of this early notational freedom to ensure that the formalization of requirements is simple and well-structured so that, together with its informal explanation, it obviously describes what is really wanted, and not something else. There can never be any formal method of checking this vital correspondence, because there should not be any more obviously correct description to check it against. Clarity is our only defence against the embarrassment felt on completion of a large project when it is discovered that the wrong problem has been solved.

The most important mathematical notations needed in requirements specification are also the simplest – for example, the familar Boolean connectives $\wedge$ (AND), $\vee$ (OR) and $\neg$ (NOT). The connective $\wedge$ (known as *conjunction*) is needed to put together the separate requirements imposed upon a product. In the example above, we want the answer z to be a divisor of x and we want it to be a divisor of y. Sometimes we need *universal quantification* ('for all x'), which is a generalization of $\wedge$. The connective $\vee$ (known as *disjunction*) is needed to achieve simplicity and symmetry by maintaining a high level of abstraction. Sometimes we need *existential quantification* ('there exists'), which is a generalization of $\vee$. For example, in clause (D1.4) above, we want there to exist a w exactly dividing x, but we don't care if there is more than one, and if so we don't care which one is chosen. And we certainly don't want to describe in gory detail how a computer is to find one. Finally, it is often easier and clearer to say what we want the product not to do. For example there must be no divisor of x and y greater than z. In the formulation of requirements, we certainly need the simple Boolean connectives $\wedge$ and $\vee$, and especially $\neg$.

By using such a powerful specification language, we run the risk of writing a falsehood, inconsistency, or other absurdity which could never be implemented. This risk can be eliminated by an early consistency check. In our example, what we need to check is that for every pair of positive numbers x and y there exists a number z with the properties specified in D1.3. A proof of this has three steps:

(P1.1) The number 1 is a divisor of every number. So it is a common divisor of every pair of numbers. This shows that the set of common divisors of two numbers is non-empty.

(P1.2) Each number is its own greatest divisor, so every set of divisors is finite. The common subset of any two finite sets is also finite. So the set of common divisors of two numbers is both finite and non-empty.

(P1.3) Every finite non-empty set of integers has a greatest member. So the maximum used to define the greatest common divisor always exists.

At the end of requirements analysis, we aim to have a mathematically precise, complete, consistent, and above all obviously appropriate mathematical description of the result we want. It would be very nice to input this description into some suitably programmed computer, and get the computer to translate it automatically into a subroutine. On each call of the subroutine, it would return the greatest common divisor of any pair of numbers supplied as arguments. If we are willing to overlook the problem of efficiency, there is an easy way of doing this, known as the British Museum algorithm. A computer can be programmed to start with some standard set of axioms of mathematics, and to use them to generate at random all provable mathematical theorems. It will therefore eventually generate such startling theorems as

One is the greatest of all numbers which divide both two and three.

So if we want to know the greatest common divisor of two and three, all we need to do is to program another computer to recognize when the British Museum computer has produced a result of this form. Then we just wait for it to do so. We may have to wait a very long time – under reasonable assumptions, all the particles in the universe will decay to photons before our fastest computers can carry out even the most trivial calculations. And if the theorem-generator attempts a strategy much better than random generation, it is difficult to avoid the risk that some true theorem will never be generated. In mathematics, the question of efficiency is rightly considered irrelevant, but in using computers to do mathematics, efficiency cannot forever be ignored – or else it will really be forever. Efficiency is therefore the main driving force in the development of an acceptable program to meet its mathematical specification, as shown in the following sections.

22.2 Logic program

A solution to the unavoidable problem of efficiency is to recast the specification of requirements into some notational framework less powerful and less general than the whole of mathematics. This restricted notation is so designed that its use will be rewarded by more efficient execution on a computer. One of the concepts of mathematics that is most difficult to implement effectively is negation of specification. For example, if you want a program that does not trigger a holocaust, you cannot hope to write a program that does trigger a holocaust and just negate it before submitting it to the computer. For this reason, even the highest-level logic programming languages prohibit or severely restrict the use of negation, requiring the programmer to implement it whenever needed.

Here is an idealized logic program to compute the greatest common divisor of two positive integers. To help in checking its correctness, it has been designed to preserve as far as possible the structure and clarity of the original requirements. We assumed that *isproduct* and *differsfrom* are available as built-in predicates on positive integers.

(L2.1) *isdivisor*(x, z) if there exists a w not greater than x such that *isproduct*(z, w, x)
(L2.2) *iscommondiv*(x, y, z) if *isdivisor*(x, z) and *isdivisor*(y, z)
(L2.3) *isgcd*(x, y, z) if *iscommondiv*(x, y, z) and for all w from z to x *isnotcommondiv*(x, y, z)
(L2.4) *isnotcommondiv*(x, y, z) if *isnotdiv*(x, z) or *isnotdiv*(y, z)
(L2.5) *isnotdiv*(x, z) if for all w from 1 to x *isnotproduct*(z, w, x)
(L2.6) *isnotproduct*(z, w, x) if *isproduct*(z, w, y) and *differsfrom*(y, x)

This program is a great deal more complicated than the requirements specification in the previous section. The obvious reason is that the absence of negation in the programming language requires explicit programming of a search through all possibilities before a negative answer is given. In order to ensure termination, a finite range for each search has to be specified, and setting this limit requires knowledge of the application domain. For example, in (L2.3) we rely on the fact that the common divisor of two numbers cannot exceed either number.

Note that in the best-known programming language, PROLOG, it would be permitted to replace (L2.3) to (L2.6) by the single clause

(L2.3′) *isgcd*(x, y, z) if *iscommondiv* (x, y, z) and
not(*iscommondiv*(x, y, w) and *isgreater*(w, z))

This restores the brevity of the specification of requirements, but when submitted to a standard implementation of PROLOG, this program may turn out to be slightly worse than the British Museum algorithm because it does not terminate at all. The trouble is that the *not* of PROLOG does not mean the same as the $\neg$ of mathematics, logic, or even normal technical discourse, and its meaning cannot be fully understood except in terms of the way that PROLOG programs are executed. In fact, in PROLOG the *and* and the *or* also have peculiar meanings, as a result of which they are not even symmetric. The motive for this was to achieve greater efficiency of execution, particularly on traditional sequential computers.

In spite of considerable ingenuity of implementation, logic programs are inherently inefficient, particularly if the specification takes proper advantage of the power of the available combination of conjunction and disjunction. The reason is that in principle all combinations of possibilities described by each disjunction have to be explored, in order to be sure of finding one that is consistent with the rest of the specification. Consider the conjunction of (A or B) with (C or D). This gives rise to four alternatives, (A and C) or (A and D) or (B and C) or (B and D), all of which may have to be tried. An existential quantifier multiplies the number of cases by a larger factor, and if recursion is involved, the number of cases to be explored increases exponentially. All but one of these cases will eventually be discarded.

22.3 Algebra

A possible way of improving efficiency is by restricting yet further the power of the language, for example by avoiding disjunction as well as negation. This is the major restriction imposed when formulating a specification in the algebraic style. In an algebraic specification, fresh names (such as *gcd*) must be introduced for each function to be specified. The specification is formalized as a set of algebraic equations, each of which must be true of all values of the variables they contain. These equations are connected implicitly by $\wedge$. Only this form of conjunction is allowed – no negation and no disjunction. As a result, it is even more difficult or even impossible to write a program which preserves the clause structure or content of the original requirements. Instead, the algebraic equations have to be derived as needed by mathematical reasoning from the whole of the original specification. This is illustrated in the case of the greatest common divisor:

(L3.1) The greatest divisor of x is x. So the greatest common divisor of x and x is also x:

$$x = gcd(x, x) \qquad \text{for all } x.$$

(L3.2) If z divides x and y, it also divides $x + y$. So every common divisor of x and y is also a common divisor of $x + y$ and y. Similarly, every common divisor of $x + y$ and y is also a common divisor of x and y. So the greatest of these identical sets of common divisors are the same:

$$gcd(x, y) = gcd(x + y, y) \qquad \text{for all } x, y.$$

(L3.3) Every common divisor of x and y is also a common divisor of y and x:

$$gcd(x, y) = gcd(y, x) \qquad \text{for all } x, y.$$

The three laws given above can serve as an algebraic specification of the *gcd* function. The *consistency* of the specification has been guaranteed by proof, which shows that the laws follow from a set of requirements already known to be consistent. But the question remains, are the laws a *complete* specification, in the sense that there is only one function satisfying them? Or do we need to look for more laws? A proof of completeness has to show that for any given positive numerals p and q there is a numeral r such that the equation

$$r = gcd(p, q)$$

can be proved solely from the algebraic specification and the previously known laws of arithmetic.

This can be shown by mathematical induction: We assume the result for all p and q is strictly less than N, and prove it for all p and q less than or equal to N. For such numbers, four cases can be distinguished:

(1) Both p and q are strictly less than N. In this case, what we have to prove is the same as the induction hypothesis, which may be assumed without proof.

(2) Both p and q are equal to N. Then the result

$$N = gcd(p, q)$$

is proved immediately by law (L3.1).

(3) $p = N$ and $q < N$. It follows that $p - q$ is positive and less than N. By the induction hypothesis, there is an r such that

$$r = gcd(p - q, q)$$

is deducible from the algebraic laws. One application of (L3.2) then gives

$$r = gcd((p - q) + q, q)$$

which by the laws of arithmetic leads to the required conclusion:

$$r = gcd(p, q)$$

(4) $p < N$ and $q = N$. There there is an r such that

$$r = gcd(q, p)$$

is provable in the same way as in case (3) described above. One application of (L3.3) then gives

$$r = gcd(p, q)$$

That concludes the proof that the algebraic specification is complete.

Clearly there is no structural correspondence between the three clauses of the algebraic specification and the five clauses expressing the original requirement. As a result, some mathematical ingenuity and labour has been needed to prove that the two orthogonal specifications describe (and completely describe) the same function. This labour could be avoided by simply leaving out the original formalization of requirements in the general notations of mathematics, and by starting instead within the more restricted equational framework of algebra.

But this would be a mistake. In the example we have been considering, the mistake can be explained as follows. The purpose of the specification is to tell the user of a subroutine the properties of the result it produces, and to do so in a manner conducive to the wider objectives of the program as a whole. Clearly, the user of a subroutine to compute the greatest common divisor will be very directly interested in the fact that the result of every subroutine call divides each of its two arguments exactly. But the algebraic law tells us only that the same result would have been obtained if the two arguments had been permuted (L3.3) or added together (L3.2) before the call. These facts by themselves seem a lot less directly useful.

It would also be a mistake to regard the different specifications, the abstract one and the algebraic one, as rivals or even as alternatives. They are both needed; they are essentially complementary, and they can be used for different purposes at different stages in the progress of a software project. Algebraic laws are relevant in the design of an efficient algorithm; they are useful even at an earlier stage, because they help to decide how a program should deal with extreme or exceptional cases. For example, if one of the arguments of the *gcd* subroutine is zero or negative, the result should obey the same laws as the greatest common divisor of positive numbers, as far as mathematically possible.

For specifications of the highest quality and importance I would recommend complete formalization of requirements in two entirely different styles, together with a proof that they are consistent or even equivalent to each other. For example, a programming language can be defined axiomatically, by giving methods of proving correctness of programs expressed in the language. A language can also be defined algebraically, by giving algebraic laws from which equivalence of programs can be proved. A language for which two consistent and complementary definitions are provided may be confidently taken as a secure basis for software engineering.

Like the original requirements specification, a set of algebraic laws can be input to the British Museum computer, which will add these laws to the previously known axioms of mathematics and then start deriving theorems from them. Provided that the laws are complete (as we have proved our laws for *gcd* to be), the computer will eventually discover any fact that we want, for example, that the greatest common divisor of three and two is one. Furthermore, the amount of time we have to wait for this earth-shattering result will be millions of times less than the original British Museum algorithm applied to the original requirements. But we would still have to wait too long – on reasonable assumptions, the whole universe will reach a uniform temperature around four degrees Kelvin long before any interesting calculation is complete.

22.4 Functional program

Again an enormous increase in efficiency is required. And again, it can be obtained by restricting yet further the set of notations in which the mathematical equations are expressed. These restrictions are designed to prevent the pursuit of deductions irrelevant to the required result. That is achieved by use of an applicative or functional programming language.

Here is a functional program to compute the greatest common divisor of positive integers:

(F4.1) $gcd(x, y) = x$ if $x = y$
(F4.2) $gcd(x, y) = gcd(x - y, y)$ if $x > y$
(F4.3) $gcd(x, y) = gcd(y, x)$ if $x < y$

In structure and content, this is very similar to the algebraic laws, but it conforms to the restrictions imposed by a functional programming language. A typical restriction is that the left-hand side of each equation must consist of a single application of the operator being defined (gcd) to distinct simple parameters (x and y). There is no such restriction on the right-hand side, which may even contain occurrences of the operator being defined. In the evaluation of an expression, a computer treats each equation of the program as a substitution rule. At each application of the rule, a call of the function is replaced by a copy of the right-hand side of the definition, with appropriate substitution of arguments for parameters.

For example, here is a sequence of substitutions which calculates the greatest common divisor of 10 and 6:

$$\begin{aligned} gcd(10,6) &= gcd(4,6) && \text{(by F4.2)} \\ &= gcd(6,4) && \text{(by F4.3)} \\ &= gcd(2,4) && \text{(by F4.2)} \\ &= gcd(4,2) && \text{(by F4.3)} \\ &= gcd(2,2) && \text{(by F4.2)} \\ &= 2 && \text{(by F4.1)} \end{aligned}$$

This trace of execution of a functional program is nothing but a proof of the fact that $gcd(10,6) = 2$. It is the same proof as would eventually be discovered by the British Museum algorithm. But the British Museum algorithm starts from the axioms and generates vast numbers of hopelessly irrelevant truths. The implementation of a functional programming language starts from the left-hand side of the theorem to be proved, and every intermediate step should lead directly towards the goal. However, the responsibility for controlling this goal-directed behaviour is placed upon the programmer, who has to prove that there is no infinite chain of substitutions. For example, as an algebraic formula,

$$gcd(x, y) = gcd(y, x)$$

is quite correct, but if this is executed as part of a functional program, it leads to an infinite chain of substitutions. In the program shown above, this cycle is broken by ensuring that the dangerous substitution is made only when y is strictly greater than x.

Proof of termination of a functional program is very similar to proof of completeness of algebraic equations. It requires knowledge of the domain of application, and it may also require knowledge of the strategy used by the language implementor for selecting between substitutions when more than one is possible. A simple strategy (of lazy evaluation), which is also the one that most often succeeds, is not generally the most efficient one.

Let us now consider how long the program will take to terminate. In the calculation of $gcd(N, 1)$, the number 1 will be subtracted from N until it reaches 1, and this will be done $N-1$ times. On a typical 32-bit microprocessor, N is limited to about 10^{10}, so the calculation will take a few hours, which might be acceptable for a program or prototype intended to be used only once. On our largest and fastest supercomputers, numbers range up to about 10^{20}, and we might have to wait around a million years or so for an answer. It seems we are still left with a problem of efficiency, and we need to look for an improvement of at least twenty orders of magnitude.

22.5 Optimization

Use of a more restricted and more efficient programming language might gain us one or two orders of magnitude in efficiency, which is hardly worthwhile. What we need is a method of calculation inherently faster than the one we have first stumbled upon; for example, one requiring a number of steps proportional only to the logarithm of the arguments to which it is applied. For this, we need to go back to the earlier stage of analysing the algebra, and take advantage of our knowledge of the nature of the mechanism used to execute the algorithm. On modern computers, division and multiplication by two are extremely fast, and it is equally fast to test whether a number is odd or even. We are therefore led to derive algebraic laws involving these operations.

Three new laws will be sufficient:

(L5.1) If z divides x, then $2z$ divides $2x$. So if z is the greatest common divisor of x and y, then $2z$ is a common divisor of $2x$ and $2y$. It is therefore not greater than their greatest common divisor:

$$2gcd(x, y) \leqslant gcd(2x, 2y)$$

Conversely, if z is the greatest common divisor of $2x$ and $2y$, then z is even and $z/2$ is a common divisor of x and y:

$$gcd(2x, 2y)/2 \leqslant gcd(x, y)$$

From these two inequations it follows that

$$2gcd(x, y) = gcd(2x, 2y)$$

(L5.2) All divisors of an odd number are odd, and if an odd number divides $2x$ it also divides x. If y is odd, the greatest common divisor of $2x$ and y is odd, so it is also a common divisor of x and y:

$$gcd(2x, y) \leqslant gcd(x, y) \qquad \text{if } y \text{ is odd}$$

Conversely, every divisor of x divides $2x$:

$$gcd(x, y) \leqslant gcd(2x, y)$$

From these two inequations it follows that

$$gcd(2x, y) = gcd(x, y) \qquad \text{if } y \text{ is odd}$$

(L5.3) If both x and y are odd, and x is greater than y, it follows that $x - y$ is positive and even. So under these conditions,

$$gcd(x, y) = gcd((x - y)/2, y)$$

Similarly, if x and y are odd and y is larger,

$$gcd(x, y) = gcd((y - x)/2, x)$$

When these equations are coded as a functional program, it becomes clear that the number of operations required when the argument is of size 2^N has been reduced to about N. The question arises whether this is the very best that can be done, or whether it might be worth trying to find a better algorithm. This is the kind of question studied by complexity theory. But experts in complexity theory tell me that they do not know whether a better algorithm for *gcd* exists, so we shall have to do the best we can with this one.

22.6 Procedural program

Pursuit of the very highest efficiency yet again requires adoption of a restricted notation in which conjunction is disallowed. Such a restriction is imposed by a procedural programming language like FORTRAN or Pascal. The component parts (P and Q) of a procedural program are joined not by any propositional connective, but rather by sequential composition, usually denoted by a semicolon:

$$P; Q$$

which instructs a computer to execute P first, and to continue with Q only when P terminates.

Sequential composition is the secret of the efficiency of procedural programs. All of the computing resources, storage, and communication capacity which have been used by the earlier component P become available immediately, without overhead of reclamation and reallocation, for reuse by the later component Q. However, the responsibility for planning the use and reuse of resources is placed on the programmer, and much opportunity is offered for subtle errors. Perhaps the main attraction of functional and logic programming is that the claiming of new resources and the reclaiming of unused resources are automatic, once the overhead of garbage collection is accepted.

The replacement of conjunction by composition means that the sequential structure of a program will in general be radically different from the conjunctive structure of a specification, and the necessary correspondence between them must be established by mathematical calculation or proof. Fortunately, these calculations can be carried out stepwise during the early stage of the design of a program, and each design decision can be proved correct before embarking on the next. Each design step transforms the structure of the specification to correspond more closely to the structure of the eventual program. After this, work on the component parts of the structure can proceed concurrently and independently, because each of them has been fully specified, with the same precision as the whole of the original requirements. When the implementations of the parts are delivered, they can be assembled together with reasonable confidence that the system as a whole will work. This confidence is obtained not by laborious integration testing when the code is delivered, but rather by a proof that was conducted before a word of code was written. Reliable assembly of prespecified parts is an essential mark of maturity in any engineering discipline.

A procedural program or subprogram can be specified by a pair of assertions, a precondition and a postcondition. A precondition describes properties of the program variables which may be assumed to hold when the program starts. For example, let the lowercase letters x and y stand for the values of the arguments supplied on entry to the *gcd* subroutine. The precondition states that these are positive:

(P6.1) $x > 0 \wedge y > 0$

In fact, the program will not change the values of x and y, so this assertion remains true throughout execution.

A postcondition describes properties of the program variables that must be true when the program terminates. For example, let Z be the program variable introduced to hold the result of the subroutine. Then the postcondition is

(P6.2) $Z = gcd(x, y)$

The first step in the design of a sequential program $(P; Q)$ is to formalize separate specifications of P and of Q and to prove that the combination of these separate specifications will meet the original specification of the whole program. This is easily achieved if

(1) the precondition of P is the same as the precondition of the whole program (or is implied by it);
(2) the postcondition of Q is the same as the postcondition of the whole program (or implies it); and
(3) the postcondition of P is the same as the precondition of Q (or implies it).

So the design of a sequential program involves only the discovery of an appropriate intermediate assertion which will be true when control passes the semicolon which separates the parts of the program. The intermediate assertion may contain new program variables local to the subroutine, which are introduced to assist in the calculation; we will denote these by capital letters, for example, X, Y, and N. In general, the discovery of a suitable intermediate assertion requires all the skill and judgement of the program designer. Though there are a number of useful heuristics, this is not the right place to explain them; so without further ado, here is an intermediate assertion for the example program to compute the greatest common divisor:

(P6.3) $2^N gcd(X, Y) = gcd(x, y)$

Now the two parts of the program may be considered independently. The task of the first part is to make (P6.3) true on termination. That is easily accomplished by just one multiple assignment:

$$N, X, Y := 0, x, y$$

If proof is needed, it may be obtained by substituting the final values for the assigned variables in the postcondition, and observing that

$$(2^0) gcd(x, y) = gcd(x, y)$$

The second task is harder, and will again be split into two parts by the intermediate assertion

(P6.4) $2^N Z = gcd(x, y)$

The second of the new subtasks would already be accomplished if N were zero. If N is non zero, it can be made closer to zero by subtracting one. But that would make (P6.4) false, and therefore useless. Fortunately, the truth of (P6.4) can easily be restored if every subtraction of one from N is accompanied by a doubling of Z. This can be checked if it is felt necessary by proving that

$$n > 0 \wedge 2^N Z = gcd(x, y)$$
$$\Rightarrow 2^{N-1}(2Z) = gcd(x, y)$$

Since termination is obvious, we have proved the correctness of the loop

while $N > 0$ **do** $N, Z := N - 1, 2Z$

On termination of this loop, the value of N is zero, and (P6.4) is still true. Consequently, the postcondition of the whole program has been established.

Having completed the first and last of the three tasks, the time has come to confess that the middle task is the most difficult. Its precondition is (P6.3) and its postcondition is (P6.4). I suggest that the task be split yet again into four subtasks, in accordance with the following series of intermediate assertions:

(P6.3) $\wedge$ (X odd $\vee$ Y odd)
(P6.3) $\wedge$ (Y odd)
(P6.3) $\wedge$ (Y odd) $\wedge$ $X = Y$

The coding of these parts can be derived almost entirely from the algebraic laws, and is left as an exercise.

When this coding has been done, we will have a complete program expressed in some mathematically meaningful programming notation such as Pascal. In suitable circumstances, a reliable automatic translator will be available to translate the program into binary machine code of an available computer, and this will be fast enough for most general purposes. If still higher speed is required, it may be necessary to carry out yet another stage of formal design, optimization and verification. For example, the Pascal program may be converted into the even lower-level language of a horizontal microcode, or other hardware description for custom-built VLSI. In this context, the cost of design errors is extremely high, and the competent hardware engineer will warmly welcome the extra confidence that can be gained by the formal manipulations and proofs conducted at earlier stages in the design.

In a software project, the process of formal design may also have a beneficial influence on delivery dates and on reliability of the finished product. This will be important in safety-critical applications. But as in other branches of engineering, the full benefit of documentation will be most clearly felt in the long years of maintenance following first delivery of a large program. Apart from easing the removal of any remaining errors, a well-documented program can be more readily and confidently improved or altered to meet changing requirements. As in other branches of engineering, the documentation should be kept up to date. This is likely to become more and more difficult as the changes accumulate, and when it becomes impossible, this should be the signal that the time has come to re-write or replace the whole program.

22.7 Conclusion

In selection of formal notations for the various phases of a software engineering project, the following criteria are relevant:

(1) For original capture of requirements, only clarity and precision are of importance.
(2) In intermediate documentation used by the implementor, we have the related objectives of clarity and correctness.
(3) In finally delivered code, we require correctness and also see efficiency of execution.

The final code of the program must, of course, be expressed in a formal notation that can be automatically translated and executed by computer. But there is no need for any of the preceding documents to be executed, or even input to a computer. Their main purpose is clarity and convenience for communication, calculation, and proof. A premature insistence on execution (on a less than cosmological timescale) may stand in the way of these more important objectives.

It is obviously sensible to use for final coding a language which is as close as possible to that of the original specification, so that the number of steps in the design process is kept small. But the programming language must not be so inefficient that clever and complicated coding tricks are needed to compensate. This seems to be a major problem with logic programming. My view is that a modern functional programming language can provide a nice compromise between the abstract logic of a requirements specification and the detailed resource management provided by procedural programming.

Such a high-level language may also be used for rapid implementation (partial or total) of the original requirements, and so provide a rapid check of the adequacy and completeness of the specification of requirements. A similar role is played by wooden models and perspective drawings in architecture or car design. But it is advisable to plan to throw away such models after use. The overriding need for rapid implementation gives scope for the talents of an experienced hacker rather than the formal precision of an engineer, and it is unlikely that the model can be taken as the basis or framework for subsequent development of the delivered product.

The example which I have used to illustrate these conclusions is one which has been used over and over again in textbooks on computing science. Because it is such a small and familiar example, it does not complicate the explanation of more general and more important ideas. For this reason, it has also revealed (all too clearly) the full weight of the notations and complexity of the mathematical proofs involved in formalization of the process of program design. The reader may well be discouraged from applying these methods to problems of a scale more typical of software engineering. And there are many other serious concerns which are not addressed directly by formalization, for example, cost estimation, project management, quality control, testing, maintenance, and enhancement of the program after delivery.

Nevertheless, I conjecture that such pessimism would be premature, and that a more formal understanding of the decisions involved in program design will provide a more secure framework within which solutions to the other problems can be fitted. The reason for my optimism is that formal methods find their most effective application in splitting large and complex projects into shorter phases, and in splitting large and complex products into smaller components, which may then be designed and implemented independently. This splitting may be repeated as often as necessary, until each subtask is no larger and no more complex than the simple example treated above.

And maybe this was not such a simple example after all. The reader who finds it too simple is invited to improve the program so that it accepts and deals sensibly with negative numbers and zero. There are two ways of doing this:

(1) The traditional method of program maintenance is to re-test the final program on the new range of arguments, change the program as little as possible, and describe the resulting program behaviour in the user manual.
(2) The method which I recommend is to re-examine the specifications and proofs presented above, to see where they have relied on the assumption that the arguments are positive; these are the places where the design and the program must be altered. This method is in accordance with sound engineering principles, and is therefore more likely to deliver a product of high quality.

The main purpose of this article has been to show the all-pervasive role of mathematical reasoning throughout all stages of a product life cycle, and to show the need for an appropriate range of mathematical notations to communicate design decisions with other people, with a computer, and even with oneself.

22.8 Acknowledgements

To Richard Karp for advice on computational complexity, and to all seven referees of this article.

22.9 Further reading

This brief overview of formal methods for program design has necessarily omitted some important topics, for example, data refinement. No mention has been made of concurrent or distributed programming, for which some kind of formal development method is almost essential. No adequate instruction has been provided to enable the reader to put into practice the methods described. And finally, no acknowledgement has been made to the brilliant researchers who have contributed to progress in the field. I hope the reader may remedy some of these deficiencies by consulting some of the books listed in this personally selected bibliography.

(1) *Requirements*
Hayes (1987)
(2) *Logic programming*
Kowalski (1979); Clark and McCabe (1984)

(3) *Algebra*
Martin (1986)

(4) *Functional programming*
Henderson (1980); Abelson and Sussman (1985)

(5) *Procedural programming*
Gries (1981); Backhouse (1987)

(6) *Data refinement*
Jones (1986)

(7) *Parallel programming*
Hoare ([94]), Chandy and Misra (1988)

(8) *Computational complexity*
Aho *et al.* (1974)

(9) *General*
Gries (1978).

Envoi

I enjoy writing. Ideas come to me at random times on random days – exciting and hopeful, but vague and insubstantial. I then look forward to the next occasion when I can sit down for a few uninterrupted hours in front of a pile of good blank paper, with a couple of soft-lead pencils, a sharpener, an eraser, a large paper-clip, and a very necessary waste-paper basket. The idea gradually crystallizes from the surrounding vagueness, and acquires substance on the written page. It is subjected to a series of tests, by formalization, by explanation, by proof, and by application to simple examples. But during this process, completely new ideas suggest themselves, with new approaches, definitions, axioms and examples, all begging to be explored. Gradually the waste-paper basket fills, the desk is littered with the detritus of multiple erasure, and a few surviving scribbled sheets are collected in the paper-clip, to be laid aside for future development. Or else the whole idea has turned out to be unworkable, too complicated, or just plain silly; at the end of a session, nothing has survived.

Fortunately, the idea sometimes looks better after it has been written down than before. It continues to churn over in my mind, until the next opportunity to sit down and work on it. The paper-clipped sheets are taken from their drawer, and work continues from where it left off. Or perhaps, by that time I have thought of another method of presentation, new examples, or even a new idea, any of which can require a fresh start. Or worse still, a second reading through the previous draft leaves me unexcited or unconvinced, or unprepared to accept it as the right foundation for further advance. So at the end of a session, the paper-clip may contain less material than at the beginning. That too is progress.

After a series of sessions spread over several months, it begins to appear that the original idea, or one of its successors, is viable. The criteria for success are strict: the definitions must be clear, the axioms self-evident, the theorems proved and the implementation efficient. The examples should be simple yet obviously typical of the much larger problems that arise in practice; and above all, the accompanying English prose must be clear, terse, and convincing. When these objectives appear achievable, the time has come to write a conclusion. This is the most difficult part: to summarize the technical material, to confess to deficiencies, to make moderate claims of success, to discuss alternative approaches, to pay tribute to previous researchers, and to point in directions for future research. It is in the conclusion that the flow of argument must be most convincing, to leave an abiding impression upon the mind of the reader. It is often necessary to redraft or restructure an earlier section to cover a point whose relevance has become clear only while writing the conclusion. At last the paper-clip contains the scribbled sheets of the whole paper, full of untidy insertions and deletions, with repetitions, omissions, and inconsistencies arising from the long intervals which separate each writing session.

I enjoy rewriting. At the next opportunity, I sit before a fresh pile of paper and start to rewrite everything from the beginning in long-hand. Now the task is to differentiate the sections, and relate the message of each of them to that of the whole; to select the best position of each paragraph in the light of the contribution it makes to its section; to weigh carefully the rôle of each sentence in the paragraph, and the choice of each word in the sentence. The rewriting of the article again spreads over several sessions, during which new ideas are explored in the search for simpler explanations, easier examples, and more familiar analogies. The rewritten article, which was supposed to be so neat and tidy, ends with almost as many insertions, deletions and corrections as before.

On the next and subsequent rewrites, the same story is repeated. The process begins to converge, and complete sheets can migrate almost unchanged from the old draft to the new. Eventually, it is possible to reread the whole article at a single session, with reasonable satisfaction and without significant alteration. Only at this stage is it worthwhile to get the article typed; and this prevents further work on it for several weeks. It is amazing how often a neatly typed version, or possibly the enforced rest before seeing it, can reveal deep technical flaws, which were previously concealed by the untidiness or familiarity of the draft. So the typescript is often returned to the typist with significant additions or alterations.

It is at this stage that a modern word processor offers the greatest assistance, but with an equally insidious danger. A word processor tempts the author to make changes as slight as possible, and to formulate them as insertions rather than deletions; whereas what is needed is to rethink, redraft and retype whole paragraphs and even sections. I hope to continue to resist these temptations.

At last the typescript is complete. I am rather proud of it, and want to show it to my friends and colleagues, and invite comments. In this way I gain many welcome suggestions for improvement of the paper; and the unwelcome ones are even more valuable. The article waits in a bottom drawer, joined by responses as they accumulate. After six months or so, the task is resumed with fresh ideas and enthusiasm. Sometimes a method has been found to tackle problems previously left unsolved. Sometimes I am appalled by the complexity of what I have written; I cannot bring myself to read it again, and I am ashamed and sorry that I have already distributed it so widely. This has often saved me from publishing a paper I would have later regretted. A similar service is performed by referees of a paper when it is eventually submitted for publication. And when it appears in print, the feeling is one of relief rather than rejoicing: I am relieved from the duty of further reassessment and revision.

The development of many ideas has been greatly assisted by the preparation and delivery of lectures before a sympathetic but initially uncomprehending or even sceptical audience. New insights, new examples, new explanations and new turns of phrase occur to me while talking; and earlier arguments are suddenly exposed as lame and unconvincing. On the next delivery, the mistakes are avoided and the improvements are consolidated. In the ideal, such lectures should be suitable for a wide variety of audiences, for example, a seminar in front of university students and staff, a keynote address for a specialist conference, or an evening talk for a local branch of a professional society. Sometimes a written contribution is requested for publication in a magazine or in proceedings, and the current draft must be handed over. So the same material gets published again, in different formats and sometimes under different titles. Or sometimes the same title is reused to describe completely different material. As a result, my bibliography is a mess; I must really take more care in future.

Some articles require many less iterations. For example, the first draft of 'Proof of correctness of data representations' was submitted to *Acta Informatica*; the second draft, with a new section requested by the referee, was actually published. At about the same time the seventh draft of 'A structured paging system' was submitted, and it was rightly rejected. It was the eighth draft that appeared in print.

Throughout the development of an idea from vague inspiration to ultimate publication, the most important requirement has been that it can be clearly and convincingly explained. Sometimes this has led to oversimplification, for example by omission of proof of termination from 'An axiomatic approach to computer programming'. And in all cases, there is still the danger that I am deluding myself and my reader. Those who are gifted with a certain facility with words can think up splendid arguments in favour of positions which have turned out (or may yet turn out) to be untenable. I find it relatively easy to tell a consistent and coherent story within the confines of a journal article, for example, describing a single feature of a programming language. It is a much more rigorous test to maintain the same consistency and conviction over several hundred pages of a book, or the design of a complete programming language.

But the ultimate test of an idea, and the one that deserves most trust, is when it has been applied successfully in some important project, where a useful product is promised on a fixed time-scale and budget, and where an unfavourable outcome will be detrimental to the project team as well as their customers or clients. These more substantial tests have always been left to my readers. I salute the bravery of those who accept the challenge of being the first to try out new ideas; and I also respect the caution of those who prefer to stick with ideas which they know and understand and trust.

If any of my ideas is of lasting value, this can only be because they have had benefit of assistance from many scientists and colleagues, both in their early formulation and in subsequent development. I have made this confession of my methods of conducting research as a means of saying 'thank you' to those who have over many years supported my work: to secretaries and typists, to students and research assistants, to colleagues, correspondents and referees, and to my wife and family, who have over many years respected my wish for periods of uninterrupted quiet. To them I owe an unrequitable debt of gratitude. Now my gratitude extends to Cliff Jones who has made this selection of my writings, and has adorned them with his perceptive preambles; and to Allison McCauley who has made sense of my tangled bibliography. This collection of essays represents the very best of more than half a lifetime of research. I have greatly enjoyed writing each of them; and hope you have as much enjoyed reading them.

C. A. R. Hoare
February 1988

References

This lists consists solely of works not by C. A. R. Hoare and not contributed to by him. Works of which he is author or part-author are listed separately on p. 398.

Abelson, H. and Sussman, G. J. (1985) *Structure and Interpretation of Computer Programs*, MIT Press, Cambridge, Mass.

Aho, A. V., Hopcraft, J. R. and Ullman, J. D. (1974) *The Design and Analysis of Computer Algorithms*, Addison-Wesley, Reading, Mass.

Anderson, D. B. (1973) Private communication.

Apt, K. R. (1981) Ten years of Hoare's logic, A survey, Part 1, *ACM Trans on Programming Languages and Systems*, **3**(4), 431–83.

ASA Standard COBOL (1968) *Codasyl COBOL Journal of Development, National Bureau of Standards Handbook 106* ANSI X 3.23, 1968.

ASA Standard FORTRAN (1964) *Comm. ACM* **7**(10).

Atkinson, R. and Hewitt, C. (1976) Synchronisation in actor systems. Working Paper 83, MIT, Cambridge, Mass.

Backhouse, R. C. (1987) *Program Construction and Verification*, Prentice Hall, Hemel Hempstead.

Bakker, J. W. de (1968) *Axiomatics of simple assignment statements*, MR94, Mathematical Centre, Amsterdam.

Birtwhistle, G. M., Dahl, O.-J., Myhrhaug, B. and Nygaard, K. (1973) SIMULA BEGIN, *Student Literatur*, Auerbach.

Bjørner, D. and Oest, O. N. (1980a) *Formal Definition of the Ada Programming Language*, INRIA (November).

Bjørner, D. and Oest, O. N. (1980b) *Towards a Formal Description of Ada*, Lecture Notes in Computer Science No. 98.

Brinch Hansen, P. (1972a) A comparison of two synchronizing concepts, *Acta Informatica* **1**, 190–9.

Brinch Hansen, P. (1972b) Structured multiprogramming, *Comm. ACM* **15**(7), 574–8.

Brinch Hansen, P. (1973) *Operating System Principles.* Prentice Hall, Hemel Hempstead.

Brinch Hansen, P. (1975) The programming language Concurrent Pascal. *IEEE Trans. Software Eng.* **1**(2), 199–207.

Burstall, R. (1968) *Proving properties of programs by structural induction*, Experimental Programming Reports, No. 17 DMIP, Edinburgh.

Burstall, R. M. (1969) Proving programs by structural induction, *Comp. J.* **12**(1), 41–8.

Campbell, R. H. and Habermann, A. N. (1974) *The Specification of Process Synchronisation by Path Expressions.* Lecture Notes in Computer Science 16, Springer, pp. 89–102.

Chandy, K. M. and Misra, J. (1988) *Parallel Program Design: A Foundation*, Addison-Wesley, Reading, Mass.

Clark, K. L. and McCabe, F. G. (1984) *Micro Prolog: Programming in Logic*, Prentice Hall, Hemel Hempstead.

Clint, M. (1973) Program proving: Coroutines, *Acta Informatica* **2**, 50–63.

Cohn, P. M. (1965) *Universal Algebra*, Harper & Row, New York.

Conway, M. E. (1963) Design of a separable transition-diagram compiler. *Comm. ACM* **6**(7), 396–408.

Courtois, P. J., Heymans, F. and Parnas, D. L. (1971) Concurrent control with readers and writers. *Comm. ACM* **14**(10), 667–8.

Courtois, P. J., Heymans, F. and Parnas, D. L. (1972) Comments on Courtois *et al.* (1971). *Acta Informatica*, **1**, 375–6.

Dahl, O.-J. (1972) Hierarchical program structures. In Dahl *et al.* ([29]).

Dahl, O.-J. *et al.* (1967) *SIMULA 67, Common Base Language.* Norwegian Computing Centre, Forskningveien, Oslo.

Dahl, O.-J., Myhrhaug, B., Nygaard, K. (1970) *The Simula 67 Common Base Language*, Norwegian Computing Centre, Oslo, Publication No. S-22.

Darlington, J. and Burstall, R. M. (1973) A system which automatically improves programs. In *Proceedings of Third International Conference on Artificial Intelligence* 479–85, Stanford, California.

Dijkstra, E. W. (1968a) A constructive approach to the problem of program correctness, *BIT* **8**, 174–86.

Dijkstra, E. W. (1968b) Cooperating sequential processes. In Genuys, F. (ed.), *Programming Languages*, Academic Press, New York, pp. 43–112.

Dijkstra, E. W. (1972a) A class of allocation strategies inducing bounded delays only. *Proc AFIPS SJCC*, **40**, 933–6, AFIPS Press, Montvale, N.J.

Dijkstra, E. W. (1972b) Hierarchical ordering of sequential processes. In Hoare, C. A. R. and Perrott, R. H. (eds.) [20].

Dijkstra, E. W. (1972c) Notes on structured programming. In Dahl *et al.* ([29]), pp. 1–82.

Dijkstra, E. W. (1972d) Information streams sharing a finite buffer. *Information Processing Letters* **1**(5), 179–80.

Dijkstra, E. W. (1975a) Guarded commands, nondeterminacy, and formal derivation of programs. *Comm. ACM* **18**(8), 453–7.

Dijkstra, E. W. (1975b) Verbal communication, Marktoberdorf.

Dijkstra, E. W. (1976) *A Discipline of Programming*, Prentice Hall, Hemel Hempstead.

Floyd, R. W. (1967) Assigning meanings to programs, *Proc. Amer. Soc. Symp. Appl. Math.* **19**, 19–31.

Foley, M. (1969) *Proof of the Recursive Procedure Quicksort: a Comparison of Two Methods*, Master's Dissertation, Queen's University of Belfast.

Gries, D. (1978) (ed.) *Programming Methodology*, Springer-Verlag, New York.

Gries, D. (1981) *The Science of Programming*, Springer-Verlag, New York.

Hayes, I. (ed.) (1987) *Specification Case Studies*, Prentice Hall, Hemel Hempstead.

Hehner, E. C. R. (1984) Predicative programming, Part 1. *Comm. Ass. Comput. Mach.* **27**(2), 134–43.

Henderson, P. (1980) *Functional Programming: Application and Implementation*, Prentice Hall, Hemel Hempstead.

Igarishi, S. (1968) An axiomatic approach to equivalence problems of algorithms with applications, Ph.D. Thesis, 1964. *Rep. Compt. Centre*, University of Tokyo, pp. 1–101.

Jones, C. B. (1971) Formal Development of Correct Algorithms. An example based on Earley's Recogniser. *Proc. ACM SIGPLAN Conf. Proving Assertions about Programs*, 150–69.

Jones, C. B. (1983) Specification and design of (parallel) programs. In Mason (1983).

Jones, C. B. (1986) *Systematic Software Development Using VDM*, Prentice Hall, Hemel Hempstead.

Jones, G. (1987) *Programming in OCCAM*, Prentice-Hall, Hemel Hempstead.

Kahn, G. (1974) The semantics of a simple language for parallel programming. In *Proc. IFIP Congress 74*, North-Holland.

King, J. C. (1969) *A Program Verifier*, Ph.D. Thesis, Carnegie-Mellon University, Pittsburg, Pa.

Kleene, S. C. (1952) *Introduction to Metamathematics*, Van Nostrand.

Knuth, D. E. (1967) Remaining troublespots in ALGOL60, *Comm. ACM* **10**(10).

Knuth, D. E. (1973) *A Review of Structured Programming*, CS-73-371, Department of Computer Science, Stanford University:

Knuth, D. E. (1974) Structured programming with GOTO statements, Technical Report, Computer Science Dept, Stanford University, STAN-CS-74-416.

Knuth, D. E. (1973) *The Art of Computer Programming, Vols 1, 2 & 3*, Addison-Wesley, Reading, Mass.

Kowalski, R. (1979) *Logic for Problem Solving*, North-Holland, Amsterdam.

Laski, J. (1968) Sets and other types, *ALGOL Bull* **27**.

Liskov, B. H. (1974) *A Note on CLU*. Computation Structures Group Memo. 112, MIT, Cambridge, Mass.

McBride, F. V., Morrison, D. J. T. and Pengelby, R. M. (1970) A symbol manipulation system. In *Machine Intelligence*, Vol. 5, Edinburgh University Press.

McCarthy, J. (1960) Recursive functions of symbolic expressions and their computation by machine, Part 1, *Comm ACM* **3**(4), 184–95.

McCarthy, J. (1963a) A basis for a mathematical theory of computation. In Braffort, P. and Hirschberg, D. (eds), *Computer Programming and Formal Systems*, North-Holland, Amsterdam.

McCarthy, J. (1963b) Towards a mathematical theory of computation, *Proc. IFIP Cong.*, 1962, North-Holland, Amsterdam.

McIlroy, M. D. (1968) *Coroutines*, Bell Laboratories, Murray Hill, N.J.

Martin, J. J. (1986) *Data Types and Data Structures*, Prentice Hall, Hemel Hempstead.

Mason, R. E. A. (ed.) (1983), *Information Processing '83*, Elsevier Science Publishers B. V. (North-Holland) IFIP.

Michie, D. (1967) Memo functions: a language feature with 'rote learning' properties, Report MIP-R-29, Edinburgh University.

Milner, A. J. R. G. (1971) *An Algebraic Definition of Simulation Between Programs*. Stanford Computer Science Dept. CS205.

Milner, A. J. R. G. (1980) *A Calculus of Communicating Systems*. Springer LNCS Vol. 92, Springer-Verlag, Berlin.

Misra, J. and Gries, D. (1978) A linear sieve algorithm for finding prime numbers, *ACM* **21**(12), 999–1003.

Morris, F. L. and Jones, C. B. (1984) An early program by Alan Turing, *Annals of the History of Computing*, **6**(2).

Naur, P. (1960) (ed), Report on the algorithmic language ALGOL 60, *Comm. ACM* **3**(5), 299–314; *Num. Math.*, 106–36.

Naur, P. (1963) (ed.): Revised report on the algorithmic language ALGOL 60. *Comm. ACM* **6**, 1–17; *Comp. J.* **5**, 349–67 (1962/63); *Numer. Math.* **4**, 420–453 (1963).

Naur, P. (1966) Proof of algorithms by general snapshots, *BIT* **6**(4), 310–16.

Naur, P. (1969) Programming by action clusters, *BIT* **9**(3) 250–8.

Nipkow, T. (1986) Non-deterministic data types: models and implementations, *Acta Informatica* **22**, 629–61.

PL/I Language Specifications, IBM Order Number GY33-6003-2.

Pritchard, P. (1981) A sublinear sieve algorithm for finding prime numbers, *ACM* **24**(1), 18–23.

Pritchard, P. (1987) Linear prime-number sieves: a family tree, *Science of Computer Programming*, **9**(1).

Reynolds, J. C. (1965) *COGENT*. ANL-7022, Argonne Nat. Lab., Argonne, Ill.

Reynolds, J. C. (1981) *The Craft of Programming*, Prentice Hall, Hemel Hempstead.

Ross, D. T. (1961) A generalized technique for symbol manipulation and numerical calculation, *Comm. ACM* (March).

Samelson, K. (1965) Functionals and Functional Transformations, *ALGOL Bulletin* 20, pp. 27–8.

Schwartz, S. T. (ed.) (1967) *Mathematical Aspects of Computer Science*, American Mathematical Society, Providence.

Scott, D. S. (1970), *Outline of a Mathematical Theory of Computation, PRG-2.* Programming Research Group, Oxford University.

Scott, D. S. (1971) The lattice of flow diagrams. In Engeler, E., (ed.), *Symposium on Semantics of Algorithmic Languages*, Springer Verlag.

Scott, D. S. (1981) *Lecture Notes on a Mathematical Theory of Computation*. PRG 19, p. 148. Oxford University Computing Laboratory.

Steel, T. B. (ed.) (1966) *Formal Language Description Languages for Computer Programming*, North-Holland, Amsterdam.

Stoy, J. (1977) *Denotational Semantics: The Scott–Strachey Approach to Programming Language Theory*, MIT Press, Cambridge, Mass.

Thompson, K. (1976) The UNIX command language. In *Structured Programming*, Infotech, Nicholson House, Maidenhead, England, pp. 375–84.

Turing, A. M. (1949) Checking a large routine, *Report on a Conference on High Speed Automatic Calculating Machines*, University Math. Lab., Cambridge, pp. 67–9.

Waldinger, R. and Levitt, K. N. (1973) Reasoning about programs. In *Proceedings of ACM Sigact/Sigplan Symposium on Principles of Programming Language Design*, Boston.

Welsh, J. and McKeag, M. (1980) *Structured System Programming*, Prentice Hall, Hemel Hempstead.

Welsh, J. and Quinn, C. (1972) A PASCAL compiler for the ICL 1900 Series Computers. *Software, Practice and Experience* **2**, 73–7.

Wijngaarden, A. van (1965) *Orthogonal Design and Description of a Formal Language*, MR76, Mathematical Centre, Amsterdam (October).

Wijngaarden, A. van (1966) Numerical analysis as an independent science, BIT **6**, 66–81.

Wijngaarden, A. van (1969) (ed.) Report on the algorithmic language ALGOL 68. *Num. Math.* **14**, 79–218.

Wirth, N. (1965) Proposal for a Report on a Successor of ALGOL60, MR75, Mathematical Centre, Amsterdam, August 1965.

Wirth, N. (1968) PL/360, *JACM* **15**(1).

Wirth, N. (1971a) The design of a Pascal compiler. *Software, Practice and Experience* **1**, 309–33.

Wirth, N. (1971b) Program development by stepwise refinement, *Comm. ACM* **14**(4), 221–7.

Wirth, N. (1971c) The programming language PASCAL, *Acta Informatica*, **1**(1), 35–63.

Wirth, N. (1973) *Systematic Programming: An Introduction*, Prentice Hall, Hemel Hempstead.

Wirth, N. and Weber, (1966) *Comm. ACM*, **9**(2), 89.

Wulf, W. A., London, R. L. and Shaw, M. (1976) *Abstraction and Verification in ALPHARD*. Dept. of Computer Science, Carnegie-Mellon University, Pittsburgh, Pa.

Yanov, Yu, I. (1958) Logical operator schemes, *Kybernetika* **1**.

Bibliography of works by C. A. R. Hoare

This list consists solely of works by C. A. R. Hoare or contributed to by him. Works of which he is neither author nor part-author are listed separately on p. 393.

[1] Iu. Ia. Basilevskii (ed.). *Theory of Mathematical Machines,* Pergamon Press (1961). Translated from Russian by C. A. R. Hoare.

[2] C. A. R. Hoare. Об одном способе осуществления синтеза предложения при МП на основе синтагматического анализа (1961). In *Foreign Develop. Mach. Translat. Info. Proc.* No. 95 (Translated from *Mashinnii Perevod i Prikladnaya Lingvistika* No. 6, pp. 80–8).

[3] C. A. R. Hoare. Algorithm 63, Partition; Algorithm 64, Quicksort; Algorithm 65, Find. *Communications of the ACM,* **4**(7), 321–2 (1961).

[4] C. A. R. Hoare. Quicksort. *BCS, Computer Journal,* **5**(1), 10–15(1962). Chapter 2 of the current book.

[5] C. A. R. Hoare. Report on the Elliott ALGOL translator, *BCS, Computer Journal,* **5**(2), 127–9 (July 1962).

[6] C. A. R. Hoare. The Elliott ALGOL input/output system. *BCS, Computer Journal,* **5**(4), 345–8 (January 1963).

[7] C. A. R. Hoare. The Elliott ALGOL programming system. In P. Wegner (ed.), *Introduction to Systems Programming,* Academic Press (1964), pp. 156–66.

[8] C. A. R. Hoare. A note on indirect addressing. *ALGOL Bulletin,* **21**, 63–5 (November 1965).

[9] N. Wirth and C. A. R. Hoare. A contribution to the development of ALGOL. *Communications of the ACM,* **9**(6), 413–32 (June 1966). Chapter 3 of the current book.

[10] C. A. R. Hoare. Single pass compilation. PL/I. In *Proceedings of the ACTP Summer School on Software* (June 1966).

[11] C. A. R. Hoare. Record handling. In F. Genuys (ed.) *Programming Languages,* Academic Press, 1968, pp. 291–397.

[12] C. A. R. Hoare. Limitations on languages. *Computer Weekly* (1968).

[13] C. A. R. Hoare. Critique of ALGOL 68, *Algol Bulletin*, **29**, 27–9 (November 1968).

[14] C. A. R. Hoare. Data structures in two-level store. In *Proceedings of the IFIP Congress, Edinburgh, 1968,* North-Holland (1969), pp. 322–9.

[15] C. A. R. Hoare. An axiomatic basis for computer programming. *Comm. ACM* **12**(10), 576–80, 583 (October 1969)
Chapter 4 of the current book.

[16] C. A. R. Hoare. Proof of a program: FIND. *Comm. ACM,* **14**(1), 39–45 (January 1971)
Chapter 5 of the current book.

[17] C. A. R. Hoare. Procedures and parameters: an axiomatic approach. In E. Engeler (ed.), *Symposium On Semantics of Algorithmic Languages.* Lecture Notes in Mathematics 188, Springer-Verlag (1971), pp. 102–16.
Chapter 6 of the current book.

[18] C. A. R. Hoare. Computer Science. New Lecture Series 62, 1971.
Chapter 7 of the current book.

[19] M. Foley and C. A. R. Hoare. Proof of a recursive program: QUICKSORT. *BCS, Computer Journal,* **14**(4), 391–5 (November 1971).

[20] C. A. R. Hoare and R. H. Perrott. *Operating System Techniques.* Academic Press, 1972.

[21] C. A. R. Hoare. Operating systems: their purpose, objectives, functions and scope. In [20], pp. 11–28

[22] C. A. R. Hoare. Towards a theory of parallel programming. In [20], pp. 61–71.

[23] C. A. R. Hoare and R. M. McKeag. A survey of store management techniques: part 1. In [20], pp. 117–31

[24] C. A. R. Hoare and R. M. McKeag. A survey of store management techniques: Part 2. In [20], pp. 132–51

[25] C. A. R. Hoare. Prospects for a better programming language. *Infotech State of the Art Report: High Level Languages,* **7**, 327–43 (1972).

[26] M. Clint and C. A. R. Hoare. Program proving: jumps and functions. *Acta Informatica* **1**(3), 214–24 (1972).

[27] C. A. R. Hoare. The quality of software. *Software Practice and Experience,* **2**(2), 103–5 (April 1972).

[28] C. A. R. Hoare and D. C. S. Allison. Incomputability. *ACM, Computing Surveys,* **4**(3), 169–78 (September 1972).

[29] O.-J. Dahl, E. W. Dijkstra, and C. A. R. Hoare (eds.) *Structured Programming.* Academic Press, 1972.

[30] C. A. R. Hoare. Notes on data structuring. In [29], pp. 83–174.

[31] O. -J. Dahl and C. A. R. Hoare. Hierarchical program structures. In [29], pp. 175–220.

[32] C. A. R. Hoare. Proof of correctness of data representations. *Acta Informatica,* **1**(4), 271–81 (1972)
Chapter 8 of the current book.

[33] C. A. R. Hoare. A Note on the FOR Statement. *BIT,* **12**(3), 334–41 (1972).

[34] C. A. R. Hoare. Proof of a structured program: 'The Sieve of Eratosthenes'. *BCS, Computer Journal,* **15**(4); 321–5 (November 1972).
Chapter 9 of the current book.

[35] C. A. R. Hoare. A general conservation law for queueing disciplines. *Information Processing Letters,* **2**(3), 82–5 (August 1973).

[36] C. A. R. Hoare. A structured paging system. *BCS, Computer Journal,* **16**(3), 209–15 (August 1973).
Chapter 10 of the current book.

[37] C. A. R. Hoare and N. Wirth. An axiomatic definition of the programming language PASCAL. *Acta Informatica,* **2**(4), 335–55 (1973).
Chapter 11 of the current book.

[38] C. A. R. Hoare. Tomorrow's men: the role of the university. *Computer Weekly, Educational Supplement,* **7** (26 July 1973).

[39] C. A. R. Hoare. Computer programming as an engineering discipline. *Electronics and Power,* **19**(14); 316–20 (August 1973).

[40] C. A. R. Hoare. High level programming languages, the way behind. In Simpson, D. (ed.), *High Level Programming Languages – The Way Ahead,* NCC Publications, Manchester (1973).

[41] C. A. R. Hoare and P. E. Lauer. Consistent and complementary formal theories of the semantics of programming languages. *Acta Informatica,* **3**(2), 135–53 (1974).

[42] C. A. R. Hoare. Monitor: an operating system structuring concept. *Communications of the ACM,* **17**(10), 549–57 (October 1974).
Chapter 12 of the current book.

[43] C. A. R. Hoare. Hints on programming language design. In Bunyan, C. J. (ed.), *State of the Art Report 20: Computer Systems Reliability,* Pergamon/Infotech (1974), pp. 505–34.
Chapter 13 of the current book.

[44] C. A. R. Hoare. Optimisation of store size for garbage collection. *Information Processing Letters,* **2**(6), 165–6 (April 1974).

[45] C. A. R. Hoare. Software design: a parable. *Software World,* **5**(9–10), 53–6 (1974).

[46] C. A. R. Hoare. Program correctness proofs. In Shaw, B. (ed.), *Formal Aspects of Computing Science,* Newcastle upon Tyne, 3–6 September, 1974 (1975), pp. 7–45.

[47] C. A. R. Hoare and H. C. Johnston. Matrix reduction – an efficient method (school timetables). *Communications of the ACM,* **18**(3), 141–50 (March 1975).

[48] P. H. Enslow, C. A. R. Hoare, J. Palme, D. Parnas, and I. Pyle. *Implementation Languages for Real-Time Systems – I. Standardisation – its Implementation and Acceptance.* Report No. ERO-2-75-Vol. 1, European Res. Office, London, UK (15 April 1975).

[49] P. H. Enslow, C. A. R. Hoare, J. Palme, D. Parnas, and I. Pyle. *Implementation Languages for Real-Time Systems – II. Language Design – General Comments.* Report No. ERO-2-75-Vol. 2, European Res. Office, London, UK (15 April 1975).

[50] P. H. Enslow, C. A. R. Hoare, J. Palme, D. Parnas, and I. Pyle. *Implementation Languages for Real-Time Systems – III. Command and Control Languages – Specific Comments.* Report No. ERO-2-75-Vol. 3, European Res. Office, London, UK (15 April 1975).

[51] C. A. R. Hoare. Recursive data structures. *International Journal of Computer and Information Sciences,* **4**(2), 105–32 (June 1975). Chapter 14 of the current book.

[52] C. A. R. Hoare. Parallel programming: an axiomatic approach. *Computer Languages,* **1**(2), 151–60 (June 1975).
Chapter 15 of the current book.

[53] C. A. R. Hoare. Data reliability. In *Int. Conf. Reliable Software, Los Angeles*, pp. 528–33, ACM SIGPLAN Notices (June 1975).

[54] C. A. R. Hoare. Software engineering. *BCS, Computer Bulletin,* **2**(6), 6–7 (December 1975).

[55] W. H. Kaubisch, R. H. Perrott, and C. A. R. Hoare. Quasiparallel programming. *Software Practice and Experience,* **6**(3); 341–56 (July 1976).

[56] C. A. R. Hoare, Structured programming in introductory programming courses. *Infotech, Structured Programming*, 255–63 (1976).

[57] C. A. R. Hoare. The high cost of programming languages. *Software Systems engineering,* 413–29 (1976).

[58] C. A. R. Hoare. The structure of an operating system. In *Language Hierarchies and Interfaces,* Springer-Verlag (1976), pp. 242–65.

[59] E. A. Ashcroft, K. Clint, and C. A. R. Hoare. Remarks on 'program proving: jumps and functions'. *Acta Informatica,* **6**(3), 317–18 (1976).

[60] C. A. R. Hoare. Hints on the design of a programming language for real-time command and control. In Spencer J. P. (ed.), *Real-time Software: International State of the Art Report,* Infotech International (1976), pp. 685–99.

[61] A. M. MacNaughten and C. A. R. Hoare. Fast fourier transform free from tears. *BCS, Computer Journal*, **20**(1), 78–83 (February 1977).

[62] C. A. R. Hoare. Introduction. In Perrott, R. H. (ed.), *Software Engineering – Proceedings of a Symposium held at the Queen's University of Belfast 1976* Academic Press (1977), pp. 7–14 (APIC Studies in Data Processing No. 14).

[63] J. Welsh, W. J. Sneeringer, and C. A. R. Hoare. Ambiguities and insecurities in PASCAL. *Software Practice and Experience,* **7**(6), 685–96 (November–December 1977).

[64] C. A. R. Hoare. Software engineering: a keynote address. In *3rd International Conference on Software Engineering, Atlanta, GA., USA*, 10–12 May (1978), pp. 1–4.

[65] C. A. R. Hoare. Some properties of predicate transformers. *Journal of the ACM,* **25**(3), 461–80 (July 1978).

[66] C. A. R. Hoare. Communicating sequential processes. *Communications of the ACM,* **21**(8), 666–77 (August 1978).
Chapter 16 of the current book.

[67] C. A. R. Hoare. Communicating sequential processes. In Shaw, B. (ed.) *Digital Systems Design. Proceedings of the Joint IBM University of Newcastle upon Tyne Seminar, 6–9 September 1977,* Newcastle University (1978), pp. 145–56.

[68] N. Francez, C. A. R. Hoare, D. J. Lehmann, and W. P. de Roever. Semantics of nondeterminism, concurrency and communication. *Journal of Computer and System Sciences,* **19**(3), 290–308 (December 1979).

[69] C. A. R. Hoare. A model for communicating sequential processes. In McKeag, R. M. and MacNaughten, A. M. (eds.), *On the Construction of Programs*, Cambridge University Press (1980), pp. 229–54.

[70] C. A. R. Hoare and J. R. Kennaway. A theory of non-determinism. In *Proceedings ICALP '80,* Springer-Verlag, Lecture Notes In Computer Science, No. 85 (1980), pp. 338–50.

[71] C. A. R. Hoare. Hoare on programming. *Computer World UK* (22 October 1980). Text of an interview.

[72] C. A. R. Hoare. Synchronisation of parallel processes. In Hanna, F. K. (ed.), *Advanced Techniques for Microprocessor Systems*, Peter Peregrinus (1980), pp. 108–11.

[73] C. A. R. Hoare. The emperor's old clothes. *Communications of the ACM,* **24**(2), 75–83 (February 1981).
Chapter 1 of the current book.

[74] Zhou Chao Chen and C. A. R. Hoare. Partial correctness of communicating sequential processes. In *Proceedings of 2nd International Conference on Distributed Computing Systems,* IEEE Computer Society Press (8–10 April 1981), pp. 1–12.

[75] C. A. R. Hoare and Zhou Chao Chen. *Partial Correctness of Communicating Processes and Protocols.* Technical Report PRG 20, Oxford University Computing Laboratory, Programming Research Group (May 1981).

[76] C. A. R. Hoare. A calculus of total correctness for communicating processes. *The Science of Computer Programming,* **1**(1–2), 49–72 (October 1981).
Chapter 17 of the current book.

[77] C. A. R. Hoare. Professionalism. *BCS, Computer Bulletin,* **2**(29), 2–4 (1981).
Invited Talk given at BCS 81.

[78] C. A. R. Hoare. Is there a mathematical basis for computer programming? *NAG Newsletter,* **2**, 6–15 (1981).

[79] C. A. R. Hoare and Zhou Chao Chen. *The Consistency of the Calculus of Total Correctness for Communicating Processes.* PRG Monograph 26, Oxford University Computing Laboratory, Programming Research Group (February 1982).

[80] C. A. R. Hoare and R. M. McKeag, Structure of an operating system. In Broy, M. and Schmidt, G. (eds.), *Theoretical Foundations of Programming Methodology – Lecture Notes of an International Summer School, Germany, 1981,* Reidel (1982), pp. 643–58.

[81] W. H. Kaubisch and C. A. R. Hoare. Discrete event simulation based on communicating sequential processes. In Broy, M. and Schmidt, G. (eds.), *Theoretical Foundations of Programming Methodology – Lecture Notes of an International Summer School, Germany, 1981,* Reidel (1982), pp. 625–42.

[82] C. A. R. Hoare. *Specifications, Programs and Implementations.* Technical Report PRG-29, ISBN 0-902928-17-1, Programming Research Group, Oxford University (June 1982).

[83] C. A. R. Hoare. Programming is an engineering profession. In Wallis, P. J. L. (ed.), *State of the Art Report 11, No. 3: Software Engineering,* Pergamon/Infotech (1983), pp. 77–84. Also Oxford PRG Monograph No. 27.; and *IEEE Software* **1**(2).
Chapter 18 of the current book.

[84] C. A. R. Hoare and E. R. Olderog. Specification-oriented semantics for communicating processes. In *Automata Languages and Programming 10th Colloquium,* Springer-Verlag (1983), pp. 561–72.

[85] C. A. R. Hoare. *Notes on Communicating Sequential Processes.* Monograph 33, Oxford University Computing Laboratory, Programming Research Group (August 1983).

[86] E. R. Olderog and C. A. R. Hoare. Specification-oriented semantics for

communicating processes. In Diaz, J. (ed.), *Automata, Languages and Programming – Proceedings of the 10th International Colloquium, Barcelona July 18–22.* Lecture Notes in Computer Science 154, Springer-Verlag (1983) pp. 561–72.

[87] C. A. R. Hoare. 1983 technology forecast. *Electronic Design* (January 1983).

[88] E. C. R. Hehner and C. A. R. Hoare. A more complete model of communicating processes. *Theoretical Computer Science,* **26**(1–2), 105–20 (September 1983).

[89] C. A. R. Hoare. Programming: sorcery or science. *IEEE Software,* **1**(2), 5–16 (April 1984).

[90] S. D. Brookes, C. A. R. Hoare, and A. W. Roscoe. A theory of communicating sequential processes. *Journal of the ACM,* **31**(3), 560–99 (July 1984).

[91] C. A. R. Hoare and A. W. Roscoe. Programs as executable predicates. In *Proceedings of the International Conference on Fifth Generation Computer Systems, November 6–9 1984, Tokyo, Japan,* ICOT (1984), pp. 220–8

[92] C. A. R. Hoare. Notes on communicating systems. In Broy, M. (ed.), *Control Flow and Data Flow: Concepts of Distributed Programming. Proceedings of NATO Advanced Study Institute International Summer School, Marktoberdorf, 31 July–12 August, 1984,* Springer-Verlag (1985), pp. 123–204.

[93] C. A. R. Hoare. A couple of novelties in the propositional calculus. *Zeitschr. f. Math. Logik und Grundlagen d. Math.,* **31**(2), 173–8 (1985).
Chapter 19 of the current book.

[94] C. A. R. Hoare. *Communicating Sequential Processes.* Prentice Hall (1985). 256 pages, ISBN 0-13-153271-5.

[95] C. A. R. Hoare and J. C. Shepherdson (eds.) *Mathematical Logic and Programming Languages.* Prentice Hall (1985). ISBN 0-13-561465-1. The papers in this book were first published in the *Philosophical Transactions of the Royal Society,* Series A, **312** (1984).

[96] C. A. R. Hoare. Programs are predicates. In Hoare, C. A. R. and Shepherdson, J. C. (eds.), *Mathematical Logic and Programming Languages,* Prentice Hall (1985), pp. 141–54.
Chapter 20 of the current book.

[97] *$H^3.M.S^4$. Data refinement refined* (May 1985) Typescript, Programming Research Group, Oxford University.

[98] C. A. R. Hoare and C. Morgan. Specification of a simplified network service in CSP. In Denvir, B. T., Harwood, W. T. and Jackson, M. I. (eds.), *LNCS 207 – The Analysis of Concurrent Systems, Cambridge, September 1983, Proceedings,* Spinger-Verlag (1985), pp. 345–53.
There are a number of other contributions by Hoare to the discussions recorded in this volume.

[99] C. A. R. Hoare and J. He. The weakest prespecification i. *Fundamenta Informaticae,* **9**(1), 51–84 (March 1986).

[100] C. A. R. Hoare and J. He. The weakest prespecification ii. *Fundamenta Informaticae,* **9**, 217–252 (1986).

[101] C. A. R. Hoare. *The Mathematics of Programming.* Oxford University Press (1986).
Chapter 21 of the current book.

[102] A. W. Roscoe and C. A. R. Hoare. *Laws of occam Programming*. Monograph PRG-53, Oxford University Computing Laboratory, Programming Research Group (February 1986).

[103] He Jifeng, C. A. R. Hoare, and J. W. Sanders. Data refinement refined: resumé. In Robinet, B. and Wilhelm, R. (eds.), *ESOP '86*, Springer-Verlag (1986).

[104] C. A. R. Hoare and He Jifeng. Algebraic specification and proof of properties of a mail service. In Meertens, L. (ed.), *IFIP WG 2.1 Working Conference on Program Specification and Transformations, Bad-Tölz, W. Germany 15–17 April,* North-Holland Publishers (1986).

[105] E. R. Olderog and C. A. R. Hoare. Specification-oriented semantics for communicating processes. *Acta Informatica,* **23**(1), 9–66 (1986).

[106] C. A. R. Hoare and He Jifeng. The weakest prespecification. *Information Processing Letters,* **24**(2), 127–32 (January 1987).

[107] C. A. R. Hoare, He Jifeng, and J. W. Sanders. Prespecification in data refinement. *Information Processing Letters,* **25**(2), 71–76, May 1987.

[108] C. A. R. Hoare, I. J. Hayes, He Jifeng, C. C. Morgan, A. W. Roscoe, J.W. Sanders, I. H. Sørensen, J. M. Spivey, and B. A. Sufrin. The laws of programming. *Comm. ACM* **30**(8), 672–87 (August 1987). See Corrigenda in *Comm. ACM,* **30**(9), 770.

[109] A. I. Enikeev, C. A. R. Hoare, and A. Teruel. **Модель теории взаимодействующих последовательных процессов для меню-диалоговых систем** *Mathematica,* **3** (1987) (In Russian)

[110] He Jifeng and C. A. R. Hoare. Algebraic specification and proof of a distributed recovery algorithm. *Distributed Computing,* **2**(1), 1–12 (1987).

[111] C. A. R. Hoare and He Jifeng. Design and proof of a mail service. In Friesen, O. and Golshani, F. (eds.), *6th Annual International Phoenix Conference on Computers and Communications – Conference Proceedings Scottsdale, AZ, USA 25–27 February, 1987,* IEEE (1987), pp. 272–5.

[112] C. A. R. Hoare. An overview of some formal methods for program design. *IEEE Computer Journal,* **20**(9), 85–91 (September 1987).
Chapter 22 of the current book.

Index